THE PHILOSOPHY OF SOCIAL SCIENCE

D0139698

Now in its second edition, this comprehensive textbook offers an exceptionally accessible yet in-depth introduction to the philosophy of social science. Students with no previous knowledge will find themselves taken on an engaging philosophical journey: the book's unique dialogue format anticipates their most frequently asked questions and provides clear explanations of specialised terminology and essential contextualisation of contemporary debates.

Encompassing both traditional and contemporary perspectives, the book explores the questions and debates raised by all the major theoretical positions in the philosophy of social science, including positivism, empiricism, rationalism, hermeneutics, feminist epistemology, postmodernism and critical realism.

The first edition of this book had a Eurocentric bias, as do virtually all other textbooks covering this subject matter. This has been corrected in the second edition and includes a new chapter on the contributions of Islam to philosophy, natural science and social science including sociology. The second edition also has a newly written chapter on pragmatism and neo-pragmatism, as well as strengthened coverage of hermeneutics, postmodernism and critical realism.

The book's rich pedagogic support includes:

- point-by-point summaries introducing the scope of every chapter;
- discussion questions;
- further reading lists;
- and a glossary of key terminology.

This excellent textbook is designed to provide every student with a clear understanding of important and complex issues. It is essential reading for all students of philosophy of social science, whether at undergraduate or Masters level, and regardless of their disciplinary background.

Garry Potter is a professor in the Faculty of Arts at Wilfrid Laurier University, Canada. He is also a documentary film-maker.

THE PHILOSOPHY OF SOCIAL SCIENCE

New perspectives

Second edition

GARRY POTTER

Routledge
Taylor & Francis Group

LONDON AND NEW YORK

Second edition published 2017
by Routledge
2 Park Square, Milton Park, Abingdon, Oxon, OX14 4RN

and by Routledge
711 Third Avenue, New York, NY 10017

Routledge is an imprint of the Taylor & Francis Group, an informa business

First edition published by Pearson 2000
and by Routledge 2013

British Library Cataloguing in Publication Data
A catalogue record for this book is available from the British Library

Library of Congress Cataloging in Publication Data
Names: Potter, Garry, 1955– author.
Title: The philosophy of social science : new perspectives, 2nd edition /
    by Garry Potter.
Description: Edition 2. | New York : Routledge, 2017. | Revised edition of
    the author's The philosophy of social science.
Identifiers: LCCN 2016025751 | ISBN 9781138998391 (hardback) |
    ISBN 9781138998407 (pbk.) | ISBN 9781315658704 (ebook)
Subjects: LCSH: Social sciences—Philosophy. | Sociology—Philosophy.
Classification: LCC H61 .P618 2016 | DDC 300.1—dc23
LC record available at https://lccn.loc.gov/2016025751

ISBN: 978-1-138-99839-1 (hbk)
ISBN: 978-1-138-99840-7 (pbk)
ISBN: 978-1-315-65870-4 (ebk)

Typeset in Times
by Apex CoVantage, LLC

CONTENTS

PREFACE TO THE FIRST EDITION

This book presents a survey of issues and debate within the philosophy of social science. It is, of course, by no means a comprehensive survey. The field has not only become increasingly vast and complex in its own right but is now so thoroughly entangled with other theoretical and substantive research questions that any attempt at a comprehensive survey would be doomed to failure. However, this book's survey of the issues is also intended as an introductory one. Its introductory nature not only limits the range and depth with which the subject matter may be engaged but has also guided the mode of exposition. This initial qualification is not intended as an apology. It is merely a clarification of the book's objectives. I don't wish to suggest that there will be nothing in it for the more advanced student, or even for experts in the field. However, its starting point is an assumption of no previous knowledge on the part of the reader.

Not only is this survey of debate not comprehensive, it is not wholly objective. Again no apology is intended by this admission. Amongst the range of positions considered, the critical realist position is given pride of place. Objectivity is conceived, on the one hand, as an objective to be strived for; certainly a 'fair' presentation of all the non-realist positions is attempted. On the other hand, the very notion of objectivity forms a significant aspect of the subject matter itself. It is an issue upon which the critical realist position recommends the declaration of biases without believing that that in itself resolves the complexity of a very problematic issue.

There is a good deal of irony intended in both form and content of this book. Critical realism is a philosophical position that emerged out of a critique of both the positivist and hermeneutic traditions. It was felt for some time that, broadly speaking, these two contrasting positions were exhaustive. That is, though a vast range of carefully nuanced points of view were available within each 'camp', so to speak, the most fundamental aspects of the philosophy of social science debate were a bi-polar affair. Recent developments, of which the emergence of the critical realism position is only one, have destroyed that duality. They are also responsible for my conscious intention of irony.

Realism emerged first as a critique of positivism, of positivism within natural rather than social science. Increasingly today, philosophy of social science debates must make reference to the philosophical problems and issues of natural science in a different manner than previously. In the past, natural science was also a reference point for the most significant issues within the philosophy of social science. Questions concerning the possibility and desirability of social science were considered in relation to the natural science model, or rather they were considered in relation to the (broadly speaking) positivist view of natural science. Today, we are said to be in a 'post-positivist era'.

Positivism's view of natural science cannot form the same reference point for the discussion of social science's scientificity. Yet it is important all the same. Its very inadequacies demonstrate much that is also wrong with the alleged polar opposition of the hermeneutic or 'humanist' camp. Postmodernist epistemology can be seen as an evolution of some of the earlier interpretivist criticism of positivist social science. It is not necessarily that it is taken to greater extremes of relativism. Such extremes had already been reached by earlier thinkers. Rather the perspective shifted. What was felt to be a very serious problem, by Peter Winch for example, is not resolved but simply celebrated by some later postmodernist thinkers. Thus, demonstrations of ironic ambiguity are sometimes propounded as philosophical solutions.

The current state of play within the philosophy of social science debate thus created the (perceived) necessity for a number of embedded ironies within this book. First, though critical realism grew out of a critique of positivism, it was felt that a much more sympathetic presentation of it was required than the 'straw man' caricatured critiques that may sometimes be found within the humanist/hermeneutic postmodernist camps. The positivists have many criticisms to answer. However, the point is that they do (in most cases) have some plausible answers. Second, the sharp polarity between positivist description (and prescription) of scientific forms of explanation and theory is somewhat illusory. In Chapter 4 the re-framing of Max Weber's theory of understanding and ideal types in Karl Popper's terms of situational logic and falsification rather dramatically makes this point by demonstration.

Making points through demonstration, the so-called performative critique of deconstruction, seems to be believed by postmodernists to be their exclusive property. As are also wit, irony, playfulness, a literary turn of phrase and innovative forms of presentation. Unfortunately, however, such innovation seldom manifests itself in terms of increased accessibility to students new to the field. Perhaps this explains the scarcity of the postmodernist form of lecture or introductory text. Perhaps they feel that such dry dusty stuff can be left to old modernist dinosaurs or that they can slip back into it occasionally just to bring the student up to speed. At any rate, this is the ironic background to my decision as to form of presentation. I wish to demonstrate, and demonstrate above all to students, that philosophy with all its abstraction need not be dry and dusty. I have chosen an innovative form of presentation – dialogue – an innovative form of presentation with a 2,000-year-old history! How much more postmodernist can you get?

The form of presentation is that of a dialogue between a social science student, code-named Socrates, and a professional 'on-line' philosophical consultant, code-named the Goddess of Delphi – acronym G.O.D. It is not a true Socratic dialogue, of course. The original Socratic belief that we already possess all knowledge, and merely need to be teased into remembering it, is not a belief shared by the author. No, the relationship between G.O.D. and Socrates is most definitely that of teacher and student.

Information needs to be imparted; straightforward explanations need to be given. However, the relationship evolves during the course of the book. Socrates refers back to material presented earlier and gradually begins to think critically, sometimes formulating excellent objections to the positions G.O.D. is outlining. This perhaps serves as a performative reminder to teachers and students alike that teachers and authors are not God.

The dialogue form and the 'characters' chosen to enact it serve other demonstrative purposes as well. For example, in the chapter on feminist epistemology, G.O.D. reminds Socrates of her gender. Repeated exposure to the acronym G.O.D. reveals Socrates's acculturated unconscious association of both 'God' and scientific rationality with a male perspective. Socrates is then partially persuaded of a feminist standpoint epistemology only to abandon it in response to the 'goddess's' critical objections. Her conclusion is that neither science nor rationality are inherently gendered, though there are epistemological advantages associated with both particular sorts of experiences and structural positions in society. This is, in fact, the mainstream (though there are some with reservations) critical realist position on the subject, and my own. However, the fact that I have in effect falsely gendered myself in the dialogue should cast some doubt in the readers' minds.

This book possesses two goals, one of which, in fact, is very much connected to doubt. Students need information. It is G.O.D.'s role in this book to provide such information; that is, the explanation of terminology, the framework and basic positions in a host of debates and their interconnections – in short, a survey of the field. There is intrinsic difficulty in the subject matter. Some of the issues are very complex and also seem to possess a conundrum-like quality. One problem is solved only to create another, whose solution in turn possesses an irritating similarity to the first problem's starting point. This intrinsic difficulty can be compounded for the student by an unfamiliarity with philosophical thinking. To teach people to think would be far too arrogant to set forward as a goal. However, the attempt to teach people to think in a manner to which they perhaps have not been accustomed is one of the aims of the book. Socrates's questions and contributions have the effect of simplifying, clarifying and bringing to the discussion an intelligent common sense combined with an unfamiliarity with the issues. As the book unfolds, this role changes somewhat. It is hoped that Socrates provides by demonstration some of the learning process involved in beginning to think philosophically.

However, just as in the book G.O.D. cannot provide a comprehensive overview of all the debates, neither is it maintained that Socrates provides all the necessary questions, objections and so forth, which the student readership might. They will, inevitably, have questions and objections of their own. Again no apology is intended by this admission. It is exactly what is hoped for. They should by the end of the book have an idea of what is at stake in these debates, an understanding of perhaps why many of them remain unresolved, and an ability and interest in asking further questions. The awareness that G.O.D. does not have all the answers,

·nor Socrates all the questions, is not a bad starting point for further study in the philosophy of social science.

Throughout the book readers will come across terms given in bold; this indicates that further clarification can be found in the Terminology Glossary at the end of the book.

PREFACE TO THE SECOND EDITION

I have a friend, who at the time of this writing, has just finished the fourth edition of a textbook on the subject of race and ethnicity in Canada. I asked him how different his fourth edition was from the first. 'Completely different' was his answer. 'Everything has changed so much since when I first wrote the book'. I think this is likely the case for successive editions of most books dealing with empirical science. The analyses must change because the underlying facts, statistics and experiences have changed.

This is not the case for the philosophy of social science. In the sixteen years since the first edition of this book, the actual practices of social science have not changed significantly. Perhaps *the* most significant change in social science practice would be the more frequent utilisation of email and the Internet for surveys and interviewing. But that was already being done sixteen years ago, just not to the same degree. People's use of social media and other technologies has of course opened up entirely new fields of social phenomena for social scientific study. This has not, however, had as dramatic an effect upon the *philosophy* of social science, as one might be inclined to think. Baudrillard's notion of hyperreality is still about as far as playful speculative philosophy has yet been carried, and my own thoughts concerning it have changed little since I wrote about it in the first edition of this book.

So the changes in this book, the justification for a second edition to succeed the first, have more to do with *me* than to do with any dramatic changes that have occurred in the social sciences in recent years. However, my change in perspective has been profound. Mostly this change in perspective has manifested itself in the content of the two new chapters of the book.

Likely most professors reading this preface will have had some experiences of disappointment with their students. It is the case in most universities that you frequently find yourself looking hopefully for intellectual enthusiasm and perhaps even, upon occasion, a sense of wonder. Yet all too often you are met with blank looks of boredom or of perplexed confusion without a consequent desire to really understand. I taught undergraduates long before I taught graduate students, and thus had an experience of unfortunate disillusionment; grad students too, I discovered, could lack all desire to engage with theoretical questions, let alone meta-theoretical ones. So I am sure most professors, like me, absolutely cherish intellectual enthusiasm among our students when we encounter it.

But intellectual enthusiasm, while necessary on the road to understanding and intelligent critical thought, is not sufficient in itself. Knowledge is also required. So it is that professors are seldom really challenged by their students.

In the fall of 2015 I was teaching a graduate course in the philosophy of social science. Though supplemented by original source readings, the first edition of this book was the course's principal textbook. I structured the course rather like the structure of the book with regard to subject matter. Having taught such a course quite a few times over the years I was, of course, well used to receiving questions of clarification. Critical questions, truly thoughtful, well-grounded critical questions, I have found to be quite rare. But this time I received not one but a suite of questions that together formed a critique of the course as a whole, including its textbook! It was fairly damning! It was also pretty much true! It was also grounded in my ignorance and a horrible kind of cultural conceit!

Even as we discussed Lyotard's critique of the Enlightenment myth, of his assertion that we no longer believed 'grand narratives'; I placed that too, into a part of a story I was telling, a narrative of the history of the philosophy of science and social science in which Lyotard too, had his little chapter. This story, this 'grand narrative' that my course was providing, that my book was providing was what the student critiqued in its entirety. The critique was detailed but yet can be expressed in a single phrase: Eurocentrism. It was not merely that the thinkers with whom the book and course engaged came from that background; it was that the story I was telling was implicitly, and perhaps to some degree explicitly, proclaiming a particular cultural history as a *universal* cultural history.

I knew immediately that my student's critique was justified; I knew immediately that I was wrong. I knew that in a sense I had committed a crime. My student introduced me to the term 'epistemicide'; a vast cultural heritage of thought and achievement had not simply been ignored but had effectively been written out of the history books, my own included. The result of this experience was that I asked this student, Noor Baig, if she would be co-author with me on a chapter about this in a revised edition of the book. She agreed, and the result is the new Chapter 8.

The new edition thus now has a chapter in which not only are many of the achievements of Islamic science celebrated, but the historical story has also been corrected. The book is, of course, primarily a book of philosophy rather than history, and thus the 'corrections' to the history of the philosophy of science and social science serve to cast all the rest of the book in a different light. The Eurocentric story is told, but then it is both corrected and reflected upon as to how the omissions and errors came to pass.

The second new chapter (Chapter 9) has several doses of irony attached to its content and production. In the chapter itself there is the observed ironic connection between what I call the 'pragmatic epistemological guarantee' as part of the *foundation* of an ontology-based realist theory of knowledge on the one hand, and the anti-foundationalist stance of neo-pragmatism's most famous theorist: Richard

Rorty. Rorty's position is not only anti-foundationalist but particularly critical of correspondence ('mirroring') theories of truth.

But the irony is not only that to be found within the text but in its conditions of production. I have not changed my extremely critical conclusions concerning Rorty's thinking in the sixteen years since the writing of the first edition of this book. I still find his views to be crude, a form of anti-intellectual sophistry. I still consider the 'default' secular orientation of the academy to be a good thing (though my Chapter 8 co-author Noor Baig has gone some way in convincing me of the manner in which Christianity continues to influence the academy's secularism). I am still an atheist, and I still believe that my critique of Roy Bhaskar's 'proof' of reincarnation is correct. And yet after Bhaskar's death – he died in 2014 – I find that I still evaluate him as one of the greatest thinkers of the twentieth century! I find that I am still not in tune with the direction critical realism evolved in after Bhaskar's 'spiritual turn'. But yet my respect for Margret Archer, Andrew Collier (who also died in 2014) and Doug Porpora – authors of *Transcendence: Critical realism and God* – has only increased over the years. So perhaps that critical cutting edge of enthusiasm for a focusing upon differences kind of critique has dulled in me over the years . . . or perhaps Richard Rorty was right. I don't think so, but my own sense of certainty about many ideas has diminished over the years.

The neo-pragmatist chapter in the book considers a lecture Rorty gave on the compatibility of science and religion. He examines possible contradictions between the truths of science and the truths of religion. They are not incompatible, in his view. This is because he and other pragmatists define truth not in terms of correspondence to reality but rather in relation to human purposes. I am certainly *not* in agreement with this view, and the argument is critiqued in the chapter . . . *but* . . .

As I said, I am now less certain of my own views and thus perhaps more tolerant concerning the views of others. So Roy Bhaskar's work, for example, I now see more in terms of the importance of what he got right about the nature of science and social science and the possibilities of human emancipation, than in any (in my ever so fallible a view) mistakes he may have made concerning philosophy, science and spirituality.

One of the early reviews of the first edition of this book (Ruth Groff in the *Journal of Critical Realism* in 2001) was titled 'Yes Socrates, G.O.D. Doesn't Have All the Answers'. The review was fair enough, though I thought the title was rather misleading. In the dialogue Socrates is a female student, the name chosen because she didn't know the names of any female philosophers. G.O.D. is not 'God' but rather is an acronym: Goddess of Delphi. So, there was certainly no claim to omniscience, either then or now. But perhaps Groff did detect a certain arrogance concerning the correctness of my views in the first edition. But that arrogance is gone; very definitely neither G.O.D. nor I have all the answers.

CHAPTER 1

THE IMPORTANCE OF SCIENCE AND THE IMPORTANCE OF UNDERSTANDING WHAT SCIENCE IS

But, after all, it is the blunt truth that we want. The final content of our aims requires something more than vulgar substitutes, or subtle evasions, however delicate . . . Apart from blunt truth, our lives sink decadently amid the perfume of hints and suggestion.

Alfred North Whitehead

If then, Socrates, we find ourselves unable to make our discourse of the generation of gods and the universe in every way wholly consistent and exact, you must not be surprised. Nay, we must be well content if we can provide an account not less likely than another's; we must remember that I who speak and you who are my audience, are but men and should be satisfied to ask for no more than the likely story.

Plato

OUTLINE OF MAJOR POINTS TO BE COVERED

The philosophy of science consists essentially of asking and answering the question 'what is science?'

1   The philosophy of science is important for the following reasons:
   a   Science possesses enormous 'rhetorical authority' in contemporary society. Scientific knowledge claims possess immense power to compel belief. Claims to the scientificity of any particular discipline, method or body of assertions about the world likewise increase their credibility. It is thus important to be able to decide whether a particular knowledge claim being made, method being used or discipline's alleged scientificity is deserved. For example, it is often claimed that astrology is a science, and this goes some way towards establishing its credibility. Yet astrology is not a science.
   b   The credibility given to scientific disciplines and particular knowledge claims really is deserved, in the sense that generally speaking scientific knowledge claims are more reliable than most others, and the methods used to arrive at them are likewise so. It is thus important to come to an understanding of what science is, in order not only to reproduce it but also to refine it.

1

2   The philosophy of science consists essentially of four interrelated philosophical subject areas: **logic**, **ontology**, **epistemology** and **methodology** (see glossary for meaning of terms given in bold).

3   The philosophy of science also contains a moral and/or political dimension. This works both ways insofar as specific philosophies of science both reflect the political concerns of their time and the positions of their proponents and also have political implications. For example, **positivism** as a philosophy of science both reflects the conservatism of its expositors and has an implicit conservative prescriptive dimension to its conclusions with regard to scientific practices and the understanding in general of claims to scientificity.

4   There is a need for the philosophy of science because the practical understanding of scientists themselves is not wholly adequate. It is frequently the case, for example, that the explicit understanding of the nature of science that a scientist might articulate is not in harmony with that which is implicit in his or her actual practice.

5   The first descriptions of **realism**, **idealism** and **empiricism** are given.

6   The particular importance of the philosophy of social science is argued for and related to the general importance of the philosophy of science. The question is particularly urgent because social scientific disciplines are uncertain of their status in this regard. Four general positions are sketched out:

   a   Social science can be scientific in broadly speaking the same way as natural science.

   b   Social science cannot be scientific at all, and it is harmful even to make the attempt. **Interpretative understanding** is what should be striven for.

   c   Social science can and should be scientific. However, many of the most important questions with which it is concerned cannot be approached by such means. Interpretative understanding utilises scientific causal analysis but must go beyond this.

   d   All of the above positions accept more or less the same understanding of natural science, i.e. a version of **positivism**. This understanding is mistaken. From this point of view, then, the whole question of social science is transformed. The **critical realist** philosophy of science also sees a unity of the natural and social scientific enterprises, but this is cast in very different terms.

DIALOGUE

The Scene: Somewhere in virtual reality a social science student, pseudonym 'Socrates', commences a dialogue with one of Microsoft's online philosophy professors, pseudonym 'Goddess of Delphi' (hereafter designated as G.O.D.).

Socrates: I need some answers!

G.O.D.: That's what they pay me for.

Socrates: I want to know about the philosophy of science, the philosophy of social science in particular.

G.O.D.: Why?

Socrates: Why what?

G.O.D.: Why do you want to know about the philosophy of science?

Socrates: I don't really. I've been told I need to know about it. There's a course in it I'm taking. It's simultaneously boring, difficult and confusing. I can't see the relevance. I just want to get out in the real world and do some research. But my tutors all tell me I need a better theoretical framework for it. They tell me that underpinning all research are some at least implicit philosophical assumptions, that by making them explicit, carefully considering them will be of practical benefit. But I have as yet to see how; anyway, they've made us do this course.

G.O.D.: I see. The real world. Hmm. You see reality as 'out there', eh?

Socrates: There's a problem with that?

G.O.D.: Some people have a problem with that. It's not as straightforward as you might think.

Socrates: No?

G.O.D.: No. Anyway, you're not convinced the philosophy of science is important, and your only interest in it is of the narrow **instrumental rationality** kind.

Socrates: Instrumental rationality?

G.O.D.: Instrumental rationality. It's a form of rational thought focused purely upon 'means to an end calculations'. You want to get to the other side of a river. Should you attempt to swim across, build a boat, a bridge, etc.? You calculate to the best of your ability the means at your disposal, the advantages and drawbacks of each possible course of action, and then select the best available. But, arguably, at least there are other forms of rationality; arguably, instrumental rationality is inappropriate to be applied to all spheres of life. It may be fine for building bridges and doing accounting, but the application of this form of rationality to other spheres of life creates problems; it turns everything into an object, a means to an end. It's even argued by some that this is a specifically male form of rationality and that both science and philosophy have been dominated by it. But we're getting way ahead of ourselves. We'll consider different forms of rationality later on.

Questions about the nature of rationality are part of the subject matter of the philosophy of social science. What I want you to realise at this point is simply that the philosophy of science is important.

Socrates: Okay, it's important. I'll take your word for it.

G.O.D.: No! Don't take my word for it. You need to be convinced by the arguments. That is what doing philosophy is all about. And for another thing, not everyone believes it is important. There is a kind of tension between philosophy and science sometimes. This is particularly true of natural science. Philosophical debate seems to be more directly interwoven with social science's subject matter. Some people have even argued that essentially social science is philosophy, or at any rate social scientific practice should be seen as more akin to doing philosophy than science. But on the other hand, a great many scientists, including social scientists, have taken a position similar to what seems to be yours at the moment. That is, that we can easily dispense with philosophy's convoluted and highly abstract questions and as you put it 'simply get out there in the real world and do some research'.

Professional philosophers are inclined to dismiss this point of view as naive. One can point out, for example, that an 'anti-philosophical' standpoint is actually a philosophical standpoint itself and thus needs to be philosophically justified.

Socrates: Couldn't one simply refuse to play that game? I mean, couldn't one forget about philosophy and simply do the research? You could then let your results stand as a response to the philosopher's 'quibbles'.

G.O.D.:   That is a very good point. A philosopher, David Hume, produced an argument, one that still greatly troubles philosophy today: the problem of **induction**. We'll be considering this problem later on in some detail. But suffice it to say at this point that it is a very serious problem, serious enough for Alfred North Whitehead to call it the 'refutation of science'. But science continued quite productively nonetheless, apparently blandly indifferent to this 'refutation'. It achieved very impressive results.

The results have been impressive enough to suggest philosophy's refutation rather than science's.

However, in spite of this, I would nonetheless argue that whatever scientists themselves might think, the philosophy of science is very important. The 'get out there and do it' anti-philosophical view is naive.

Socrates: What makes you so sure? Why do you think you know better? Surely the scientists themselves would know whether the philosophy of science is worthwhile or not.

G.O.D.:   They ought to. And a great many of them do. Others think they've got all the answers to the philosophical questions concerning science, without even realising that they're philosophical questions.

Socrates: What do you mean?

G.O.D.:   Well, essentially it's this. The philosophy of science asks and answers the question 'What is science?'. Now, it might appear reasonable to think that a scientist would have to know what science is. And this is, of course, true on one level. They would have to know what science is, simply in order to practice it. But it's a very localised and limited sort of knowledge. Merely to have knowledge of the practices of their own area of specialised expertise, or more generally of their discipline, leaves a lot of questions unanswered. Is science simply a method or does it also consist of a body of knowledge? Is biology a science in the same way as physics? Or meteorology, economics or sociology? What is the relationship between one science and another, one set of scientific knowledges and another? Is science the same now as it was in the past? Must explanations conform to a specific logical form? What should count as a justification for the acceptance or rejection of a new scientific theory? What is the difference between a scientific and non-scientific theory or explanation?

Socrates: Scientists don't know the answers to these questions?

G.O.D.: Well, some of them do and some of them don't. Some of them have thought about it a great deal more than others. Some of them think they have the answers to these questions . . . and some of their answers are quite simply wrong. Others simply haven't reflected closely enough upon their own practice.

Socrates: Well, at least they've got a clear idea about what the **scientific method** is, haven't they?

G.O.D.: The scientific method? You seem to have some idea already what science is.

Socrates: No, not really. I'm just starting to get impatient. Everybody has heard of the scientific method.

G.O.D.: I'd like to ask you to tell me what it is then, because I don't believe there is one. Do physicists do the same things as archaeologists?

Socrates: No, of course they don't do exactly the same things or even the same sorts of things, but all science must have some very broad general characteristics in common or else . . .

G.O.D.: Or else it wouldn't be science? Yes, that's true, but we're getting ahead of ourselves. Understanding what science is, is important for basically two reasons. First, there is its rhetorical authority . . .

Socrates: Rhetorical authority?

G.O.D.: Yes, credibility. In contemporary Western culture science is king. In the credibility stakes it has beaten out God, politicians and even pop stars. To assert that 'x has been scientifically proven' carries more compulsion to belief than any pronouncement to the contrary by Mick Jagger, a parliamentary sub-committee or the Pope. Even the pronouncements of papal infallibility are now usually couched in such a manner as not to contradict science's ultimate rhetorical authority.

Socrates: About some things perhaps. Not others.

G.O.D.: That's true. But science is held to be the ultimate authority on a very great many important things. Does smoking cause cancer? If we use this material instead of that one, will the building collapse or not?

Socrates: Okay, I see your point. But what about global warming? Some scientists say it's happening; some say it's not. There are a lot of areas where scientists disagree. They don't know everything. What about love, poetry, the human spirit?

G.O.D.:   Well, we might have to wait a while before we reach poetry or the human spirit. Perhaps we'll get there eventually, if you're really interested. But who said that scientists know everything? Why shouldn't they disagree? However, you make my point by bringing up global warming. Scientific experts and their various theories are in conflict about many aspects of the issue. However, it is to scientists that you'll turn to make your mind up on it. Yes?

Socrates: I guess so. You're saying that science doesn't know everything, that scientists disagree, but even so we should take them as the ultimate authority.

G.O.D.:   Not exactly. There is a political dimension to that question that we're not quite ready to consider. We will though. For the moment let's just say that science occupies a very powerful discursive status in our society; so much so, that many borderline, dubious and outright bogus claims to scientific status are made. These claims to scientific-ity are often used to sell products, convince politicians or fool the general public. Scientificity claims are made both for particular alleged knowledges and for various practices and disciplines. How do we judge whether such claims are justified or not?

Some claims are arguably valid though not universally agreed. Other claims, clearly and simply, are completely false.

Socrates: Give me some examples.

G.O.D.:   Okay. Here are two: sociology and astrology. The scientific status of sociology is contested. There are quite powerful arguments on both sides. However, astrology often claims to be a science. It is not! In fact, within the history of the philosophy of science, it has frequently been used as a kind of lodestone to demarcate the scientific and non-scientific realms.

It is used as such because it has many of the trappings of science yet still is not scientific. This is so, in spite of the many claims for its scientificity by its numerous adherents.

Socrates: What's not scientific about it? How can you say so definitely that it's not a science? You just said that many people claim it is.

G.O.D.:   Those are good questions. I promise you, we'll look at astrology's scientific pretensions later on. We'll spell out precisely how it fails to be scientific. But just take my word for it for the moment.

Socrates: Take your word for it! But you said . . .

G.O.D.:   I know what I said. But there is a difference between taking on board something provisionally while you see how the argument develops and believing something as true simply on the basis of authority.

Socrates:	I know that. I'm just trying to catch you in a contradiction.
G.O.D.:	That's good. Pointing out contradictions is very much part of the process of critical thought. But back to astrology. Many pseudo-sciences attempt to cash in on science's authoritative rhetorical status to increase their own credibility. Thus, we need to have an understanding of what science really is to be able to evaluate such claims. Claims to scientificity are not identical to claims to truth, but they are importantly related.
Socrates:	Okay. I'll buy that. But is that it? Is that the only reason why understanding the nature of science is considered so important?
G.O.D.:	No. I said earlier that there were two important reasons. The second reason is deceptively simple. Science's rhetorical authority is deserved! There are very good reasons why we should accept its claims to knowledge. It has a well-established track record of being a good way to find things out about the way the world works. Why do I assert this, you ask?
Socrates:	No, I didn't. I'm quite ready to accept that.
G.O.D.:	Well, perhaps you accept it too easily. It is not an assertion everyone would agree with. People have become increasingly suspicious of science. Understandably so. Some of the early romanticists' fears of science have become realised. Science is (indirectly) responsible for the production of horrors that make Frankenstein's monster pale in comparison. Some of the technological applications of science have indeed been truly monstrous, while others are certainly at least potentially dangerous. An attitude of suspicion is definitely warranted.
	Yet at the same time technology, the most blatantly obvious and visible manifestation of the practical application of scientific knowledges, is a powerful reason for according science the rhetorical authority it possesses in our culture.
	There are those who would disagree. They would assert that science is simply the dominant belief system of our culture. This is itself a point of view within the philosophy of science, a particularly ill-thought-out and fallacious point of view, but a point of view nonetheless. We shall consider it in more detail later on, and I'll show you why this is so. But for now let us simply say that it is circular in its reasoning. It is equivalent to saying that we tend to believe in science because we believe in it.
Socrates:	Okay, now wait a minute. Science has produced good technology. Science has produced bad technology, nuclear bombs and so on. I can see how it has had diverse effects. But are you equating science with technology?
G.O.D.:	No, definitely not! It is simply that technology is the most obvious manifestation of the practical utility of scientific knowledges. There are other scientific knowledges that didn't require any technological

developments for their usefulness to be apparent. The importance of clean hands for performing surgery, for example, may perhaps seem only common sense now, but its implementation as consistent medical practice waited upon the production of scientific knowledges concerning infection. What I'm really trying to get at is that we live in a world not only of technology but in a world where an enormous multitude and variety of scientific knowledges affect our daily lives in very fundamental and crucially important ways. Contemporary living depends upon a cumulative and disparate mass of applied scientific knowledge. Man, so it has been said, does not live by bread alone. But science delivers far more than bread, though even wheat farming is very heavily dependent upon a host of scientific knowledges and techniques. By comparison, irrespective of its prevalence and influence, religion scarcely touches our daily lives on a practical level. A devout Muslim on his way to Mecca may demand a special diet from the airline, but the fact that he is flying at all, relies upon a host of scientific principles. The most avid Baptist demonstrates her 'faith' in science whenever she inserts her bankcard into a cash machine and waits expectantly for her money to arrive. It is not that religion isn't still very, very important to most of the world's population. It is. But in the world of mundane, very practical day-to-day living, scientific knowledges lie behind almost all the activities we engage in.

Science has been very successful. For good or ill its achievements dominate the world we live in. It has thus rather dramatically and practically proven itself to be a particularly good way of learning about the nature of reality. But exactly what is this particularly good way of learning about reality? What are its characteristics? Answering these questions thus seems crucial if we want to know how to replicate that success in the future.

Socrates: Hold on. If I understand you correctly, it does all come down to a question of method. Perhaps the scientific method? But if I remember correctly, you said that that was a mistake. You said there wasn't any single scientific method, but rather methods.

You have definitely contradicted yourself this time!

G.O.D.: Very good. Very good indeed! You're beginning to think philosophically now.

Socrates: Don't be condescending. Answer the question. I'm right, aren't I? You're arguing that we need to know what science is so we can continue to reproduce its earlier successes. That sounds to me like discovering what the scientific method is.

G.O.D.: There are some people who would agree with that. But I'll say again that there isn't a single scientific method. Marine biologists don't perform the same activities as astronomers, or even the same sorts of activities.

Socrates: Well then, you are contradicting yourself. If we can't learn what the scientific method is . . . because there isn't one, then surely it is a matter of learning the techniques of the particular discipline – radio astronomy, biochemistry or whatever. And isn't that a matter for science itself rather than the philosophy of science? Okay, we can say that science is important. You've convinced me of that. Actually, no; you didn't convince me of that. I always knew science was important. But it doesn't convince me that the philosophy of science is important!

G.O.D.:   Again. Very good. And I'm not being condescending. I mean it. You're beginning to think like a philosopher. The position you've just articulated is itself a position in the philosophy of science. A rather naive one, but a position nonetheless.

Socrates: Yeah, right. Thanks.

G.O.D.:   No, really. It's a position a great many scientists would agree with. They are, however, wrong. Look, if we accept that there are a diversity of methods currently being utilised by the various sciences, and if we observe that they have been developed, revised and refined over a period of time, in short that they are changeable, we are still left with a very important question. Isn't there some general criterion or criteria by which we can evaluate whether sets of practices are scientific or not? How are we to evaluate these various methods? Should we be doing things this way or that? Which method is better?

Socrates: Well, that's easy. Whichever method works best. Whatever produces the results.

G.O.D.:   Once again you are articulating a position in the philosophy of science. It is called **pragmatism** and was developed initially by William James and others. Later on Paul Feyerabend articulated a rather more sophisticated argument for a kind of 'anything goes' approach to science, with pragmatic criteria as the only guidelines. More recently Richard Rorty has argued for a somewhat different version of pragmatism. We will look at all of this later on.

   However, let's for a moment consider the possibility that there may be quite unscientific methods for acquiring knowledge, which nonetheless are sometimes quite successful. We then perhaps need to consider short-term versus long-term success. We can also further observe that the question of success is one that can be enquired into on various levels.

Socrates: What do you mean levels?

G.O.D.:   Well, I think the time has come to give you a bit more of a detailed answer as to what the philosophy of science actually is. I think then that the answer to your question will begin to become clear. All right, the philosophy of science consists essentially of four interrelated fields of inquiry: **epistemology, ontology, logic** and **methodology.**

There is also a related series of questions that connect these to politics and/or ethics.

Socrates: Epistemology?

G.O.D.: Don't be frightened by the word. I'm aware that comedians like to use words like 'epistemological' as examples of pretentious intellectual incomprehensibility. Actually, these words have perfectly understandable meanings. If you pursue your study of the philosophy of science very far, they'll become as much a part of your daily speech as words like chocolate and ice cream.

Socrates: I doubt it.

G.O.D.: No, it's true. I'm going to give you a general idea, if not exactly a precise definition of them now. But you'll really begin to learn what epistemology is as you begin to consider epistemological questions, ontology as you consider ontological questions and so on. The philosophy of science, just like any other discipline or specialism, has its own technical vocabulary. You do need to learn it, but it's not very mysterious, and it is certainly not incomprehensible.

Socrates: No? I remain to be convinced.

G.O.D.: Each of the words – and you already know many, many of them – that end in 'ology', have something of the same meaning. The ending 'ology' simply means the study of. Thus, biology, from the root 'bio', meaning 'life', is simply the study of life.

Methodology is the study of method. Epistemology, from the root 'episteme', which means 'to know', is the study of knowledge.

Socrates: What's that from? Latin?

G.O.D.: Greek, actually. And ontology is . . .

Socrates: The study of ont?

G.O.D.: Very funny, but you're actually right. Ont means 'being or existence'. Ontology is an engagement with that very question.

Socrates: I don't know what you mean by that.

G.O.D.: All right, I'll give you a couple of examples. You're looking at something, some simple object, let's say a rock. You see it, but how do you know it's there? You know it's there because you see it. Right?

Socrates: Well, yeah . . . right. But that seems circular to me.

G.O.D.: You're right, it is. But never mind that for the moment. You know the rock is there because you see it. But how do you really know it's there? All you really know for sure is that you have a sense impression, sight, of the rock. How do you really know that there actually is a real material object 'out there' that is causing you to have that visual sense impression? All you know for sure is that you have it.

Socrates: Well, if you were seeing something that wasn't there, you'd be hallucinating. If you didn't see something that really was there, you might bump into it. Then you'd know for sure that something was there!

G.O.D.:   Why? Because you could touch it? But touch is simply another one of our senses. We know we have the sensation, but how can we know, know for sure anyway, that there is a reality outside ourselves that is causing these sensations?

Socrates: Oh, come on! This is why philosophy drives me crazy. It's obvious that there is something out there that we have sense impressions of. It's sheer lunacy to think there might not be.

G.O.D.:   As it happens I agree with you. But lunacy or not, a well-respected philosophical tradition is based upon very similar arguments. When I asked you how can we know that there is actually a material 'thing', the rock, 'out there' in reality, something external to us that is causing our sense impression of it, sight, touch or whatever; when I asked you that, I was asking an epistemological question. There is a very important philosophical school of thought that asserts that our senses, our experience of such sensations as we have, is the prime basis of all knowledge, the sole source of knowledge we have of the **empirical** world. Now when you confidently answered my question about the rock, you were also taking a very definite onto-logical position. You were asserting the material existence of reality outside of our awareness of it.

Socrates: Was I? I guess I was. How could there not be a reality outside of ourselves? And of course it is material. Our senses tell us that.

G.O.D.:   You're sounding like an empiricist with that last statement.

Socrates: What does that mean? You make it sound like a dirty word. You're accusing me of something before I even know what it means.

G.O.D.:   Sorry. You're right though. I'm not particularly fond of **empiricism** as a philosophy. However, it's very important that you should know about it. It has been the single most influential philosophical school of thought with respect to science. But we'll get to that later. Don't worry about trying to remember all the names of the schools of thought I'm giving you now. For one thing, there is considerable disagreement about exactly what these labels imply. For another, different people use them differently in different contexts. And most certainly memorisation is the worst of all possible ways to approach this subject. You'll simply acquire a general idea of what is involved with the various philosophical schools of thought as we go along. We'll be gradually engaging with questions in ever greater detail and depth. By the time we've finished you'll be accusing people who disagree with you of empiricism and idealism and many other 'isms' at the drop of a hat. You'll be able to philosophically swear with the best of us.

Socrates: I look forward to that.

G.O.D.:   Okay, now seriously, when questions are asked about the nature of knowledge, the status of different claims to truth, or even the question 'What is truth?', it is epistemology that is being engaged in.

On the other hand, assertions about the nature of existence and reality are ontological assertions.

Socrates: Wait a minute. I'm still not sure I get this. If I ask, for example, 'What is this house made of?', and then someone answers, 'It's made of bricks', is that ontology?

G.O.D.: No, it's not . . .

Socrates: Somehow I knew you were going to say that.

G.O.D.: Don't worry. I think you'll find that when we get further into this, you'll be able to see that even the so-called experts in science and philosophy sometimes make the same sort of mistake. No, when you claim that a house is made of bricks, you are making a **substantive assertion**. You are making a claim about the nature of the world. Ontological assertions are also claims about the nature of the world, but they are claims on a different level. They are claims about the nature of the sort of 'thing' they are, houses, bricks or whatever. Ontological claims are claims about the nature of reality, not the specificity of its composition, but rather the nature of the form of its composition.

Socrates: Sorry, I'm still not there.

G.O.D.: Well, you asserted earlier that, of course, there is a reality outside ourselves. There is a rock, and we have sense impressions of it. The rock is something existing. Our sense impressions are sense impressions of it. Yes?

Socrates: Yes.

G.O.D.: Well, that is an ontological position. One way of putting a different and contradictory ontological position to yours would be to argue that only the sense impressions in your mind exist. The rock itself, at least as you were conceiving it as a thing in its own right, does not really exist. Only the sense impressions are real. The sense impressions are in your mind. So it's fair to say that they are (more or less) ideas. Reality is wholly a mental phenomenon. This is an ontological position called **idealism**. Your view, that the rock (or whatever) exists in its own right completely independently of us, is called **materialism**. Also sometimes it is called **realism**. These last two terms sometimes get used interchangeably and sometimes not. But never mind that now.

Socrates: So, some philosophers actually ask whether there are any real objects in the world! No wonder people think they're weird! How can we know there are really objects in the world? They really don't think the obvious answer 'because we can see them, hear them, touch them, etc.' is good enough.
          Incredible!

G.O.D.: Wait a minute; let's get things straight. When you assert that there are actually real objects, 'things' that exist in the world whether you perceive them or not, that is an ontological assertion. When someone denies it, when they assert that there are only our sense impressions, when they say that reality is a mental phenomenon, that too is an ontological assertion. But when you ask the question, "how can we know that things exist independently of us?", it is an epistemological question. The answer that we know that things exist because we can see them or hear them is an empiricist epistemological position. There are a variety of both ontological and epistemological positions. They can be put together in a variety of combinations. So, for example, you could have an empiricist epistemological position paired up with either a materialist or idealist ontology.

Socrates: I think I've got it about epistemology, at least, with respect to empiricist epistemology. I wouldn't go so far as to say 'seeing is believing' maybe, but I think I believe something like that. And I feel pretty sure the world is not just in my mind. So that makes me a . . . which is it? Materialist or realist? I mean ontologically.

G.O.D.: Either one will do for now. Another label for your position would be empirical realist.

Socrates: Empirical realist. Okay, I like the sound of that. But it's this idealist position that I find hard to fathom.

G.O.D.: Okay. There is the rock; there is your mental impression of the rock. This you would maintain is caused by the actuality of the rock. The rock exists whether you taste it, feel it, see it or not. Yes?

Socrates: Of course.

G.O.D.: Okay. Now what if I said that it is the idea, the mental image, that is the real reality. Take, for example, a triangle. Well, we have many examples of triangular shaped objects. But none of them, even with the most precise engineering available to make them, is perfect. None of them are really triangles. They are approximations of triangles.

The period, or full stop mark, in this text, is not a real point but an approximation of a point. If you look at a geometry textbook, the points and lines and circles and squares you find in the book aren't really such; they are representations which approximate the reality. We can never find the real thing in what you would maintain is reality. We don't find them in the empirical world, that is, in the world that is observable by our senses. Plato maintained that it is the triangles, the points, the lines, etc. that are real. The material world is illusion. Variations on this theme belong to the philosophical school of idealism. Asserting that the mental impressions you have of the world are its reality, and that the world's materiality is illusory, is another form of idealism.

Socrates: Okay. Wait a minute now. Some of this is ringing a bell. But Plato, idealism . . . well, I think I've started us down the wrong track. There's something I forgot to mention. I should've said it at the beginning.

G.O.D.:   Yes? What's that?

Socrates: Well, I should have told you I'm a sociology student. It isn't the philosophy of science that I need to know about. It's only the philosophy of social science that I really need to find out about. I don't think Plato is very relevant.

G.O.D.:   Well, you're wrong there. I don't mean he is a philosopher of social science exactly, but a lot of his thinking is of enduring relevance – even if we want to reject it. We frequently find some classical idealism (Plato is the archetype idealist philosopher) smuggled in to contemporary theories under quite different labels. We need to be able to recognise it when we see it. Most of all we need to have good answers to the questions it poses. It's fine for you to reject idealism. But you need to be able to do so in such a way that an idealist couldn't immediately poke all kinds of holes in your position. You need to be able to justify it.

Also, even if our main interest in the philosophy of science is specifically focused upon social science, it is absolutely essential to have some understanding of the philosophy of natural science. Absolutely essential! In fact, a lack of understanding of the nature of natural science – its logic, epistemology, ontology and methodology – is responsible for a good deal of the confusion many people have about the nature of social science. No, we haven't gone down the wrong track at all. I think we've made a good start.

Socrates: Really. I'm glad you think so. But I don't really feel I've learned anything at all.

G.O.D.:   We've actually covered more than you think. Just a little bit more and some things will fall into place. I'll give you an idea where we are going.

Socrates: That would be a help.

G.O.D.:   Okay. Back to ontology once again; I can give you the classic ontological question for sociology. What is the nature of society? On the one hand, you have Dürkheim who insists that society, social facts, social structures and so on have a real existence. He asserts that they have a **sui generis reality**. Society is not reducible to the individuals within it. Its existence may depend upon the existence of the collectivity of individuals and their activity, but society is nonetheless something other than the individuals and their activities. One way of putting it would be to say that the whole does not equal the sum of its parts; it is something other than that, something in its own right. Society, social structures, these are emergent phenomena in reality. Exactly how they emerged is another question. But we cannot say they simply emerged from a plurality of individuals. This is because the very construction of the identities of individuals and the way their social behaviour is framed presupposes the necessary existence of a set of social relations, a structure. This, at least, is the sort of argument Dürkheim and others have put forward.

Weber, on the other hand, categorically denies this. His argument is very much good common sense. Society exists through the activities of the individuals that compose it. No individuals, no society. This is true of any alleged supra-individual entity. We may for convenience refer to various institutions as though they have an existence above and beyond the individuals who are their members.

But this 'convenient fiction' is just that – a fiction. The whole does equal the sum of its parts. Now people sometimes come to believe very strongly in the existence of various institutions – the nation or the university or the team or whatever – and their belief in such, their collective belief in such, may well have some real causal force in the world. However, so Weber argues, we must never forget that these alleged entities only exist through our activities. They really are only our collective activities and beliefs about them.

Now, on the one hand, Weber's argument seems intuitively sound. We know that without the collection of players, there would be no football team. It makes sense to assert that really the team is simply the collectivity of its players, coaches and so on. On the other hand, it makes trying to understand some things very difficult. It is a hard position to maintain consistently. Weber himself quite frequently appears to forget just what he enjoins us never to forget. He begins to discuss various institutions and forms of social organisation as though they existed as entities in their own right.

Both men have very powerful arguments for their positions. Both have inconsistencies within their application of them. This is the crucial point here; one's position on such ontological questions is going to have a profound bearing upon the way one goes about studying social phenomena. You see that, don't you?

Socrates: I guess so. I guess if you don't see social structure as anything other than the activities of individuals, then you'd go about studying it differently than if you saw it as something other than that.

G.O.D.:   That's it. This also applies to other philosophical questions. Method is going to be influenced by one's ontological and epistemological positions even though scientists may or may not be fully conscious of some of their underlying positions with respect to this. One can discover some apparent logical contradictions in a piece of substantive research. These actually reflect the way ontology, epistemology and methodology are implicitly related to one another in the underlying assumptions of the research.

You see, as well as examining actual scientific practice and describing what science is, the various philosophies of science are also prescriptive. They present an idealised version, a model if you like, of what science should be. One of the guiding notions is that epistemology, ontology and methodology should be coherently related to one another and that actual scientific practice should be in harmony with this.

Socrates: That makes sense. Listen, I think I need to stop for a while and think about all this.

G.O.D.:   Wait, one last point and we're there. Well, there at the beginning actually. But at least you'll know where we're going. Now Weber and Dürkheim, for all their differences, shared something in common, something very important to understanding the nature of social science.

Socrates: What's that?

G.O.D.:   They held in common a mistaken view of the nature of natural science.

Socrates: Yes?

G.O.D.:   Yes, essentially they both shared a positivist understanding of natural science. And the positivist view of natural science is mistaken!

Socrates: You sound pretty confident of that. But what difference does it make? They were both sociologists.

G.O.D.:   Is sociology a science?

Socrates: Well . . . I don't know.

G.O.D.:   Consider the answer to that question in the light of all that we were discussing earlier. I argued that science is an exceptionally good way of finding out about the nature of reality. If nothing else, we have some technological success as demonstration of this. Certainly on a practical level, natural science seems to have been a great deal more successful in this regard than the social sciences. If natural science's practical applications serve as its vindication, it seems fair enough to enquire of social science's practical achievements, and social science appears by comparison to have a pretty poor record. At any rate, the achievements of natural science seem a great deal more obvious. I mean compare, for example, the success of astronomers predicting eclipses with that of economists predicting upturns or recessions in the economy. Sometimes the economists get it right, but it seems that just as frequently they don't. They certainly disagree amongst themselves about such things a good deal more than do astronomers.

    Maybe social science isn't so successful because it is failing to be sufficiently scientific. On the other hand, maybe its subject matter just isn't amenable to a scientific approach. Or maybe, regardless of its possible practical success, a natural science approach to social phenomena isn't desirable for other reasons. Social science, too, has had some aspirations to achieve the equivalent of the engineering applications of natural science – social engineering. This is widely regarded with suspicion today. At any rate, virtually all the debates concerning social science have initially been posed with reference to one particularly dominant view of natural science. That view is called **positivism**. It is a variant of **empiricism**. It is also, for all its influence, nonetheless a mistaken view.

Socrates: Positivism. Okay, hold on. You're going too fast.

Let's go back a bit. You compared economics and astronomy. Astronomy looks much better with respect to its predictions. Fine. But what about meteorology? Everybody makes jokes about how bad the weather people are with their predictions. And is this the bottom line with respect to science? Prediction?

G.O.D.:   Not to me. But it is in fact a key feature of the positivist understanding of scientific explanation. The positivist would insist that prediction is crucial to science, that there is a symmetry between prediction and explanation. In fact, they over-play prediction's role. It is one of their errors. But we'll leave positivism and prediction to next time.

Socrates: Good.

G.O.D.:   But I want to say this about it at least: positivism in one form or another has been until recently, and even arguably still is, the dominant understanding of natural science, held by most philosophers and scientists alike. It is definitely the dominant view of natural science held by social scientists and philosophers of social science. When they speak of us being in a '**post-positivist era**' they really mean that positivism has gone out of fashion as a theory of the nature of social science. Well, actually, upon occasion they are also questioning the value of science full stop. However, positivism still has its adherents even amongst social scientists. Understanding the positivist conception of the nature of science is thus absolutely crucial for the philosophy of social science.

As a philosophical theory (in all its variations) it has strong points and weak points. However, apart from that, it demarcates the field of inquiry for us. We can divide up the various positions in the philosophy of social science in the following way. There are those who argue that the social sciences can be, should be and (perhaps only sometimes) actually are scientific. Most (but as we shall see not all) of those who believe this are positivists. What I said rather crudely about the philosophy of science in general, that it asks and attempts to answer the question 'what is science?', becomes translated in the realm of the philosophy of social science into the questions 'can the social sciences be scientific in the same way as the natural sciences?' and 'should they even attempt to be?'.

We thus have, as I said, on the one hand, the positivists who strongly believe the answer to these two questions is yes. Thus, for them, sociology, for example, can and should attempt to find **analogues to the role of experiment** in natural science. On the other hand, we have what is sometimes called the **humanist tradition**, which would, by and large, answer no to these two questions. Thinkers in this tradition would argue that there are unique features adhering to the human condition, our capacities for self-reflection and choice, for example, which render the methods of the natural sciences either inappropriate or impossible.

Others would argue that the very nature of human beings requires social phenomena to be explained in a different manner; that to speak of **understanding** rather than **explanation** is really more appropriate. To accomplish this, an entirely different way of proceeding, a completely different sort of methodology, is required.

Still others believe that the methodology of natural science is applicable and useful, even necessary to some degree, but real explanation cannot stop there. The sociological analogues of experiment (statistical comparison and analysis, for example) are valuable and necessary. However, such methods cannot tell us much of what we really wish to know. For that, a different type of method is required; we must seek **interpretative understanding.** We must above all concern ourselves with meaning. Human action, unlike molecular behaviour for example, is inherently meaningful. The stars, as Tennyson said, blindly run; human beings do not.

There is thus this fundamental divide in terms of understanding what social science could be and should be with respect to scientificity. Broadly speaking there are the positivists and the anti-positivists. However, most of the positions on both sides of the divide share a common set of beliefs crucial to the whole question. They accept the positivist conception of the nature of natural science. They are thus both wrong in their fundamental assumptions about the possibility of a scientific social science. Because positivism, in all its variations, is fundamentally mistaken not only about the nature of social science, but about the nature of natural science as well!

Socrates:	Who believes that?
G.O.D.:	Me.
Socrates:	No, I mean what's this position called?
G.O.D.:	**Critical realism.**
Socrates:	Okay, I'll try to remember that.
G.O.D.:	Don't bother; we've got a long way to go before we get there. I'm just trying to give you an idea where we're going. Anyway, you may well disagree with it.
Socrates:	I'm too tired to disagree with anything right now.

DISCUSSION QUESTIONS

1   Give a brief outline of what you feel the popular understanding of science to be. In what ways can you think it might be inaccurate or at least inadequate?

2   What differences might there be between a scientist's understanding of the nature of science and a philosopher's? How could it possibly be the case that scientists might not really know what science is?

3   What advantages and disadvantages might there be to a social scientific discipline such as sociology or economics endeavouring to be scientific? If such disciplines are not to be considered scientific, how else are we to describe them?

4   What basis might there be for the claim that astrology is a science? In what ways does it fail to be one?

FURTHER READING SUGGESTIONS

The literature on the history and philosophy of science is vast! Any literature search in a decent library will almost certainly turn up more than almost anyone could handle. Later chapters will give a more extensive bibliography broken down into subject areas. However, these will also very definitely be a small selection (and arguably a rather arbitrary one) of what is available. Very few of these books could be described as easy reading, even those intended as introductions. Part of the difficulty of the reading in this area is due to the inherent difficulty of the subject matter. However, this difficulty is compounded for those relatively new to the subject by the fact that most of what is written on it refers to what has gone before as though it were common knowledge. For the beginner it can be much like coming in on the end of a conversation that has been going on for a long time, during which all the common reference points were established and are now simply referred to in a kind of shorthand. For this reason I have made a point of listing a great many of the early 'classic works' in the field.

The wise student would be advised to be modest in terms of quantity of reading but ambitious in terms of quality of comprehension. For example, Benton's book listed below is better described as clearly written than easy. It covers in some detail a range of the problems of the philosophies of both natural science and social science, as well as making the connections between the two very apparent – a good book to read slowly and thoughtfully.

Journals

Philosophy of Social Science
Philosophy of the Social Sciences (Sage)
International Journal of Philosophy and Social Sciences (IJPSS – Research India Publications)
Radical Philosophy
Journal for the Theory of Social Behaviour
Signs
Isis (University of Chicago Press) – deals with the history of science and raises many interesting philosophical problems concerning both history and science.
History of Science (Sage)
Philosophy of Science
Telos
British Journal for the Philosophy of Science – the philosophy of science has become increasingly technical over the years, and this journal reflects this. A look through some

of the recent issues should make apparent the relatively simple and basic level in which we are engaged in this book. However, some articles are nonetheless quite accessible.

Philosophy of social science

Benton, T. and Craib, I. (2010) *Philosophy of Social Science: The Philosophical Foundations of Social Science* (2nd edition), Palgrave Macmillan, New York.

Giddens, A. (ed.) (1974) *Positivism and Sociology*, Heinemann, London – see especially the essays by Weber, Schutz, Gellner and Habermas.

Halfpenny, P. (1982) *Positivism and Sociology*, Allen and Unwin, London – quite accessible but focused as the title indicates.

Hughes, J. (1997) *The Philosophy of Social Research*, Addison Wesley Longman, London – covers quite well the material engaged with in the first five chapters of this book from a quite different perspective.

Keat, R. and Urry, J. (1975) *Social Theory as Science*, Routledge & Kegan Paul, London – especially Chapters 1–4, probably the most accessible of the books listed.

Mantzavinos, C. (2009) *Philosophy of the Social Sciences: Philosophical Theory and Scientific Practice*, Cambridge University Press, Cambridge, UK.

Philosophy of science in general

Butterfield, H. (1957) *The Origins of Modern Science*, G.H. Bell, London – explains well the early stages of the historical development of science.

Cartwright, N. (1983) *How the Laws of Physics Lie*, Oxford University Press, Oxford.

Couvalis, G. (1997) *The Philosophy of Science*, Sage, London – a good overview of the philosophy of natural science.

Klee, R. (1997) *Introduction to the Philosophy of Science*, Oxford University Press, New York.

Lakatos, I. and Musgrave, A. (eds) (1970) *Criticism and the Growth of Knowledge*, Cambridge University Press, Cambridge – a classic in the history of the philosophy of science.

Putnam, H. (1978) *Realism and Reason*, Cambridge University Press, New York.

Whitehead, A.N. (1967) *Science and the Modern World*, Free Press, New York – taken from a series of lectures given to Harvard graduate students but still accessible to undergraduates. Very good explanations of relativity and quantum theory for the layperson. Whitehead also has his own unique view as to their philosophical implications.

History of science

Chant, C. and Fauvel, F. (eds) (1980) *Darwin to Einstein: Historical Studies on Science and Belief*, Longman [in association with the Open University Press, Harlow] – the book was used in the past as a text in an Open University course. It contains interesting selections of past scientific controversies, debates, discoveries, theories and philosophical reflections upon them. The historical detail provides a more concrete contextualisation of some of the issues considered very abstractly in the philosophy of science debate.

CHAPTER 2

RATIONALISM AND EMPIRICISM: SCIENCE'S WEAK FOUNDATIONS

. . . the worst that happened to men of science was that Galileo suffered an honour-able detention and a mild reproof, before dying peacefully in his bed. The way in which the persecution of Galileo has been remembered is a tribute to the quiet com-mencement of the most intimate change in outlook which the human race had yet encountered. Since a babe was born in a manger, it may be doubted that so great a thing has happened with so little stir.

Alfred North Whitehead

In a word, then, every effect is distinct from its cause. It could not, therefore, be discovered in the cause; and the first invention or conception of it, a priori, must be entirely arbitrary.

David Hume

OUTLINE OF MAJOR POINTS TO BE COVERED

1   Review of central points in first chapter (expressed somewhat differently).
   a   The practical value of understanding the nature of science and of creat-ing broad demarcation lines between the scientific and non-scientific.
   b   The philosophy of science is essentially theory concerning the nature of knowledge, the nature of the sort of activities most likely to produce knowledge and conceptions of the nature of reality (e.g. whether it is a phenomenon of mind or matter).
2   A brief historical sketch of the **Enlightenment** (eighteenth century) and its relation to the **scientific revolution** (seventeenth century).
   a   Pre-Enlightenment thought is religiously grounded in the authority of the Church.
   b   Two broad epistemologies emerged from the scientific revolution and Enlightenment: **rationalism** and **empiricism**.
3   Rationalism locates the source of knowledge in the human capacity for rational thought.
   a   The political implications of epistemology are illustrated through the example of Descartes, i.e. locating the source of knowledge in a human capacity implicitly undermines the absolute authority of the Church and in a sense democratises the production of knowledge.

4   Empiricism locates the source of knowledge in human experience.
   a   Empiricism is more influential in the development of science because of its stress upon human activity and sensory observation. Thus, measurement and experimentation are held to be key features of scientific practice.
5   The difference between epistemology and ontology is illustrated through demonstrating how one could either subscribe to a realist (or materialist) ontology or an idealist ontology equally well with an empiricist epistemology. The example of Berkeley is used to illustrate this.
6   The difference between **induction** and **deduction** is clarified through a reflection upon Hume's notion of causality and his 'refutation of science'. Hume argues that we infer causality through a psychological process of association based upon repeated observation of constant conjunctures of events. This is thus relying upon induction, i.e. inferring general rules from numbers of particular instances. Deduction moves in the other direction, i.e. we conclude what a particular case will be by starting from a generalisation. Thus, if to be rational is to be logical, and logic is understood (strictly speaking) to be deductive and not inductive, then science is not rational.

DIALOGUE

The Scene: Time does not pass. It never does in virtual reality. Time's irreversible arrow is easily subverted here; one can scroll backwards and forwards in the digital transcript to exactly the point one chooses. At this point, the sociology student Socrates and the on-line philosophy professor G.O.D. (Goddess of Delphi) recommence their dialogue.

Socrates: I'm back. Can I ask you a question? Are you always on-line?

G.O.D.:   Only for the time I'm paid. I've definitely got a life in the real world! You're not going to ask me about it, are you? We're not supposed to talk about our real lives – unless they're philosophically relevant of course.

Socrates: Don't worry. I'm not even curious. Even if I was I wouldn't have time. I've got to get a grip on the philosophy of social science. I'm still a little confused over our last chat, but I re-read the file and I think I've got a general idea where we're going. It does seem to be taking a rather long time to get to what I really need to find out about though.

G.O.D.:   There's a reason for that. Where do you think we've got to so far? What do you think are the major points we've covered so far?

Socrates: Well, most of the major points seemed to come towards the end of our last session. But let's see . . . all right, the philosophy of science is basically important for two reasons. First, it's important for political and rhetorical reasons. The claim to scientific status enhances the credibility of any body of alleged knowledge, discipline or school of thought. A claim to scientific status is not exactly the same as a claim to truth, but it enhances the credibility of truth claims if the scientific status can be justified. Right?

G.O.D.: What else?

Socrates: We need to have a good idea what science is in order to judge whether particular claims or even whole bodies of beliefs are in fact justified in their claims to scientificity. Even more importantly, the powerful rhetorical status of science is justified. It really is a good way, perhaps the best way, to discover information about the world. It's got an excellent track record in producing useful knowledges. We need to know what science is, in order that we can keep doing it, apply it to other areas and perhaps even improve it.

But this is one of the points I'm confused about. When I say something like 'the best way to discover information', it sounds to me as though we're talking about the **scientific method**. But you said that there wasn't any one scientific method.

G.O.D.: Wouldn't it be possible that rather than a single universal method, there were other criteria for determining scientificity, for creating a demarcation line between the scientific and non-scientific?

Socrates: Maybe. But I was never saying that there was a single scientific method, that a physics experiment is going to be the same as a chemistry experiment. Rather what I mean by the scientific method is a general method.

G.O.D.: I understand what you mean. But it depends upon how general and perhaps even how you mean 'general'. But your example is actually revealing. You said, 'physics experiment and chemistry experiment'. Experiment is generally incorporated as a key feature, usually the key feature, of the scientific method. Now assertions of this kind about the scientific method are, first of all, principally associated with one particular philosophy of science – positivism.

Some sort of explanation or general description of the scientific method is usually found in the opening chapters of introductory textbooks for virtually all the sciences, including the social sciences. The perspective presented is usually positivist. The features of scientific experiments usually figure prominently as well. However, experimentation is simply not possible in many fields of inquiry, particularly social scientific fields of inquiry. For example, experiments in macroeconomics or sociology are simply not possible for obvious reasons.

Socrates: What obvious reasons?

G.O.D.: Well, could we deprive a group of children of all education to see if they really learn anything of lasting benefit in school? Could we legalise prostitution to see if the divorce rate goes up or the crime rate down?

Socrates: Okay, okay. I guess the reasons are obvious. We can't control human beings and play about with them like chemistry sets – even if it sometimes seems like the politicians do that.

G.O.D.:   There are also other reasons that aren't so immediately obvious. But we'll leave that until we consider critiques of positivism and then look at the issues again when we consider arguments about the impossibility of social science.

Socrates: You mean my question wasn't so stupid after all?

G.O.D.:   No, it wasn't. My apologies.

Socrates: Couldn't social science approximate experiment? Obviously there are things that couldn't be done exactly like the classic experiments of physics. But sociology has some sort of **analogues of experiment**. For example, we formulate concepts and then **operationalise** them. This means finding some way of testing them against the world. We develop techniques of statistical comparison and analysis of correlations between variables. From this we might be able to infer causality, even make predictions and approximations of scientific laws.

G.O.D.:   Very good. You remember some of your first year social science.

Socrates: Actually I was looking at one of my textbooks. I don't really remember much of it at all.

G.O.D.:   I'm sure you remember more than you think. Also I'm sure it made a deeper impression on you than you think. Therein lies a future problem. It's one of the things that make the philosophy of science quite difficult for those just coming to the subject.

We begin to explore the issues concerning the nature of scientific explanation and so on with some degree of sophistication after a while. But all the time, in the back of most students' minds is an obstacle to really coming to grips with the subject properly. They learn about a variety of perspectives upon the nature of scientificity, but somehow they manage to retain the understanding of science they had when they first began. It's a kind of intellectual schizophrenia. A kind of 'double think' is employed. The person develops on one level a fairly sophisticated picture of science. Yet on another level they simultaneously retain their earlier crude notions, as though somehow that is what science really is. Beginners in the philosophy of science don't come to it fresh even if they may think so. Actually to achieve any knowledge of the subject they constantly have to fight the confusion generated by fairly deeply ingrained misconceptions. Ah, well, there's no way around it really.

Socrates: You philosophers really are something! You imply that I'm crazy. You label me a positivist. Which, I'll say again, you make sound like a dirty word.

You label me before I even know what the words mean!

G.O.D.:   I didn't say you're crazy; schizophrenic was the term used, and I wasn't being literal. Anyway, I'm sure you can take it. More importantly, if I make positivism sound like a dirty word, I don't mean to, not at this point anyway. Positivism as a philosophy of science has a lot to be said for it. In many respects it is quite a well-thought-out, sophisticated account of science. At least some of its variations are. There's another thing to be wary of, by the way. Positivism is a term that gets quite a variety of different usages. It can be used very broadly and very narrowly. You need to attend pretty closely to the context it is in and to who is using it. But don't worry. I'll keep reminding you of that as we go along.

The main thing is that some version of positivism, whether very crude or very sophisticated, forms most people's understanding of science. The problem is that people forget (if they ever knew) that positivism is merely one general account of the nature of scientificity amongst others. It is an explanation of a complex topic, which must compete with others. It has things to recommend it. But on the other hand, it has weaknesses, fairly serious weaknesses.

Socrates: Okay, so I'm a crude positivist, while even sophisticated versions of positivism have flaws in them – but I still don't know what positivism is yet!

G.O.D.: Yes, I'm sorry, but you're just going to have to be patient. I've got a question to ask you first. Why is it that we need to have a good understanding of what natural science is before we can proceed to engage with social science directly?

Socrates: Because the field of debate in the philosophy of social science is structured around questions as to whether social science can be, or even whether it should attempt to be, scientific in the same way as natural science. We thus need to have a pretty good idea of what natural science is before we can answer these questions.

G.O.D.: Very good.

Socrates: So now will you tell me what positivism is?

G.O.D.: Well, I'll begin to. Positivism is basically a sub-species of empiricism. You remember I told you that the philosophy of science basically consisted of epistemology, ontology, logic and methodology, with a dash of politics and ethics tied on to either end?

Socrates: I don't know what you mean by 'tied on to either end'.

G.O.D.: These questions not only have political implications, they usually also reflect the political biases and context the philosopher began with. For example, Marxism's scientificity is challenged by the criteria for scientificity Karl Popper developed. He develops good reasons and arguments for the applicability of these criteria, which apparently have nothing to do with politics. Yet the fact that he didn't like Marxist politics and that Marxism is categorised along with astrology as unscientific, perhaps might not be coincidental. Similarly, Comte's notions of a positive social science of society can be seen to connect up with his concern with the problem of social reforms and social order in a manner that reflects the aftermath of political revolution. But that too we'll look at later.

The point is that epistemology and ontology are very longstanding and central subject areas of philosophy. Philosophers asked questions about the nature of both being and knowledge a long time before science was born. Epistemology and ontology merely become somewhat modified and specifically focused within the philosophy of science. They did so in response to science itself, its knowledge-producing success and one of the most significant cultural phenomena of human history – the **Enlightenment**.

Socrates: I've heard of that, but I don't know much about it.

G.O.D.: You should. It marks the beginning of the **modern era**. Or so it is sometimes characterised as doing. All right, now for a little twenty-second history lesson. Event is probably not the best way of describing the Enlightenment. Or even events. It is not one single occurrence, and what most significantly occurred happened within the sphere of ideas. A new way of conceiving of the world came into being. Some of this came about as a result of the Reformation, which allowed some relaxation of the Catholic Church's monopolistic control of thinking within Western Europe. Some of it came about as a result of the **scientific revolution** of the preceding century, which demonstrated not only new knowledges of the world but new ways of acquiring knowledge of the world. At any rate, in the eighteenth century a virtual explosion of new thinking occurred within the realms of morality, politics, and most significantly for our focus here, epistemology. It was not a question of a single set of ideas or a single subject matter that was transformed. To study the Enlightenment as a phenomenon is to study a whole range of subject areas – the political thought of Rousseau and Paine, the American and French revolutions, philosophy, literature and art. All of this combined to effect a transformation of the Western world, a new **cosmology**.

This new cosmology was inherently more democratic in its attitude to knowledge. Now, there you go, my first direct reference to a political connection with the philosophy of science. You'll find that democracy, in some sense or another, is an issue quite crucially bound up with epistemology and in very complex ways.

Socrates: You mean, for example, issues to do with the social control aspect of knowledge?

G.O.D.: Yes, but I'm not going to go into that in very much detail at this point. We're not quite ready yet. But I don't want to give you the idea that in the eighteenth century the production of knowledge was a very democratic process. It was, and still is now (though of course it's organised rather differently), very much the activity of an elite. No, what changed profoundly in the Enlightenment was the conception of the source of knowledge, the conception of how knowledge might potentially be produced. It was, in a sense, democratised.

Socrates: I don't want to interrupt your history lesson. But I just thought I'd point out that you're contradicting yourself.

G.O.D.: No, I'm not. The actual production of knowledge, certainly scientific knowledge at any rate, is undertaken by a relatively small community. It is undertaken within a hierarchical system and subject to dynamics of power relations that are certainly far from democratic. However, within the Enlightenment, different conceptions of the source of knowledge came to the fore. It was these that were more democratic. Prior to the Enlightenment the source of all knowledge was held to be God.

This is, of course, an over-simplification but not too terrible an over-simplification. Thus, knowledge (leaving aside some, but not all, practical everyday knowledges) could only be acquired in one of two ways. It could either come through divine inspiration, both a dubious and rather dangerous source. Or it could come through the interpretation of sacred texts. For Christian Western Europe this meant, of course, principally the Bible. But it could also mean certain other canonical texts, including philosophical texts, most notably Aristotle.

Socrates: Just a minute. You said divine inspiration was dubious. Okay, I can see that. When someone tells me they've got a direct line to God, I'm inclined to be sceptical. But why dangerous?

G.O.D.: Well, the Church was a very authoritarian structure. People's relationship to God was supposed to be mediated through the Church. This explains the significance of the Reformation, with respect to the Enlightenment. Anyway, claiming direct knowledge from God could easily be interpreted as an attempt to usurp Church authority. Knowledge, both then and now, is a social product. Claims to knowledge have to be socially certified as genuine. The Church was the institution, officially accredited so to speak, to do this. Claims to knowledge from within the perspective of pre-Enlightenment cosmology ultimately derived from authority – the ultimate authority, of course, being God Himself. Now, leaving aside direct communication, knowledge was thus to be found in canonical texts – the words of God, if you like.

Hermeneutics, a discipline about which we'll have a lot to say later, derived its initial meaning from this history. It was the 'science' of interpretation. Knowledge was produced through the process of wresting the meaning from these sacred texts. Later on, in more contemporary times, hermeneutics became more generally the science of meaning and interpretation whereby society itself can be seen as being a sort of text.

Socrates: Why did it need a special science to discover the meaning of these sacred texts? Couldn't God have been clearer?

G.O.D.:   I don't know whether you're trying to be funny or not. But it doesn't matter. One can provide either a sociological historical answer to that question or a literary one. One even might give a theological answer, if one was so inclined. But these would all take us off the subject. I'm only giving you the basic gist in fairly crude terms of a complex historical phenomenon. Cosmological history has a great many dimensions to it. But for our purposes the central point is this – God, the Church and sacred texts being the sources of knowledge ensured two things. First, they ensured a certain rigidity to the knowledge acquisition process, an innate conservatism if you like. And second, they ensured an authoritarian structure to the very essence of the process.

The Enlightenment brought a different orientation to the manner in which knowledge was conceived. I said earlier it 'democratised' the very understanding of the knowledge production process. By that I meant it rooted knowledge, the source of knowledge, in human rather than divine capacities.

Socrates: Okay, I see your point. Which human capacities?

G.O.D.:   The capacity for rational thought, which we all possess, and in our capacity to learn from experience.

Socrates: Well, that seems rather obvious. Of course we learn from experience – well, we should. But I think I'm missing the significance here.

G.O.D.:   Only because you don't know the history of ideas. Or rather, because on an unconscious level, you know it too well. You simply take for granted now what were originally quite revolutionary ideas. The two dominant post-Enlightenment Western philosophical traditions, **rationalism** and **empiricism**, were based upon these two human capacities. Rationalism was founded upon the notion that all human beings possess the capacity for rational thought. Empiricism alleges the source of all knowledge is to be found in experience. Both of these are human capacities, basic facts inherent in the human condition. I think I can make my point about democracy more easily through a rationalist example. Have you read Descartes?

Socrates: He's the 'I think, therefore I am' guy.

G.O.D.:   Yes, the **cogito**. 'Cogito ergo sum'. He attempted to subject everything he knew to a radical sceptical doubt. He wished to found his philosophy only upon that which he could not doubt. He felt that it would only be those ideas that he held most clearly and distinctly that would be true. Well, his line of reasoning can be and has been subjected to considerable criticism. However, what is perhaps most crucially important was, good reasoning or bad, it was reasoning! Not that medieval scholars and philosophers didn't engage in reasoning; they did, and some of it was pretty sophisticated too. But though they reasoned, they were always appealing to a source beyond and outside of reason for the legitimacy of their conclusions. Descartes was appealing to Reason itself. Reason rather than Faith was the source of knowledge.

Now, there is reason to believe that perhaps Descartes was writing with one eye cast over his shoulder at ecclesiastical authority. He was aware of, and probably not a little concerned by, the Church's treatment of Galileo, who was forced to recant his heretical views on astronomy. Perhaps this was why Descartes managed, after doubting everything all the way to the cogito as the sole foundation of his philosophy, to reason his way back to God. Perhaps not. The point is that while staying on the safe side of the Church, whether from prudence or genuine conviction, he actually produced a more radical undermining of its authority than if he had concluded God's non-existence. It may even have been the case that such a conclusion was not merely politically dangerous but literally impossible to think. The project of doubting everything is not quite so easy as Descartes supposed it was.

Socrates: I don't quite know what you mean. But never mind that. I don't think I'm with you on the main point here. How is his work more radically subversive than if he had denied God's existence?

G.O.D.: Because although he concluded God's existence, and a great deal else that went along with the conventional ideas of the day, including the Church's authority, his source of such conclusions came from enthroning his own power of reason as the supreme arbiter of what is true. The human capacity to reason, not a faith in divine wisdom, is the source of knowledge. He reasoned his way to God's existence, but he didn't begin there! Whether God exists or not, it is through Reason rather than sacred texts by which we are going to acquire knowledge of the world. If the Church had been paying closer attention, they ought to have burnt him at the stake. Such thinking proved far more radically subversive in the long run.

Socrates: So it's the process one uses to reach conclusions rather than authority and power that gives them their legitimacy, their validity. Yes? And process, in Descartes's case, is reason and logic. This is taking us down the road towards the scientific method, right?

G.O.D.: Well, let's say it's one of the approach roads. Science, as I said before, even science recognisable as such in today's terms, was well under way before the eighteenth-century Enlightenment.

Immense scientific achievements had occurred much earlier, making the seventeenth the real century of scientific revolution. Enlightenment epistemology was really only articulating the implications of a scientific outlook already implicit and applied in the work of such men as Galileo, Kepler, Boyle and Newton (above all Newton!).

People as early as the late sixteenth century were already articulating some kind of notion of what science was that could be recognisable in today's terms. Francis Bacon's view, a kind of early empiricism, again undermined the Church's authority through subtle subversion rather than any frontal assault. Bacon's stance could be seen as a kind of ironic inversion of Christ's encounter with Roman authority. Christ's command 'Render unto Caesar what is Caesar's' was expressed by Bacon in relation to Church authority as an injunction to leave 'to faith what is faith's'. The realm of God and theology could belong to the Church (or rather to the churches, because the English Revolution's Protestant sectarian struggles were the social backdrop to this line of thinking). However, nature, and the knowledges of it that human beings could discover, were held to be the provenance of science. And these were to come from their practical activity and experimentation.

Socrates: I still haven't quite got what empiricism is. You were saying before that it was to do with sense impressions, perception – 'seeing is believing'.

G.O.D.: In its most basic formulation empiricism is simply this: experience is the source of all knowledge. 'Seeing is believing' is simply a common-sense expression of this epistemological position. It oversimplifies, but yet it actually gets at the most important aspect of empiricist philosophy quite well, even to the tendency to prefer sight over our other senses. There are two important aspects to empiricism's putting experience as the foundation of knowledge with respect to science. The first is crucially important in coming to understand what science really is, though it tends to get lost sometimes by the empiricist philosophers. That is, experience is active. One learns about the world through interacting with it. Science is a practice, a human activity. This is true whether that activity is classifying, measuring, experimenting or even simply theorising. But a number of empiricist philosophers, though deriving their position on knowledge from this central proposition concerning experience, tended to transform this necessarily active component of experience into a more passive view of the nature of knowledge.

Socrates: In what way?

G.O.D.: Through their concentration upon the second aspect or implication of experience as the source of knowledge. The focus upon experience, as the old saying 'seeing is believing' implies, focuses upon the sensory nature of experience. We see the world, hear it, touch it and so on. This provides us with the evidence of what it is like. We are thus something akin to a blank slate to be written upon. There is no **a priori** knowledge of the world.

Socrates: *A priori*?

G.O.D.: Yes, it literally means 'before experience'. It is knowledge that is held to be innate or true by definition. For example, two plus two equals four is true because the numbers, the operation of addition and the meaning of 'equals' can all be defined in relation to one another. But we need experience to tell us anything about the world.

Socrates: Well, that seems only obvious.

G.O.D.:   Yes, it's obvious and true too – to a certain degree. But nonetheless one is left with a lot of problems concerning the nature of knowledge still.

Socrates: Like what? I kind of like the 'seeing is believing' idea.

G.O.D.:   You also liked the grounding of knowledge in the human capacity for rational thought, didn't you?

Socrates: No, not so much.

G.O.D.:   Why not?

Socrates: Well, who is to say what is rational anyway? What do you mean by rationality? People are crazy. I think most people are crazy anyway. Sometimes I even think I'm crazy.

G.O.D.:   Yes, well okay. You've hit on a big question there, I'll grant you. What exactly rationality is, is indeed not so easy a question to answer. And it is a question that I'd like to leave for a while. I've got a plan as to where we're going, and I'd like to leave some of the issues concerning rationality until later. Is that okay with you?

Socrates: Sure, whatever you say. But empiricism, at least as far as you've got with it, just seems to make better sense. I don't think most people think very logically. Do you?

G.O.D.:   Well, no, a lot of the time they don't. But the central idea was not that people thought rationally all the time, just that it was a human capability. Let's just say for the time being that rationality is something like logic and that human beings have the capacity for logical thought. Mathematics is logical. And mathematics is crucial to science and the production of many different sorts of knowledge about many different aspects of reality.

One of the central questions concerning knowledge is how to put together these two different viewpoints concerning knowledge. Perhaps a better way of expressing it would be to say 'emphasis' rather than 'viewpoint'. Rationalist epistemology as manifest in the philosophy of science certainly does not rule out empirical evidence being of considerable significance. Don't make the mistake of equating the terms empiricist and empirical by the way. Empiricism is the label for an epistemological position, one that emphasises a particular relationship to experience, the observable, the empirical world. But all philosophies of science of necessity must give some account of our relationship to the empirical domain. It is simply a fact that science engages with it. Possibly for this reason empiricism, at least early on in the history of the philosophy of science, was most influential. However, empiricism must also give some account of the utilisation of logic, mathematics, etc. in scientific practice. In other words, it too must take account of the importance of our human capacity for rational thought.

Socrates: Wait a minute, I think I've got it. It is simply that the empiricists emphasised experience and the rationalists emphasised people's rational processing of that experience. Is that it?

G.O.D.: More or less. Yes.

Socrates: Okay, that makes sense. Though you certainly took a lot of words to say so. Is that what philosophy is all about? Taking a long-winded way to say something pretty simple.

G.O.D.: No, it's not. Though I can see why it might seem so to you. The fault is probably mine.

Socrates: Don't get offended. It just really seems like that sometimes. Let's see if I've got this right. So the empiricists emphasised the reality of the world out there, the world that we see and touch. The rationalists saw reality as a mental phenomenon. Yes?

G.O.D.: No. Now you're conflating and confusing two different philosophical territories again – epistemology and ontology. You see? Perhaps things aren't quite so simple as you thought.

Socrates: Don't sound triumphant when I get things wrong! You're not really God you know.

G.O.D.: Don't I know it! I'm just a poor, underpaid and exploited employee of Microsoft. But seriously you have got things wrong a bit.

Socrates: And just when I thought I had a hold on it too.

G.O.D.: Don't worry. Some of the world's most prominent philosophers have made just this sort of mistake. The thing is that ontology and epistemology have to fit together coherently. This is much more difficult than it might first appear. One can be a rationalist, for example, and emphasise the logical conceptual component of knowledge. One can do this without denying either the existence or importance of an empirical world. But just as, on the one hand, being a rationalist doesn't necessarily commit you to idealism, though frequently they go together . . .

Socrates: Sorry, what's idealism again?

G.O.D.: No, it's my fault. It's actually difficult to discuss these subjects without slipping into 'isms'. Remember earlier, when we talked about Plato and points and triangles? Which is real, the concept of the triangle or the triangularly shaped thing in the world?

Socrates: Plato said it was the idea of the triangle that was real. The thing in the world was just a representation. That's idealism, isn't it?

G.O.D.: Right. And it is an ontological perspective. It's a philosophical assertion about the nature of reality rather than an epistemological assertion about the nature of knowledge. Empiricism, 'seeing is believing', is an epistemological position. The three most famous empiricist philosophers, sometimes known as the British Empiricists, John Locke, George Berkeley and David Hume, all held quite different ontological positions. Berkeley, for example, was an idealist.

Socrates: Really. You mean he didn't think there was a world out there. What was he seeing when he was believing then?

G.O.D.: The mind of God.

Socrates: What? Oh, come on now! Was he doing a Descartes kind of deal and pulling some kind of a dodge with the Church authorities?

G.O.D.: No, definitely not. We actually don't know for sure how far Descartes was going to disguise his ideas. But Berkeley was a bishop. And totally sincere. He got to his position in quite a different manner from Descartes. Earlier we discussed sense impressions as being mental phenomena. You remember? When you look at a rock, you receive a visual impression of the rock in your mind. But how do you know that there is a rock 'out there' in the real world?

Socrates: Yes, that sounds vaguely familiar.

G.O.D.: Okay, well if you are asserting that experience, sensory experience is the source of all knowledge; the answer to the question 'how do you know there is a rock out there in the real world?', or more generally 'how do you know that there is any real world out there at all?', could be quite simply that you don't. You only know that you have sensory impressions – of rocks, houses, people, the stars, whatever. Are there 'things' that really exist that cause these sensory impressions? Berkeley would argue that it is an unwarranted presumption to assert that such is the case. We only have the sensory impressions as the source of knowledge. These are essentially mental phenomena; ergo, it makes sense to speak of reality being a mental phenomenon.

There is a classic philosophical question: does a tree make a sound when it falls in the forest if there is no one there to hear it? Berkeley's answer would be no. In fact he would argue that there is no tree at all if there's no one to perceive it. The perceptions are reality.

Socrates: But that's silly.

G.O.D.: Well, maybe, I'm rather inclined to think so, but . . .

Socrates: I mean, if things didn't exist unless there was someone to perceive them, then things would be coming in and out of existence all the time. I look at the wall; I look away from it; I look back at it. It goes in and out of existence, back and forth; the world is appearing and disappearing. It's ridiculous! I see a friend. I look away. He disappears. What happens when he looks away from me? Do I disappear? No, the idea is silly. I mean really! Is this what philosophy is about? I'd have a real simple way of refuting Berkeley if he were around today.

G.O.D.: Oh yes, and how would you do that?

Socrates: I'd just give him a smack on the back of the head. There's reality for you, Bishop, I'd say; it's there whether you look at it or not. It can sneak up behind you.

G.O.D.:   Hmm. Interesting approach. But actually it wouldn't do as a refutation.

Socrates: No? Why not?

G.O.D.:   Well, you'd be just reproducing, in somewhat more dramatic form, the classic story of Berkeley's friend Dr. Johnson's attempt to refute him. He and Berkeley were out on a walk together, and Berkeley was explaining this idea to him. Johnson kicked a stone and exclaimed, 'I refute it thus', thus demonstrating to Berkeley and future generations of philosophy students that he'd totally failed to understand Berkeley's arguments. Touch, you see, is every bit as much a sensory perception as is vision. The argument works just as well whatever sense you might be referring to. You were actually on a better track when you were talking about reality appearing and disappearing – except that Berkeley had an answer to that too.

Socrates: What's that then?

G.O.D.:   Well, sense impressions are mental phenomena. But there is an inter-subjectivity involved. The individual's mind, the individual sense impressions are not all there is. Rather it is simply that the basic stuff of reality is a phenomenon of mind, universal mind, God.

Socrates: Okay, I get it. But I'm still not impressed.

G.O.D.:   No? Fair enough. But it's not quite so simple a matter to refute his logic either. Anyway, I only brought up Berkeley to demonstrate the fact that there are a variety of ontological positions compatible with an empiricist epistemology. There are empirical realists too.

Socrates: That's what you said you were, isn't it?

G.O.D.:   No, I said I was a critical realist. I said you were an empirical realist. Remember? Critical realists are also empirical realists, but their understanding of the nature of the real, embraces far more than merely what is empirically perceptible, and their view of knowledge is not empiricist – of whatever variety. There are varieties of realists, and there is a long history of philosophical confusion as well as different schools of thought utilising this term.

There are also varieties of empiricist philosophies – phenomenologists, instrumentalists, positivists and others. There's also a variety of positivist positions. Don't worry, I haven't forgotten where we're going; we're going to get to positivism eventually.

Socrates: Thanks for reminding me. I'd forgotten all about it. Positivism is a brand of empiricism, eh?

G.O.D.:   That's right. It is a way of explaining the problem of the relationship between our rational conceptual capacity and our sensory experience, which together constitute our production of knowledge. Knowledge itself is a mental phenomenon. It is something that we as individuals acquire and possess. But it is not merely subjective. Its objectivity derives from the sensory observations of our experience and the logical conceptual procedures we utilise to analyse these observations.

Socrates: That seems reasonable.

G.O.D.: Yes, it certainly is. But, as you pointed out earlier, rationality isn't quite so simple a matter to conclude upon. But even if you take it simply to mean being logical, it's not a simple matter putting the two together. In fact, there's a very serious problem involved.

Socrates: What's that?

G.O.D.: **Induction**. Alfred North Whitehead called it the bane of philosophy.

Socrates: What about **deduction**? Isn't it more central to logic?

G.O.D.: Well, yes. And if we want to see science as being the relation of reason to experience, we want to go in that direction. But there's a problem. A huge problem! Hume, one of the classic empiricist philosophers I mentioned earlier, was the first to identify it. But people have been grappling with it more or less unsuccessfully ever since.

Socrates: What is it then?

G.O.D.: The problem essentially is this. Deduction is a form of inference where you move from the general to the particular, from the universal to the particular. For example, the **syllogism** is the classic form of deductive inference. You have a statement 'All A's are B'. You then have a second statement, 'This is an A'. You are therefore logically justified in the conclusion that it is also a B. A favorite example of philosophy textbooks uses your computer code-name – well probably they had the original Socrates in mind when the example was used. Okay, here it is: 1) All men are mortal. 2) Socrates is a man. 3) Therefore, Socrates is mortal. The syllogism is not the only form of deductive argument, of course, but it expresses the essence of deduction. One moves from the general to the particular. Scientific laws, as usually understood, are formulated and applied in this fashion. This understanding of scientific law and explanation, by the way, is generally referred to as the **deductive-nomological** or **'covering law' theory**. Okay, let me give you an example, Newton's first law of motion: 'Every body continues in its state of rest, or of uniform motion in a straight line, except so far as it may be compelled by force to change that state' (in A.N. Whitehead, *Science and the Modern World*, 1967, p. 46). This is the general statement – the scientific 'law'. Now an experimental observation: the steel ball-bearing rolling along a horizontal plane slowed and came to a stop. Conclusion: some force must have been applied to it to cause it to do so. You see the reasoning involved here. The behaviour of the rolling steel ball is a particular instance of the universal condition expressed in the law. Thus, we know, know absolutely, that our conclusion must be true. That is, it must be true if Newton has correctly discovered and formulated a universal law of nature. Yes? The reasoning involved is deductive.

Socrates: Makes sense to me. What's the problem?

G.O.D.: Where did the law come from in the first place? We can apply it deductively to form conclusions and make predictions, but how did we arrive at it? Did we deduce it the way we reached our conclusion about the behaviour of the steel ball?

Socrates: Didn't we? Or rather didn't Newton?

G.O.D.: Well, I am sure he reasoned and used deduction as well as experimentation in order to discover his laws of nature, but what is the starting point? Deduction moves from the general to the particular. And if we are utilising our experience of the world as the basis of knowledge, we are apparently forced to move in the other direction. That is, we are moving from the particular to the general. We do not experience the universe; we experience small samples of it. We conduct an experiment. We expect the experiment to tell us something beyond itself. We wish to generalise from it. With respect to science, the positivist view of science anyway, we understand scientific laws in terms of such generalising from experience and experiment.

Socrates: Yeah, I'm with you, but I still don't see the problem.

G.O.D.: Let's go back to Hume. Let us look at his take on causality. Hume turned the world upside down, or at least the philosophical world, with his observations about rationality, science and causality. Okay, we observe an event A occurring repeatedly, after which event B invariably occurs. We conclude that event A caused event B. Hume used one billiard ball striking another as an example. One ball hits a second one; the second one moves. Simple. The collision caused the second ball to move. This occurs every time we observe it. There is a constant conjuncture of events. Science, in just the same way as we appear to do in everyday life, apparently concludes causality from the observation of constant conjunctures of events.

Socrates: That seems reasonable to me.

G.O.D.: Hume doesn't conclude that this is an unwarranted conclusion exactly. But he argues that it is logically unwarranted. He explains our conclusions of this sort in psychological terms. We have a psychological association of the one event with the other and conclude a causal relation. Now this may be sensible (in one sense of the word sensible) to conclude both in science and in everyday life. Certainly Hume aimed his intentions and his billiard balls in the same way everybody else would do if they wished to knock one into a pocket. But at root, the sort of inference we are making is not at all deductive in form; it is inductive.

Socrates: Now just a minute. Hume plays billiards the same way as everybody else. He believes that the collision of one ball into another causes the second ball to move. Yes? But he's saying we don't deduce this, we don't use deductive logic in coming to this conclusion. Yeah? Well, so what? It's obvious what is causing what. We don't need

	logic to come to a conclusion. And what was the bit about psychological association?
G.O.D.:	Okay, so you believe the collision of the first ball causes the motion of the second. Why?
Socrates:	What do you mean why? I told you it's obvious. Don't you think so?
G.O.D.:	Yes. Hume believed it too. But why? Saying it's obvious doesn't answer the question. By the way, this *is* what philosophy is all about: trying to enquire into things that are apparently obvious, that everyone takes for granted.
Socrates:	It seems to me that a lot of what philosophy is about is answering simple questions with more complicated ones.
G.O.D.:	Well, that's true. But there is a lot to be gained by doing so. All right, I'll give you again Hume's answer to the billiard ball causality problem. Our belief in causality essentially derives from observed repetition. We observe a constant conjuncture of events. In this case it is the collision of billiard balls as one event followed by a second event, the motion of the second ball. It is the constant association of one event with another in our minds that leads us to infer causality.
Socrates:	Well, maybe so. But the inference is correct, isn't it?
G.O.D.:	Yes, I think it is. But try putting your question a different way? Is the inference valid?
Socrates:	What do you mean?
G.O.D.:	I mean, is it logically a valid inference? And the answer is no. It is an inductive inference. Induction is a form of inference where you move from the particular to the universal. You observe x number of flowers are red. You then conclude all flowers are red.
Socrates:	Yeah, all flowers aren't red. Seeing a lot of red flowers could lead me to a false conclusion. Fine. But that's not the same as the billiard ball conclusion.
G.O.D.:	No?
Socrates:	No. To put it in your language, I'm moving from the particular to the particular.
G.O.D.:	Very good. Very good indeed. I appreciate the difference. Except that that form of inference is merely a sub-species of induction. The term for it is **eduction**. But it is essentially the same form of reasoning and equally logically invalid.
Socrates:	How so?
G.O.D.:	Because underwriting the move from the particular to the particular is a generalisation for which you have no basis. You pick twenty or thirty round white marbles from a jar. Your inference is that the next one will be the same. Yes? You're inferring that all the marbles in the jar are white – which is why the next one you pick will also be so.

Socrates: No, I'm not. I'm thinking that it probably will be.

G.O.D.:   Good, good, I think you're really beginning to get the hang of thinking philosophically.

Socrates: But I'm still wrong, right?

G.O.D.:   I'm afraid so. You've introduced probabilities into the equation. And prematurely. You would need to know what colour all the marbles in the jar were to know the probabilities of choosing any colour. And as you don't know that, you're making a universal generalisation based upon only a particular sample. Probabilistic reasoning is fundamentally deductive in form and quite different from induction, or eduction.

Socrates: I'm afraid I'm getting confused here.

G.O.D.:   Don't worry about it. Confusion between probabilistic and inductive reasoning is also a common mistake. Some quite famous philosophers have gotten confused on just this point. Just take your time and think about it. The essential thing to concentrate on is that induction and deduction move in opposite directions. We've seen thousands and thousands of examples of many repeated instances and never seen a counter-example. But do we know for sure that there will never be one? That is the way induction works. It is the exact opposite of deduction. If you know for sure all x's are y and that something is an x, then you know absolutely for sure that that x is y. But our observations of events are almost always samples; whether large or small it doesn't matter. We seldom perceive all of anything, or at least we don't know that we perceive all of it.

Socrates: Okay, I get that. So we can't know for sure. We can't really know anything for sure. Is the point that we don't have any knowledge at all?

G.O.D.:   Actually, I mentioned earlier that some have said that Hume produced science's 'refutation'. But he wasn't suggesting that we haven't any knowledge. And he was also quite willing to believe that science does produce knowledge of causality. His argument is more subtle. It is that if we identify rationality with logic, that is, with deduction, then strictly speaking, science is not rational.

Socrates: What's the big problem with that?

G.O.D.:   One could say there are two big problems with that, though I suppose in the end they come down to the same thing really. The question concerns science's special claim to authoritative knowledge. I mean authoritative in quite a different sense here than that of deriving authority in terms of the socially sanctioned attribution of 'expertise' to scientists as a particular social group. They do have that authority with respect to knowledge. But remember I also argued that that authority was deserved!

They are not the equivalent of the Church, merely a new secular priesthood. Though some of the thinkers we shall later consider might argue that that is precisely the case. Religion doesn't base its claims upon its rationality. It bases them upon faith. We wish to justify science's special claim to credibility. But we don't want to base it simply on faith. And Hume has apparently shown us that science seems to rest upon just that.

Socrates: Who is this 'us'?

G.O.D.: Well, philosophers of science, scientists themselves.

Socrates: That sounds rather wet to me.

G.O.D.: Yes, exactly. On the one hand, it doesn't accord well with the general recognition and powerful conviction that the rational method is somehow intrinsic to science, and on the other, it doesn't answer the question of why science seems to be such a successful method of producing knowledge. One can exclude many sorts of questions from the remit of science. We can, if we wish, concede, as Bacon did, 'to faith that which is faith's'. But at the very least, we want to be able to demonstrate that there are good *reasons* for accepting that scientific knowledges do have a special status concerning claims about the natural world. At the very least! This is before we even ask questions about the status of knowledges about social reality. So Hume's argument is very disturbing. There may be problems with it; for instance, in his insistence on our ascriptions of causality being merely a psychological phenomenon. But the problem of induction remains a serious problem in the philosophy of science.

Socrates: You mean nobody has succeeded in solving it?

G.O.D.: Lots of people have solved it. They've solved it in all manner of ingenious ways. But there isn't one universally accepted solution. Essentially the problem remains. There is one solution that is probably dominant. It is to be found at the core of the most generally accepted account of natural science amongst contemporary natural scientists, and though it too emerged out of a critique of twentieth-century positivism, it is broadly positivist in outline itself. I think the time has come to give you an outline of some of the positions in contemporary positivist thought.

Socrates: Finally!

DISCUSSION QUESTIONS

1   How do you know that anything or anyone exists? Could not your whole experience of the world (including other people) simply be something like an elaborate three-dimensional 'film' (including the sensations of touch, smell and taste) being produced (by an unknown creator perhaps) for your benefit alone?

2   Most of the things we know about the world have been told to us by others – our parents, teachers, friends, the media, etc. However, we believe different things with varying degrees of conviction depending upon who is telling us. What are the factors influencing our confidence in believing what we are told is true? Is accepting the authority of scientists with respect to knowledge the

same as accepting the authority of the Church or the government? What differences might there be with respect to the credibility of these authorities?
3   Exactly what is the problem with inductive reasoning? Why is it said to be not wholly logical? Is Hume's argument, that our understanding of cause and effect is based upon induction and psychological association, correct? If he is correct in this, is he also correct in further arguing that science is not rational?
4   Why is it that empiricism as a philosophy has been more influential in the historical development of science than has rationalism?

FURTHER READING SUGGESTIONS

Lakatos, I. and Musgrave, A. (eds) (1970) *Criticism and the Growth of Knowledge*, Cambridge University Press, Cambridge.
Whitehead, A.N. (1967) *Science and the Modern World*, Free Press, New York.

The Enlightenment

Butterfield, H. (1957) *The Origins of Modern Science*, G.H. Bell, London.
Cassirer, E. (1951) *The Philosophy of the Enlightenment*, Princeton University Press, Princeton.
Heilbron, J. (1995) *The Rise of Social Theory*, Polity, Cambridge (Parts I & II).

The scientific revolution

Heilbron, J. (1995) *The Rise of Social Theory*, Polity, Cambridge (Chapters 8–10).
Shapin, S. (1996) *The Scientific Revolution*, University of Chicago Press, Chicago.

Classic early thinkers

Empiricism
Andreski, S. (ed.) (1974) *The Essential Comte*, Croom Helm, London.
Berkeley, G. (1963) *The Principles of Human Knowledge*, World Publishing Company, Cleveland.
Comte, A. (1976) *The Foundations of Sociology*, ed. K. Thompson, Nelson, London.
Dürkheim, E. (1964) *The Rules of Sociological Method*, Macmillan, London.
Hume, D. (1984) *An Enquiry Concerning Human Understanding, and An Inquiry Concerning the Principles of Morals*, Clarendon Press, Oxford.
Locke, J. (1976) *An Essay Concerning Human Understanding*, Clarendon Press, Oxford – contains a glossary, introduction and critical commentary by P.H. Niddich.
Mill, J.S. (1961) *Auguste Comte and Positivism*, University of Michigan Press, Ann Arbor.
——— (1961) *A System of Logic*, Longman, London.

Rationalism
Descartes, R. (1976) *Discourse on Method*, Bobbs-Merrill, Indianapolis.
——— (1986) *Discourse on Method, and the Meditations*, Penguin Books, New York.

Kant

Kant, I. (1983) *Critique of Pure Reason: An Introductory Text*, ed. H. Palmer, University College Cardiff Press, Cardiff.

———— (1983) *Kant's Promogena, and Metaphysical Foundations of Natural Science*, trans. E.B. Bax, G. Bell and Sons, London – contains a biography and introductory overview by the translator.

———— (1996) *Critique of Pure Reason*, Hackett, Indianapolis.

Phenomenonalism and materialism

Lenin, V.I. (1972) *Materialism and Emperio-Criticism*, Foreign Languages Press, Peking – presents a cutting critique of Mach and the 'Machians' as well as a classic formulation of a naive materialism. Debate has moved on from both Mach and Lenin on these points, but they still serve as a good introduction as to what is at stake between materialism and idealism.

Mach, E. (1959) *The Analysis of Sensations, and the Relation of the Physical to the Psychical*, Dover, New York – turn-of-the-20th-century exponent of the sort of empiricist idealism as espoused by Berkeley (as described briefly in this chapter). He was able to convince many scientists as well as philosophers.

More contemporary thinkers are to be found in the further reading lists of later chapters.

■ SM AND ITS PROBLEMS: S NOT ALL THERE IS TO ᴅᴄʟɪᴇVING

When I was giving expression to my joy that the results coincided with his calcula-tions, he said quite unmoved, 'But I knew that the theory is correct'; and when I asked, what if there had been no confirmation of his prediction, he countered: 'Then I would have been sorry for the dear Lord – the theory is correct'.

Ilse Rosenthal-Schneider, one of Einstein's students

The one thing I've learned about history is that no one has learned anything from history.

G.W.F. Hegel

OUTLINE OF MAJOR POINTS TO BE COVERED

1 The philosophy of science is both a description of what science is and a prescription of what it should be. The positivist account of science has been particularly influential. Even though sufficient scepticism has been directed at it, so as to give the label 'post-positivist era' to the present and recent past some purchase as a description, the humanist opposition to positivism within social science still retains a positivist account of natural science. Thus, understanding the basics of positivism is crucial to the understanding of the philosophy of social science debate.

2 The **deductive-nomological or covering law account** of scientific explana-tion is one very influential understanding of it. It explains scientific laws as standing in a deductive hierarchy of ever more basic and general explanatory purchase.

a Scientific theory and explanation may be understood in terms of a deductive argument consisting of a generalisation (the putative law or specific explanation), observational premises (expressed as statements) and a conclusion expressive of predicted observations. These latter observations are the empirical testing and confirmational proof of the theory.

3 The Humean notion of causality is explained in terms of observed successions of events. This is understood as a problem for the deductive-nomological account

of scientific explanation – the problem of induction. Strictly speaking, inductive inferences are not logical. Therefore it follows that science is not rational.

4 Falsification and the **hypothetico-deductive model of science** are explained in terms of being a potential solution to the above problem. All knowledge must be held provisionally. Scientific laws are seen as our best unfalsified hypotheses. With this qualification, though elaborated as a critique of positivism and the deductive-nomological account of science, its basic features are maintained, most notably a symmetry between explanation and prediction. The hypothetico-deductive account merely substitutes attempts at falsification for attempts at verification or confirmation.

5 The symmetry between explanation and prediction in positivist accounts of science is criticised through examples given of explanations that are not predictive and predictions that do not explain.

6 The role of probabilities in scientific explanation is considered through a reflection upon **Reichenbach's 'law'**: If two phenomena A and B occur with a statistical correspondence significantly greater than chance, then either there is a causal connection between A and B directly, or some third set of phenomena C, D, E, etc. had an independent causal connection with them both.

7 Various other features of the positivist explanation are described and criticised.

   a A distrust of metaphysics. This is itself a metaphysical position.

   b An insistence upon objectivity. Observation is itself theory-laden.

   c Explanations are conceived of deductively as relations between statements. There is great difficulty connecting up theoretical statements and observational statements, particularly in the light of point b above.

   d The empiricist emphasis upon experience and observation calls into question the instrumental enhancement of human faculties in this regard. No criticism is made here as contemporary positivism generally accepts instrumental enhancement as allowable. Nor is a criticism made of the methodological imperative to operationalise concepts.

   e Observational **anomalies** or anomalous experimental results should be treated as falsifications. The actual history of science shows this not to be the case. There are both potentially good reasons for this and bad ones. This issue is taken up in the next chapter when the work of Thomas Kuhn is considered.

8 A distinction between **naive falsificationism** and a more **conventionalist** account is given. Falsification procedures and goals do not actually wholly solve the problem of science's utilisation of induction, i.e. falsified theories and their procedures also stand upon inductive inferences. A conventionalist understanding of the hypothetico-deductive model of science, however, merely postulates it in terms of the scientific community's quite desirable norms and conventions of practice.

DIALOGUE

The Scene: Time does not pass. It never does in virtual reality. Time's irreversible arrow is easily subverted here; one can scroll backwards and forwards in the digital transcript to exactly the point one chooses. The astute reader will of course have observed that this is in no way dependent upon virtual reality or the new computer technologies. One can do exactly the same with a book. The sociology student Socrates and the on-line philosophy professor G.O.D. (Goddess of Delphi) recommence their dialogue.

G.O.D.: All right, to begin with, the term positivism did not originate in the twentieth century. It was coined by Augustus Comte.

Socrates: I know him. The 'father of sociology'. He came up with that name too.

G.O.D.: Yes, he tried to carve out a place for sociology as an autonomous discipline with its own distinct subject matter. Whether describing that effort in terms of fatherhood is the best way to go about understanding the process is another question. However, it's not a question we need go into here. He also tried to make the discipline into what he termed a 'positive science'. We do need to look at that. However, we'll leave that until later. The understanding of social science has some particular difficulties, and we are not yet through with natural science. Putting the two together can confuse issues that are complicated enough on their own.

Socrates: Okay, but just remember that that is where I need to go. We've talked for a long time and barely even mentioned social science.

G.O.D.: I think you'll find that we haven't been wasting our time. It's a necessary preparation. Remember I told you that the predominant views concerning the scientificity of social science are all principally based upon a particular understanding of natural science – positivism. At least broadly so. I also told you that some of the new positions on the subject would assert that that view is mistaken. Much sociology and other social science undertaken today could be said to be positivist, but nonetheless it is widely maintained, for a variety of reasons, that we are now in a post-positivist era. So before we can possibly begin to understand these debates, it would behoove us to have a clear understanding of positivism in natural science. So, are you with me? '

Socrates: Go for it.

G.O.D.: Okay, the first thing we can say about positivism is that it is an application of, or a version of, empiricism. We've already discussed empiricism more generally. Broadly speaking, positivism accepts the premise that experience is the source of knowledge but also somewhat more narrowly interprets what is meant by experience in terms of empirical observation.

The positivist, like all philosophers of science, reflects upon the practice of science and tries to make clear and explicit some of the things which are understood by the scientific practitioner in a rough and ready, practical kind of way. He or she attempts to make more precise the meaning of terms, to refine our understanding of the most important of those aspects of scientific practice perhaps most taken for granted, and thus hopes to improve scientific practice. So, positivist philosophers of science have given accounts of, for example, the form of scientific explanation, the precise meaning of terms such as scientific law and theory. Within such work, therefore, there is both prescription and description. The philosopher of science is providing a careful description of the nature of scientific explanation in general terms, a construction of an idealised model, if you like, of what form a scientific explanation actually takes. This model, though, is not merely descriptive but is prescriptive as well. The model is not only showing us what science is like but is also prescribing what science should be like. The model of scientific explanation is, on one level, an **abstraction** from actual scientific practice and, on another level, a refinement of how it ideally should be done. It cuts out what may be confused and contradictory in particular cases. Thus it is a guide to future practice as well as a description of past and present practice. Do you follow me here?

Socrates: I think so. Scientists produce particular explanations of some phenomenon or another. The explanation typically takes a certain form. But they haven't necessarily reflected carefully on the nature of their form of explanation. The philosophers take up the common points and what they see as essential to all scientific explanations and construct some kind of a model. Yes? This model can then serve to prescribe what are and what are not good scientific explanations.

G.O.D.:   Very good. So, you see, the philosopher is thus also providing a demarcation line between the scientific and the non-scientific.

Socrates: So, there is one positivist model of scientific explanation? We're back to the scientific method again.

G.O.D.:   Well, yes and no. I don't want to confuse the issue, but I don't want to give you false information either. There have been a lot of positivist philosophers, and they all put their own particular spin upon things. However, there is what you could call a dominant model. The dominant model of scientific theorising is called the hypothetico-deductive model, and the dominant model of the form of scientific explanation is the . . .

Socrates: The deductive-nomological or 'covering law' model.

G.O.D.:   Right. I'm impressed. You've got a good memory.

Socrates: Nah. I'm using a split screen so I can look back at our previous discussions. I want to see if I can catch you out in any contradictions. So you'd better be careful.

G.O.D.:   I will be. So, you can check on this. The second, and really for our purposes most significant model, is called the **hypothetico-deductive model of theory**. It is basically a refinement of the deductive-nomological model that we need to look at more carefully. Check on whether or not I've misled you. I fear I might have.

Socrates: Admitting you made a mistake, eh?

G.O.D.:   No, I said misled you. The deductive-nomological model of scientific explanation was being presented to you in another context. I was trying to make some points concerning generalisation and induction that we'll also need to return to when we consider the hypothetico-deductive model. However, I was correct when I asserted that scientific laws according to the 'covering law' model were essentially empirical generalisations from which one could deduce and predict specific behaviour and events. However, with my emphasis upon empirical generalisation, you might have got the idea that any old generalisation might do, and this isn't the case. In fact this is a problem for this theory of explanation. Scientific laws must be **non-trivial universalisations**.

Socrates: What do you mean?

G.O.D.:   I mean by that that they must in some sense 'speak beyond themselves'.

Socrates: You're certainly speaking beyond me. I have no idea what you're talking about.

G.O.D.:   Well, let's go back to my 'white marbles' example. Leaving aside the problem of how we obtained our universal statement 'all the marbles in this jar are white', it still would not qualify as a scientific law.

Socrates: Why not? I mean, I see what you mean by trivial. But I don't see the principle as to why it shouldn't be considered a law.

G.O.D.:   Good point. And not a trivial one either. This is a difficulty with the deductive-nomological model. Well, let's say we do know absolutely that all the marbles in the jar are white; we've taken them all out and looked at them perhaps. Okay, we know the generalisation is true. Now we produce the secondary statement, 'this is one of the marbles in the jar' and deduce the astounding conclusion that it is also white. We haven't really accomplished anything, have we?

Socrates: No, but . . .

G.O.D.:   All we have is concluded that our example fits our generalisation. We have a generalisation with the statement 'all the marbles in this jar are white' but not one that is capable of generating predictions. The positivist model of science places a great deal of stress upon prediction. There is a symmetry between explanation and prediction.

Socrates: Isn't it a prediction to say that any particular marble that you will find in the jar will be white?

G.O.D.: Not much of a prediction, is it? What you say is true enough though, and that's one of the problems with the deductive-nomological model of explanation. To qualify as a law it must somehow 'speak beyond itself', and yet in so doing it introduces problems with respect to its ostensibly purely deductive character.

Socrates: How so?

G.O.D.: Let's look back at Newton's first law of motion again. We can deduce any number of things from it. We can deduce that some force must be constantly exerted on the planets, for example, to keep them orbiting the sun instead of flying off into space in a straight line. From one law we can deduce other laws in a kind of deductive hierarchy; hence the name 'covering law'. But think about it. To explain the motion of the planets is neither trivial nor obvious. In conjunction with some other laws, most importantly concerning gravitational attraction, the motion and future relative position of the planets can be predicted.

Socrates: Okay, to qualify as a law a statement must have a number of characteristics. It must be universal. It must stand in a logical relationship to other scientific laws, and it must not be trivial but rather predictive . . . I'm still not sure I'm quite with you on the last point though.

G.O.D.: No, I think you've got the general idea. As I said there are problems with this 'speaking beyond itself' notion. We want to be able to exclude both tautologies and 'accidental' generalisations from our notion of law. To assert that 'all dogs are animals' is **tautological**, if dogs are partially defined in terms of their animality. To assert that 'all of the dishes on a particular restaurant's menu are vegetarian' may well be quite interesting to a non-meat-eating diner, but it would hardly qualify as a scientific law. It is in some sense 'accidental'. But it is not so easy to exclude it on purely formal grounds from qualifying as a scientific law. We seem to be introducing some other criteria in doing so. Formalising exactly what this is can be quite difficult. There are also problems to do with postulating a symmetry of explanation and prediction. I also want to draw your attention to another feature of twentieth-century positivism that your summary reminded me of. You said 'to qualify as a law a statement must' . . . do something. The key word is 'statement'. We need to understand how logical relationships between statements made about the world are connected to our empirical observations of the world. Which of these would you like me to discuss first?

Socrates: Which is more important?

G.O.D.: They are all tremendously important.

Socrates: Well, let's do explanation and prediction first then . . . get that one out of the way.

G.O.D.: Well, I don't think we'll actually be able to 'get it out of the way' as you so neatly put it. It's going to keep coming back in different guises. But I'll present for you some of the most obvious problems. Okay, the symmetry of explanation and prediction notion seems to work quite well in some cases. Planetary motion, gravitational force – there are countless examples where the symmetrical relationship between prediction and explanation seems obvious. Prediction and explanation are so inextricably interwoven that it seems almost fair to say that prediction is explanation and vice versa. The existence of hitherto unobserved planets was predicted upon the basis of careful observation and an application of scientific laws. Not only was their existence later confirmed by observation, but the particularities of their orbits, relationship to other bodies, etc. seemed to be explained wholly adequately. It can really seem in some cases that explanation is prediction and vice versa. Yes?

Socrates: If you say so.

G.O.D.: Don't say that. Are you following the reasoning here or not?

Socrates: Yes, I'm just kidding you. Look, I'll even predict what you're going to say next. You're going to say that there are other cases where the idea doesn't seem to hold up so well.

G.O.D.: That's right. In both directions. There are things we can predict quite well without being able to explain them and things we can explain yet can't use the explanation as a basis for prediction. Take evolutionary theory, for example. Natural selection, mutation, genetic inheritance etc. etc.; we have a pretty good understanding of the evolution of life, genetic diversity and so on. Yes? But we certainly cannot predict the emergence of any particular new species.

Socrates: No? I thought we could.

G.O.D.: Some things can be predicted as far as adaptation to particular conditions, such as increased insect resistances to pesticides, for example. But this is a long way from predicting the emergence of new species. Our understanding of the mechanisms at work in evolution and biological change is pretty good. But on the whole, it is a non-predictive form of understanding and explanation.

Okay, now on the other side of prediction and explanation, we can also quite confidently make many predictions which fall a long way short of what we consider might constitute an explanation. For example, there is such a strong statistical correlation between cigarette smoking and cancer that it is now concluded that smoking causes cancer. Okay, we can predict probabilities of people contracting the disease in the future in relation to past and present smoking habits but . . .

Socrates: Excuse me for interrupting but . . . 'predict probabilities'?

G.O.D.: Oh dear. I didn't pick a very good example, did I? It opens up a whole new can of worms. It's one we do need to consider but . . .

Socrates: Well, just use a different example then.

G.O.D.:   No, I may as well continue with this one. Maybe I can kill two birds, or even three or four, with one stone. But just forget the probability part of it for the moment. To know that smoking is linked to cancer is not the same as understanding just what it is about smoking that causes cancer. We don't know the reason why it has the effect it does. If there was 100 per cent correlation between cigarette smoking and cancer, it would cancel out our statistical probability problem, but even if we knew for sure that every smoker would get cancer, this still doesn't explain why. It doesn't explain the 'how' of it either. It doesn't explain the process whereby the smoking behaviour generates the cancer. Scientists are working on that one, and I believe have made some headway but it's a different problem. Do you see what I mean about prediction and explanation here? People were predicting on a daily basis the rising and setting of the sun for centuries before they were able to explain the phenomenon correctly.

Socrates: Okay, I get the point. So why didn't you just use that example to begin with? Never mind. So now we're left with statistics and probability and whatever you were on about before – something about 'statements'. You said it was important.

G.O.D.:   It is. And I've thought of a way to connect up statistics and probability with the question of language and meaning from a positivist perspective. I'll use one of the Vienna Circle of positivists [see further reading suggestions], a man named Reichenbach. The Vienna Circle developed to an extreme one of twentieth-century positivism's most important characteristics, a distrust of **metaphysics**.

Socrates: I've heard of metaphysics. A branch of philosophy, isn't it? But I don't know exactly what it is.

G.O.D.:   Well, according to the **Vienna Circle** of thinkers, metaphysics is basically nonsense. They developed a perspective upon language and meaning that was very influential within the philosophy of science. Essentially scientific explanations and theories are sets of scientific laws, theoretical and observational statements governed by logical relations; hence the names which are sometimes given to this line of thinking – **logical positivism** or **logical empiricism**. As good empiricists, they believed that empirical observation was the key to science. Relatively straightforward and simple statements, observation statements, could be made with respect to empirical observations. This is unfortunately a good deal more difficult than it might first appear. But leaving that aside for the moment, you can perhaps see the appeal of this position. It grounds science in both empirical observation and logic. The view they maintained concerning meaning was that the meaning of any statement was the set of possible observations sufficient to demonstrate its truth. The beauty of this position is that they have developed a theory of meaning such that

| | logical validity, truth and falsity are directly connected to observations about the world. And with that they categorised a whole class of possible statements – most importantly for philosophy, metaphysical statements – as strictly speaking meaningless. |

Socrates: You've lost me entirely. I'm not even sure what we're talking about any more.

G.O.D.: Right. I'll try again from a different angle, as there is a very practical set of consequences that follows from this point of view. All right, the source of knowledge ultimately lies in the observations you make about the world. Right? This is the cornerstone of empiricism. Now we make statements about the world, about our observations. These can be vague and nebulous or quite precisely connected to our observations. Well, I'm skirting over the problems and difficulties of this, but the imperative is to make the sort of statements that can be connected to the observations in hopefully some clear and unambiguous way, some testable way, some way that removes some of the inherent subjectivity of our sensory impression of the world. Let us say, for example, that rather than simply saying 'warm', we give a thermometer reading instead. This is something that is quantifiable, that is produced by a quite definite set of operations and which can be exactly compared with others. Some scientists have gone so far as to say that 'if you can't measure it, it doesn't exist'. What they mean by this, is that strictly speaking for phenomena to be rendered scientifically meaningful, one must be able to make statements about them precise enough to be logically manipulated – that is, in some sense or another, measured. Otherwise, they would say, you're just talking nonsense. Metaphysical statements, as for example 'God is just', would be classed as meaningless as it is inherently unverifiable by any conceivable observation.

Socrates: But I know what it means. There's obviously something wrong with a position that says something is meaningless that is perfectly understandable to millions of people. However, I think I see what they are on about. Statements that are purely speculative or at least cannot be proved or disproved by any appeal to empirical evidence are according to them meaningless. They are trying to restrict science and philosophy's field of investigation. Fine. I don't agree with it. But I think I understand it. But it's the notion of meaning having to do with the verification, or truth or falsity, of observations that I don't understand. And what does measurement have to do with it?

G.O.D.: I understand it's a little confusing. Let's go back to the idea of statements about the world connecting up with observations. I said before that this is actually problematical. Not only is the world complex, but our observations of it are rather complex too. A theory of meaning, now discarded, but nonetheless very influential in the development of positivism, was called **logical atomism**. This philosophy asserts that both scientific and ordinary language observation statements are actually compounds of extremely simple statements, the 'atoms' if you like, to which they are related through definition. Thus the most subtle and complex assertions of qualities could, at least potentially, be broken down into much simpler straightforward observation sentences with a clearly demarcated observational referent. To be meaningful, then, all statements must in the end be capable (even if apparently very indirectly) of connecting up with a definitely specified referent. These 'logical atoms', so to speak, can conversely be compounded to make our more complex scientific propositions. Thus, we have at root a simple straightforward relation of reference between observational statements and empirical observations. The more complex statements are merely logical constructions using these simple statements as building blocks. The meaning of such assertions is thus essentially their truth-values as governed by the laws of logical inference. The meaning of statements about the world thus ultimately comes down to whether or not they are verified by the observations we make of the world. Yes?

Socrates: I think so. Every meaningful statement ultimately says something about the world that at least in theory could then be either confirmed or denied by means of an observation. Statements that couldn't be tested out in this manner are regarded as meaningless. But it's still not entirely clear.

G.O.D.: Well, as I said, this is very problematical, and this philosophy of meaning has largely been abandoned. But it demonstrates the overall thrust of the positivist program. Scientific explanation is the logical manipulation of statements, some theoretical, some observational. Okay, now perhaps discovering these simple straightforward 'logical atoms' is not so easy; breaking up or compounding all sentences in this manner is extremely difficult, if not impossible. But what might be the easiest way to approximate it?

Socrates: I don't know.

G.O.D.: Well, basically there are two routes. Classification and measurement. Let's return for a moment to the abbreviated intellectual history of thought I gave you. It was, of course, extremely oversimplified and for that reason in some senses false. I may have implied that prior to the Enlightenment, prior to Descartes, no one had much use for reason. If I did, I was being extremely misleading. Scholastic philosophers were very much concerned with reason. They did in fact believe quite strongly in a reasoned ordered universe. In fact we can go back to the Stoics for the cornerstone of this belief. Seneca asserted that 'the Divinity has determined all things by an inexorable law of Destiny, which He has decreed, but He Himself obeys' (in A.N. Whitehead, *Science and the Modern World*, 1967, p. 83). But much of European thought prior to the Enlightenment was dominated for centuries by the thought of one Greek philosopher. Not Plato but Aristotle. And Aristotle's doctrines, as far as the development of science is concerned, entailed an injunction to classify! This was truly unfortunate and could be argued to be the principal intellectual obstacle to the development of science. Throughout the Middle Ages, for example, Aristotelian principle dominated. Reason manipulated abstractions whose relation to the observable world, while apparently clear, in fact blocked scientific advance. The prime methodological injunction said classify. It should have said measure.

This is the strength of the empiricist philosophical program. This is particularly the strength of the positivist refinement of it. Logic and analysis are used, and used quite rigorously, but the emphasis is upon observations, which first of all can be spoken of very precisely, and which second, can be manipulated logically very precisely. This logical operation is most significantly mathematical. Scientific technique comes down to a search for ways and means that reproducible operations can be specified, such that observation is most significantly measurement. This perspective is basically what paved the way for the significant scientific advances (most notably in physics) of the seventeenth century. Essentially positivism is all about formalising a philosophical framing and justification for what classical science had been operating with only semi-consciously.

Socrates: I think I follow you. Though I think I'll need to think about it a bit to digest it. But let's leave that. What about probabilistic reasoning? You mentioned this guy, Reichenbach.

G.O.D.: Oh yes, Reichenbach, one of the Vienna Circle. He formulated an important principle as concerns statistical reasoning. The use of statistics, you see, is quite important to science. Yet as far as I've explained it to you, statistical inferences couldn't qualify under deductive-nomological criteria as candidates for scientific laws. The deductive nature of such laws insists that they take the form of statements, something like 'if ever x then y'. However, almost all scientists and philosophers, including positivists, would like to include statistical inferences within the sphere of science, even if they do not take precisely this form. Such inference might take the forms, for example, 'if x then 20% of y', or 'if 60% of x then y', or finally 'if 25% x then 10% y'. There are a number of different ways in which science utilises statistics. Statistical inferences are often combined with either probabilities or a usage of induction. There is considerable confusion on this matter. But let me give you the most important and straightforward manner in which statistics can be used to determine causality with respect to Reichenbach's principle. It also somewhat redeems my earlier use of cigarette smoking as an example.

Socrates: Oh yeah. You don't like to admit mistakes, do you?

G.O.D.: Well, if you can turn vice into virtue, it's a pretty good trick isn't it? Okay, the scientific world has pretty much accepted that a causal linkage between cigarette smoking and certain forms of cancer has been definitely established. Yet, as we discussed before, the nature of the **causal mechanism**, how it works, etc., is a long way from being fully understood. Why then is the scientific community convinced of the causal linkage? The evidence is purely statistical. Reichenbach's principle provides a formalisation of the principle by which the causality is 'proved'. He asserts that for every statistical correlation between two phenomena significantly greater than chance, then either one has causally influenced the other, or some third phenomenon or set of phenomena has causal influence upon them both. The statistical correlation between smoking behaviour and incidence of cancer is considerably greater than chance. Hence cigarette smoking causes cancer. Yes?

Socrates: What about the third possibility? I mean I believe the experts. Smoking causes cancer. But isn't there, at least theoretically, the possibility that some third set of conditions is responsible for both smoking and cancer in some way and that actually smoking doesn't cause cancer?

G.O.D.: A very good question. And one with both practical and philosophical implications. Okay, a sociology example comes to mind here that brings out both. You may have heard of it already. It's quite often brought up in North American introductions to sociology courses. Apparently for many years in New York City there was a strong statistical correlation between the crime rate and ice cream sales.

Socrates: Oh yeah, I know this one. Hot weather is responsible for them both. When the weather is warm, people tend to eat more ice cream. More crimes are also committed when it's hot out.

G.O.D.: Good. You understand the principle. Okay, now why wasn't it concluded that people eat more ice cream if they commit crimes or that ice cream eating tends to cause people to commit crimes?

Socrates: Well, that would be silly, wouldn't it?

G.O.D.: Quite so. But in many other cases it wouldn't be. Cigarette smoking, for example, was believed for many years actually to be good for you! Just as you asked, why didn't they conclude some third factor was causally responsible for both smoking and cancer? The answer to that is simple. Scientists deliberately set out to exclude that possibility through trying to allow statistically for any possible relevant variables. That is, they are doing statistically what is analogous to a scientifically controlled experiment. This is familiar to you, yes?

Socrates: Yeah.

G.O.D.: Okay, it also points us towards a philosophical problem. How could we ever know for sure that all the other (potentially infinite in number) variables have been controlled for? It also further weakens the

'symmetry between explanation and prediction' orientation of positivism, in terms of what might conceivably account for an adequate
understanding of scientific explanation. In the ice cream/crime
example, a causal connection between the two is immediately ruled
out. The warm weather factor on the other hand immediately 'makes
sense' to us. It would seem that there are other utilisations of logic
and reason at work. The exercise of logic involved in scientific theorising simply cannot be restricted to the deductive relationship
between laws, theories and observational statements.

Socrates: Yes, I can see that. I have another question. You frequently say
'causally influenced' rather than simply saying 'caused'. Is that just
accidental or is something at stake in your choice of words?

G.O.D.: Very observant of you. No, it wasn't accidental. There is something
quite important implied. But just let me say something else fairly
obvious about statistics first. It is this: statistics may feature in scientific explanations, yet not in any way be either theories or laws.
They are sometimes simply evidence. That is, they are more or less
equivalent to observational statements. They are simply observations
of a particular kind; a set of procedures is engaged in to produce
information with reference to samples. The statements, instead of
taking the form 'I have observed five white marbles', take the form
'x% of the marbles in this jar are white'. The scientific interest in
such statements depends upon the context of employment. That is,
they may or may not be of interest, they may or may not have causal
implications.

More interesting is when statistics are employed in a causal argument supportive (or not) of a particular theory. A reflection upon
this will bring out the answer to your question. There are other cases
besides probability that bring out this feature of causality. But statistics and probability illustrate the feature very well. In fact the
smoking/cancer example does so. The simplest form of a causal
relationship is one where there is a single cause, and the effect is
produced every time, i.e. every time I hit one billiard ball into another,
the second one moves. This is a case whereby the cause is said to
be sufficient. There are, of course, many other sorts of causes whereby
the motion of the second billiard ball is induced. Thus, the billiard
ball case is one whereby the first ball's collision with the second is
considered sufficient but not necessary. There would be cases, however, whereby a single cause is both necessary and sufficient. The
effect will only be produced by one particular cause, and it will
always be produced. This, as I said, is the simplest causal relationship and takes the form 'if and only if A then always B'. Then there
is the case whereby some particular cause is identified as necessary
but yet is not sufficient; and finally there is the case whereby a
causal relationship between two variables may be established, but

the identified causal variable is neither necessary nor sufficient. Statistically established relationships quite frequently fit this last situation and illustrate some of the difficulty of probability and causality. That is, we quite frequently don't actually know whether causality is present or not.

Socrates: I don't know what you mean. Can you give me an example?

G.O.D.: Yes, as I said, the smoking/cancer illustrates the situation perfectly. Following Reichenbach's principle, we know there is some sort of causal relationship between smoking and cancer. The behaviour and incidence of the disease correlate with one another very significantly. Too much so to be mere chance. Yes? Okay, we know that smoking is not a necessary condition for contracting cancer. We know this because many people who have never smoked get the disease. So we know there are other causal influences. We also know it is not a sufficient cause either. Many smokers do not get the disease. So, apparently smoking is neither a necessary nor sufficient cause of cancer.

Socrates: Apparently?

G.O.D.: Yes, only apparently. We only really know that there is some causal force or linkage between the disease and smoking behaviour. We know a certain, very high percentage of smokers do get cancer. But Reichenbach's law only tells us that one phenomenon may have caused the other. Okay, in this case we know in which direction it is working. Getting cancer doesn't cause smoking. The smoking precedes the cancer – well I suppose someone who never smoked before might take up smoking as a consequence of being diagnosed with the disease, but let's not complicate things unnecessarily.

Socrates: No, let's not.

G.O.D.: But the thing is that Reichenbach's third possibility is still open. There are in fact an infinity of possible third phenomena and complexes of phenomena that might be producing both the smoking behaviour and the contraction of cancer.

Socrates: Yeah? Like what?

G.O.D.: I don't know. That's just the point! It could be something wholly unexpected, some kind of connection we've never even dreamed of, something which after the fact of discovery makes perfect sense but which simply hasn't occurred to anyone yet. Clean hands and sterile instruments as a requirement for surgery didn't occur to anyone for a very long time. It seems only obvious to us now, but connecting up death through infection with the surgeon's dirty hands or instruments certainly wasn't obvious to earlier generations. It required an understanding of infections. And this is, of course, precisely what we're lacking with respect to cancer.

Socrates: Are you really doubting that smoking causes cancer?

G.O.D.: No, I'm not. I'm pretty sure it does. I am also optimistic that, sooner or later, a proper understanding of the process by which it does so will be arrived at. No, I'm merely using the example to illustrate some of the formal difficulty with this sort of reasoning. Positivist science stresses controlled and replicable observational situations, whether through experiment or not. But logically this can in principle never be wholly successful as there are, in principle at least, an infinite set of variables to control for. On a practical level, there is also a problem. That is, we are guided by theory in our selection of variables to control for, and the theory may be quite mistaken. If so, we perhaps control the wrong variables, and other causally significant phenomena are present in an unknown and wholly uncontrolled way. We simply fail to take notice of them. In some kind of general way this shifts the emphasis positivism places upon observation back onto theory. So where does theory come from?

Socrates: Are you asking me?

G.O.D.:   No, it was just a rhetorical question to lead us back to the **hypothetico-deductive model of theory**. You see the statistical and probabilistic reasoning is deductive or can be expressed in deductive form, but it is still reliant upon that bugbear of philosophy – induction. We can use statistical correlation as part of a deductive argument, but there is always a concealed inductive premise. We may be presuming, for example, that the statistical correlation that holds for a sample is also maintained generally, or that the statistical relationship observed in the past will hold good for the future. Yes, we hypothesise that it will do so. Note the emphasis upon the word '**hypothesis**'.

Socrates: Yeah, okay. What then?

G.O.D.:   Hence, the label 'hypothetico-deductive'. Induction poses a problem for the deductive-nomological model of scientific explanation. We have our laws and observations and may deduce conclusions as predictions, which may be later confirmed by observation. But no amount of confirmation would formally support the law or theory. Yes?

Socrates: Kind of like the 'all the marbles in the jar are white' example? That's your general law. It licenses the prediction that the next marble you pick out of the jar will be white. When it is, the 'law' is confirmed. But if there is only one black marble in the jar, the law is false.

G.O.D.:   Exactly. Truth and falsity in this sense are not symmetrical. A universalisation can never be absolutely confirmed.

Socrates: But it can be absolutely falsified by only one example. Right?

G.O.D.:   No. That is, in fact, one of the things that is wrong with the naive falsificationist view.

Socrates: Come again! You're not telling me that the observation of one black marble doesn't absolutely falsify the proposition 'all marbles are white', are you?

G.O.D.: No, I'm not doing that. And I'm sorry if some of the examples I use to make my points are sometimes misleading. I'm afraid the marble example has passed its sell-by date. It's too simple a case to illustrate what's wrong with the falsification view, or, at least the naive **falsificationist view of scientific theory**. Think of our statistical examples again. What was true of them is actually true of any scientific experiment or **analogue of experiment.**

Socrates: Analogue?

G.O.D.: Approximation. Equivalent. Something that is not actually the same thing, but yet possesses all the formal features of an experiment, or at least sufficient of them to stand in an experiment's place. Positivist social science, as we shall see, consists very significantly of the attempt to develop just such analogues of experimentation.

Socrates: Okay, but I still don't see what's wrong with what I said about a single counter-example rendering a theoretical generalisation as false.

G.O.D.: Well, think of experiments and how they attempt to control for variables. As I said before, there are, at least theoretically, an infinite set of potentially unknown but nonetheless relevant variables. Were they adequately controlled for? We don't know. We can't know. There is always the possibility that we have missed something, that our counter-example is not really such. You certainly wouldn't decide to scrap an accepted and well-established law of physics on the basis of a school kid's experimental refutation.

Socrates: No, but . . . I think that's carrying things to absurdity. We take steps to ensure the experiment is performed reliably.

G.O.D.: Okay, on a practical level how do we know if this is in fact the case?

Socrates: I don't know.

G.O.D.: We repeat the experiment and see if the falsification is confirmed.

Socrates: Yes, I see. But there's still something that bothers me about this. It kind of feels as though you're cheating.

G.O.D.: Yes, I see what you mean. But it really is true that because of the myriad factors one can't control for, the ostensibly straightforward deductive falsification is always dependent upon inductive reasoning as well. There's another point connected to this as well, which I want to bring out now – the question of facticity and interpretation.

Socrates: Facticity?

G.O.D.: I mean by that questions as to what counts as a fact. What is a fact anyway? The hypothetico-deductive model of theorising, you see, posits theory as standing between the high-level abstract generalisations of scientific laws and the immediate observational facts of the world. Theory, as well as being a constructed hypothesis which one can test, which can be either confirmed or falsified, is also a kind of **bridging operation** between the immediate 'brute facts' of our experience and the universal laws that scientific knowledge produces. Theory specifies the operations, provides the definitions, whereby observation is transformed into something which can be confirmed or denied in terms of the hypothesis. Typically many more than one scientific law may be relevant to the hypothesis. Frequently the observational 'entities' involved are not clearly defined in any kind of immediately obvious way. Often the 'entities' are not directly observable in practice, or may even in theory be unobservable. So you see theory has a big job to do.

Socrates: Yes, I see that. Especially if you want to ground knowledge in terms of observation. But I still like the idea of scientific knowledge being as yet un-falsified hypotheses. It gets rid of the idea of science producing absolute knowledge. Something always bothered me about that.

G.O.D.:   Good. It's in fact one of the most pernicious popular misunderstandings of the nature of science. However, we're getting off the subject. Facts. Let's get back to facts. That's what a positivist would say.

Socrates: Okay. Facts then. By the way, does this have any connection to 'naive falsificationism'? Is there such a thing as 'non-naive falsificationism'?

G.O.D.:   Yes, to both questions. Though 'non-naive' isn't the label for it. But, I'll say it again. Let's get back to facts. Well, it is easy to say, much harder to do. What would be a fact for an empiricist? It would be a sensory observation, yes?

Socrates: Yeah. I guess for the empiricist the sensory observation would be the basic stuff, if not of the world, of that with which we build our knowledge of the world. The observations are the facts.

G.O.D.:   Very good. But once again there is a problem. Observations are theory-laden.

Socrates: What do you mean?

G.O.D.:   We don't simply observe the world. The very act of observation involves placing an interpretation upon it. Interpretation doesn't even have to be conscious. It can be an unconscious process as well. I'll give you a few examples. Take a photograph or drawing. Here we have a two-dimensional representation of three-dimensional reality. People generally have no difficulty in interpreting two-dimensional images as representations of three-dimensional reality. Yes?

Socrates: Nope, it's easy. We do it automatically with photos and paintings – if they're drawn skillfully enough, that is.

G.O.D.:   What would you say if I told you that this process of three-dimensional/two-dimensional 'translation' isn't quite so straightforward as it might seem, that it isn't 'natural' but rather something we have to learn. I don't know if this story is true or not, but it could be. T.E. Lawrence ('Lawrence of Arabia') tells of showing some photographs to a group of Arab nomads, pictures of them actually. They apparently had never seen photographs before, and they could not recognise their own images.

Socrates: I don't think I believe that.

G.O.D.: You see a dog in front of a television set. He responds to the dog on the screen that is barking. He stares fixedly at the television. You would say he's watching the dog on the television. Yes?

Socrates: Sure.

G.O.D.: But, so psychologists studying animal perception tell us anyway, animals such as dogs are not capable of resolving two-dimensional images into representations of the three-dimensional world. The image on the screen consists really of thousands of coloured moving dots forming changing patterns. This is the reality of what's there. This is what the dog sees. He doesn't see another dog running through a field.

Socrates: Are you saying the dog on the screen isn't really there? I don't mean really there in the room in front of the dog watching the television. I mean the image. Isn't it really there?

G.O.D.: That is a question that can be answered quite differently on different levels. I'll give you another example. But first consider this. We both see a dog in front of a television. You'd report the apparent fact that he was watching another dog on the screen. I wouldn't because of what I'd read about the dog's psychological cognitive capacities. Our 'facts', which derive from the same observation, apparently contradict one another. They're not quite the raw data they might first appear to be. They've been subject to a process of interpretation. Okay, here's another example. I'm going to send you a picture. Ready?

Socrates: Okay, I'll print it out and take a look at it. [See Figure 3.1.]

G.O.D.: Okay, now what do you see?

Socrates: I see two women in profile looking at one another.

G.O.D.: Look again. Can you see a vase?

Socrates: Oh, yeah. I can see that now.

G.O.D.: Some people have a lot of trouble seeing one of the images or the other. Sometimes people have difficulty to the point of once being able to get the second take on the picture, they can't then get the first one back without extreme concentration.

Socrates: No, I can shift back and forth from one to the other without too much difficulty.

G.O.D.: All right, there's lots of these sort of pictures. Now what is really there is ink on a page. But this is only one level. On another, both images are there. Perhaps there are still other ways of interpreting this drawing, ways another culture would see immediately but which remain completely hidden to us. This question of levels will be extremely important later on by the way. But never mind that now. You see the point concerning observation and interpretation?

Socrates: Yes. But I don't think I would describe it as 'theory-laden'.

Figure 3.1

© Shutterstock

G.O.D.:   What about the example of the dog watching television? Your interpretation and mine?

Socrates: Okay, yeah. I forgot about that one. But it's a little different.

G.O.D.:   True. But the overall point is that observations, facts, are not simply
given to us in an unmediated fashion. We apprehend them through
various sorts of 'filters' – cultural filters, psychological filters, etc.

Socrates: Yeah, I see that. What's the significance of this then?

G.O.D.:   Well, there are many different implications and many different ways
to understand them. First off, you can see the connection to the
falsification problem, can't you?

Socrates: Yes. As the observations are not simply indisputably there, without
any prior interpretation – interpretation of some kind anyway – then
their relevance to a hypothesis could be quite variable. So the falsificationist view, because of ignoring, or at least oversimplifying
this problem, can be justly accused of being naive.

G.O.D.:   Very good. However, a word of caution. In recent times, positivism,
the hypothetico-deductive account of theory, falsification, particularly

as associated with the work of Karl Popper (who provided its initial theorisation), have all been subjected to oversimplification themselves. Positivism, particularly in social science circles, has become increasingly unpopular. These positions have all been subjected to intentional and unintentional caricature. It has been said, for example, that positivism grounds its notions of objectivity in theory-neutral observation. This is, of course, partially true. But only partially. In other ways, it is a very crude over-simplification and casts positivists in the role of being completely insensitive to issues to which in fact they are extremely sensitive. They have expended considerable energy in deriving ingenious solutions to some of these problems.

Socrates: Well, let's hear some of their solutions then.

G.O.D.:   I'll give you one. It's perhaps the most important one as it demonstrates most clearly the positivists' recognition of some of the inherent difficulties within their own program, while at the same time it allows them not to abandon it. Objectivity is seen as a goal. The scientific community provides normative guidance for achieving this (ultimately practically unachievable) ideal goal. The construction of agreed sets of replicable procedures that will minimise individual subjectivity are formalised. The falsification notion of hypotheses is seen not quite so much as successfully providing an ultimate philosophical grounding for scientific practice. Rather, scientific practice that enthrones risk of potential falsification as a kind of normative ideal, grounds the validity of theory and explanations jointly in the scientific community's conventions and in science's practical successes. There is both a kind of **relativism** and some circularity involved here. But it is of a very self-consciously self-reflective sort.

Socrates: I'm not sure I follow.

G.O.D.:   Scientific theories that allow the most precise testing, that is, those which are definitively predictive and thus potentially subject to clear experimental falsification, are understood as models of scientificity not always achievable in practice. But this goal, and the sets of procedures that best allow of its approximation, are in fact the norms of the scientific community with respect to practice. Objectivity is thus procedurally and normatively defined. There is a kind of relativism in this, and this is recognised. But the validity of these norms in terms of any real achievement of objectivity is further buttressed by science's undeniable practical success.

Socrates: Hmm. I'll have to think about that, but I don't think I'm convinced.

G.O.D.:   Well, that doesn't bode well for your future as a positivist because I still haven't given you the full thrust of the critical attack upon positivism. That will have to wait until we begin our examination of positivist social science. Before that, though, we still have to ask where theory comes from.

Socrates: Two questions. First, okay, where does theory come from? Second, what do you mean 'where does theory come from?'.

G.O.D.:   Well, so far all our consideration of the reasoning involved in scientific explanation has been to do with the falsification or confirmation of scientific law or theory. Where do the ideas come from? Do they in fact just come from experience? Do we just stumble into scientific discoveries? Is discovery a very good term for referring to scientific achievements? Or is it misleading?

Socrates: Is it?

G.O.D.:   Is it what?

Socrates: Misleading.

G.O.D.:   Yes, I would say that it is. I can give you an example, one used by Thomas Kuhn, whose ideas we'll be examining next. Our present-day scientific understanding of oxygen is basically a joint effort. Priestley discovered it before Lavoisier invented it.

Socrates: Come again?

G.O.D.:   Yes, something of a paradox, isn't it? At least that is the way Kuhn presents it. But we'll leave Kuhn until our next go. Suffice it to say here that Priestley first isolated it as a substance but completely failed to understand what he'd actually done. Lavoisier put together the theory that explained everything. As I said, we'll come back to this when we look at Kuhn's work. But for now let's just ask where did his theory come from? The obvious empiricist answer is that it flowed upwards from the observations. But as we have seen, this seems to be inadequate as most of the positivist attention seems to be on the confirmation or falsification of hypotheses. Where do the hypotheses come from?

Socrates: I'm sure you're not really asking me.

G.O.D.:   No. I'm going to give you a couple of answers. Here's the first. The inspiration of genius. We have a whole historical mythology attached to that answer. You know, Newton getting hit on the head by an apple, Archimedes leaping up from his bath and shouting eureka, eureka, that sort of thing.

Socrates: Yeah, I've heard the stories. Are you trying to say these people weren't geniuses?

G.O.D.:   Nope. I'm sure they were. But genius as an explanation is next to worthless. Newton may well have been a genius, but an apple banging him on the head, whether it actually happened or not, doesn't tell us very much. I'm sure hundreds of people were banged on the head by apples without it leading to a theorisation of gravity. Surely there is reasoning involved in the construction of hypotheses. It's surely not confined to the attempts to validate them. There must be a logic to scientific speculation and conjecture.

Socrates: That makes sense. But if this is going on entirely within people's minds, how could we ever know what it is?

G.O.D.: Well, some of them have tried to articulate the reasoning process that led them to their important breakthroughs. However, in so doing, most of them have stressed the importance of the extra-rational influences.

Socrates: Extra-rational? Is that a word?

G.O.D.: It is now. I just made it up. What I'm getting at here is that those scientists who have been most self-reflective upon the process of hypothesis and theory generation have stressed the number of outside factors, outside the specific problem area in which they were work- ing that is, which led to their breakthroughs. Historical study of science shows another sort of logic working side by side with that directly focused upon specific research problems.

Socrates: What's that?

G.O.D.: A kind of sociological logic. Scientific theory production is framed within the development of particular discourses, within wider socio-economic factors. The production of scientific knowledge is a social phenomenon. There may well be individual aspects to it. Newton's achievements are, of course, in some sense his and his alone. But in many other very important senses they are not. The achievements may be a product of his genius. But they are also a product of his genius very firmly rooted in his time with all that that entails.

Socrates: 'With all that that entails'! You make it sound like a lot. Like it's very important.

G.O.D.: It is! It is where Thomas Kuhn comes in. But perhaps we'd better leave it to next time.

Socrates: Good idea!

DISCUSSION QUESTIONS

1   The methodological imperative to operationalise concepts, that is, for exam- ple, to transform the vague qualitative notions of descriptions such as warm or cool into something precise and measureable (e.g. mercury thermometer readings), has obvious advantages in some situations. What possible disad- vantages or limitations might there be to such methods?

2   Does understanding scientific proof in terms of attempts at falsification, rather than confirmation of hypotheses, successfully resolve the problem of induction?

3   Why might explanations that fail to make any predictions be considered less than satisfactory? Could the positivist stress upon prediction be at least partially justified, even if there are cases where we have non-predictive explanations?

4   What is the difference between an inductive inference and one based upon probabilities?

FURTHER READING SUGGESTIONS

The deductive-nomological and hypothetico-deductive accounts of science

The discussion in the text generally focused upon Popper. However, Hempel has likewise been enormously influential. Their views are probably closest to how most natural scientists (excluding perhaps those in biology and a few other disciplines) understand their own activity.

Hempel, C.G. (1965) *Aspects of Scientific Explanation, and Other Essays in the Philosophy of Science*, Free Press, New York.
——— (1966) *The Philosophy of Natural Science*, Prentice-Hall, Englewood Cliffs, NJ.
——— (1972) *Fundamentals of Concept Formation in Empirical Science*, University of Chicago Press, Chicago.
Popper, K. (1959) *The Logic of Scientific Discovery*, Hutchinson, London.
——— (1989) *Conjectures and Refutations*, Routledge, New York.

Vienna Circle theorists

Carnap, R. (1967) *The Logical Structure of the World (and) Pseudoproblems in Philosophy*, Routledge & Kegan Paul, London.
Kraft, V. (2008) *The Vienna Circle*, Philosophical Library, New York.
Nagel, E. (1961) *The Structure of Science*, Routledge & Kegan Paul, London.
Reichenbach, H. (1961) *Experience and Prediction: An Analysis of the Foundations and Structure of Knowledge*, University of Chicago Press, Chicago.
Zolo, D. (1990) 'Reflexive Epistemology and Social Complexity: The Philosophical Legacy of Otto Neurath', *Philosophy of Social Science* 20(2) pp. 149–169.

Language

Ayer, A.J. (1946) *Language, Truth and Logic*, Gollancz, London.

This is an important book but from a very particular perspective only. There will be more 'further reading suggestions' on the topic of the philosophy of language from other perspectives in later chapters.

Functionalist explanation

Functionalist explanations are generally accepted as scientific by positivists. They are also enormously important in social science. As I did not deal with this subject at all, the articles listed below should provide useful reference points for what is at issue.

Hempel, C.G. (1965) 'The Logic of Functional Analysis' in *Aspects of Scientific Explanation*, Free Press, New York.
Nagel, E. (1956) 'A Formalisation of Functionalism' in G.K. Zollschan and W. Hirsh (eds), *Explorations in Social Change*, Houghton Mifflin, New York, 1964.
Zolo, D. (1986) 'Function, Meaning, Complexity', *Philosophy of Social Science* 16(1) pp. 115–127.

Perhaps the most important of sociological explanations of this sort would be Talcott Parsons' structural functionalist theory as expounded in his two classic works: *The Structure of Social Action* and *The Social System*.

Parsons, T. (1949) [1937] *The Structure of Social Action*, The Free Press, Glencoe, Illinois.
_____ (2012) [1951] *The Social System*, Quid Pro, LLC, New Orleans.

Induction

Hanson, N.R. (1965) *Patterns of Discovery*, Cambridge University Press, Cambridge.
Lessnoff, M. (1974) *The Structure of Social Science*, Allen & Unwin, London – contains a useful introduction to inductive generalising.
Nidditch, P.H. (ed.) (1968) *The Philosophy of Science*, Oxford University Press, Oxford – a good selection of articles covering what have become the 'classic' problems to do with induction.
Salmon, W.C. (1967) *The Foundations of Scientific Inference*, University of Pittsburgh Press, Pittsburgh.
Tavanec, P.V. (1970) *Problems of the Logic of Scientific Knowledge*, Springer, Dordrecht, Holland.

Distinctions between theoretical and observation statements

Hanson, N.R. (1965) *Patterns of Discovery*, Cambridge University Press, Cambridge – especially Chapters 1, 2 and 4.
Quine, W.V.O. (1953) *From a Logical Point of View*, Harper & Row, New York – especially see 'Two Dogmas of Empiricism'. This has been a particularly influential essay in the movement towards a 'post-positivist era' in the philosophy of science. Quine advocates what he calls 'ontological relativism', the implication of which is that we must abandon the notion of linking theory with observation statements.

General

Korner, S. (ed.) (1975) *Explanation: Papers and Discussions*, Blackwell, Oxford.
Lakatos, I. and Musgrave, P. (eds) (1970) *Criticism and the Growth of Knowledge*, Cambridge University Press, Cambridge.

Operationalism

Some of the philosophical difficulties of empiricism and the distinctiveness of positivism's solutions to them were only barely alluded to in the text. A variety of positivism is associated with an interesting theory that asserts that the meaning of scientific concepts is equivalent to the set of practical operations by which they can be used, i.e. the meaning of heat is to be understood through the operations used to measure temperature and is to be restricted to specifying the nature of such operations.

Bridgeman, P.W. (1927) *The Logic of Modern Physics*, Macmillan, New York.
Harré, R. (1972) *The Philosophies of Science*, Oxford University Press, London – especially pp. 76–8 and 161–3 for a succinct discussion of quite a technical issue. This is a very useful book generally, particularly so for understanding realism. A larger selection of readings in the realist philosophy of science, including more of Harré's books, is listed at the end of Chapter 8.

CHAPTER 4

EXPLANATIONS OF SOCIAL SCIENTIFIC UNDERSTANDING AND SOCIAL SCIENTIFIC UNDERSTANDINGS OF NATURAL SCIENTIFIC EXPLANATIONS

'The stars,' she whispers, 'blindly run.'

Alfred Lord Tennyson

. . . whether or not a proposition is, as it were, up for grabs as a candidate for being true-or-false, depends on whether we have ways to reason about it.

Ian Hacking

Paradigm Shifts . . . In its most general terms, it means that people just decide to stop looking at the world in one way and start looking at it in another. So feel free to throw in T.S. Kuhn if you're ever caught between a conversational rock and a philosophical hard place.

from Jim Hankinson, *Bluff Your Way in Philosophy*

OUTLINE OF MAJOR POINTS TO BE COVERED

1 Positivism propounds a unity of the natural and social sciences. Very broadly speaking, the basis of that unity is method. Methods are, however, specific to their subject matter and disciplines. Social scientific methodology attempts as far as possible to approximate the rigour attainable in the natural sciences and retains the emphasis upon measurement and quantification, precision in classification, prediction, some sort of possibility of falsification and so on.

2 Positivists are aware of the criticisms put forward in the last chapter and, as far as possible, attempt to overcome them. They are thus not nearly as naive concerning objectivity and the value impregnation of observational statements, classifications, etc. as they are sometimes made out to be. Humanist criticism of positivist social science is thus sometimes a straw man argument, aimed at a caricature of positivist social science rather than its reality.

3 The positivist desire for precision, measurement, etc. does however limit the selection of problems with which it engages. Also, the positivist distrust of metaphysics extends to some degree of scepticism concerning the evidential basis for conclusions in disciplines such as history.

4   The assertion that human behaviour is inherently unpredictable is simply false. Leaving science aside, much of human daily life depends upon our capacity to predict the behaviour of others.

5   The self-reflective nature of human beings, which is rightly given as an objection to certain aspects of understanding causality, nonetheless possesses a double edge to it. Social science does possess one huge advantage to natural science in one respect – we can ask human agents about their intentions, something we cannot do with molecules or planets. Our access to our own consciousness is also an advantage in arriving at an understanding of social action and meanings.

6   The distinction is made between **understanding** and **causal explanation**. These two terms frequently serve as a demarcation line in the debate between a positivist social science that stresses the latter and humanist social science that emphasises acquiring an understanding of the rules (as opposed to laws) that govern human actions and the meanings they attribute to them.

7   A clear distinction is drawn between the perspective of Max Weber and those in the interpretativist tradition in social science who see all attempts to utilise the positivist notions of causal explanation as pernicious. Weber definitely saw a place for statistical comparison and utilised it himself.

8   Weber also believed that social science needed to go beyond merely causal explanation to seek understandings of the meaning of social actions. Towards this end he articulated the procedures whereby **ideal types** are constructed and used as a rational tool of investigation.

9   To demonstrate how positivism is not nearly so narrow as is sometimes supposed, a comparative description of the respective approaches to a problem of Weber and Popper is given, which stresses their similarities. A hypothetical example of the sort of problem Weber might investigate is described in Popper's language of situational logic, deduction, empirical evidence and falsification. Note: this description is undertaken to make a particular point and possibly could be misleading (see the 'intellectual health warning' at the beginning of the chapter). Popper and Weber are also placed upon the same side as methodological individualists as opposed to Dürkheim's view of society as being *sui generis*.

10 Dürkheim, while frequently considered a positivist, is perhaps more accurately described as a realist. The assertion is made that strictly speaking there are no applications of positivist social science as it contains a basic incoherence. However, this criticism is not taken up until the last chapter and is only hinted at here.

11 Thomas Kuhn's historical description and social theory of scientific revolutions is outlined.

   a   The history of science does not reveal a linear progressive accumulation of knowledge. It has long periods of puzzle-solving normal science, which are punctuated by scientific revolutions.

   b   **Normal science** proceeds from a single **paradigm**, a set of agreed-upon problems and means of solving them. However, scientific revolutions occur when a radically different paradigm is conceived and established. Adherents of different paradigms frequently talk past one another because of how fundamentally different their assumptions are.

c   Anomalies are seldom treated as falsifications (as they should be from a positivist perspective), but may be simply ignored. This is because paradigm shifts are (arguably) most significantly determined by sociological determinants – everything from the economy to the career motivations of individual scientists.

12   Are there different realities corresponding to each paradigm, or is it merely the same reality seen differently? The sociological determinants referred to in point 11c above can be taken to support an extreme relativism. That is, truth disappears and knowledge can be seen as wholly socially determined and dependent upon belief. Different beliefs, different realities, seems to be a possible conclusion. This point is considered from a number of different perspectives in the next chapter.

13   An example of different paradigmatic understandings of a particular problem is given – the **oxygen/dephlogisticated air problem.** A realist solution is given whereby a rational choice between two competing theories can be sensibly made on the basis of criteria that are certainly not sociological.

14   It is explained why the realist solution in point 13, while adequate to explain that particular problem (and others), does not wholly resolve the challenge levelled by an extreme relativist interpretation of Kuhn. There are many problems, particularly in social science, where there is no identity of substance and agreed-upon procedures as there were in the oxygen/dephlogisticated air example. Oxygen and dephlogisticated air are the identical substance and may be produced by the same procedures either way it is conceived. However, Weber's classes and Marx's are not. Here we have some overlap of reference (how much is arguable) but not identity. This problem – and there would be many others – is much more complex. The relationship between concept and reality in such cases is far more complex.

Intellectual health warning

The discussion of Karl Popper and Max Weber in this chapter could potentially be misleading. First of all, they were not contemporaries of one another. More importantly, the practices of interpretativist sociology and positivist social science are in general vastly different. Positivist social scientific practice does tend to be quantitative in nature, and the opposition between quantitative and qualitative social science, while a misguided and false opposition, nonetheless persists to this day to some degree. The description of a Weberian sort of analysis described in Popperian terms which follows is there only to make the point that positivist philosophy of social science is neither as naive nor as narrowly conceived as is sometimes supposed. But Popper is not a Weberian or vice versa!

The Scene: A spatio-temporal void filled with ideas. In the real world, time has passed.

G.O.D. and Socrates (not their real names) have been living their lives. They have been eating, watching television, playing sports, having sex, and having arguments (not philosophical). G.O.D. has had to look up the answers to some other students' questions. Socrates has read a book or two. Neither has much curiosity about the other's life. Neither do we. Their dialogue begins where it left off.

Socrates: So, we're going to consider social science at last.

G.O.D.: Yes, and we will begin with positivist social science. Probably you'll be relieved to know that I haven't too much to say about it that we haven't already covered in our earlier discussions of natural science. Or rather, I don't have too many positive things to say about it.

Socrates: You don't like it much, eh?

G.O.D.: No, that's not it. I have serious criticisms to make about it from my own realist point of view. But we'll leave those until much later. No, what I meant was that I think you've already got most of the basic ideas. The more interesting things to say are all critical or responses by positivists to that criticism rather than a positive statement of their point of view. I think you've got that already. Essentially, the positivist position asserts a unity of the scientific enterprise, a unity of both natural and social science. The basis for that unity is method.

Socrates: Ah ha. The scientific method again.

G.O.D.: Yes, but I hope by this time you won't see that in simplistic terms. It is only on the broadest and most abstract level in which there can be seen to be methodological unity. Each discipline develops its own methods and criteria for judgment. It is rather an overall perspective upon the nature of scientific explanation and the approach to it. Social science, because of the unique characteristics of its subject matter, has problems quite specific to it. Many of these are immediately apparent and quite obvious. Positivist social scientists, contrary to the viewpoints sometimes expressed by their opponents, were certainly not oblivious to them. It is a real mistake to view them as entirely naive.

Socrates: You mean they understood there are some differences between studying human beings and rocks or molecules.

G.O.D.: They certainly did. But they also realised that along with the difficulties of studying the behaviour of self-reflective actors capable of choice, the subject matter also gives the social scientist some advantages over the natural scientist. The positivist understanding of explanation, you remember, places a great deal of stress upon prediction. One of the criticisms of positivist social science asserts the inherent unpredictability of human behaviour. But . . .

Socrates:	Well, that's true, isn't it. We think and make choices before we act. We aren't going to be governed by invariant laws, like molecules are. Human history is an open system, isn't it? And people who've tried to predict the future have had a bad track record. Besides that, most of the people who have done so haven't been scientists either.
G.O.D.:	That's not entirely true. It depends upon what sort of predictions we are talking about. To say that human behaviour is inherently unpredictable is just plain false. Our day-to-day living very much depends upon the successful prediction of the behaviour of others. And making those predictions, in the greatest number of cases, just isn't that difficult. One of the advantages in predicting human behaviour over that of predicting molecular behaviour is that we can simply ask people what they intend to do. We can't ask the molecule.
Socrates:	But people don't always do what they say they're going to do, whether they really intend to or not. They also quite often lie about what they're going to do.
G.O.D.:	That is true. But do you think that such obvious notions didn't occur to positivist social scientists?
Socrates:	I suppose they would've.
G.O.D.:	Positivists understand very well the specific difficulties of social scientificity, and even perhaps the limits to possible scientific explanation of social phenomena. Some might say that they over-emphasise these limits.
Socrates:	What do you mean by that?
G.O.D.:	Well, first of all they know very well what scientists can and can't do. They know you can't perform macro-sociological experiments. They know, for example, that comparative statistical analysis only approximates the degree of rigorous control possible in closed laboratory conditions. They know that social scientific theory only approximates the notion of explanation and law utilised in natural science. But pretty close approximations are in fact possible. Reichenbach's statistical principle can easily be utilised to produce falsifications. The ice cream example we referred to earlier can illustrate this point as well. Let us say that (for some daft reason or another) the idea of ice cream consumption causing crime was seriously entertained. It is supported by the statistical correlation between the two variables in New York. Fine. Well, we look at other (as far as can be ascertained) comparable situations and see if the statistical correlations still hold. We find they don't. We still don't know what was causing the original correlation between the variables, but at least this relationship was restricted in its generality. So much so that the 'ice cream causes crime theory' can be rejected. It has, so to speak, been falsified by counter-example. Now, this was a trivial, even ridiculous example. But the same general principle would hold for a great many other more serious cases. The general form of

explanations, theorising, testing and so on, as are utilised in the natural sciences, can be maintained.

Positivist social scientists spend a great deal of time attempting to make social scientific techniques as rigorous as possible. Included in this is a very conscious awareness of potential limits. They do the best they can to refine their methods of observation, analysis and criteria of judgment. They do this in full awareness that there are limits as to how far this can be taken. The key word here would be rigour. Positivist social science attempts as far as possible the precision of mathematical relationships. However, there are aspects of social life that even in theory are unapproachable with such degrees of technical rigour. Here one could say positivists are too aware of human limitations. The distrust of metaphysics propounded by the **Vienna Circle** of logical positivists took that distrust to an extreme. However, the positivist approach, however broadly conceived, still retains elements of that mistrust. While few social scientists would be prepared to push it as far as the original logical positivists, there still is a general view that scientific explanation is the only valid form of knowledge, and that to some degree or another if you move outside the terrain approachable by such techniques, you're basically talking nonsense.

Socrates: Really! So what about history, literature, culture, etc. These aren't sciences. Don't they produce any knowledge? And what about anthropology, sociology and economics? All social science isn't positivistic. Many of these disciplines don't even attempt to follow natural science guidelines, do they?

G.O.D.: No, indeed not.

Socrates: But positivists hold the knowledges of these disciplines in contempt, yes?

G.O.D.: Well, I wouldn't want to go as far as that. Certainly, all positivists are not philistines, though there is an element of philistinism inherent in their outlook. It basically comes down to their placing hierarchical status upon types of explanations, with respect to the degree of confidence we can have in them. Most positivists would be rather circumspect with respect to declarations about the impossibility of historical understanding being achieved at all. Still, they would also be rather wary of the breadth of generalisations attempted by historians on the basis of what they would see as rather dubious and limited evidence. Perhaps a certain degree of such scepticism is salutary. No, their conception of scientificity works as a kind of regulatory ideal. It prioritises certain forms of technique over others. As far as possible, explanations should be based upon careful observation. Thus, the accessibility of observational evidence also becomes a guideline as to what sorts of phenomena can be scientifically investigated. The positivist is inclined not merely to use classification procedures but as far as possible to achieve precise classifications. Explanations take a logical form describing the relations between carefully defined categories. Wherever possible, mathematics should be employed, along with rigorous techniques of measurement. Rigour, as defined in such a way though, simply isn't possible with respect to many aspects of life in which we are interested. So, if the positivist wouldn't exactly be entirely derisive about many historical theories and so on, there is an ever-present aspersion upon their status as 'real' knowledge.

There is a key word that I have used a few times before that I now want to draw your attention to. It is a marker for a basic division of sides in the philosophy of social science debate. The word is '**understanding**'.

Socrates: Understanding. Hmm. What is the significance? You mentioned it briefly in comparison with the word **explanation**.

G.O.D.:   Yes, we have been talking about explanations. These have been conceived of as having some kind of basic form and purpose, i.e. to explain causality. But understanding involves more than this.

Socrates: What's the difference? Surely, if you've explained something, you've understood it.

G.O.D.:   Well, that depends upon your understanding of explanation. Sorry, I was trying to be cute there; sometimes I get carried away with my own cleverness.

Socrates: I've noticed.

G.O.D.:   Yes, well . . . No, explanation, as we've been considering it thus far, is rather exclusively concerned with cause and effect. In a limited fashion perhaps, it can consider reasons as causes. But the **interpretativist** tradition in social science completely reverses the emphasis. It is primarily concerned with meaning. Weber, for example, would assert that you have not really understood a social phenomenon until you have understood the meaning it has for the actors involved. This is a much broader, richer notion of explanation than merely determining causal relationships.

Socrates: You mean if I explain why people do something, this is different from giving a causal explanation. What if the reason for the people's action is the cause? Why did I pour water in the trashcan? Because it was burning. That was the reason for my action. Reason, cause, they are one and the same.

G.O.D.:   Yes, that is a good example. Other cases are less clear-cut. But in any case, the question of whether reasons can be causes is a slightly different argument. It is one that is relevant, but nevertheless I'd like to save it until later. You keep jumping to realist positions.

Socrates: Sorry.

G.O.D.:   No, no, that's a good thing. It shows your instincts are sound. It's just that we've got some ground to cover first. Let me give you a

clear example of the difference between the sort of positivist understanding of a causal explanation and an interpretativist perspective
upon understanding. Weber both clearly articulates this distinction
and demonstrates it in his own work.

Socrates: **Verstehen,** right?

G.O.D.: Yes, but let me continue. The statistical differences with respect to
relative economic success between members of different religious
affiliations were such that many in Weber's time suspected a causal
relation between different religious belief systems and economic
achievement. It is this statistical comparative evidence that is the
foundation of Weber's famous book *The Protestant Ethic and the
Spirit of Capitalism.* You've read this book, yes?

Socrates: I know the general argument. A particular attitude towards work,
saving, investment and so on, 'the spirit of capitalism', was required
to 'kick start' capitalism's development. This spirit derived from a
particular theological orientation towards the accumulation of wealth,
the denial of sensual pleasure, spending and so forth. This attitude
was not specifically capitalist. Rather it was a set of beliefs about
God and redemption, which rather accidentally seems to be particularly appropriate for instigating the sort of behaviour and attitudes
required to really get capitalism up and rolling. This is the so-called
'Protestant ethic'. Weber's argument is not that it is required for
capitalism, because once capitalism is fully established it's not necessary any longer. Capitalism possesses its own internal dynamic.
But what Weber does argue is that this spiritual dimension, the sets
of beliefs that emerged in the Reformation, had a causal influence
upon capitalism's development. His proof of this is that in many
other historical times and places, all the other relevant conditions
for capitalism's emergence were present, yet it did not emerge.

G.O.D.: That's pretty good as a summary of his argument. But you've left
out a crucial dimension to it.

Socrates: Well, I've only read bits of it and summaries by other people.

G.O.D.: No, no, I'm not criticising you. You presented quite a good summary
of the salient points. Actually, your summary works very well to
illustrate some of the differences between the sort of causal explanation the positivists are concerned with, and the dimension of understanding to which interpretativist sociology addresses itself. You
presented what could be described as the causal explanation dimension of the book. You see, the interpretativist tradition takes a number
of different stances towards the sort of explanations that are prescribed by positivism. Some would argue that such explanation is
impossible. Others argue that not only is it inappropriate for attempting to understand the human world but that the attempt itself is
actually pernicious. We'll be considering these arguments later.
Weber exemplifies a much more balanced position. He believed that

such causal explanations were not only possible with respect to social reality but also necessary. However, he also felt that such explanations frequently do not tell us what we want to know, even what we most importantly want to know. This is the dimension of meaning! Explaining the meanings of social action is a rather different task from merely explaining causality.

Socrates: I still don't think I understand the difference. How is this so?

G.O.D.:   Well, a significant portion of *The Protestant Ethic* is directed at an analysis of religious doctrine, particularly the doctrine of salvation. But Weber does not merely look at what sort of actions would be prescribed by such doctrines but analyses what it must have felt like to have such beliefs. He considers, for example, that to have maintained certain beliefs would have generated an immense loneliness, to a degree that such belief would be psychologically unsustainable. Accordingly, the beliefs would have to be modified after a while.

Socrates: Why?

G.O.D.:   Well, imagine that you believed in predestination. You are either saved or damned. There is nothing to be done about it. Not only is there nothing you can do to achieve salvation, but there is no way you can know which state, eternal damnation or salvation, you are predestined for. No one else knows your state either, only God. But it is your duty to maintain a faith in your own state of grace.

Socrates: Yes, I see what you mean. Pretty grim.

G.O.D.:   Now, of course, what Weber is doing is adding another dimension to the explanation. He is interpreting the meanings social actors place upon their actions. Elsewhere he articulated a coherent methodological procedure by which we can do so. I'll speak about that in a moment. First, I just want to quote for you one of his most famous statements concerning interpretative understanding: "One need not be Caesar in order to understand Caesar". I think you can see how positivists might reject this claim. At least, they would very likely rule out of bounds as unscientific the sorts of operations that would be required to arrive at this sort of claim.

Socrates: Yes, I can see that. It would be too subjective for them. Also, it is something that is inherently unverifiable – or falsifiable, for that matter. How did Weber say this could be done?

G.O.D.:   I'll come to that in a moment. First, I want to introduce a new term to you – **scientism**. It is used differently and means different things to different people; usually it is understood as a pejorative term. The nature of the pejorative varies according to the different perspectives people have about scientificity. Anyway, I want to give you a few definitions of this term as pertains to our consideration of the relationship between natural and social science. One definition is that scientism is the fetishisation and inappropriate slavish imitation of the methods of natural science. This would correspond to a philosophy of social science position that stressed the unique aspects of social phenomena and the consequently inappropriate nature of natural scientific methods. Scientism, then, is a term of abuse that humanists can throw at positivistic sociology, for example. They would see that positivist rigidity concerning explanation and method relegates them to the study of only that which can be approached by overly restrictive sorts of method, and they would argue that that which can be approached in such a fashion is usually trivial, obvious and of little interest. The insult implies that positivist sociology and other positivist social science is thus only pseudo-scientific.

Socrates: How does this relate to Weber?

G.O.D.: Well, many positivists would be unwilling to describe his procedures for coming to 'understand Caesar' as scientific. The interpretativist reply to this could well be that such critics are being scientistic and want to replace the interesting work done by such as Weber and others in the interpretativist tradition with their own pseudo-scientific studies of trivia.

Socrates: Ah, yes, I see. So would all positivists reject Weber's work?

G.O.D.: No. In fact Karl Popper has a rather interesting perspective upon the topic and a different definition of scientism too. I've already cautioned you concerning people underrating Popper and positivism. I've told you he was a critic of the **Vienna Circle** of logical positivists. Yet frequently he is labeled a positivist himself.

Socrates: Yeah, I remember. What's his definition of scientism then?

G.O.D.: Popper defines scientism as 'the aping of what is *widely mistaken* for the method of science' (Popper, K. {1972} [1994] *Objective Knowledge: An Evolutionary Approach*, 1972, Oxford University Press, p. 18, my italics). Interestingly enough, he would thus likely see those who would rule out Weber's methodology as unscientific as being scientistic. Weber's method of analysis he would see as being eminently logical and even falsifiable.

Socrates: Falsifiable! How?

G.O.D.: Well, as I've told you before, one needs to be cautious about writing positivism off too easily and most particularly so with respect to Karl Popper's version of it. The notion of science many critics attribute to positivism may well be held by some positivists but actually corresponds very well to Popper's definition of scientism. That is, that it is a mistaken view of natural science, most particularly so with respect to objectivity. Objectivity, the objectivity of either natural or social science, is not grounded in the relative detachment of the individual scientist. The relationship of science to values is a complex matter. However, Popper would at least agree with Weber that scientificity is a value itself! He'd further argue that scientific activity is immersed in human interests, that it is guided by our interests in problems. Most significantly, objectivity arises through science's responsiveness to criticism. This susceptibility to criticism Popper holds up as a regulatory ideal to which science as a social practice aspires. But what does criticism involve? The deductive nature of scientific explanation implies a two-way street between conclusions and premises with respect to truth. We suspect the truth of a particular conclusion. This is the basis for all critical theoretical engagement, Popper would argue. Well, if a conclusion is not true then it follows that the theory that asserts it must be false – false with respect to either its evidential premises or its theoretical logic. So criticism essentially attempts a refutation either through the exposure of logical contradiction in the argument itself or through a demonstration of the falsity of some of the evidential premises that are necessary steps in the argument. Let me try to give you an example of what is practically meant by this in the sort of case Weber might be attempting to argue.

Verstehen has often been described as an empathetic understanding, an achievement of some sort of emotional empathy with the individual or group or social situation one is trying to understand. Weber was deeply suspicious of this. Emotional empathy is not the basis for his assertion that we can 'understand Caesar'. He doesn't use the same terms as Popper, but he has a set of perfectly rational procedures for attempting to achieve this sort of understanding in an objective fashion. Popper describes it as developing a situational logic. We describe as best we can, using what evidence is available to us, a situation. The set of logical relations between the various pieces of evidence is essentially what our theory is composed of. What the actor does in the situation, according to the theory, is essentially what we or anyone else would do – given the same information. There is a logic of the situation, so there are thus reasons for the actors behaving in a particular way. All right, there is our theory. Now a criticism of it amounts to demonstrating some logical flaws in the way we have constructed the relations between the various pieces of evidence that apparently compose the situation. Or alternatively it can be criticised through the presentation of some new piece of evidence. Say, for example, that a letter is later found that shows that the actor did indeed, contrary to our original theory, have some pre-knowledge of some relevant aspect of the situation, which we did not take into account. We thus must change our theory. In either case this composes something of a falsification of the theory.

Now whether Weber would be entirely happy with this logical formalisation of the process that Popper implies is another question. However, it does show that Popper is actually much more in tune with someone such as Weber than is popularly supposed. What is Weber doing in *The Protestant Ethic*? He is creating **ideal types**.

Socrates: Sorry, ideal types? Is this an ethical concept then?

G.O.D.: No, it has nothing whatsoever to do with the normative sense of the word 'ideal'. One could just as easily have an ideal type prostitute or axe murderer as anything else. No moral judgment is implied. Ideal types are theoretical constructions. They are a kind of typification of some sort of person, group, institution or other social phenomena that we are interested in. However, they are typical in one sense only. They are not typical in every respect. They are not the 'average'. They are only typical in some sense relevant to a particular research problem. Thus, in his theorising the beliefs and feelings of a Calvinist, Weber is not interested in every aspect of Calvinist theology. He is only interested in those aspects that directly bear upon the evolution of the 'spirit of capitalism'. His ideal types are very particular sorts of abstractions, and their theoretical construction could be said to significantly compose what Popper calls the situational logic of a phenomenon. Weber gives us evidence of Calvinist or Puritan theological doctrine through a selection of their writings. He gives us reasons for why a certain attitude would be taken to life and ultimately to economic activity.

This is, of course, potentially criticisable on a number of grounds. We can attempt to fault Weber's logic as he leads us through aspects of theological doctrine and its evolution to conclude certain more general attitudes and understandings of the world would be held by a set of social actors. Or we could show other aspects of doctrine and show how they contradict his argument. Weber's Protestant ethic theory has in fact been criticised on both grounds. Whether such criticism could ever be so decisive as to constitute a falsification is another matter. However, Popper has made a valuable point insofar as he pins his notion of scientific objectivity on the social process of rational debate about such matters.

Socrates: All right, I think I'm in danger of losing the plot again. I'm getting Popper's and Weber's positions confused. They're actually in complete agreement?

G.O.D.: No, I wouldn't go that far. Perhaps I shouldn't have tried to combine my explanation of their positions. But I wanted you to avoid some common misunderstandings. They are simply much more compatible than many people suppose. And Popper and positivism . . . well I am hoping you will reject them in the end. But I don't want you to reject them too easily. Positivism can be extremely sophisticated and easily deal with the sort of criticisms that are commonly made of it. Very frequently such criticism is a form of '**straw man argument**', i.e. very brilliant refutations of positions that actually no one holds. Also, I very much wished to emphasise that Weber's position is actually much more balanced than that of many others who would argue that social scientific explanation is radically different in kind from the sort of explanation applicable to natural phenomena.

Socrates: So would you describe Weber as a positivist then?

G.O.D.:   No, no, no! Perhaps I have over-emphasised some similarities. I wanted to show how Weber's approach could in fact be re-described in Popper's terms. I wanted to show how some, at least, of the apparent antimony between positivism and interpretativism is unnecessary. The classic way in which these distinctions are made is to line up Comte and Dürkheim on one side as positivists, while placing Weber on the other. Comte made the original formulation of the positivist position. His is an expression of the empiricism inherent in positivism, with a particular twist concerning sociology and a hierarchisation of the sciences. He placed sociology on top. As sciences developed in a logical relationship to one another, the full development of sociology had to wait upon that of psychology. It is an argument that need not seriously concern us here, as no one accepts it any longer. His positivism is not nearly as sophisticated or interesting as Popper's and has not had much effect upon twentieth-century sociology.

Dürkheim is much more interesting, and he does directly contradict Weber's position. But whether or not he can accurately be described as a positivist is another matter. I'm later going to argue that really there are no coherent applications of positivist science, as positivism is not an entirely coherent philosophical position. But we'll leave that for later. Where he does contradict Weber directly is with respect to ontology and thus also methodologically. Interestingly enough, Popper and Weber are in agreement upon that as well. Dürkheim bases his argument for the necessity of developing sociology as an autonomous discipline because of the **sui generis** existence of social reality.

Socrates: Sui generis? Oh yes, he argues that social phenomena are not reducible to the sum of individual behaviours. They exist in their own right above and beyond the individual as external phenomenon. Yes? His most famous methodological postulate was to 'treat social facts as things', arguing that social facts were really in some sense 'things' themselves.

G.O.D.:   Popper and Weber, on the other hand, are methodological individualists. Weber stresses that such social entities as institutions are actually only convenient fictions. They do not in fact exist except insofar as they are realised through the actions of individuals and the meanings they ascribe to those actions. People speak of various social entities as if they had a real existence. Thus, it is necessary to take such a popular misconception on board, as it has real effects concerning actions and the meaning ascribed to them. However, Weber enjoins us never to forget that such apparent real entities are only meaningful abstractions, labels for fictions; really they are no more than the sum of the individuals and their activities.

Weber and Popper share with Dürkheim, however, the conviction that a clear demarcated discipline of sociology is important. While ontologically, for them, social phenomena can be reduced to the collectivity of individual action and meaning, this does not mean that sociology can be reduced to questions of individual psychology. This is where Weber has his own suspicions of Verstehen.

Socrates: But I have always heard of Weber as the initiator of Verstehen.

G.O.D.: You were somewhat misinformed. Weber's sort of Verstehen is not some sloppy form of empathy. Interpretative understanding is reached through reasoning and evidence.

Socrates: I see . . . I think. Could I try to sum up what I've got so far? Broadly speaking, you've given me the basics of empiricism and positivism. The latter can be relatively sophisticated or unsophisticated, but the best of the positivists, someone like Popper for example, have a way of demonstrating some fundamental unity of natural and social science with respect to method (very broadly conceived). The worst sort of positivism would perhaps rule out (as unscientific) many sorts of valuable social scientific inquiry. However, the best sort of positivism can embrace even a kind of interpretative understanding.

The emphasis upon understanding and meaning, as opposed to merely cause and effect explanation, forms the basis of the main argument that there can't be a unity of the sciences. However, Weber – an interpretativist – does not use it as such. There is a kind of objectivity involved, even in approaching questions of meaning and understanding. Essentially, Weber avoids what are the dominant oppositions in the philosophy of social science debate; that is, he avoids the opposition between explanation and understanding. Rather he attempts to provide objective explanations of understanding. This is the reason you attempted to describe his methodology in Popper's terms. Yes?

So, thus far, positivism looks pretty good. However, later on you're going to poke all kinds of holes in it. Is that about it?

G.O.D.: Well, you left out a great deal of detail, but yes, that's basically it. Your formulation of Weber's project as the explanation of understanding is excellent.

Socrates: Thank you. But I'm also right that though you've made him sound very good, you're later going to poke holes in him.

G.O.D.: Yes, I'm even going to poke some holes in Popper. But we haven't yet examined the more extreme humanist positions that deny the possibility of unity between natural and social science.

Socrates: Is that what comes next?

G.O.D.: Not quite. We have to return to natural science again first.

Socrates: Oh no! I thought we were done with that.

G.O.D.: No, not by a long shot. I mentioned Thomas Kuhn to you the last time we talked and said we'd be considering his work this time.

Socrates: So you did.

G.O.D.: Now Kuhn mainly discusses natural science, but what he had to say is of tremendous relevance to social science as well. His book *The Structure of Scientific Revolutions* is perhaps one of the most influential books of the twentieth century and will likely continue to be discussed and debated in the next. Also, although he doesn't discuss social science very much, he is himself more of a social scientist than either natural scientist or philosopher. He presented a selective history of science, in order to illustrate some important points about notions of scientific progress. These points, while if not exactly shaking the world, certainly shook up our understanding of science and did so in a way that has particularly affected debates in social science.

Socrates: Okay, let's have him then. What's his line on things?

G.O.D.: One of the features of science commonly associated with positivism that we haven't spoken about very much is its inherent notion of progress. The progressive accumulation of knowledge is implicit in the deductive-nomological model of scientific explanation. Scientific laws stand in a hierarchical logical relation to one another. This is the basis, by the way, for Comte's hierarchisation of the various disciplines. Laws may be subsumed by laws of still greater generality and simplicity. Implicit in this notion is an ever-increasing accumulation of knowledge. This can also be linked to the emergent worldview associated with the Enlightenment, a rather optimistic view of a general progress for humanity.

Socrates: Progress towards what?

G.O.D.: Civilisation? Well, progress can be articulated in various ways. You of course know Marx's position; he saw capitalism as a stage on the way to humanity becoming truly civilised. This sort of general idea took many other different forms, not only in politics, but in other realms of life as well. Where Marx posited socialism, other people had different endpoints, still others didn't have such specific ideas as to where we were going; there was just an overall belief that we were going somewhere. The understanding of science is interwoven with these more general notions of progress. We'll be returning to this topic when we come to discuss postmodernism because the notion of progress can be disputed on many grounds. There are many debates. Kuhn's work has had a substantial impact upon most of them.

The debates are complicated, but Kuhn's most fundamental conclusion is very simple. Science, if in any sense we can say that it has progressed, has certainly not done so in a straightforward linear and accumulative fashion. Kuhn's presentation of scientific history shows it to be a much more complicated affair. As such, it casts doubt on the very notion of progress.

Socrates: You know, I'm beginning to see how philosophy works. You'll say something like 'the fundamental conclusion is very simple'. And it is. Science doesn't progress in a linear accumulative fashion. But then this has to be hedged somehow, qualified. Everybody will agree on this simple conclusion – sort of. That is, they'll see it as partially true and partially not. And a whole lot of people will disagree upon the degrees of partial truth and falsity and their implications. And it becomes very complicated.

G.O.D.: Yes, you've got it. Kuhn's own work has a lot of ambiguity within it. The history of science is a very complex affair, and drawing conclusions from it can be very contentious. However, I'm going to give you a brief overview of Kuhn's basic ideas, a couple of examples and point to where some of the controversy lies. You'll be able to grasp what's at stake immediately, I'm sure.

Socrates: Oh, I'm sure.

G.O.D.: You will. Right, the basic argument is organised around three inter-related concepts: normal science, scientific revolutions and paradigm. Normal science, according to Kuhn, is essentially puzzle-solving. It corresponds in some senses to what someone, such as a positivist for example, might naively conceive the whole of science to be about. We have a constellation of various problems, questions for which we don't have an answer as yet. But we do have a common body of agreed-upon knowledge to begin with. Within this agreed-upon body of knowledge are a number of things. There is an agreed-upon set of criteria for what counts as knowledge. There are agreed-upon procedures for obtaining further knowledge, for evaluating theories, evidence and so on. There are agreed-upon sets of problems that confront the particular disciplines, for deciding not the answers, but what the questions are. Included in this latter set of assumptions are ideas as to what form both questions and answers should take. All of this constitutes an overall viewpoint, one of the ways at least (there are others which are narrower) in which Kuhn's concept of paradigm can be understood. All these common assumptions form a paradigm from which normal science can proceed. Normal science consists of going about fairly un-dramatically solving the problems that are set for it. The most frequently used analogy for this activity is the jigsaw puzzle. During periods of normal science, scientists are simply going about putting together the pieces of the jigsaw puzzle. Are you with me on this?

Socrates: I've got a few questions, but they can wait a bit.

G.O.D.: Okay, well the history of science, according to Kuhn at any rate, consists of fairly long periods of this normal science, where scientists share the same paradigm. But periodically this calm history is punctuated with bursts of revolutionary upheaval. It is somewhat like the *Bluff Your Way in Philosophy* epigraph at the beginning of the chapter quite simply puts it, some people stop looking at the world in one way and start looking at it in another. A new paradigm appears. Some people embrace the new paradigm and some do not. Some scientists are working within it, while some are still working within the old one. Now this new paradigm does not simply dispute the alleged knowledges of the old one, but, in some sense or another, it disputes its fundamental assumptions, quite possibly its unconscious assumptions.

This often results not in the sensible rational debate you might hope for between scientists but rather in them simply talking past one another. The debate between proponents of each paradigm can be likened to a dialogue of the deaf. Words, arguments, etc. are exchanged, but it is as if each side fails to hear the other because their mutual misunderstandings are so basic. The different paradigms are said to be incommensurable. It is like that diagram of the vase and the faces. One side sees it one way and the other vice versa. Okay, before I go any further with this, you said you had some questions.

Socrates: Yeah, I do. But my earlier questions can still wait a bit. I've got a more important one now. What's the evidence for this? I mean, what's Kuhn's evidence that the history of science is like this? Can you give me some examples?

G.O.D.:   Sure. There's the change from Newtonian to Einsteinian physics. Einstein transformed our whole conception of time and space, the behaviour of light, gravity and so on.

Socrates: But can't the two be fitted together? Isn't it the case that the laws of Newtonian physics continue to apply to just about everything, except for speeds approximating the speed of light, some micro particle behaviour and maybe some other special cases. They don't really contradict each other, do they?

G.O.D.:   Good point. Maybe Einsteinian physics is just a refinement of Newtonian physics. But on the other hand, maybe it's much more than that. I'll give you another example – the Copernican revolution. There was a profound shift in human consciousness associated with the idea that the earth is not the center of the universe, that the earth orbits the sun rather than vice versa. Now here's a question for you: all right, two people are watching a sun rise; one sees the world from within a pre-Copernican paradigm, the other from within our present-day view; now are they seeing two different realities or are they seeing the same reality differently?

Socrates: They're seeing the same reality differently. And our present-day view wouldn't exactly say the pre-Copernican viewpoint is wrong either. The earth goes around the sun; the sun goes around the earth. One can describe their relative motion either way, depending upon what geometry you use. Wouldn't relativity theory, with its conception of time and space, allow you to pick any point you please as the centre of the universe and describe everything else in terms of relative motion, position, etc. in relation to it? It's just a question of frame of reference.

G.O.D.: You have been reading your popular science, haven't you? Okay, those are good points you raised. I'm in agreement with your basic argument, but there are objections to be raised against it. Now remember when we were discussing falsificationism, I brought up the case of a schoolboy chemistry experiment coming out with unexpected results?

Socrates: Yeah, obviously we're not going to overturn a well-established theory or law on the basis of school kid sloppiness.

G.O.D.: All right, but how has science historically treated **anomalous** instances or apparently bizarre theories? I mean, even if such were produced by allegedly 'respectable' scientists?

Socrates: I don't know.

G.O.D.: Well, frequently, perhaps most frequently, anomalies are merely treated as anomalies. Strictly speaking, according to falsificationist criteria, experimentally produced anomalous results should be treated as counter-instances, as falsifications. Yes?

Socrates: You mean they aren't?

G.O.D.: Frequently not. And what has been the fate of those who have produced new and, according to the wisdom of the day, 'off the wall' theories and conclusions? It's quite often the case that by the standards of any particular time, a scientific breakthrough will have its ridiculous, absurd-seeming aspects.

Socrates: So, the people are dismissed as cranks or nuts?

G.O.D.: Sometimes. More frequently, and this is the case with anomalous results as well, the unpalatable is simply ignored. Sometimes the results will be explained and used by others later on, others working within a new and different paradigm perhaps, where the case now suddenly makes perfect sense. The previously ignored theory sometimes later comes to seem of great importance and thus absurd no longer. It may come to form the basis for a new paradigm of understanding. So what is the significance of such examples?

Socrates: Well, one thing is that science doesn't progress in such a linear straightforward fashion. Okay, I don't have a big problem with that. It's not perfect. Another thing would be that it's not really fair. It doesn't live up to its own standards.

G.O.D.: Yes, well, fairness is one aspect of it, I suppose. But there is something else even more fundamental to be learned from such examples. Come on, you're a budding sociologist. What is the main point of significance here?

Socrates: The social dimension of science?

G.O.D.: Very good. We've introduced a social dimension into the equation. How to understand this and how far we want to take it is really what all the debate is about.

But let's look at it a little closer. The first thing we can say philosophically is that the perspective on knowledge of an individual 'knower' is misguided. We don't start each generation anew with a blank slate. We start with common assumptions, commonly held beliefs. Individual scientists may produce theories, insights, new concepts; perform experiments; and so on, all by themselves. They can do this, but they don't from a void. They begin with knowledge – and errors – which others have produced. Second, whether their theories get taken up or ignored, whether their experimental results are replicated, accepted, rejected or even looked at at all, is a social process. The criteria for judgments are socially arrived at. The mechanism for the dissemination of knowledge is social. Individuals may sometimes produce knowledge, but even so it is a social process. And most frequently today, the work of experimental science is actually a team effort. Scientific equipment, scientific activity, costs money. This is not an insignificant fact.

Socrates: Okay, I can see all that. But perhaps I'm still missing some of the significance of it.

G.O.D.:   Let's carry it a step further. Imagine the various scientific specialisms as searchlights trained upon particular areas of reality. Now, one of the factors determining the direction these searchlights are pointed will be the specific demands of industry perhaps. Another factor will be the set of assumptions currently in vogue as to which is the best direction to look in. So, scientific discovery will be frequently linked to apparently quite unrelated factors of the cultural and socio-economic system. These links can be traced. This is one of the activities of the sociologist of knowledge.

All right, now what of the community of scientists themselves? Scientific reputations, jobs, salaries, etc. are competitively linked to achievement. A scientist may have both reputation and livelihood linked to a particular theory. This is going to make him or her rather unreceptive to a theory that overturns their earlier work and its accompanying prestige. When they conduct experiments they are actively looking for certain results and may be blind to other potentially important factors.

Socrates: Well, this is coming back to what I said about fairness, isn't it? It is coming back to the question of people living up to their own standards, that is, to scientists living up to the standards of science, to engaging in that ongoing critical exchange upon which Popper places so much stress.

G.O.D.:   Yes, but not only that. Let's take the case of apparent falsification and a journal editor who refuses out of spite or self-interest to publish this research. Well, such examples are actually the least interesting cases. Bias is bias; fraud is fraud. What is more interesting is how deeply implicated is the whole process in the social dimension of reality. If it's not just a case of 'people failing to live up to their own standards', as you put it, but rather of the socially constructed nature of the standards themselves, then we are on the road to a potentially thorough-going sociological relativism. We are very close to saying that all of reality itself is socially constructed. Do you see the significance? If the history of science can be seen to be a series of transformations between one paradigm and another, and the most significant factors involved in choosing between paradigms are shown to be social factors, then knowledge itself is most significantly a social construction. This is the point of view taken by the **conventionalist philosophy of science**. The connection to an independently existing reality has been cut, or at least seriously weakened. Different paradigms, different realities, is one possible conclusion.

Socrates: Nah, I can't buy that. You mean I've got my reality; you've got yours? Nope. Can't buy it.

G.O.D.: Well, okay, good. I think your scepticism and common sense is going to see you through. Your instincts are sound. But what do you base your argument on? How do you prove that that view is wrong?

Socrates: Well, let me give you an example then. I did some reading about that **oxygen/phlogiston problem** you referred to earlier. All right, one theory calls the substance produced, the one that Priestley 'discovered', dephlogisticated air. The other theory, Lavoisier's, ours, calls it oxygen. Same substance right?

G.O.D.: Right. But it's more than a question of labels.

Socrates: I was getting to that. We know it's the same substance to which the labels of either theory refer for a simple reason. They can both be produced by the same set of procedures. Yes? Further, each theory comes up with a different set of predictions concerning the substance's behaviour in specific cases. Okay, the phlogiston theory asserts, predicts, that in burning, a substance is lost – phlogiston, i.e. dephlogisticated air. Our chemical theory sees burning as rapid oxidisation, a chemical process that should produce weight gain rather than weight loss as the phlogiston theory suggests. Deciding upon the better of the two theories can be easily done by a simple procedure that doesn't in itself presuppose anything one way or the other – weigh the substance.

G.O.D.: Wow! That's very good!

Socrates: I know. I got it out of a book by a realist author (T. Benton, *Philosophical Foundations of the Three Sociologies,* 1977). But I haven't quite finished it. If it is the case that this sort of judgment can be made, then the other cases that you refer to are ones where people, scientists, are just failing to play by the rules. So, sometimes for social reasons, some things that aren't really knowledge get socially certified as such, and sometimes real knowledge doesn't. Well, that only proves that science isn't perfect, that scientists are only human. It doesn't prove that reality is entirely socially constructed or simply relative to points of view either.

G.O.D.:   I'm impressed. I really am.

Socrates: Thank you.

G.O.D.:   I still have some thoughts to leave you with before we move on though. First off, an observation: I don't know if you noticed it or not, but your example is far more 'localised', so to speak, than the Copernican revolution or Einstein's. This is one of the problems with Kuhn's concept of paradigm. It is unclear how general to make it and how far to extend the notion of radical breaks between one paradigm and another. Now, I think your example clearly resolves the issue of relativism in the more 'localised' contexts. It demonstrates an underlying continuity to the scientific enterprise and sets limits to the influence of social factors. It reaffirms a notion of scientific progress in coming to an increasing knowledge of the world. Or at least it demonstrates the basis for such. But what about cases where the common elements of your example are lacking?

Socrates: What do you mean?

G.O.D.:   Well, I think I can use the answer to that question to bring us back to social science actually.

Socrates: Well, hurrah for that. But I'm still intrigued by what you said. Don't you have any natural science examples?

G.O.D.:   Yes, I do. I'll give you one of those as well. Okay, there were three things held in common by both sides in the oxygen/phlogiston debate. First, a common body of shared assumptions and knowledge to begin with. Second, the identical substance could be produced by the same set of procedures without choosing between the competing theories. Third, there was further agreement upon criteria of judgment, measurement, observation and so on. Well, what of cases whereby one or all of those three areas of agreement are lacking? For a starter here's an example that straddles both natural and social science. You know about the controversy over the alleged condition of M.E. (Myalgic Encephalomyelitis)?

Socrates: Yeah, I think so. Some people claim it is a real physical illness, some kind of viral thing. Others claim it's purely psychosomatic, that those affected are a bunch of lazy hypochondriacs really.

G.O.D.:   You've rather drastically over-simplified the terms of the debate. Hypochondria may form part of the popular conception of it – the use of such pejorative terms as 'yuppie flu' is indicative of this – but it is not one of the seriously contending explanations of the phenomenon. There's a general recognition that the suffering, the symptoms experienced, are real. The disagreement is over the source, the nature of the cause. Is it physical in nature or is it a psychological/

social phenomenon or a combination of the two? I'm over-simplifying here as well, but that's the gist of it.

Okay, there's an immediate linkage between the epistemological questions involved here and some very practical political ones. There seems to be in the general public's mind, and in the perspective held by most M.E. sufferers' minds as well, that somehow illnesses with an identifiable physical mechanism are more real than psychological phenomena. The popular derogatory notion of hypochondria connects up with that epistemology implicitly. It also politically connects up with the sufferers' quite real fears of stigmatisation. Then, too, there are the effects upon social policy with respect to the way it is categorised – treatment, funding, compensation and so on. So there is quite a lot at stake for the sufferers, dependent upon which 'paradigm' becomes dominant.

For scientists themselves there are also issues concerning 'territory' and legitimacy. For example, the psychoanalytical profession's orientation towards understanding (and treating!) the phenomenon demonstrates some of their concern about their own legitimacy as a science. All in all there are a lot of conflicting social interests involved. Okay, the social interests and conflict with respect to M.E. is perhaps both sharper and more obvious than was the case with the oxygen example. However, for our purposes here, that is not the most significant difference. Rather, it is the absence in the M.E. case of those three areas of commonality we discussed with respect to the oxygen/phlogiston example.

First of all, what is the equivalent of the common 'substance'? What we have instead is a collection of sufferers' descriptions of symptoms. Where is the common body of knowledge that the different paradigms share? Psychoanalysis has its own historically constituted collection of criteria for comparative judgment, diagnosis and so on. These are quite different from those of virology. Could both 'sides' be right? Could there be a physical, virus-based M.E. and also a psychologically caused collection of symptoms? Could all the 'sides' be wrong? Consensus seems to be forming among doctors of there being a dual social and viral dimension to the phenomenon. Well, all of this is very difficult to pronounce upon. Do you see the weakness in your example for explaining all cases of comparative judgment between paradigms? Such relatively simple cases as the oxygen/phlogiston example are likely merely a subset of the wider, more complex situation that usually pertains.

Socrates: So you mean that we can't judge which is the better theory for describing the phenomenon because there may actually be more than one phenomenon involved. Unlike the oxygen/phlogiston case, the equivalent of the 'substance' here is one of the unknowns.

G.O.D.: Exactly so.

Socrates:	And the conflicting theories don't start from the same set of shared knowledges either.
G.O.D.:	A good deal of what psychoanalysts accept as established knowledges are highly contentious outside their school of thought. A good many virologists would likely be inclined to dismiss the whole discipline as a load of tosh and see their claims to scientificity as ludicrous. They might do this yet still deny there is a viral basis to M.E. and categorise it as psychological.
Socrates:	Thus, there would be no agreement upon criteria for judgment by which one could choose between the theories without presupposing the superiority of one set of criteria over another.
G.O.D.:	That's it.
Socrates:	Wow. So it's a hopeless mess then.
G.O.D.:	It sometimes can appear so.
Socrates:	So are you saying there is no way in which we can comparatively evaluate theories which derive from fundamentally different paradigms?
G.O.D.:	No. I would just argue that it is extremely difficult. There is a basis for doing so, but I don't want to put my argument for it just yet.
Socrates:	You want to wait until we go on to discuss realism, right?
G.O.D.:	That's right. Let me give you another example, exclusively from social science this time. One of the ways in which Kuhn's notion of paradigm is applied to sociology is frequently through the assertion that sociology has yet to produce any dominant paradigms, as the field is so rife with fundamental disagreements. This can be taken as a good thing, a sign of its intellectual health and self-reflexive questioning nature. On the other hand, this can be presented as a bad thing, a sign of its immaturity as a discipline, of perhaps its pre-scientific status. Fundamental concepts are conceived of and utilised so very differently by different schools of thought within the discipline that the notion of incommensurable discourse is often used to describe the state of play. But this is a reflection not only of confusion and dissension within the discipline, but also within its subject matter, the social world itself. Class is one of sociology's basic concepts. When class is being discussed, the term is used as a label not only for different phenomena as identified by different theoretical matrixes but for different understandings of the world employed by social actors themselves. Thus, it is not only a theoretical tool, subject to different conceptualisations and usage by different schools of thought, but it is also part of the subject matter that the conflicting analyses are trying to explain.
Socrates:	Yes, I can see that. Marx and Weber define class differently, and also their respective theories place different emphases upon people's own categorisation of themselves and others.

G.O.D.: Not merely emphasis. People's self-definition plays quite different roles in the various theoretical frameworks. And Marx and Weber are only two amongst the many who employ notions of class in quite different ways. Perhaps most importantly of all, quite apart from substantive differences between different theorisations of class, there can be quite fundamental ontological differences as well.

Socrates: What do you mean?

G.O.D.: Well, class as part of a classification scheme is one thing. It can be used to categorise groups of individuals. Different definitions, different categories, ergo the groups and individuals are categorised differently. However, the Marxist would argue that class exists. It is not merely a theoretical category but is something of the order of a Dürkheimian social fact. It exists regardless of whether theorists employ it as a conceptual tool or whether people define themselves in this matter. The disagreements are thus so fundamental between this viewpoint and those who would dispute it as to indicate that Marxists are operating from within a wholly different and incommensurate paradigm in relation to other social scientists studying apparently similar problems.

Socrates: Okay, I can see that. So what is the solution then?

G.O.D.: Ah, solutions are premature at this point. We still have a long way to go. I want to leave you with an even more fundamental notion of **incommensurability**, one that is probably too big to be captured by the concept of paradigm. Here's something that you can go away and think about. What about rationality itself? Is it not possible that our notions of rationality, of science and so on, are merely our culture's social constructions? Might not other cultures have other notions of rationality, other modes of knowledge, which work equally well for them? Isn't it possible that we are merely imposing our culturally inherited notions of science and rationality, our belief system, upon other cultures? Perhaps we are simply being ethnocentric. We are prioritising our values simply because they are ours.

Socrates: I don't think I believe that.

G.O.D.: Well, the easy answer to you would be to say, 'Well, you would say that wouldn't you; that's your culture's perspective and part of their history of colonial domination'.

Socrates: Yes, well they'd have to do better than that to convince me.

G.O.D.: That's okay. Some people definitely have. Next time we'll take a look at the work of Wittgenstein and Peter Winch. I think you'll find they'll give you a run for your money on these points.

Socrates: Oh boy; I get to have my whole world turned upside down, eh?

G.O.D.: Well, we'll see.

DISCUSSION QUESTIONS

1   Choose any quantitative social scientific method. In what ways can it be considered to be analogous to experimentation in natural science? In what ways not?

2   Choose a historically significant event. On what grounds could it be argued that even if we fully understand and can explain what caused the event to occur, we still have not fully understood it?

3   Weber did not believe he was originating a new method of understanding social action with his technique of using the construction of ideal types. Rather he felt he was merely making systematic and rigorous a form of reasoning that is frequently used anyway. Can you think of some examples of using some approximation of an ideal type methodology that you have used in everyday life while trying to understand others' meanings and motivations?

4   Why might philosophers and scientists be disturbed by the argument that social factors determine which scientific conclusions about the natural world are accepted and which ones not?

5   A clear rational choice can be made between competing scientific theories if identical procedures can be accepted by both and the predictions of one are accurate and the other not. Is this sort of answer sufficient to resolve the problems of paradigm shifts in science?

FURTHER READING SUGGESTIONS

Journals

Journal for the Theory of Social Behaviour
Philosophy of Social Science
Radical Philosophy

General

Adorno, T. (ed.) (1976) *Positivist Disputes in German Sociology*, Heinemann, London – especially articles by Popper and Habermas. This book has something of a classic status now.

Benton, T. (1977) *Philosophical Foundations of the Three Sociologies*, Routledge & Kegan Paul, London.

Giddens, A. (ed.) (1974) *Positivism and Sociology*, Heinemann, London – especially essays by Weber, Schutz, Gellner and Habermas.

Halfpenny, P. (1982) *Positivism and Sociology*, Allen & Unwin, London.

Hughes, J. (1997) *The Philosophy of Social Research*, Addison Wesley Longman, London.

Keat, R. and Urry, J. (1982) *Social Theory as Science*, Routledge & Kegan Paul, London.

Lessnoff, M. (1974) *The Structure of Social Science*, Allen & Unwin, London.

Popper, K. (1960) *The Poverty of Historicism*, Routledge & Kegan Paul, London – this book has also become something of a classic.

Sociological classics

Andreski, S. (ed.) (1974) *The Essential Comte*, Croom Helm, London.

Comte, A. (1976) *The Foundations of Sociology*, ed. K. Thompson, Nelson, London.

Craib, I. (1997) *Classical Social Theory*, Oxford University Press, Oxford.

Dürkheim, E. (1964) *The Rules of Sociological Method*, Macmillan, London.

Heilbron, J. (1995) *The Rise of Social Theory*, Polity, Cambridge (Part III) – good discussion of Comte.

Hughes, A.J., Martin, P.J. and Sharrock, W.W. (1995) *Understanding Classical Sociology*, Sage, London.

Leat, D. (1972) 'Misunderstanding Verstehen', *Sociological Review* 20, pp. 29–38.

Mill, J.S. (1961) *Auguste Comte and Positivism*, University of Michigan Press, Ann Arbor.

———— (1961) *System of Logic*, Longman, London.

Rickert, H. (1962) *Science and History, a Critique of Positivist Epistemology*, Van Nostrand, New York – presents the classic critique of positivism from a hermeneutic perspective.

Weber, M. (1949) *The Methodology of the Social Sciences*, Free Press, New York.

———— (1968) *The Protestant Ethic and the Spirit of Capitalism*, Allen & Unwin, London.

———— (1978) *Economy and Society*, Bedminster Press, New York, Vol. 1, *Chapter 1*.

Kuhn

Hacking, I. (1981) *Scientific Revolutions*, Oxford University Press, Oxford.

Kuhn, T.S. (1970) *The Structure of Scientific Revolutions*, University of Chicago Press, Chicago – perhaps the most widely read and quoted book on the history and philosophy of science. It is enormously influential and quite accessible.

Historical epistemology

Bachelard analysed science and arrived at very similar conclusions to Kuhn much earlier. The school of thought known as 'historical epistemology' was enormously influential in France and thus indirectly to the rest of the world through the work of people such as Althusser and Foucault.

Bachelard, G. (1964) *The Psychoanalysis of Fire*, Routledge & Kegan Paul, London.

———— (1969) *The Philosophy of No: Philosophy of the New Scientific Mind*, Orion Press, New York.

Canguilhem, G. (1961) 'The Role of Analogies and Models in Biological Discovery' in A.C. Crombie (ed.), *Symposium on the History of Science*, Oxford University Press, Oxford, pp. 507–520.

———— (1988) *Ideology and Rationality in the History of the Life Sciences*, MIT Press, Cambridge, MA.

Gutting, G. (1984) *Michel Foucault's Archaeology of Scientific Reason*, Cambridge University Press, New York – good on both Bachelard and Canguilhem.

Lecourt, D. (1975) *Marxism and Epistemology: Bachelard, Canguilhem, and Foucault*, NLB, London.

Tiles, M. (1987) 'Epistemological History: The Legacy of Bachelard and Canguilhem' in P. Griffiths (ed.), *Contemporary French Philosophy*, Cambridge University Press, New York, pp. 141–156.

CHAPTER 5

HERMENEUTICS AND SCIENCE: 'THE LINGUISTIC TURN'

In our language a whole mythology is laid down.

Ludwig Wittgenstein

For it was believed that he who possessed the true name possessed the very being of god or man, and could force even a deity to obey him as a slave obeys his master.
from J.G. Frazer, *The Golden Bough*
(about the beliefs of the Ancient Egyptians)

OUTLINE OF MAJOR POINTS TO BE COVERED

Cultural relativism developed in part as a response to the previous ethnocentric social science that evolved in conjunction with the colonial age of imperial conquest. It is a useful corrective to the limitations of attempting to understand other cultures in terms of the standards of one's own. This lesson applies beyond attempts at inter-cultural understandings of history (i.e. 'the past is a foreign country') to the understanding of sub-cultures within one's own society. It does throw up many conceptual and ethical/political problems, however, of a very fundamental nature. This chapter focuses upon these and the related debates that arise from them.

1   The distinction is further made between understanding and causal explanations with a consideration of the views of Peter Winch.
   a   Social science is and should be much more like understanding a language than understanding the workings of a machine.
   b   Social action is rule-governed rather than law-governed because of the capacity of actors to make meaningful choices.
   c   Laws of nature are understood in a positivist sense of expressing invariance, as generalisations of **constant conjunctures of events.** Rules are understood as human-created frameworks for both guiding and socially structuring the meanings of decisions and action.
2   The above views imply an extreme relativism with respect not only to judgment but to the possibilities of ever understanding another culture.
   a   Rationality itself is given a relativist nature and understood in terms of a specific Western cosmology.

b   Some alternative examples are given whereby two significant points are observed.

  i   The alternatives to Western science and rationality seem to function perfectly well for other societies in terms of social functionality and practical engagement with nature.

  ii The extremes of difference between some belief systems and Western scientific rationality when framed in Peter Winch's understanding of cultural relativism are such as to indicate the impossibility of understanding other cultures at all.

3   Winch offers a tentative solution to the problems raised by the last point above. Birth, death and marriage are suggested as universals of the human condition through which a bridge of understanding may be forged to allow us the possibility of understanding other cultures.

a   A fourth feature is added to the above three: the necessity for human beings to engage with the natural world to provide for the practical necessities of life.

4   The implications of moral relativism are explored through examples where our inclination to make moral judgment is so strong because of the negative extremity (from our perspective of judgment) of the other culture's practice that it suggests a serious problem with cultural relativism and its refusal of moral judgment.

5   Jürgen Habermas's position is articulated, in part as a specific response to the above views articulated by Winch and in part as an alternative to the postmodernist viewpoints examined in Chapter 7.

a   Habermas is situated in relation to the **critical theory** of the Frankfurt School. The latter's concept of instrumental reason and critique of the Enlightenment is sketched out.

b   Habermas's theory of the relation between knowledge and **human interests** is briefly outlined.

  i   The **empirico-analytic sciences** arise from our cognitive interest in developing practical knowledges in order to harness nature to serve our practical needs and desires.

  ii The **hermeneutic sciences** develop from our practical needs to communicate and interact with our fellow human beings.

  iii **Critical reason** develops from our common *emancipatory interest*.

c   Habermas's notion of the **ideal speech situation** is considered in relation to the above three forms of interest. It provides an ideal standard whereby the distortions of communication occur through the inequalities inherent in the distribution of power.

6   Habermas's position gives us a basis for ethical judgments of both our own and other cultures, as judgment is in reference to an ideal standard rather than merely our own inherited cultural values.

7   Habermas's depiction of forms of rationality allows us to understand and historically locate instrumental reason as merely a form of rationality that has become too dominant and applied to spheres of life where it ought not to be.

8   The various negative aspects of the Western rational scientific worldview seen negatively as an expression of modernity can now be modified so as to see modernity as an unfinished product. A brief foreshadowing of the postmodernist perspectives (taken up in Chapter 7), with which this view is in contradiction, is given in this context.

9   A criticism of Habermas's position is given: that it is a procedural view of truth, which reduces questions of truth to questions of truth and ideology. A brief foreshadowing of the final chapter's critical realist argument is given in this context.

DIALOGUE

G.O.D.:	Twins are birds.
Socrates:	Sorry?
G.O.D.:	Twins are birds.
Socrates:	What?
G.O.D.:	There is a tribe of people called the Nuer who believe this. Do you know what might be meant by such a belief?
Socrates:	I have no idea. Are they nuts?
G.O.D.:	No. It is part of their culture. Human twins are believed to be birds.
Socrates:	Okay, so what in the world is meant by that?
G.O.D.:	Actually, I have no idea. I'm not part of their culture. It doesn't make sense to me.
Socrates:	I see. This is a different culture to ours, so we can't judge them by our standards of rationality. This is your lead-in to cultural relativist epistemology. Yes?
G.O.D.:	That's right. How can we possibly make sense of a belief like that? From within our framework, it is nonsensical.
Socrates:	Absolutely. Perhaps whoever translated it got it wrong somehow.
G.O.D.:	Perhaps. But we can conclude a few things from the attempt. First off, if the translation is mistaken, it wasn't a casual error, like getting the wrong word for bread in a shop in France. The anthropologist who performed the translation thought that this was a rather peculiar sort of assertion and put considerable energy into attempting an understanding of it. Second, if it is a mistranslation, that in itself is a part of the problem. That is, it goes to the heart of the problematical nature of understanding other cultures. Further, while we might wish simply to write off such apparently inexplicable phenomena as something of merely peripheral interest, we would be unwise to do so.
Socrates:	Why? Because it wouldn't be 'politically correct' to do so?
G.O.D.:	Well, there certainly is a political dimension to this question, but it wasn't what I was getting at. We know that our own society is fragmented to some degree; how much so is not entirely clear. Well,

obviously the more different another society and culture is from our own, the greater the difficulty we will have in arriving at mutual understanding. We can carry this further, to address the issue of diverse sub-cultures within our own. What is it that guarantees our own communication and understanding? One of the answers given is associated with the rationalist tradition of philosophy. Human beings all possess the capacity for rational thought. But what if the very meaning of rationality is brought into question?

Socrates: Some cultures are more rational than others. I don't see how that problematises the very meaning of rationality.

G.O.D.: Perhaps it needn't. But you'll concede there is at least a potential philosophical problem.

Socrates: Yeah, I guess so.

G.O.D.: Okay, another thing we can conclude about the 'twins are birds' belief is that in some sense or another it is symbolic. I mean, while the Nuer apparently really believe that human twins are birds, they don't seem to expect the former to be able to fly or attempt to eat them. It is obviously some kind of symbolic expression.

Socrates: It seems a pretty daft symbolic expression if you ask me.

G.O.D.: What of taking the host in Catholic communion? To assert that some ceremonial wine is really the blood of Christ could well seem equally daft.

Socrates: You're telling me!

G.O.D.: Okay, remind me later that this example connects up with an important point concerning the judgment of our own culture.

Socrates: I think our culture is pretty crazy too. That 'blood of Christ' stuff certainly seems so to me.

G.O.D.: Yes, well, we'll come back to that later. I want to present to you some of the main points of Peter Winch's critique of social science. In essence, he didn't see it as science at all.

Socrates: You mean science as conceived of by the positivists, of there being a unity of natural and social science?

G.O.D.: Exactly.

Socrates: And he stressed the difference between the task of understanding and the task of producing causal explanations.

G.O.D.: Have I told you this already?

Socrates: Yes, I'm just applying some of what we've discussed already to guess where we're going.

G.O.D.: Very good. You're definitely on the right track. Laws and rules. What would you see as the difference between them?

Socrates: One is formally codified and the other is simply informal social convention.

G.O.D.: No, no. I don't mean legislative law, I mean scientific law.

Socrates: Oh. Right. I don't know then. Wait. Is it to do with social science only being able to approximate natural scientific explanation, that

G.O.D.:
statistical tendencies, etc. can't achieve the same degree of rigour and precision?

No, that's not it. It's a good try though. No, I'm afraid I've sent you down the wrong track. Human society, social reality, so Peter Winch would argue, is rule-governed. Rules may be formalised in the form of laws, but this is a different meaning of the word 'law' than what we're concerned with here. Laws of nature are different in kind from **social rules**.

Socrates:
I'm sure that's true. But I'm going to ask even if it's obvious. How so?

G.O.D.:
Well, for one thing, we can break rules. You can't 'break' the law of gravity. If you could, it wouldn't qualify as a law any longer. Social action, Winch contends, is essentially rule-governed behaviour. An individual may choose to follow or break a social rule, but we can't come to an understanding of the action in either case without being aware of the rule. This factor changes the relation of social scientists to their subject matter, from that of natural scientists. It is through our social rules that meaning is given to social actions. The natural scientist carefully observes and looks out for regularities in nature.

One view of scientific explanation, as we've discovered, is that its ultimate aim is to be able to universalise observed regularities in the form of laws. This would not be possible with respect to social behaviour because rules are not generalisations of invariant behaviour but rather are part of the meaning system of the actors. One could observe very carefully the constancies of social activity at wedding ceremonies, for example, but this would not tell you very much concerning the meaning of the ritual.

Socrates:
Oh, I don't know. I think you might be able to learn a lot from careful observation, even if you were unaware of the meaning of some other culture's ritual. If you observed sufficient examples, I think you might learn a good deal concerning the meaning of the ritual.

G.O.D.:
Well, I think you've got a point there. It is in fact just the sort of reply a positivist might make. But I don't think Winch would buy it at all. Anyway, I think you can probably see now why I began this discussion with 'twins are birds'. Winch's points become more apparent with extreme examples. His argument actually amounts to an attack upon the possibility of social science in general. But he makes a great many of his points through anthropological examples.

Socrates:
Yeah, I can see that with other cultures, simply observing might not be sufficient. You could easily get misled.

G.O.D.:
Quite so. And one could argue that early anthropology did a very bad job of coming to understand other cultures. Initially it kept

trying to read other cultures through our own cultural matrix and judged them accordingly. The notion of **cultural relativism** is in part, quite a significant part, a response to an earlier tradition of **ethnocentric** anthropology that went hand in hand with empire. But we'll come back to cultural relativism later.

I want to tell you another of Winch's main contentions. He asserts that coming to an understanding of social phenomena is much more like understanding a language than it is like giving an explanation of the workings of a machine. Actually, with respect to our understanding of social science, this idea goes far beyond merely Winch's ideas. It is part of a larger shift in philosophical and social scientific perspectives. It is sometimes referred to as the '**linguistic turn**' in theorising.

Socrates: Who else went down this road then?

G.O.D.: In some fashion or another, just about everybody, except maybe the positivists, and perhaps you could even say them too. Though they did so in a different way; for example, language was very important to the logical atomists, which we discussed before. Actually, a lot of Winch's thinking is influenced by Wittgenstein. He developed a very distinctive view upon the nature of language, thought and communication. He did so, in part, as a response to the Vienna Circle, but more generally through engaging with the problems of logic and truth. Can you see how there might be a connection?

Socrates: Yes, I can see how questions concerning logic, understood as relations between propositions, and the problem of linking this up with observations about the world could bear on this issue – sort of. Understanding the nature of language would be very fundamental. But how does this connect up with seeing social actions as rule-governed, as distinct from laws of cause and effect?

G.O.D.: There are a number of ways to make this connection. Actually, as you are perhaps beginning to see, all of the issues with which we are engaged in the philosophy of social science are interconnected. Anyway, here are two ways of making the connection. First, the notion of scientific law, at least the positivist notion of such, is very much bound up with the notion of **constant conjunctures of events**. Well, the grammatical rules of English could be said to govern the word order of sentences in the same way as Newton's laws of motion govern the behaviour of planetary motion – with one very significant difference. Someone speaking English can easily make a grammatical error. Further, this can be done, yet the speaker can still be understood. You could not possibly make an error with respect to gravity. That is, one can make an error in understanding how gravity works, but understand it or not, it will affect us just the same. Though the Frazer epigraph at the beginning of this chapter rather suggests otherwise (as though the naming of things gives us direct control over them), this is not the case with respect to language. In fact, this is the second major difference. Inter-subjective and subjective understanding play a wholly different role with respect to linguistic rules and physical laws. Understanding is itself a part, indeed the most important part perhaps, of the phenomenon we are wishing to understand.

Socrates: Okay, let's see if I've got this. We come to explain physical phenomena through observation of regularities, what you just termed 'constant conjunctures of events'. (I know, I know, it's more complicated than that!) On the other hand, social phenomena, while not simply being helter-skelter, are not going to be invariant; we can't simply observe and look for regularities and so on.

G.O.D.:   That's part of it. But what if you did see a great deal of repetition, some unvarying regularities? In natural science you would be on the road to somewhere with that, wouldn't you? You would have a starting point for theorising at least? Yes?

Socrates: Yes. Are you trying to suggest that that would not be the case with social phenomena?

G.O.D.:   Twins are birds.

Socrates: I wish you'd quit saying that.

G.O.D.:   Well, let's say you observe this tribe, and they always make this assertion (at least so far as you've observed) in the same context (as far as you can tell). Would that necessarily tell you what it means to them?

Socrates: No, I suppose not, though it might tell you a great deal.

G.O.D.:   It might. But then on the other hand, the exact same physical actions can have drastically different meanings. To understand the meanings one really needs to know a great deal about the context. For example, one probably needs to understand English culture quite well to stand much chance of getting served in a busy pub. Do you ever watch *Star Trek*?

Socrates: Yeah, sometimes. Why?

G.O.D.:   Well, there was one episode where they met an alien civilisation which, on the one hand, did not appear to be unfriendly, but on the other hand, all previous encounters with it had been basically unsuccessful in establishing communication. There were two quite interesting aspects to this episode that are relevant to our discussion. The first was that while they did not wholly succeed in coming to an understanding with the aliens, their partial success at least informed them of the basis of the alien communication system. The aliens communicated through metaphoric reference to their history, with respect to even quite simple day-to-day type communication. This allegedly reflected the way they thought and felt – or at least so concluded the *Star Trek* crew. They likened this to having discovered the basis of the alien grammar. It followed the principle, for example, when referring to sexual romantic love, of saying perhaps 'Juliet on the balcony'. However, this still did not enable them to communicate with the aliens very successfully. They thought they had discovered the equivalent of the grammar of the alien communication, but of course they did not possess any of the vocabulary, i.e. the aliens would not use 'Juliet on the balcony', as they did not know the story nor the *Star Trek* crew know what their equivalents would be.

An interesting observation can be made about this. The alien communications, and thus apparently their mythology, seemed perhaps rather less obscure and easier to figure out than assertions such as 'twins are birds' and the like. That is, our real world human beings seem capable of considerably more bizarreness from the point of view of our culture than *Star Trek*'s imaginary aliens.

The other interesting aspect of the episode was that first contact between our (*Star Trek*'s Federation, that is) civilisation and theirs was established through the transmission of a mathematical progression. This principle is actually practised by human scientists in connection with a search for extraterrestrial intelligence. The assumption underlying it is that mathematics is universal, either in the sense of governing all possible reasoning on a certain level, or of mathematical relationships structurally embedded in the universe itself. This places a limit on the possible extremes of relativism. But it is only an assumption. If we extend Kuhn's notion of paradigm to the most extreme possible interpretation, then the very notion of rationality becomes potentially subject to cultural variation. This is in fact what Winch does. Though he found his own conclusions rather disturbing.

Socrates: You've made reference to extreme relativism before. I think I know what you mean by it, but I'm not sure.

G.O.D.: Well, I'll give you Winch's example of the Azande. It makes quite clear what is at issue at any rate. The Azande believe in magic. It forms a part of the fabric of their everyday life. It's a part of their unquestioned assumptions about the nature of reality; they don't question it any more than you wonder about the lights coming on when you flick a switch. But from the perspective of Western rationality and science, their assumptions are absurd, and their beliefs in supernatural forces simply false.

Socrates: I wouldn't be so quick to dismiss another culture's beliefs.

G.O.D.: Perhaps that is because you've grown up in the post-colonial era. Perhaps it's because you live in a university environment where cultural relativism has become nearly as much of an unquestioned orthodoxy as previously was the ethnocentric position. Perhaps . . .

Socrates: Perhaps you just think I'm an airhead?

G.O.D.: Don't be silly. But let's see if you do dismiss their beliefs or not. To determine guilt or innocence of someone suspected of a crime, or in other cases where supernatural wisdom is called for, the Azande administer poison to a chicken. A question is asked and the answer understood in the affirmative or negative according to whether the chicken lives or dies.

Socrates: Okay, you've got me. That does sound pretty silly. I'm sure there must be more to it than that.

G.O.D.: Well, of course. The action is undertaken in correspondence with a set of social rules prescribing exactly how it is to be performed and so on. The action is connected to an elaborate set of beliefs concerning nature – and the Azande wouldn't make the same sort of distinction between the natural world and the supernatural as we would of course. What we might term supernatural is as real to them as dirt and grass. The Azande not only all know and understand these beliefs but have them very deeply ingrained within them; they are part of what they would perceive to be simply common sense.

Socrates: Okay, now you're presenting this simply as two belief systems – ours and the Azande's. But this seems to go beyond culture. Let's say someone commits a crime. He knows he has committed this crime but denies it. The chicken oracle is consulted. He's deemed innocent because the chicken dies. Well, it would seem that something is wrong there, even within the context of their own belief system. The thief would know that the oracle is wrong.

G.O.D.: Very true. But remember our discussion of falsification and anomalies? Sometimes experimental evidence is treated as a falsification, sometimes it is ignored, sometimes a series of *ad hoc* modifications to related theory is made, sometimes adjustments are made and the experiment re-performed, etc.

Socrates: You're saying the Azande engage in a similar procedure?

G.O.D.: Exactly so. The chicken dies or doesn't. Yes or no. But it is not that simple. There are, so to speak, a lot of 'get out clauses' to deal with unanticipated outcomes. Winch argues that with respect to a belief system fulfilling the function of providing social cohesion, intragroup harmony, etc., there is every evidence to suggest that the Azande system works every bit as well as ours. He further observes that with respect to dealing with the natural world, regardless of the fact that from our perspective their beliefs seem absurd, they seem to behave perfectly sensibly in their practical engagement with it, i.e. they plant at the right time of year and so on.

Socrates: So, you're saying that their belief system is as good as ours, that we would be foolish to make judgments about the superiority of our system.

G.O.D.: Well, so Winch would say. I have some serious objections.

Socrates: Like what?

G.O.D.: From Winch's perspective the Azande system works perfectly well and really can only be judged by **immanent criteria**.

Socrates: By what?

G.O.D.: Immanent criteria. That is, from within the context of their own system, not by criteria from outside it. This is in fact a major part of his argument for the difference between science and social science. Our relationship as social scientists to the subject matter is intrinsically different. As social scientists we are looking at people, at their social actions. But as these are perhaps most significantly only to be understood in the context of belief systems, then beliefs themselves are perhaps the most important aspect of social reality. Nature is something for which as scientists we may produce better or worse explanations. Social reality, on the other hand, is already pre-understood, so to speak, by the social actors themselves. The social scientific framework is merely one system amongst others and holds no special priority. With respect to another culture's belief system, one could say, for example, that the beliefs simply are the reality. This social scientist is aiming at achieving the understanding, for example, that the Azande already possess about their own culture. When he puts it into social scientific language he is in effect merely offering a translation. It cannot in any way be regarded as a superior account. The Azande may through various magic rituals be re-affirming their social solidarity, as Dürkheim might argue, but they are also simply performing a rain dance if that is what they believe they are doing.

Socrates: Wow, I've got a host of questions now. The first one would be, and maybe this one is the most important, why are we bothering to study them in the first place? Or rather if we want to learn about the Azande beliefs, why ask an anthropologist? Why not simply ask one of the Azande? Okay, how do we do that? We don't speak the language; we don't understand the culture. The anthropologist gives us the translation. But isn't the difficulty in translating where we started from? I mean, if their culture is so different from ours that the very notion of rationality, nature, etc. is so fundamentally different from ours, how could we ever come to understand it? It seems to me we might have got to a point the opposite of Weber's – 'to understand Caesar one needs to be Caesar'.

G.O.D.: Yes, very good. You are beginning to draw out some of the implications of Winch's argument. Do you think you could sum them up?

Socrates: I'll try. First, there is the fact that social actions are rule-governed. This makes trying to understand social reality much more like trying to understand a language than understanding the workings of a machine – which presumably is the manner in which Winch conceives of the scientific enterprise.

G.O.D.: Yes, there was a popular conception of reality that derived from the science of Newton's time, which I'm sure you've heard of – 'the clockwork universe'. Producing explanations of cause and effect could be very easily likened to learning about the workings of a machine.

Socrates: Yes, and I can see why Winch wouldn't like that perspective taken to the study of human beings. So, like others in the interpretativist tradition, he placed his emphasis upon understanding rather than explanations of cause and effect. Understanding the meanings of social actions is the goal of social science. It is thus an inherently different sort of activity than providing causal explanations of natural phenomena. So, social science becomes something very much more like philosophy than natural science. Well, that's not such a big problem. Not to me anyway, though I see how it could upset the positivists.

G.O.D.:   It is a big problem and not only for positivists! For three reasons. You've already got at all of them to some degree.

Socrates: All right, for one thing it places all the emphasis upon the meaning individuals, or at least groups of individuals, place upon their actions themselves. Social scientists are just one grouping among many. It doesn't give their meaning system any priority over that of the group they are studying. In fact, it seems to imply the opposite. I suppose this places the very role of social scientists in question. If their account of social reality is not in some sense superior to that of the people they are studying then it raises questions about what they are doing at all.

G.O.D.:   Very good. And where might that lead you?

Socrates: Ah, I see it! First of all, if the meaning system being studied is different enough from our own to question the very nature of ratio-nality, then it raises questions about the very possibility of com-munication and understanding. Perhaps only the Nuer could ever understand what is meant by 'twins are birds'. You'd have to be one of them to understand it. That extreme can be carried over into questioning the understanding any social group has of another. This actually is something I have some experience of. That is, I've read some poverty studies by sociologists. You academics don't really have a clue. You think you do. But you don't. You don't know what it is like to be poor! You live in a different world!

G.O.D.:   Well, I'm a philosopher. I'll let the sociologists defend themselves on that one. But your language is revealing.

Socrates: I know how relativistic I'm sounding. You don't need to take every-thing I say entirely literally – especially when everything you say apparently has levels and levels of subtle shades of meaning to it. I really doubt that philosophers are any better than sociologists. It was academics in general I was criticising. But I'll leave my personal resentment out of this and make my last point about Winch. Okay, I said academics 'live in a different world' and meant that they can't understand poverty because their own lives are too comfortable. But perhaps the most worrying implication of Winch's ideas is that the 'different world' statement should perhaps really be taken literally. He seems to be implying that about the Azande. Different meaning systems, different realities. Western science and rationality are just one possible belief system amongst many. Azande magic is as valid as science. Ultimately, they are validated in the same way, by . . . what was that word you gave for it? Immanent criteria. But why stop at the boundaries of radically different cultures? Why not sub-cultures within our own? Why not individuals? You've got your reality; I've got mine.

G.O.D.: Yes, I think you've got the picture. That is what is meant by extreme epistemological relativism. The natural world and the social world cross over. I mean there isn't a rigid demarcation between social reality and natural reality, is there? We have beliefs about nature. Is every set of beliefs about the natural world as good as another?

Socrates: I actually feel somewhat relieved to know that you are going to tell me that the answer to that question is no! You're going to tell me where Winch went wrong now, aren't you?

G.O.D.: Actually, Winch was aware of these implications and very troubled by them. Well, actually he wasn't too concerned about the prospect of social science being stripped of its scientific pretension and claimed as a branch of philosophy. But the extremes of epistemological relativism worried him. Further, the implication that we could perhaps never really understand another culture seemed to be contradicted by the fact that we do learn other languages and seem to know quite a bit about other cultures. Perhaps understanding 'twins are birds' is a little more difficult than learning French cuisine and the language to discuss it, but at least some level of inter-cultural communication and understanding seems evidently to be possible.

Winch looked for some kind of universal basis upon which this understanding could be based and rather tentatively came up with one. He thought that there were universals to the human condition itself. All societies must in some manner come to terms with birth, death and marriage. Not marriage as defined by Western culture but at least with respect to some form of social organisation for human reproduction and child-rearing. He thought that these three basics of the human condition formed a basis for inter-cultural understanding and communication because of their inherently meaningful nature.

There is a fourth possible candidate to go along with these three which Winch didn't come up with. It actually leads into a critique of Winch's cultural relativism.

Socrates: I knew this was coming. And I'll say again I'm relieved. Somehow, marriage, birth and death don't seem very adequate foundations for communication. Even if all societies must deal with these things, isn't it possible that they will do so in such extremely different ways that they would possibly, at least, be unrecognisable to the other?

G.O.D.:   Yes, a very good point. But I somehow don't think you are going to like this other possibility very much either. It could possibly sound ethnocentric. All societies, in addition to dealing with birth, death and marriage, must also interact with nature in order to provide the necessities of life. Which thinker does that proposition make you think of?

Socrates: I don't know.

G.O.D.:   Come on, you're a sociology student. We've referred several times to Dürkheim and Weber. Who is the other member of sociology's 'holy trinity'?

Socrates: Marx? Is that why you said you thought I wouldn't like this idea?

G.O.D.:   No, like most of your generation, I'm sure you have considerable knowledge and a completely open mind about Marx.

Socrates: Don't be sarcastic!

G.O.D.:   No, it's not the basic proposition that I thought might bother you; that all societies must somehow provide for their own material welfare seems incontestable as an assertion and almost too obvious to need saying. We need to eat! No, it breaks down a certain level of relativism at least and provides a basis for comparative judgment of belief systems. You remember it was part of Winch's argument that the Azande, for all their strange magic belief system, still managed to function in the natural world in a way that is quite recognisable to us as being practical, i.e. they plant their crops at the right time of year and so on. Yes? Well, evidently there is some coincidence between their belief system and ours, with regard to some of the business of practically interacting with nature. They might couch their explanation of why the harvest must be done at a certain time of year in terms of propitiating Gods or supernatural forces or whatever. We come to similar conclusions as they do; only our explanation is couched in terms of meteorology, agro-biology and so on.

Socrates: So, the fact that they are doing the same things in response to nature as us gives us a basis for understanding at least some of the meaning imparted into their various rituals, beliefs, etc. Yes?

G.O.D.:   That too. But it also gives us a basis for comparative judgment of respective beliefs. Their explanation and ours for some things have a different framework of understanding but come to the same practical conclusions. However, really explaining how nature works is required to go further. I mean that the Azande magic system may work practically enough for simple agriculture, but it is not adequate for ever building an aeroplane. On some levels it is false.

Socrates: But maybe they wouldn't want to build an aeroplane – or an atom bomb either.

G.O.D.: A good point. But it is a point in another argument really. Perhaps their society is happier than ours. Perhaps their system works just as well or better – socially. But that isn't really what is at issue with respect to an extreme epistemological relativism. It suggests that beliefs about reality are not all there is to reality. That is part of the critical realist position, by the way.

Socrates: I think I get the point. But, as you suspected, there is something about it that makes me uneasy.

G.O.D.: Good! I wouldn't want you to be convinced too easily. This point comes up again and again in different guises. As I think I told you, Winch's relativism is very much embraced by postmodernism. Postmodernists sometimes seem very pessimistic but at other times seem simply to celebrate all that worried Winch. Even when they are being pessimistic, however, they put a different spin on it from that of Winch. So, we'll definitely come back to this later on.

Right now I want to take us in a slightly different direction, though it too connects up with postmodernism. Well, as I said, everything connects up with everything on some level or another. I want to bring in the ethical dimension to cultural relativism. That is one of the things that was bothering you about my judgment of Western superiority over the Azande, wasn't it?

Socrates: Yes. You seemed to be arguing that we can build bombs and aeroplanes so we must be superior.

G.O.D.: Well, that wasn't exactly my argument. I was in more general terms claiming scientific explanation of the natural world as superior to all others. Further, I also think we can and must be able to make moral judgments about other cultures' practices.

Socrates: Really! That sounds rather Fascist to me.

G.O.D.: Interesting that you should say that. Wouldn't you condemn Nazi Germany's treatment of the Jews and Gypsies and so on?

Socrates: I think that's an absurd argument.

G.O.D.: Wasn't it part of German culture? Simply part of their belief system? There is plenty of evidence showing, if not a general knowledge about the camps, at least some passive support for a generally discriminatory policy aimed at Jews and other minorities. It may be a **reductio ad absurdum** argument, but what is your answer to it?

Socrates: The Germans are basically part of the same culture we are. They have their national idiosyncrasies, but essentially they are part of Western culture. What they did was wrong!

G.O.D.: Exactly the sort of answer Peter Winch would give. He would say that we could make judgments about the beliefs of someone practising witchcraft in our culture (where it is not part of our overall belief system). But with respect to the Azande, where it is part of the daily life of the culture, it is a different matter. Many people, in fact, do seem to take just this stance, even with respect to practices which by our standards seem very extreme and clearly wrong. For example, female circumcision. This practice creates a dilemma for many Western feminists who have flirted with postmodernism or simply do not wish to impose Western cultural values on other cultures. As I said, cultural relativism developed as a reaction to earlier ethnocentric views. Many people are very uncomfortable with the idea of making any judgments whatsoever about other cultures' beliefs and practices. It smacks of the old colonialist mentality.

Socrates: Well, it does! I'm sure the practice is understood quite differently by the cultures in which it is performed. Also, I read that it is usually women that perform the operation and demand that clitorectomies be performed on their relatives. Isn't that so?

G.O.D.:   Yes, I believe that is true.

Socrates: Well, who are we to make judgments about their culture? Ours isn't so wonderful, maybe. If they want to do it, how can we say it's wrong?

G.O.D.:   There are a number of possible arguments. But I want to give you just one. It is simultaneously a very powerful argument and one which is very easy to misunderstand. It also connects back up with some of the issues we discussed earlier with respect to rationality. It also frames the whole debate about positivism rather differently as well. I'm referring here to the work of Jürgen Habermas.

Socrates: It sounds like he covers a lot of ground.

G.O.D.:   He certainly does! But I'm only going to give you a small portion of it. Principally, I want to explain to you his idea of the **ideal speech situation**. It is the basis for his notion of universality. But I had better give you some background information first.

Habermas is of the second generation of Frankfurt School theorists. The name comes from the Frankfurt School of Social Research. The principal project of the first generation of Frankfurt School thinkers (Theodore Adorno, Max Horkheimer, Herbert Marcuse, Eric Fromm and others) was the theoretical marriage of Marxism and psychoanalysis. An interesting connection to our earlier Nazi example was their project to utilise psychoanalysis to understand the mass appeal of Fascism. They were rather personally affected by it, being forced to flee to America in the 1930s.

This first generation of Frankfurt School theorists had a great deal to say about a host of topics including the philosophy of science and positivism. However, we shall be primarily concerned with Habermas, who both in many ways carried on the same approach and in others very much struck out on his own. Critical theory is another label applied to them, by the way, and you mustn't confuse it with critical realism, though there are some affinities between the two. You'll see why it has that label in a moment.

We began our enquiry into the philosophy of science with the Enlightenment. Horkheimer and Adorno presented a massive critique of the Enlightenment. They demonstrated its dark side. Or rather they demonstrated the philosophical underpinning of some of the darker sides of **modernity**. They demonstrated some of the narrowness and limitations of the positivist conceptions of rationality, for example, and linked it to history.

Habermas extends their critique but rather ironically has become best known as the champion of modernity. Modernity, Habermas sees as being very much an unfinished project. We need more rationality, not less. This is a position he has very much come to occupy vis-à-vis postmodernist critics of Western rationality.

However, he distinguishes between types of rationality. Essentially, there are three, each of which he associates with different **human interests**. I'll come back to the notion of interests in a moment. The notion of instrumental rationality (or instrumental reason) comes from the first generation of Frankfurt School theorists. You remember our first discussion? I suggested that perhaps you had a purely instrumental motivation to learn about the philosophy of science.

Socrates: I remember. You told me it was inappropriate to the subject matter. But I'm getting some interest in the subject matter for its own sake now. However, passing my course is still my bottom line. I don't see what's wrong with that either!

G.O.D.: I don't want to be faulting you in particular for having that attitude. Rather it is a part of our culture, part of the real structure of our society. There are very good reasons why you have that attitude. However, there are also possibly reasons why it is a bad thing that such attitudes are fostered within our world. This is part of the philosophical dark side of the Enlightenment that Horkheimer and Adorno critiqued. One uses logic as a tool to calculate the best means to an end. This is fine in cases where it is appropriate. But it isn't always so. It engenders a particular sort of attitude to the world. It objectifies – can you see a connection here to positivism? One treats the natural world as a collection of objects – of objects to be manipulated for our own ends. They pre-figured modern-day environmentalists in suggesting that perhaps having such an attitude is short-sighted and limited. And to move from the treatment of the natural world in terms of objects to be manipulated for our own ends is only a step away from treating human beings as such.

Socrates: Yes, I can see that it's limited and could perhaps be a bad thing. Like I'm forced to take a particular attitude to acquiring this knowledge because I'm competing with others. I need the knowledge to further my career. I can see the narrowness of it. But that's how the world is.

G.O.D.:   Exactly. All right, instrumental rationality is a very restricted form of rationality, so they would argue. They link the development of this attitude historically to the development of natural science, to industrialisation, to Weber's disenchantment and rationalisation, to capitalism. The positivist understanding of knowledge is merely a reflection of a more general historical process. They use the term very broadly at times and at others are referring more specifically to the Vienna Circle or Popper or others. I've already warned you that people use it rather differently but bear this in mind when considering critical theory. Instrumental reason, thus you see, has two dimensions to it. It is both a way of looking at the world and a way of looking at the process of acquiring knowledge of the world. Positivism consciously presents this latter perspective, while failing to see how much of the former is located within it. It has, you see, assumptions which are not reflected upon.

All right, Habermas is more equivocal about instrumental rationality. He very much sees it as having its place. He sees it historically, in terms of human development, as did earlier members of the Frankfurt School, but he links it with a specific human interest. We all have an interest in the development of beneficial technologies, of ways and means of interacting with nature so as to provide us with our needs and desires. The development of electricity, more efficient agriculture and so on is a good thing. We, humanity, have an interest in such achievement. The sort of rationality that is developed in relation to this is developed in response to a particular cognitive interest. That is, a type of thinking, a style of thinking, develops historically in relation to our human interests in acquiring knowledge of the natural world to satisfy our wants from that world. This leads historically to the development of what he calls the **'empirico-analytic sciences'**.

But this is not our only deployment of rationality. We have practical communicative cognitive interests as well. We act upon the world collectively, socially. Habermas inherits this much Marxism, at least, from the earlier Frankfurt School Marxism. But where the Marxist emphasis is of course upon labour, Habermas shifts the emphasis to communication. We have a practical need to understand our fellow human beings. This 'interest' leads to the development of the **hermeneutic sciences**. It is, quite naturally, linked with human interaction.

I hope you can see the linkage of Habermas's first 'interest' with the development of natural science, and the second with the development of hermeneutics. He is doing two things to the usual polarisation of positivist scientific explanation and interpretativist understanding. He is grounding them both philosophically in terms of interests and historicising their development.

Socrates: I'm not sure, but I think I've got the gist of the argument. But you say he posits a third interest. What's that?

G.O.D.:   Human emancipation.

Socrates: Hold on! That seems rather a big jump.

G.O.D.:   Not really. First of all, he simply puts a slightly different inflection upon the development of instrumental reason. Adorno, Horkheimer and others link it to domination. Habermas grounds it in real human needs, in the human condition if you like, but sees it coming to 'dominate' the other forms of interest. Understanding, communication, is a practical need. Nonetheless, we often fail in the attempt. Understanding, Habermas argues, is crucially affected by social structure, relations of power. Communication is distorted by power relations. Instrumental reason becomes the only form of reason. It becomes a tool of power. Remember early anthropology? Ethnocentrism? Anthropology went hand in hand with empire and exploitation. The first understandings of other cultures were distorted by this.

Socrates: Are you accusing the early anthropologists of trying to exploit the people they were studying?

G.O.D.:   Not really. Perhaps some were consciously doing so but that is not the point. It was the context in which such research was performed. People really do want to understand one another. The third cognitive interest arises from this desire. Emancipation is connected up with understanding, understanding in an imperfect world where communication is distorted by relations of power.

Socrates: I don't think I follow that. It still seems like a big jump to me. I think you must be leaving out a few necessary steps in the argument.

G.O.D.:   Yes, I've left out how Habermas conceives the basis of communication. We all wish to be understood and to understand others. This is the real basis of communication. And what is understanding really? In some sense or another, it is agreement.

Socrates: I don't think so!

G.O.D.:   That is because you haven't understood me correctly. No, seriously, I mean that. Well, I meant it both as a joke and seriously at the same time. All right, I say something and you disagree. Yes? You tell me why you disagree. I say, 'Ah, you've misunderstood me, what I mean is this'. You still disagree. You explain to me why. Your explanation of why essentially boils down to telling me how I have misunderstood your reasons for disagreeing. I say I understand that now, but it seems evident from your statements that you are unaware of some fact or another. This process could perhaps go on to infinity in theory. But essentially what we are doing is attempting each time to explain our positions seriously. If we understood one another and were each in possession of all the relevant facts we would then agree. If not we would give reasons, further clarifications.

Socrates: That's not how people usually conduct arguments. They repeat the same thing over and over. They go off the subject entirely and bring in extraneous information. They insult each other. They threaten each other. Or they simply get tired of the discussion and agree to disagree.

G.O.D.:   Habermas isn't saying that this back and forth clarification, reasoned disagreement, additional relevant information etc. etc. sort of process is what actually happens in real life. Nor is he setting up his 'ideal speech situation' as a Utopian goal. Well, in one sense, I suppose he is, but don't get fixated upon that; it is not the most important part of the idea. No, he is positing it as being in some sense the essence of communication. This is the fundamental point of communication – to be understood, to persuade by reason and information and be persuaded by reason and information.

Now of course this isn't what always or even most often occurs in reality. Habermas is well aware of that. In fact, his whole theory is based upon that awareness. This isn't what happens in reality. Why not? Habermas has an answer to that question. It doesn't happen because of the structured nature of human society, because of power relations. Inequality with respect to access to knowledge. The power relations inherent in the instrumental reason aspect of the growth of the empirico-analytic sciences allow some to dominate others. This sort of rationality is increasingly employed as the dominant form of rationality in our society. Communication isn't undertaken in order really to communicate but rather more frequently to manipulate. Agreement isn't sought but rather simply acquiescence.

Socrates: I think I'm beginning to get the idea, but maybe you've just beaten me into submission, exerted your power over me.

G.O.D.:   I know you're just being flippant, but there is a serious point underlying what you're saying. We are communicating. We are trying to understand one another. Our communication is taking the most elementary form as well, a straightforward back-and-forth dialogue. But yes, there is an inequality present here. We are unequal with respect to possession of a certain kind of knowledge. We are certainly unequal with respect to authority in relation to philosophical knowledge. Perhaps you will simply acquiesce to something you neither agree with nor understand. And why will you do so? Because you believe that I have the authoritative answer, the one you need to pass your exam, the goal of the instrumentally motivated interest that caused you to undertake this dialogue in the first place. And am I going to give you the right answer? I'm a paid employee. I'm undertaking this dialogue as a way of making my living. Perhaps I enjoy my position of academic superiority over you and wish to amuse myself at your expense by trying to dazzle you with strange ideas, confuse you, mislead you. Do you see what I'm getting at here? Our communication is distorted by factors which derive from the nature of the social reality we inhabit.

Socrates: I do. And I sure hope you're kidding about the misleading me part! You're not, are you?

G.O.D.: No, I'm not. Not intentionally anyway.

Socrates: I do feel confused at times. But essentially I'm trusting you.

G.O.D.: Yes, that's fine. But do you see even that rather makes Habermas's point about power relations distorting communication? In a way the inequality of knowledge we have with respect to this subject gives you no choice but to trust me. This gives a dimension of power relations to virtually all communication. In the ideal speech situation everyone would have equal access to information rather than it being a commodity to be bought and sold.

When we come to look at postmodernism, by the way, we'll be looking at the ideas of one of Habermas's long-standing rivals – Jean Francois Lyotard. He very much emphasises the commodity aspect of information. He asserts that we don't really have knowledge anymore, knowledge conceived of as understanding anyway, we only have information, a commodity which is bought and sold like any other.

Okay, I need to make a few other connections now. This condition of inequality, of social structures that are distorting communication, comes historically through the development of hermeneutic understanding to give rise to the necessity of developing **critical reason**. It is connected with our **emancipatory interest**. Now I think I can make this connection clear if I return to one or two of our earlier examples concerning cultural relativism and the practices which we might wish to condemn.

We not only judge other cultures but our own as well. You said earlier that you thought our culture was crazy. From what basis were you making that judgment?

Socrates: I don't know. I wasn't completely being serious anyway.

G.O.D.: I think you were. To some degree, at least. Now, whatever standard you were appealing to, it wasn't the prevailing ethos of our culture. You must have been appealing to something else. Habermas would probably assert that it is deriving from your embryonic development of critical reason.

Socrates: Embryonic, eh?

G.O.D.: I wasn't trying to be insulting. Habermas sees this in historical terms. Humanity is gradually developing this capacity for critical judgment. This is why he sees modernity as an unfinished project. Critical judgment is rooted in our capacity to think and act self-reflexively. When we pass judgment on other points of view, we need to be able to show not merely where they are mistaken (that is, to only be able to criticise other points of view in purely cognitive terms, as the positivist might do), but we should also be able to demonstrate the social origins of the mistaken viewpoint. In essence, we should be able to explain why people hold the mistaken views that they do. This is frequently to be found through an analysis of the social situation.

The ideal speech situation can be seen as a comparative ideal standard against which we can perceive the actuality of communicative distortion. Distortion will occur, for example, as a result of exclusions from the communication process. Let us take Nazi Germany as an example again. The Jews certainly were excluded from the 'discussion' about 'the Jewish problem'. We can understand the viewpoints of those in favour of clitorectomy as a social practice quite easily from a feminist analysis undertaken of such societies. We can also understand the perspective that criticises such feminists as imposing Western values upon a non-Western situation. But in fact the feminists are not actually appealing to Western standards of judgment but ultimately human standards, universal standards linked to a notion of emancipation and derived from a critique of our own society.

Socrates: But isn't that just what ethnocentrism is? Setting up one's own particular standards of judgment as universal?

G.O.D.: Yes, indeed. But Habermas gives us some kind of philosophical grounding by which we could at least argue, in any particular case, that we are getting at something universal and not merely demonstrating the limitations of our own bias. Those from cultures other than our own would, of course, be equally entitled to participate in such a discussion and be able to dispute our claims to universality. But, if we could show that their point of view depends upon some other manipulation going on, some areas of knowledge being withheld, we would have evidence to back up our claims. In fact, argument, debate, communication is precisely the ground for such judgment. If we can see the power relations at work in bringing people around to a position which is actually not in their real interests, then we have a basis for criticism.

Socrates: Their 'real interests'? Who is to decide that?

G.O.D.: Once again, communication and debate. If the people being affected by a practice are not really setting the agenda but are excluded from the discussion or the necessary information which rational judgment requires, then it at least suggests that some manipulation or deceit may be going on.

Socrates: There seems to be something circular in this reasoning.

G.O.D.: Not circular but rather historically emergent. This is something that is collectively evolving.

Socrates: Okay, I see Habermas has a progressive view of history, and it goes directly against the various sorts of relativism. But I think I'm with Winch here. I'm not happy with the relativist idea. But I can't see how to get around it either. The female circumcision example bothers me. I can see it both ways. But there's something about Habermas's position which reminds me of the old Marxist viewpoint of false consciousness. Sure people might have false consciousness. They are ideologically influenced. But how do you step outside it? I'm not sure I buy this notion of self-reflexivity and critique. I mean don't all human beings have that capacity. And doesn't that place us right back where we started? I mean, it comes with the problem of the subject matter of social science being human beings. They reflect upon their beliefs. What gives social science a privileged standpoint from which to judge?

G.O.D.:   Well, I think Habermas has actually answered your questions there.

Socrates: Maybe. I'll re-read this later. Maybe, I'll even read some of Habermas himself. But if this dialogue exemplifies something, it isn't the ideal speech situation. No, it's the usual form of discussion people have. They quit when they get tired without ever having reached a definite conclusion.

G.O.D.:   I gather you want a break. Okay, but I'll just leave you with a couple of comments. First, we will be coming back to both the general problem of the special perspective of the social scientist with respect to human beings as subject matter in a couple more forms. It's also somewhat fortunate that the general issue of judgment that is bothering you seems particularly apparent through the example of feminist judgments upon female circumcision, because the next thing for us to consider is the various feminist viewpoints on science. Finally, just a last comment upon Habermas – the problem I see with his position. It is one you didn't mention.

Socrates: What's that, then?

G.O.D.:   Well, this is over-simplifying rather dramatically, and Habermas would certainly wish to qualify what I am stating as his position, but at least in the way I have explained it thus far, it can be said to be a **consensual theory of truth**; that is, it is truth by consent. Truth is still somehow entirely socially determined. We don't have truth and falsity any more. Rather it seems that with Habermas we have truth and ideology. Leaving aside all the problems you mentioned – it is good that you're becoming harder to persuade to the various positions I'm giving you, by the way – if we imagined his ideal speech situation we would see truth emerging through discussion all the time; it is only ideological distortion arising from power relations that prevents this. But couldn't we all be wrong? Couldn't reality be quite different from what we've all come to agree about it, even with an agreement which arose through an equal exchange of ideas, with everyone given equal access to the best information available? Couldn't we simply all make the same arithmetic error without any power relations interfering with our judgment, for example?

Socrates: No.

G.O.D.:   What?

Socrates: Well, given that we are never going to be in that situation I don't see what difference it makes.

G.O.D.:   But it does make a difference. We could all agree upon magic and witch doctors perhaps. Then electricity would never have been invented.

Socrates: I'm going to turn off the computer now.

DISCUSSION QUESTIONS

1   What is the significance of the distinction between social rules and natural laws? Does it really make social science impossible? Should we really understand social science as philosophy rather than science?

2   Different cultures have extremely different belief systems, but rationality is a universal human trait and the same for everyone. How might this assertion be defended?

3   If we accept that our Western form of rationality is not universal then understanding other cultures is not possible at all. What would be the basis for making such an assertion? What other possible basis might there be for understanding cultures quite different from our own?

4   Is the practice of making moral judgment upon the practices of other cultures itself immoral? Consider this question in relation to some of the more extreme examples of practices we might certainly wish to judge morally.

5   What standards are we appealing to when we are criticising the norms, values and practices of our own culture? Is Habermas's conception of the ideal speech situation an adequate concept for addressing this question?

FURTHER READING SUGGESTIONS

Hermeneutics

Bauman, Z. (1978) *Hermeneutics and Social Science*, Hutchinson, London.

Berger, P.L. and Luckman, T. (1967) *The Social Construction of Reality*, Penguin, London.

Bleicher, J. (1980) *Contemporary Hermeneutics*, Routledge & Kegan Paul, London.

Davidson, D. (1984) *Inquiries into Truth and Interpretation*, Oxford University Press, Oxford.

Evans-Pritchard, E. (1956) *Nuer Religion*, Clarendon Press, Oxford – as well as being the source material for the 'twins are birds' discussion in this chapter, Evans-Pritchard's anthropological works are frequently referred to in discussions concerning belief, magic, rationality, cultural relativism and so on.

Gadamer, H. (1975) *Truth and Method*, Sheed and Ward, London – perhaps *the* classic book in this subject area.

Gellner, E. (1985) *Relativism and the Social Sciences*, Cambridge University Press, Cambridge.

Hollis, M. and Lukes, S. (eds) (1982) *Rationality and Relativism*, Blackwell, Oxford.

Mantzavinos, C. (2009) *Naturalistic Hermeneutics,* Cambridge University Press, Cambridge, UK.

Newton-Smith, W.H. (1981) *The Rationality of Science*, Routledge & Kegan Paul, Boston – especially Chapters 5 and 6.

Outhwaite, W. (1975) *Understanding Social Life*, Allen & Unwin, London.

Rorty, R. (ed.) (1967) *The Linguistic Turn: Recent Essays in Philosophical Method*, University of Chicago Press, Chicago – Rorty's more recent thinking is very influenced by Derrida. However, the 'linguistic turn' in social theory came long before him, as this collection of essays demonstrates.

Tambiah, J.S. (1990) *Magic, Science, Religion and the Scope of Rationality*, Cambridge University Press, Cambridge – engages in more detail with the subject matter of the first part of this chapter through an analysis of the works of many of the key thinkers in the field.

Wilson, B.R. (ed.) (1977) *Rationality*, Blackwell, Oxford – especially good selection of articles on the subject of rationality and cross-cultural understanding. It contains Winch's article 'The Idea of Social Science' as well as an interesting critique of his position by Alisdair McIntyre in an article with the same title.

Winch

Hughes, J. (1997) *The Philosophy of Social Research*, Addison Wesley Longman, London – covers quite well the material engaged with in the first five chapters of this book from a quite different perspective; that is, the author has a general agreement with Winch's thesis that social science is not really science but something more akin to philosophy.

Winch, P. (1958) *The Idea of a Social Science*, Routledge, London.

Wittgenstein

Wittgenstein is probably best approached in conjunction with a secondary source as he is deceptively difficult.

Anscombe, G.E.M. (1996) *Introduction to Wittgenstein's Tractatus*, Thoemmes Press, Bristol – somewhat technical in nature.

Bloor, D. (1983) *Wittgenstein: A Social Theory of Knowledge*, Columbia University Press, New York – Wittgenstein can be interpreted in very strongly relativist terms or not. Bloor leans towards a radical relativism.

Wittgenstein, L. (1958) *Philosophical Investigations*, Blackwell, Oxford.

Ferdinand Saussure

Saussure, F. (1983) *Course in General Linguistics*, Duckworth Press, London – arguably one of the most influential books of the twentieth century. Saussure is known as the 'father of modern linguistics', and the science of semiology entirely derives from him. Structuralism and poststructuralism, his intellectual inheritors, have covered a lot of fields. The book is also quite accessible.

First-order and second-order knowledges

Schutz, A. (1962) 'Common Sense and Scientific Interpretation of Human Action' in M. Natanson (ed.), *Collected Papers: The Problem of Social Reality*, Martinus Nijhoff, The Hague, pp. 3–47.

Schutz, A. (1972) *The Phenomenology of the Social World*, Heinemann, London – apart from raising the above problem in an interesting way, this book is also the original articulation of phenomenological sociology.

Critical theory

Adorno, T. and Horkheimer, M. (1979) *The Dialectic of the Enlightenment*, Verso, London.

Berry, D. (2012) *Revisiting the Frankfurt School: Essays on Culture, Media and Theory*, Ashgate, Farnham.

Held, D. (1980) *Introduction to Critical Theory*, Hutchinson, London.

Habermas

Bernstein, R.J. (ed.) (1985) *Habermas and Modernity*, MIT Press, Cambridge, Massachusetts – the book includes essays by Bernstein, Giddens, Jay, Rorty and Habermas himself.

Finlayson, J.G. (2005) *Habermas: A Very Short Introduction*, Oxford University Press, Oxford, UK.

Habermas, J. (1978) *Knowledge and Human Interest*, Heinemann Educational, London.

Habermas, J. (1987) *The Theory of Communicative Action*, Polity Press, Cambridge.

Held, D. and Thompson, J.B. (eds) (1982) *Habermas, Critical Debates*, Macmillan, London.

Outhwaite, W. (1994) *Habermas: A Critical Introduction*, Polity Press, Cambridge.

CHAPTER 6

FEMINISM AND SCIENCE: A WOMAN'S PLACE IS THE MORE OBJECTIVE SPACE

Science it would seem is not sexless; he is a man, a father and infected too.

Virginia Woolf

But I doubt that even in our wildest dreams we ever imagined we would have to rein-vent both science and theorising itself to make sense of women's social experience.

Sandra Harding

OUTLINE OF MAJOR POINTS TO BE COVERED

1   Science and epistemology are both a site of political struggle for feminists and subjects for investigation. The range of differing views within the broad feminist camp on these subjects is quite extreme. At one end of the spectrum is merely a criticism of science's past and present practice with respect to the marginalisation of issues relevant to women and barriers to scientific careers. Along with this there is a general acceptance of criticisms of the positivist philosophy of science, particularly social science. At the other end of the spectrum are extremely radical positions that posit a distinctly female logic.

2   Criticisms of the moderate end of the spectrum are presented that suggest that mere criticism of past and present practices and of positivism generally does not go far enough.

3   The notion of standpoint epistemologies is explained analogously through the Marxist privileging of the proletariat's structural position in society as a potentially superior vantage point to understand social reality. The similar privileging of women's experience as possibly providing a better vantage point for knowledge production rests upon two separate arguments which may, however, be combined.

   a   The first is that it is their historically oppressed position that privileges their vantage point.

   b   The second is that the nature of their emotional experience and work gives rise to a less narrow conception of objectivity – an incorporation of hand, brain and heart. Thus, there is the possibility of a better feminist successor science, which could potentially overcome male biases in conceptualisation and research practice.

4   Three sorts of problems that arise from these positions are explored.

    a   First, Lukâcs's Marxist standpoint epistemology posits two sorts of proletariat knowledge: the limited and distorted knowledge that working-class people often actually possess and the superior knowledge production potential based upon their position historically. How does one connect the two without a measure of theoretical elitism? This problem is replicated in feminist standpoint theory in the disjuncture between feminist theorists and ordinary women who do not see themselves as feminists. This problem can be generalised as one facing all social scientists and theorists. Do we wish to privilege the first-order explanations of their activities which all human beings have? Reference is made back to the previous chapter's arguments concerning ethnocentricism in relation to this point. However, if we cannot somehow privilege the second-order accounts of social scientists over those whose activities and meaning systems they are studying, then the question is raised as to what the point is of doing social science at all.

    b   A second criticism made of **feminist standpoint epistemology** is that in the attempt to overcome some of the male-developed philosophical and social scientific oppositions (nature/culture, objective/subjective, emotion/reason, public sphere/private sphere, work/labour, etc.) feminist standpoint theory simply reproduces them, e.g. by acceding to the notion of rationality as a masculine trait.

    c   The third criticism of feminist standpoint epistemology points the way towards the next chapter's discussion of **postmodernism**. An argument criticising the essential nature of a notion of 'woman' is given. Different groups of women have had very different sorts of experiences. Black American women's experience of the family as a source of strength is contrasted with **radical feminism**'s situating of it as the prime site of women's oppression. The recognition of difference is seen as opening up the possibility of multiple and partial standpoints with respect to knowledge. The political dangers of destroying the possibility of collective political action based upon a notion of sisterhood are pointed out in relation to this point of view. The brief consideration of postmodernist feminism thus provides the bridge to the next chapter where such ideas are considered in more detail.

DIALOGUE

G.O.D.:   'All men are mortal; Cleopatra is a man; therefore Cleopatra is mortal' (J. Moulton, 'The Myth of the Neutral "Man"' in M. Veterrling-Braggin et al., *Feminism and Philosophy,* 1977).

Socrates: You like beginning our conversations with odd statements, don't you? It's not quite as bizarre as 'twins are birds', but it's still bizarre. However, I'm sure there's a point to be made.

G.O.D.: Indeed, and the bizarre nature of this 'syllogism' is part of it. It is related to an argument made by some feminists that scientific rationality is gendered, even rationality as narrowly defined in terms of logic and mathematics.

Socrates: You don't mean to say that feminists are taking a position akin to Peter Winch's, that Western rationality is just our cultural construction, and other forms of attributing meaning to social life are just as good? Is the argument that there are male and female cultures and also that there are male and female forms of reasoning?

G.O.D.: There are certain affinities with Winch's position in some feminist epistemological arguments but the emphasis is different. The focus, of course, is much more explicitly upon gender issues. But first let me emphasise the diversity of views amongst feminists themselves on epistemological issues. I know I've said that before, in reference to positivists and others, but the differences here are more fundamental and extreme. There are common themes that give a kind of unity to the positivist position, in spite of the differing views within it. This is also true of feminism – in general, in the broadest of political terms. However, whatever unity might be said to exist amongst the diversity of competing voices in feminist discourse, it is definitely not to be found in terms of epistemological positions. And that is what we are concerned with here.

Socrates: Do you mean to say there is no unity at all within the feminist camp with respect to knowledge and science?

G.O.D.: I would say there is one thing, and one thing only, upon which there would be a common perspective amongst feminists on the subject: they are all critical of mainstream scientific practice and its philosophical understanding of itself. But the manner and degree to which they are critical of these things are immensely variable. For example, at one extreme of a definitely non-linear spectrum of views, the critique is rather superficial. It consists of essentially three things. First, the lack of female representation within the scientific community; second, the marginalisation of gender-related issues within social scientific subject matter; and third, the positivist conception of science is criticised.

Socrates: Why do you say that's superficial? It sounds reasonably important to me.

G.O.D.: I am certainly not saying that it is not important. It is a question of both relative depth of critique and uniqueness of feminist perspective. For example, the critique of positivism in this form is not peculiar to feminism; it differs little from many other post-Kuhnian perspectives on science. The other two issues are not really philosophical. A reform of scientific practice could easily correct the situation.

Socrates: Are you sure it would be that easy? I don't see why you are saying it is not really a philosophical perspective. I mean there is the obvious question to be asked, both in relation to the lack of female representation in the sciences and to the lack of investigation into gender-related issues. I mean: why? Don't feminists ask that?

G.O.D.:   Yes, of course they do. And you are quite right, these questions certainly have a philosophical dimension! I am just presenting the view at one end of the spectrum – the non-philosophical and less radical end of the spectrum. This perspective has a certain affinity with **liberal feminism**. To increase female participation in higher-level scientific work and to pay greater attention to female voices in the setting of research agendas could be said to follow naturally from the wider political agenda of improving the condition and extending the influence and power of women in society generally.

Similarly the historical lack of recognition of the significance of gender within a host of social scientific subject areas can be regarded as simply an oversight. It is a dramatically huge oversight to be sure, but nonetheless it is something that might be remedied relatively easily. In fact, it is being remedied, with gender very much now being on the agenda of mainstream sociological research. Its previous absence can also be very easily explained. Social science set up a binary opposition between the public and private spheres and concentrated on the former. This simply reflected prevailing cultural assumptions based on a gendered hierarchy and the social division of labour, i.e. men inhabited the public spheres of life and women the private. The latter was accordingly marginalised.

This has become widely recognised, and attention is now directed at previously neglected areas for potential research. The importance of gender has been conceded and attempts are being made to re-examine past work, for example the sociological classics, and to reappraise them. Distortions have been unearthed in their conclusions, which can retrospectively be seen to have been inevitable, owing to the invisibility of gender in their theorising.

Socrates: Yes, I understand. Some good points were made, really important points, and now perhaps reforms are being made. But the critique doesn't go far enough. It sounds very complacent to me, in fact.

G.O.D.:   Really? Are you a feminist then?

Socrates: No.

G.O.D.:   I see. Well, I'll ask you about that later. I think you're right about it being complacent, but why do you say that if you are not a feminist?

Socrates: Well, there are two things about this perspective, at least the way you're expressing it, that surprise me. First, it sounds a little like when people say, 'Well our system isn't perfect but it's the best there is' or even 'Everything is for the best in this best of all possible worlds' (from Voltaire, *Candide*). It just doesn't sound like a very radical critique. And I've always associated feminism with a very radical stance. That's the second thing that surprises me about this position. Compared to some of the issues we discussed in relation to cultural relativism, this sounds pretty tame. I expected feminists to occupy an epistemological position much more extreme – along the lines of your 'Cleopatra logic example', which, by the way, I don't see the logic in. I mean what's the point of it?

G.O.D.: Don't worry about Cleopatra; I'll come back to her. The example is from the other end of the spectrum. But you're quite right. The reformist perspective I have been referring to does not penetrate very deeply; feminism certainly can be a great deal more radical.

The critique of positivism made by a number of feminists actually pre-dates feminism, at least second-wave feminism, in which epistemological issues were first discussed. This critique is sometimes little different from that by non-feminists arguing from a hermeneutic perspective.

However, it can be made to go a little deeper with a more specifically feminist orientation. The criticism of scientific practice and the criticism of science's self-understanding can be systematically linked to gender. The positivist orientation for explaining the natural world, as well as the social world, can be linked to a series of binary oppositions criticised by feminists, i.e. nature and culture, private and public, reason and emotion, mind and body, and so on. The critique of such oppositions postulates the necessity for transcending them, not merely investigating a neglected area, such as, for example, the private sphere of domestic life.

Socrates: How do you mean transcend them?

G.O.D.: In this case, what I mean by 'transcend' would be first to demonstrate critically the falsity inherent in the intellectual construction of such oppositions, and second, to remove their pernicious influence from future research practice.

Socrates: Well, the second part makes sense if the first part is true. Can you give some examples that show that it is?

G.O.D.: Sure. Let us look at Marxism. What are the central conceptual categories utilised by Marxist analysis? Class and labour, or more precisely, labour power. Class is defined in terms of relation to production, which is, of course, understood in analyses of capitalism in terms of the wage labour system – paid employment rather than work. Domestic work is often unpaid and undertaken in the traditional female sphere of home life, the private domain. Labour public, work private. Thus, Marxism has a theoretical absence with respect to a key aspect of social reality and its power relations. Its examination of social inequality ignores the possibly even more fundamental power inequalities of gender. Even within Marxism's own terms, the preparation of the worker's capacity to work is dependent upon a support base from the home. The failure to analyse precisely the interrelation between the home and the workplace constitutes a serious omission.

Again, let us talk about levels of critique. One level of feminist critique would simply point to this omission, stress the importance of domestic labour and reproduction as important features of social life and leave it at that. However, one could also go much deeper through an analysis of how production and reproduction are interrelated. One could examine how they 'penetrate' one another in terms of both causality and meaning. One could look at the language and metaphors used to explain, and thereby also to obscure; in short, one could demonstrate how the conceptual oppositions set up by the original Marxist analysis obfuscate an understanding of what is, in fact, a more complex reality than appears to be the case from a gender-biased perspective.

Socrates: I see. But couldn't this all be derived from within a Marxist framework?

G.O.D.:   Perhaps. But the critique and transcendence of these oppositions needn't stop there. That is, the feminist critic could also argue that Marxism falls within the broader meta-theoretical orientation of the dominant ideological gender bias of science. The centrality of production as a theoretical category reflects an orientation towards nature; Marxism's materialism can be read as a very masculine materialism. Its materialism is that of **'malestream science'**. It perpetuates its dualisms of the abstract and the concrete, mind and body, and so on. All this is arguable by the way. The dualisms proposed to be transcended can all be linked together, or not. The arguments concerning their 'falsity', 'distortion' or 'theoretically limiting' nature have been made differently by different feminist theorists.

Socrates: All right. I appreciate there are a range of very different perspectives within the feminist camp. But I have an objection to make concerning the 'falsity' of the dual oppositions.

G.O.D.:   Perhaps inadequacy rather than falsity would be a better way of expressing it.

Socrates: Whatever. My point is that there could well be valid reasons for making a demarcation between the private and public spheres. Such demarcations could be useful. For example, what use would there be in bringing child-care into the discussion if you were discussing an industrial dispute?

G.O.D.:   I almost can't believe you said that! You certainly aren't a feminist sympathiser, are you? Child-care issues are often core elements in industrial disputes and even more frequently should be when they are not. This is true even for principally male workforces. Child-care arrangements affect the general conditions of life for . . .

Socrates: Yeah, yeah. But you're missing my point. This is one of the things that bug me about feminists. Every time you are discussing an issue, if a feminist slant can be brought to bear upon it at all, however remotely, they'll give you a whole lecture. I'd almost think you were a feminist yourself. I know you are just putting forward the various arguments of different schools of thought to me and that you don't personally subscribe to every point of view. But you just sounded so shocked that I could forget about the importance of child-care issues . . .

Anyway my point is that such distinctions can be useful. I mean here you are allegedly teaching me to think analytically, and you seem to be denying this. To analytically separate the public and private spheres doesn't mean the latter doesn't exist or is unimportant. Certain cases can be excluded from consideration to look at more important variables or features of a situation. Some of the 'oppositions' you mentioned aren't just artificial abstract categories either. Ordinary people make a distinction between their home and private life and the public sphere generally, including between paid employment and washing the dishes.

G.O.D.: I'm not disputing your point that such distinctions can sometimes be useful. Virtually all theoretical categorisations are potentially valuable, providing there is a coherent and explicit theoretical justification for them. Also, I wouldn't deny that people operate upon the basis of such categories and distinctions in their daily life. The feminist point would be that some categories, some binary oppositions, have become 'reified', so naturalised as to be only common sense. The social scientific community could, and should, do better than this. This is one argument for the notion of a **feminist successor science**. It is not feminine science as opposed to masculine science. Rather, it is a better, more objective science, because it transcends the distortions inherent in current sexist scientific practice, and also sexist science's understanding of itself as universal and objective. It transforms the very meaning of what objective means.

Socrates: How does it transform the meaning of objective?

G.O.D.: It removes from it the connotation of value neutrality. It exposes the exaltation of value neutrality as a value that derives from a very particular historical and sociological position – that of white European men at a particular historical conjuncture. It demonstrates the linkage between the historical emergence of the capitalist economic system, Enlightenment thought, the colonisation and subjugation of myriad peoples throughout the world, the socioeconomic gender divisions of society and the intellectual polarisation of nature and culture. The dichotomy between an inanimate natural world and a value-laden social world is the basis for a false view of objectivity. It serves the interests of a particular social grouping and projects their worldview as universal, while at the same time concealing that it is doing so. The overtly emancipatory values that feminists would attach to scientific enquiry are thus more objective. By the way, why wouldn't you expect me to be a feminist?

Socrates: Well, you're certainly sounding like one at the moment. But you're a man, aren't you?

G.O.D.: No.

Socrates: No! No?

G.O.D.: Didn't you read what my acronym stands for?

Socrates: I didn't pay much attention. I just know that you're one of the Microsoft philosophers – and arrogant enough to call yourself God.

G.O.D.: It stands for 'Goddess of Delphi'. It's a little joke. She was the oracle whom Socrates consulted. I thought that's why you chose the code-name Socrates.

Socrates: Nope. I just chose the name of a famous philosopher. My idea of a little joke too – choosing the name of a famous philosopher when I didn't know anything about philosophy. And the only names of philosophers I could think of were all male. And here's something I bet will surprise you: I'm a woman too.

G.O.D.: You're a woman! Really! That does surprise me. Why did you pick a male name?

Socrates: I just told you. I couldn't remember the names of any famous female philosophers. I also thought there might be advantages in taking a male name. I thought you might deal with me in a better way, you know, allow me more time, be a little more patient with my ignorance because you assumed that in spite of it there is some intelligence in here somewhere – you must be able to understand that if you're a feminist; discrimination against women is your main line.

G.O.D.: Wow. You're a woman, but you're not a feminist. But you seem to be representing a lot of feminist assertions about the world.

Socrates: So? That doesn't make me a feminist. Discrimination against women still exists in the world. I'm aware of it. I deal with it. That doesn't make me a feminist. I don't center my life on it.

G.O.D.: But that is just the point. On some level you do. This is precisely the reification argument with respect to categories and conceptual oppositions. You take something that exists in the world contingently and see it as somehow natural and inevitable. For example, now that I've told you I am a woman, it probably removes some of the intellectual authority you were ascribing to my arguments. Isn't that so?

Socrates: Well, yes, maybe, some. But you've been telling me all along to be critical anyway. So that could only be a good thing.

G.O.D.: To be critical and sceptical is a good thing. But for the right reasons. My being a woman is not a good reason to be sceptical of the information I give you or the arguments I present. Your own experience, what you've just told me, should make you more sympathetic to feminism. It should show you how deeply ingrained are some of your beliefs and attitudes.

It is not simply that some of these beliefs may be false. Several different lines of feminist theory would assert that the common sense you espouse is also ingrained in the structure of social reality. That is, patriarchal ideology naturalises some partial and false beliefs, which because of their apparent naturalness are taken simply as facts – 'the way things are' – and thus are acted upon and produce real effects. Your experience is a case in point. Unconsciously you are ascribing a gender to God, Science and Reason, to everything that possesses power and authority in our society. Actually, I think you'd be better off taking a course in feminist theory than in the philosophy of social science.

Socrates: Now listen; you're starting to be insulting. Actually, I am going to take a course in feminist theory next term. But listen: first off, I don't assign a gender to God. If I have to believe in a God it certainly isn't some old man with a white beard, or any Goddess either for that matter. And I'm not the one assigning gender to science or rationality. It's you feminists who are doing that! So let's get back to the philosophy of social science, shall we?

G.O.D.:   Okay, but I can actually use your situation to explain one of the positions in feminist epistemology: standpoint theory. I'll show you how in a moment and I don't think you'll find it insulting.

Standpoint theory is derived from a sociology of knowledge perspective. All viewpoints upon reality are partial and therefore to some degree distorted, yes? This is part of the universalism versus relativism problematic. Standpoint epistemology propounds a way in which they can be conjoined. There are variations of this besides the feminist version. I'll give you a Marxist version as a lead-in to the feminist one first.

All right, the sociology of knowledge investigates the social position of the knowing subject. It takes it out of the framework that postulates an isolated individual knower for understanding the process of knowledge acquisition. It places the whole activity in a social context. One need not be an absolutist in this respect to understand knowledge as social construction. The sociology of knowledge locates the social basis for knowledge, the relationship between interests and belief. Habermas, whom we discussed earlier, was in part drawing from this tradition when he developed his theory of the relation between knowledge and human interests.

The historicisation and socialisation of belief and knowledge associates the partial aspect of knowledge with respect to the partiality inherent in the viewpoint of its social location. Thus, in Marxist terms we can speak of bourgeois points of view and proletarian points of view. The conception of an atomised individual knower is itself a part of bourgeois ideology, which because of their socio-economic and political dominance has come to seem both obvious and true, no more than common sense. But in fact it expresses the limited, partial and therefore distorted viewpoint of a particular social class.

Now I have been hinting here about notions of **social totality**. Different Marxist theorists have different conceptions of this, but none are better from the point of view of demonstrating a standpoint epistemology than Georg Lukâcs. Different belief systems and knowledges may be socially located within the class structure of society. One class's ideology may come to dominate in the sense described above, but more than that, one class's point of view may be epistemically privileged, assigned a superiority with respect to knowledge. For Marxists, this class is the proletariat. Why?

Socrates: Yeah, why? I've known a lot of so-called 'working-class' people. And if one was going to take class position into account with respect to their beliefs, it would be from the perspective of excusing their ignorance because of educational disadvantage, rather than any alleged knowledges or insights they possess. There are exceptions, of course; I know some pretty bright lads from working-class backgrounds. But they're just that – exceptions. And they don't tend to play up their working-class origins either, at least not here at university. The only people who seem to do that are those sad cases selling *Socialist Worker* in the student bar.

G.O.D.: For Lukâcs, there are two notions of proletarian class-consciousness – actual and ascribed consciousness. It is the former you have been exposed to apparently, while it is the latter we are interested in. He would not believe, for example, that you could simply go and ask the Clapham Common bus conductor for his opinion on the present state of the world political economy and be very much enlightened. The bus conductor may understand various aspects of his job and life situation very well indeed, and know some things about them that no one else would. But he would also quite likely be mistaken about other things, even aspects of his own personal situation. This is because the world political economy and his life situation compose parts of a social totality to which he only has a partial and distorted access. That is, even properly to understand important aspects of his own life situation requires a knowledge of things outside the limitations of his own personal experience. This knowledge is necessary in order to see through the ideological screens through which his experience is processed. An example would be commodity fetishism, whereby the social relationships of production and the market are reified as relations between things. This way of perceiving reality is not simply false; it has real causal consequences. It is also in a sense true on one level – in its partial nature. Nonetheless, Lukâcs maintains that it is the proletariat who have the most privileged position to potentially obtain real knowledge.

Socrates: This is the other type of class-consciousness then, ascribed consciousness? Who possesses that?

G.O.D.: The ascribed consciousness of the proletariat is really only a potential the proletariat possesses. Empirically they may or may not possess it. It derives from the universality of the proletariat's position, that is, the uniqueness of their relationship to the social totality and history. Classes have been oppressed in various ways throughout human history. The oppression of the proletariat is in some sense the apex of this changing nature of oppression. This is not in the sense of being necessarily the worst off or most unjustly treated. Rather, the nature of their exploitation through the wage labour system universalises the process of oppression with respect to fundamental aspects of the human condition. The history of class struggle is a history of one class superseding another as the dominant class. But the **teleology** of Lukâcs's Marxism breaks the repetitive nature of such transpositions of power, through the positing of an end to history.

Socrates: Teleology? An end to history?

G.O.D.: Yes, Lukâcs's version of Marxism claims to have identified a progressive direction to history. It is seen as an inexorable law-governed process moving towards a specific end. Teleology is the term used to describe such processes. The mature plant is, as it were, already present in the seed. The seed's evolution and growth is a process with a predetermined end, i.e. the mature plant. History can be viewed the same way.

Socrates: Surely there are problems with that idea. I mean, for one thing we've observed countless seeds grow into plants. History is surely a different sort of process entirely. The future has yet to be observed. How can we know in advance what will happen? And I can see some other problems with this idea as well.

G.O.D.: You are sounding like a positivist again, with your stress on being unable to know things unless they are observed. Also you are conflating epistemology with ontology.

Socrates: I don't know if I'm a positivist or not. I've still to sort out what I think about some of the criticisms of it. But while, as I said at the beginning, I kind of like the 'seeing is believing' idea, I don't know how far I'd take it. But you said, and I quote: 'all philosophies of science must take on board some consideration of the value of empirical observation'. So I don't think you can accuse me of positivism just because I want to see some proof for people's assertions and retain some scepticism concerning speculation. This teleological idea of history sounds pretty speculative to me. And I don't know what you mean by saying I'm conflating epistemology and ontology. I think I've got them sorted out now.

G.O.D.:   Well, you said history is a 'different sort of thing'. You said this in comparison with seeds and plants. Remember, ontology is to do with what sort of entities or things exist. Epistemology is to do with the basis for knowledge and other related questions.

Socrates: Yes, I know that. I just didn't express myself very precisely. But I think you actually knew what I was getting at and are just being picky.

G.O.D.:   As it happens, I believe I do understand what you are getting at, and it's a good point. But I'm not being picky. At least, I'm not being so in a personal way. Philosophy places a high premium on making careful distinctions and being consistent with them once they are made. Undetected category shifts that take place in arguments that are being carried on at a high level of abstraction can have serious consequences – confusion and bad argument being the most frequent.

Socrates: Okay, I take your point. I'll try and make my arguments more carefully in the future. But what about my objections? You said I had made a good point.

G.O.D.:   Yes, you did. Two good points really. History is a different sort of thing from seeds and plants. Or at least most of us would wish to believe so, with respect to freedom and choice, conscious human agency playing a part in history and so on. We like to think we could have some control over our future. Marxism is often accused of being excessively deterministic. However, whether the basis for such knowledge claims are warranted (i.e. the claims to uncovering the 'laws of history') is another issue. It is crucially related. But nonetheless we can maintain an analytical distinction here between the epistemological issues and the ontological ones.

The teleologically orientated Marxist does not need to have a crystal ball through which he can observe the future to ground his claims to knowledge concerning the direction of history and what is governing it. I'll give you a rather simple example to make this point. Suppose you observed an unfinished pyramid being built. Careful observation of its lower layers and the mathematical relationships between them could allow you imaginatively to project the progression at work to its completion. That is, you could 'see' the completed pyramid before it was built, even if you had never seen one before. This sort of reasoning is the basis of the theorising by which Marxists have claimed to know the destination of the 'train of history'. Now, of course, they could be wrong. In fact, almost everyone today believes that they were wrong! But that is another matter. Can you see the line of reasoning involved? Their imaginative projection of humanity's future derives from their analysis of history and what they perceive as the relevant facts of the human condition.

Socrates: Okay, I understand the argument, but I retain my scepticism.

G.O.D.:   Good! All right, back to Lukâcs. Let us just say for the sake of argument that the Marxist analysis of history and society is correct. It asserts two things that are relevant here. First, that the proletariat is the first class in history to be a universal class. It is so by virtue of its oppression being somehow the perfection, the essence of oppression. It is also universal by virtue of its future liberation. This would break the recurring chain of one class's dominance succeeding another's; that is, the coming to power of the proletariat will not be merely the change of dominant and dominated but rather human liberation.

Second, Marxism, or rather Lukâcs's and a number of other theorists' anyway, asserts that aspects of the social totality are to be found in every particular. This idea is sometimes called '**expressive totality**'. The totality is not only composed of all the particulars but is on some levels reproduced in every particular. That is, we can find in the particular an expression of the totality. So, there is in the particulars of the relations of capitalist exploitation that which is expressive of exploitation, oppression and human history universally. It is possible for the proletariat to find within the particulars of their own class situation a viewpoint by which the essential nature of the human condition and history can be understood.

Socrates: I'm following this, but at the same time I'm finding it very convoluted and peculiar. If the essential truths, the laws of history and so on, can be derived from the proletariat's 'standpoint', how come they don't see it? You admitted earlier that the bus conductor had only a partial and distorted view of both his own situation and the world economy.

G.O.D.:   This is why Lukâcs needs two notions of class-consciousness. Some of the proletariat, most of the proletariat, are unable to penetrate the ideological screens to interpret their own experience properly. Nonetheless, their class position, in relation to the most important elements of the social totality, at least allows them the potential for doing so. Here we can finally make a return to feminist standpoint theory and demonstrate, at least in part, the thinking that links the potential with the actual.

Socrates: I'm glad we're coming back to the topic. It seems to me we've come a long way from feminism.

G.O.D.:   You're wrong there. For example, Nancy Hartsock's **feminist standpoint** epistemology is very closely analogous to Lukâcs's proletarian version and derives from the same sort of meta-theory with respect to positions and knowledge. There is, for example, the same problem with respect to potential and actuality. Feminist standpoint theory privileges women's experiences and overall social situation as a superior vantage point for coming to understand the social world. Some variations of this sort of theory make it explicitly 'feminist experience' as a way of dealing with the problem.

Socrates: What problem?

G.O.D.: You.

Socrates: Oh yeah, I'm the Clapham Common bus conductor in the Marxist version. Not a Marxist and not a feminist either.

G.O.D.: Exactly. Remember with respect to our consideration of the Marxist example, we were presuming for the sake of argument that the overall Marxist analysis of history was correct. Thus, if you are not a Marxist, your views are somehow ideologically distorted. Thus, if you are not a feminist . . .

Socrates: The feminist can say: 'Your consciousness needs raising, dear!' I get it. But I don't buy it at all! First of all, it is incredibly patronising and arrogant! One might say it is the very opposite of the perspective on other cultures Winch would have us adopt. Okay, there are problems with such views. But you told me that cultural relativism developed at least in part as a response to the ethnocentric anthropology of the past. It was a repudiation of the condescension and the arrogance of the 'bad science' that went hand in hand with imperialism. The false consciousness argument, whether Marxist or feminist, seems to have a lot in common with imperial ethnocentrism.

In some ways, standpoint theory is even worse. The Western cultural claims to superiority were at least backed up on some level. It might sound nasty to say so, but such claims were at least implicitly underwritten by economic and military dominance. The feminist standpoint theory is exactly the opposite. My experience as an oppressed woman is supposed to give me a privileged access to knowledge. But the feminist decides that while that is my potential perhaps, in actuality I don't really possess such knowledge; I don't fulfill my potential because I disagree with them. What is the basis of such a judgment? They would assert that they are oppressed, that I'm oppressed. What makes their knowledge claims superior to mine? We're both women. And it's the same with the Marxist case. Our presumption of the 'truth' of the Marxist analysis was just that – a presumption made for the sake of argument. Do you see? There's a vicious circularity involved in the argument. It seems necessary to presume the truth of the conclusion in order to provide the basis for the argument to reach that conclusion.

G.O.D.: Very good!

Socrates: Don't just say 'very good' to me. Tell me what the feminists or the Marxists would have to say to that! Have I, or have I not, decisively refuted their arguments?

G.O.D.: Well, some people would say that you have.

Socrates: But you think not.

G.O.D.: No. I'm sure you are not surprised to learn that you are not the first to point out such apparent contradictions, to either Marxists or feminists. Your argument has been presented many, many times, in a variety of forms, some more sophisticated than yours, though I think you've got at its essence. The outrage at both Marxist and feminist arrogance and condescension has also often been expressed. However, both have answers to such arguments. What kind of tack do you think they might be able to take to defend their position in the face of what you called 'irrefutable arguments'? Why don't they accept your criticism of circularity?

Socrates: I don't know. Because they are just bloody-minded? Irrational? Because their position is simply based upon faith?

G.O.D.: Well, once again, such accusations have been leveled at them. But I'll give you a possibly better answer. Their position is more sophisticated than you realise and is not, in fact, circular in its reasoning. First, the Marxist and feminist analyses of history and society are not initially grounded in standpoint epistemology, but otherwise. They can be variously grounded in different epistemologies and ontologies; in fact, they can be grounded in the same sort of philosophical viewpoints as other sorts of theory and knowledge. The main body of either Marxist or feminist theory does not rest upon standpoint epistemology. Both make considerably detailed substantive claims about the world. The truth of these may be judged by other criteria. But substantive feminist explanation precedes feminist standpoint epistemology. It precedes it both chronologically and logically.

Political struggle, feminist research and theory provided argument and answers to questions about the nature of society and history, the power relations between men and women, and how these interact with other social phenomena. The epistemological questions of feminism grew out of development in substantive research into such areas. It arose from the developing awareness of the depth and complexity of such issues. Thus, while on the one hand feminist epistemology is developing as an attempt to philosophically ground feminist politics and research, on the other hand epistemology is in a sense an area of substantive research for feminists. They have, for example, examined how patriarchal power structures have distorted the falsely idealised notions of scientific explanation and practices.

So, that is one side of the equation. It is a response to the charge of circularity. But what about your experience? You don't define yourself as a feminist; you do not accept many feminist claims about the nature of society. The feminist would say perhaps something along the lines of: 'I'm sorry, sister, but you have failed to understand the true nature of your oppression'. Yes, it sounds patronising. But couldn't it be true nonetheless?

Socrates: Hmm. I would be tempted to reply with an insult. No, I don't think so.

G.O.D.:   What if a structural engineer said to you: 'I'm sorry, I don't believe you fully understand the principles concerning metal fatigue relevant to safety considerations, with respect to the ageing of materials used in this bridge'? Now, you wouldn't be insulted in that case and would be inclined to take such a pronouncement seriously. Yes?

Socrates: Yes, of course. We began this whole discussion with respect to the authority of science. But the cases aren't analogous. You're saying the feminist is an 'expert' concerning the status of women in society. I'm sure many feminists know a great deal of relevant facts concerning this that I'm unaware of. Fine. But you've also said the basis for authority needs to be questioned. Well, I question it, when it is my experience that is under consideration. And isn't that the case here?

G.O.D.:   Yes, indeed it is. So, okay, once again, just for the sake of argument let us presume that the radical patriarchy theory of society is, broadly speaking, substantially correct. You don't believe it. Thus, in a sense you are ignorant or misinformed or have only a partial distorted view even of your own personal experience. All right, you don't believe that to be true. But let us just assume for the moment that it is. Now, the radical feminist has a male colleague who by and large has been persuaded by her arguments. Now he too has, in a sense, a better understanding of some aspects of your personal experience. He is more aware of 'the true nature of your oppression as a woman' than you are. Yes? Are you following this?

Socrates: Yes, I'm following it. But I'm also remembering that our starting place is simply an assumption. An assumption that I don't actually believe is correct! But carry on. This male feminist sympathiser understands my oppression better than me. All sorts of people understand my experience better than me.

G.O.D.:   I can understand your emotional resentment of this possibility. But I can also offer you two things to consider, which should make it a less bitter pill to swallow. First, that while you don't identify yourself as a feminist, I am sure that there is much in the feminist analysis of society, even the radical feminist analysis of society, which you would accept. For example, you would likely see the sexual double standards that still persist in society as being unjust and oppressive to women. So the contrast in our hypothetical scenario, i.e. where we accept for the time being the notion that the radical feminist analysis is correct, is much less extreme than it might seem.

   Second, the idea that someone could possibly understand things about you, even very personal things about you, better than yourself needn't be so very offensive if you think about it. The structural engineering example can very easily be shifted to something more personal. How about a gynecologist? Perhaps he or she understands some aspects of your experience that you not only don't fully understand but find it is causing a problem for you? Okay, too physical an example; it is too dependent upon natural science. What about a psychoanalyst? Perhaps you might disagree with her analysis of your unconscious motivation for performing an action. But it wouldn't immediately outrage you that she could make such a presumption.

Socrates: It might. And also, of course, it would depend on the degree to which I was convinced of the validity of psychoanalytical theory in general. It seems we're back where we started.

G.O.D.: No, we aren't. I was, as I said, just trying to break down some of your emotional resistance to the argument, trying to sugar the bitter pill a little. Let us go back to the male feminist sympathiser and your experience. As we've concluded, if **radical feminism** is correct, and I haven't forgotten that this is just an assumption made to illustrate the standpoint argument . . .

Socrates: I get the feeling that such assumptions frequently do get forgotten, and that is one of the ways philosophy arrives at some of its more bizarre conclusions.

G.O.D.: Yes, I think you are right about that. But this isn't the case here. Okay, now ask yourself what the difference might be between his perspective and yours – yours after you had, so to speak, come to see the error of your ways and had a better analysis of your own experience. Now you too are a feminist. What is the difference between his understanding and yours?

Socrates: None I guess, if we're agreed.

G.O.D.: Ah, but you are wrong there. You have a concrete, experientially grounded dimension to your understanding, which he lacks. The vantage point of your real life experience gives a richer, deeper understanding than is possible from the man's position.

Imagine how you might feel after you had become convinced of the validity of the radical feminist position. Imagine how it would transform the manner in which you would then interpret your previous experience, including, of course, your previous interpretations of that experience. Perhaps this is too hypothetical an exercise for you to imagine the emotion; because once again we are, of course, simply assuming the 'truth' of the radical feminist position. But I think we could conclude anyway that the feeling of being duped would be intense. Duped by men! Duped by the patriarchal power structures of society! Now consider the possibility of that in relation to the annoyance and resentment you presently feel towards the arrogance and presumption you see involved with feminist claims to a greater understanding of your experience. This other group of people did far more than patronise you; they deceived you! They deceived you so well that you deceived yourself; all the self-understanding you thought you had was merely an expression of their understanding of you. It was so powerfully expressed that you took it on board as your own, and now you've seen through it, and seen how deeply it penetrated you, and how adversely it affected you.

Socrates: Okay, I'd be angry. So what? Why do you keep emphasising the emotional aspect of this?

G.O.D.:   Because among the (alleged) false dichotomies set up by 'male-stream' philosophy, are some outgrowths of mind-body dualisms: reason versus emotion, abstract versus embodied understandings, objective versus subjective, fact and values. Hilary Rose, among others, propounds the triad of hand, brain and heart as actually providing the grounding of knowledge. The 'hand' and the 'heart' are aspects of knowledge production which traditional epistemology excludes in its presentation of a disembodied history of ideas. Let me try to convince you of the relevance of the emotional side of this.

Let us imagine that the male feminist sympathiser has reached similar understandings to you. But he has reached them more abstractly. He could at any time forget them whilst analysing another subject area and fail to see the relevance of the connections. However, you, once having become aware of having been deceived, are unlikely to forget it!

In this way too, radical feminism and Marxism are analogous. The notion of commodity fetishism that we discussed earlier exemplifies the way in which a worldview, a worldview embracing the most elementary aspects of daily life, could potentially be transformed. What is common sense, the reified perception of relations between things, gets turned upside down, or rather it gets turned right side up. The whole world looks different once this theoretical insight is grasped. One can be critical of capitalism without this notion, but there are severe limits to such critique. One is still inhabiting, to use Kuhn's terminology, the same paradigm as the dominant ideology. Once it really and truly has been grasped, however, the world can never look the same again. It is an insight that informs virtually every aspect of social life, because it is so fundamental and so directly in conflict with the predominant 'common sense' of the time.

This would exactly be true of the various versions of radical feminism. The liberal feminist, the person like yourself, who would take some of feminism on board, picking and choosing some bits, while leaving others, is still inhabiting the dominant paradigm of patriarchy, in spite of severe criticism of some aspects of it. While radical feminism (and some other versions of feminism too, of course) involves seeing the world in a whole new way.

And how were such insights into the nature of social reality arrived at? Could the male sympathiser have originated them? Actually there was nothing but the experiential privilege of his position to prevent him. I don't mean epistemological privilege here; I mean social, economic and political privilege. Okay, you're a twentieth-century, no, a new millennium woman. You're not a feminist, but among the things you would now take for granted were once extremely radical, almost unthinkable, notions. I mean, feminist or not, you certainly wouldn't buy the 'a woman's place is in the kitchen' line of thinking, would you?

Socrates: No, of course not.

G.O.D.:   But at one time women did. Okay, so imagine the wife of a Marxist revolutionary in the nineteenth century. He affirms the materialist view of history. Man must interact with the natural world and do so socially. Before there can be ideas and abstractions, society must take care of the business of producing the necessities of life. The source of value is to be found in labour. The wife of this revolutionary catches fragments of such discussions, as the men in her parlor eat the meals she provides for them. From their perspective, the dishes appear and disappear as if by magic. That she should provide them with such services is so taken for granted that they are scarcely recognised as services at all. Years pass and the sons they (or rather she) raised in turn take their place at the discussion table, and in turn fail to notice the process whereby dishes and clothes are transformed invisibly from dirty to clean. Now, with all the emphasis upon the material aspect of the human condition and history, all the talk concerning the centrality of labour and production, why did these men fail to appreciate an undeniably important, certainly very much material, aspect of human existence and incorporate it into their socio-economic and political historical analyses? They could have. It certainly forms a part of Marxist analysis today. The analysis of domestic labour, reproduction, etc. was not (and is not) something impossible for a male to develop. But they didn't. Because, how easy it was for them to overlook it!

I am over-simplifying of course. Nineteenth-century theorists didn't miss these things entirely. However, in many respects they simply took the orthodox, 'common-sense' views of their era concerning women, at the same time as providing radical insights into other domains of social life.

It would be difficult for a woman to miss such things. Or rather, difficult for her to miss them in one sense, and difficult for her to perceive them in another. The same would be true of the factory worker in whose name these nineteenth-century men were theorising. They were excluded from the formal knowledge acquisition process and lacked the time for such intellectual endeavours. However, at the same time, their concrete situation of exploitation gave them a different concrete basis for understanding the abstractions of the intellectuals.

The point is, that while there are contradictions within the standpoint epistemologies, they are not strictly logical contradictions but embedded in social reality itself. Marxists would call such contradictions dialectical perhaps, but feminist standpoint epistemology is getting at the same thing.

Socrates: Okay, let's see if I've got the gist of this. And then I have a host of questions. Women, the proletariat, because of their situation in the hierarchy of power relations of our present-day society (and even more so in the past), frequently have a misguided and ill-informed understanding of the world. This is because first of all they have been excluded from the knowledge production process . . .

G.O.D.:   Wait, let me just interrupt you there for one moment. Women are not totally excluded from the scientific process today. And I don't mean by that merely that they have, to a limited degree, broken into domains that were traditionally all-male preserves. Rather I am referring to the historical evolution and change within the organisation of scientific research. In earlier times, it was a craft-based production process. Now it is an industrial form of organisation. The 'great men' of the scientific revolution had the ideas, but they also performed the hands-on work of scientific observation and experimentation. Scientific work today is much more of a collectively and very hierarchically organised endeavour. Women occupy a disproportionate number of the lower echelons of this process. They perform a great deal of the necessary hands-on work, the routine of laboratory work, for example. But the administration and direction of research is still predominantly in the control of men. The majority of women science workers thus are quite literally in a proletarian position with respect to the relations of scientific knowledge production. They do not control the means of this production.

Socrates: Okay, I can see the relevance of that. But my point is that they are excluded from acquiring the possession of relevant knowledge. Their real position in society disadvantages them with respect to knowledge, just as it does with respect to a great many other things.

But the flip side of this is that that very disadvantaged situation also privileges them epistemologically. This is because science's self-image is not accurate. It claims a neutrality and universality that it does not in fact possess. It distorts some things and misses others entirely. Under the guise of being value-free it incorporates sexist gendered values. This is an insight that could be realised by men as well as women. However, the very social privileges of their dominant position in society present a barrier to men arriving at such understanding. On the other hand, once given access to relevant information, the experiences of women, including importantly the experience of oppression and social exclusion, gives them a superior vantage point from which to see the flaws in current scientific research. Most particularly, it makes it easier to reject science's understanding of itself – hence the possibility of a better, feminist orientated, successor science. That's basically it, yes?

G.O.D.: That is the essence of the argument, yes. There is also the aspect of women's experience as caregivers. This makes it easier for them to unite hand and brain and heart. It allows them to see the distortion inherent in a notion of objectivity that absolutely separates facts and values.

Socrates: Right. Okay, I've got the main points then. Now some questions. Isn't the experience of the oppressed just as partial as that of the oppressor? I know you've given an answer to that, but I'm not sure if it's satisfactory. The history of 'malestream science' you referred to has, in spite of its shortcomings, produced a knowledge of nature that allows us to build computers and aeroplanes and . . .

G.O.D.: Bombs?

Socrates: And medicines. Are the socially directed harmful applications of knowledge to be blamed on science?

G.O.D.: Can we clearly separate 'applied' and 'pure' science? Is the process of producing knowledge clearly separable from the values that direct that enterprise?

Socrates: I don't know. I understand the argument, I think. But I need to think about it some more. However, I've still more questions. First, you've given me both a Marxist and a feminist standpoint epistemology argument. Which of these is to be preferred? Or can they be combined? And if there are standpoint arguments made on the basis of class and gender as oppressed groups, couldn't there be others with equally valid claims? Race, ethnicity, sexuality? Do we have a plurality of bases for knowledge? Or do we put them all together and find the most oppressed combination? Would a working-class, third world, black lesbian occupy the most privileged position of all from which to access fundamental aspects of the human condition?

G.O.D.: Are you asking that last question seriously? Or are you trying to demonstrate a flaw in standpoint epistemology by means of exaggeration?

Socrates: Both really. I mean it does seem to indicate a problem, when the position you are arguing for seems to have bizarre consequences. Which reminds me: you said you'd come back to the Cleopatra logic example at some point. And finally I'm curious: do you actually subscribe to the feminist standpoint epistemology argument? Or were you simply presenting the arguments for it and intend to poke holes in it later? As I recall, you said you are a critical realist. Can you be a feminist critical realist?

G.O.D.:   Okay, last question first. Yes, you can. Caroline New, for example, would describe herself as such. And yes, that is the position I subscribe to personally. I will give you a critical realist modified, feminist standpoint epistemological argument later.

  The other questions you raise are very interesting. One could say they reflect some of the tensions and contradictions within the feminist project as a whole. There is a desire – and indeed, it could even be argued, a necessity – for unity within the feminist emancipatory political project. Yet women do not all share the same experiences. To assume so is to acquiesce to the prevailing gender-biased epistemological notions that have propounded gender as a biological, rather than social, category. Woman is an essentialist category, which actually reflects prevalent conceptual oppositions, the very ones which a feminist standpoint epistemology would wish to transcend. The acceptance of such essentialism reflects both the social order we live in and a critical failure to go deep enough into the contradictions within the dominant viewpoint, even while attempting the apparently most radical critiques. Janice Moulton's 'Cleopatra syllogism argument' is a case in point. It represents the misguided notion that in order to create a coherent feminist epistemology, one must argue for a distinctive feminine, as opposed to masculine, logic. Such is not the case at all.

Socrates: All right then. What is the flaw in the reasoning behind the Cleopatra example? Surely the 'bizarreness' signifies something? Surely, using man as a generic term for human signifies a male bias in language at the very least?

G.O.D.:   Yes, it does that. But that is something else again. It is not the same as demonstrating a logical flaw in the expression of syllogisms.

Socrates: But doesn't it? All men are mortal; Cleopatra is a man; therefore Cleopatra is mortal. Doesn't the bizarreness of this indicate some problem?

G.O.D.:   Yes, but not a logic problem. The argument is made that if man had been used in a gender-specific sense, the original Socrates syllogism would be valid. But first it is pointed out that this was not what was intended in the original Greek, nor is it what is intended by use of this example with respect to the teaching of formal reasoning. If used in the generic sense, one would have to be able to substitute for Socrates every other possible name, male or female. The bizarreness elicited by the substitution of a female name invalidates the argument. But this is simply not true!

  Do you remember our discussion of the relation of logical statements to one another and their relation to the world? Validity and invalidity with respect to logical argument are connected to questions of truth and falsity, but they are not identical! Perfectly valid arguments can have outrageously absurd premises, and quite ridiculous, as well as patently false, conclusions. All objects that orbit the earth are made of green cheese; the moon orbits the earth; therefore the moon is made of green cheese. This is a perfectly valid logical argument. That it is untrue and ridiculous is beside the point. 'Bizarreness' simply doesn't enter into questions of logical validity or invalidity.

Socrates: Something still seems somehow wrong there to me.

G.O.D.: What you are forgetting is that the truth of the conclusion of a valid logical argument is dependent upon the truth of its premises. In any attempt to apply logical arguments to the real world, there is actually an implicit 'if' involved, concerning the truth of the premise. 'If all objects that orbit the earth are made of green cheese', is an 'if' which we clearly know to be untrue. If it was true, then the conclusion would be likewise so. But it isn't. If all men are mortal, and if Cleopatra is a man, then Cleopatra is mortal. Putting that 'if' in front of Cleopatra removes the problem.

Socrates: I guess so.

G.O.D.: You still don't sound convinced. And there is a lesson to be learned from that. It is one that speaks to science but not logic. Science involves more than merely the continued process of knowledge production. Reproduction is involved too. The insights of one generation need to be transmitted to the next. Science education is very much part of science. Perhaps the metaphors used in science's idealised presentation of itself have pernicious and misleading educational effects. The male bias in metaphor, for example, could have a detrimental effect upon the learning process of female students: your choosing the name Socrates, for example, could be seen as a reflection of some of the problems inherent in philosophy and science education. It is well established that the white middle-class children used as illustrations in early learning materials had a detrimental effect upon working-class black children's cognitive development of reading and other academic skills.

Socrates: Yes, I can see that. Maybe I have been brainwashed. But I'm still sceptical. And you still haven't answered my other questions about other oppressed groups in relation to epistemological privileging.

G.O.D.: No, I haven't, but I'm going to. The diversity of feminist views and the diversity of female experience is less a philosophical problem in itself and more a reflection of the current state of affairs. Sandra Harding argues that this is no bad thing in itself. The epistemological problems are not unimportant, she would say, but they don't need an immediate answer as their importance actually derives from their relevance to practice and relation to politics. At the moment, the diversity of views leads to a multiplicity of approaches, and that is perhaps what is required at the moment. It is not so terrible that some of these views are conflicting. This is actually a good lead into a consideration of **postmodernism**. The diversity and fragmentation of epistemological views merely reflects the fragmentation of social reality. The days of our acceptance of grand **metanarratives** are over, postmodernists argue. However, the postmodernist viewpoint also conflicts with many others. Jane Flax would argue that it certainly conflicts with the notion of a feminist successor science, as this is still in some sense what the postmodernists would label as irredeemably modernist.

Socrates: Hold on. You're getting way ahead of me. What do you mean by metanarratives?

G.O.D.:   Incredulity towards metanarrative is one of the ways of defining the postmodern condition. But perhaps we should leave that until next time.

DISCUSSION QUESTIONS

1   The outline of the major points to be covered at the beginning of this chapter is presented in the same form as the others in this book, i.e. it is in a point-by-point format. Could this linear mode of thought perhaps be seen as masculine? Can we identify other particular features of types of thinking that could be seen as gendered?

2   If equality of opportunity for women is fully achieved in terms of scientific careers, and if the previously marginalised subject areas relating to gender are now placed centre stage within social science, then surely all possible feminist political objectives with respect to science have been realised. What arguments could be given to disagree with this assertion?

3   Why should the experience of oppression give a better perspective from which to understand social reality? Is it not equally arguable that the experience of social and economic privilege gives a superior vantage point because such privilege gives a more ready access to education and knowledge?

4   If social scientists can only attempt to approximate the understandings possessed by the members of the particular social grouping they are studying, then what is the point of doing social science at all?

5   What advantages and disadvantages are there to allowing the incorporation of emotion into the scientific enterprise as opposed to attempting as far as possible to keep it out?

6   If the epistemological arguments concerning the significance of different situations and collective identities have the political consequence of weakening the unity of feminist struggle, is that sufficient reason in itself to criticise such arguments?

FURTHER READING SUGGESTIONS

Journals

There are many! Articles on myriad aspects of feminism, gender or related areas of concern are now to be found in virtually every social science and philosophical journal.

Feminist Review (Palgrave Macmillan)
Feminist Studies
Feminist Theory (Sage)
Journal of Gender Studies (Taylor & Francis)
RFR/DRF (University of Toronto Press)
Signs: Journal of Women in Culture and Society
Women's Studies Quarterly

General reference books

Andermahr, S., Lovell, T. and Wolkowitz, C. (1997) *A Concise Glossary of Feminist Theory*, Oxford University Press, New York.

Deegan, M.T. (ed.) (1991) *Women in Sociology: A Bio-Bibliographic Sourcebook*, Greenwood Press, Westport, CT.

Young, I.M. and Jagger, A.M. (1998) *A Companion to Feminist Philosophy*, Blackwell, Maiden, MA.

Feminist standpoint theory

Haibert, M. (1989) 'Feminist Epistemology: An Impossible Project?', *Radical Philosophy* 53, Autumn pp. 3–7.

Hartsock, N. (1983) 'The Feminist Standpoint: Developing the Ground for a Specifically Feminist Historical Materialism' in Harding and Hintikka's book listed below.

Heckman, S. (1997) 'Truth and Method: Feminist Standpoint Theory Revisited', *Signs* 22(2) pp. 341–365.

Holmwood, J. (1995) 'Feminism and Epistemology: What Kind of Successor Science?', *Sociology* 29(3) pp. 411–428.

Rose, H. (1983) 'Hand, Brain and Heart: A Feminist Epistemology for the Natural Sciences', *Signs: Journal for Women in Culture and Society* 9(1) pp. 73–90.

Smith, D. (1997) 'Comment on Heckman's "Truth and Method: Feminist Standpoint Theory Revisited"', *Signs* 22(2) pp. 392–398.

Feminism and sociology

Eisenstein, Z. (1982) 'Rethinking Sociology from a Feminist Point of View', *American Sociologist* 17(1) pp. 29–39.

Reinharz, S. (1992) *Feminist Methods in Social Research*, Oxford University Press, New York – gives a feminist perspective on many traditional methods of sociological research. Especially interesting is the chapter 'Original Feminist Research Methods'.

Smith, D. (1974) 'Women's Perspective as a Radical Critique of Sociology', *Sociological Inquiry* 44 pp. 7–13.

———— (1975) 'An Analysis of Ideological Structures and How Women Are Excluded: Considerations for Academic Women', *Canadian Review of Sociology and Anthropology* 12 pp. 343–369.

———— (1987) *The Everyday World as Problematic: A Feminist Sociology*, Northeastern University Press, Boston.

Philosophy of science

Harding, S. (1986) *The Science Question in Feminism*, Open University Press, Milton Keynes – a good overview of the major issues in the debate and a strong position of her own arguing that it is perhaps premature (and unnecessary) to sort out all the epistemological questions posed by feminism's opposing strands. For a critique of her position, see the article by Caroline New listed below.

———— (1991) *Whose Science? Whose Knowledge?*, Open University Press, Milton Keynes.

Harding, S. and Hintikka, M. (eds) (1983) *Discovering Reality: Feminist Perspectives on Epistemology, Metaphysics, Methodology and Philosophy of Science*, Reidel, Dordrecht.

Kourany, J.A. (2010) *Philosophy of Science after Feminism*, Oxford University Press, Oxford, UK.

Feminism and logic

Moulton, J. (1977) 'The Myth of the Neutral "Man"' in M. Veterrling-Braggin (ed.), *Feminism and Philosophy*, Littlefield Adams, Totowa, NJ, pp. 100–115.

Postmodernism and feminism

Flax, J. (1983) 'Political Philosophy and the Patriarchal Unconscious: A Psychoanalytic Perspective upon Epistemology and Metaphysics' in Harding and Hintikka's book listed above.

———— (1993) *Disputed Subjects*, Routledge, New York – especially Chapter 10.

Lovibond, S. (1989) 'Feminism and Postmodernism', *New Left Review* 178 pp. 5–28.

McLennan, G. (1995) 'Feminism, Epistemology and Postmodernism', *Sociology* 29(3) pp. 391–409.

Soper, K. (1990) 'Feminism, Humanism and Postmodernism', *Radical Philosophy* 55 pp. 11–17.

Realism and feminism

Assitter, A. (1996) *Enlightened Women: Modernist Feminism in a Postmodernist Age*, Routledge, London.

'Critical realism, gender and feminism' (2016), Special Issue of the *Journal of Critical Realism* (15)5.

Francis, B. (2002) 'Relativism, Realism, and Feminism: An Analysis of Some Theoretical Tensions in Research on Gender Identity', *Journal of Gender Studies*, Taylor & Francis 11(1) pp. 39–54.

New, C. (1998) 'Realism, Deconstruction and the Feminist Standpoint', *Journal for the Theory of Social Behaviour* 28(4) pp. 349–372.

General

Barrett, M. (1980) *Women's Oppression Today: Problems in Marxist Feminist Analysis*, Verso, London.
Sharman, J. and Beck, E. (eds) (1979) *The Prison of Sex: Essays in the Sociology of Knowledge*, University of Wisconsin Press, Madison.
Spender, D. (1987) *For the Record: The Meaning and Making of Feminist Knowledge*, Women's Press, London.
Stanley, L. and Wise, S. (1993) *Breaking Out Again*, Routledge, London.
——— (1990) *Feminist Praxis*, Routledge, London – especially Chapter 2.

Black feminism

Collins, P.H. (1991) *Black Feminist Thought*, Routledge, New York.
hooks, b. (1981) *Ain't I a Woman?: Black Women and Feminism*, South End Press, Boston.

Third wave feminism

Gillis, S., Howie, G. and Munford, R. (eds) (2007) *Third Wave Feminism: A Critical Exploration*, Palgrave Macmillan, London, UK.
Heywood, L. and Drake, J. (eds) (1997) *Third Wave Agenda: Being Feminist, Doing Feminism*, University of Minnesota Press, Minneapolis.

Some second-wave feminist classics

de Beauvoir, S. (1953) *The Second Sex*, Knopf, New York.
Firestone, S. (1979) *The Dialectic of Sex: The Case for Feminist Revolution*, Women's Press, London.
Friedman, B. (1963) *The Feminine Mystique*, Norton, New York.
Millett, K. (1972) *Sexual Politics*, Abacus, London.

Engels

Engels, F. (1986) *The Origins of the Family, Private Property and the State*, Penguin Books, London – the original Marxist theorisation on the historical position of women in society. The work profoundly influenced early second-wave theories of patriarchy.

Lukâcs

Lukâcs, G. (1971) *History and Class Consciousness*, Merlin Press, London.

CHAPTER 7

POSTMODERNISM: IF YOU SAY THERE ARE NO RIGHT OR WRONG ANSWERS AND I SAY YOU'RE WRONG, AM I RIGHT . . . OR WRONG?

Truths are illusions which one has forgotten are illusions, worn-out metaphors which have become powerless to affect the sense, coins which have their obverse effaced and are now no longer of account as coins but merely as metal.

Friedrich Nietzsche

We believe that it is possible for scientific work to gain some knowledge about the reality of the world, by means of which we can increase our power and in accordance with which we can arrange our life. If this belief is an illusion, then we are in the same position as you. But science has given us evidence by its numerous and important successes that it is no illusion.

Sigmund Freud

OUTLINE OF MAJOR POINTS TO BE COVERED

The chapter begins with the question of personal and collective identities in relation to the many varieties of feminism. The recognition of difference between groups and the shifting nature of our multiple identities are seen as central features of postmodernism. The question of the stability of an individual identity over time is explored in this context, as is a further examination of the issue of collective identities in relation to political action. The introduction to the consideration of postmodernism is complete when the question is raised concerning whether or not these issues have themselves changed in relation to profound shifts in contemporary social reality.

1 Postmodernism is described as an anti-epistemological position because of its rejection of the modes of thinking it associates with modernism. It is pointed out, however, that this is itself an epistemological position.
2 Lyotard's postmodernist perspective, as developed in *The Postmodern Condition*, is the first of these to be described.
  a There is a radical distinction to be made in terms of the different *language games* of ought and is.
  b Science belongs to the language game of 'is', that is, of providing descriptions and explanations of how things are.

c Science is dependent upon a different sort of language game from its own to legitimate itself as a human activity. In Lyotard's terms it is dependent for this upon 'narrative knowledge'. Science's legitimation is expressed in terms of the grand narratives of the Enlightenment and modernity.

d According to science's own standards, '**narrative knowledge**' is no knowledge at all.

e Breakdown of knowledge and understanding has occurred whereby knowledge has been reduced to being merely a fragmented informational commodity. And collectively we have now reached a position of incredulity towards the grand narratives of the past in which we made sense of human history in terms of progress and civilisation.

3 The contradictions between the above and Habermas's position are explored.

4 A clarification of the need (or not) to mark a distinction between **poststructuralism** and **postmodernism** is made. It is to be understood in terms of whether one is sympathetic to the views of Derrida and Foucault (as seminal poststructuralist thinkers) or not and whether one is sympathetic (or not) towards postmodernism generally.

5 A brief synopsis of Saussure's theory of **signs** is given, emphasising its synchronic nature and the arbitrary relationship between **signifiers** and **signifieds**.

6 A synopsis of Derrida's examination of signification is given with emphasis upon the notion of deferral and the potentially infinite contextualisation process of meaning. Precision of meaning is impossible.

a The elements of **deconstruction** as a technique for textual analysis are sketched out emphasising the reversal of oppositions.

7 The view that deconstruction is more than mere technique is articulated, and a brief synopsis of Derrida's problematisation of language use in the history of philosophy is given. Power is embedded in language.

a A brief criticism is made of both Derrida and Saussurian **semiology** by way of foreshadowing the final chapter on critical realism. The referent must be articulated with signification to give a proper theory of meaning.

8 Nietzsche's concept of the will to power is briefly considered. The importance of truth is attacked.

a Nietzsche's own writing style is considered in relation to the postmodernist aestheticisation of philosophy.

9 Foucault's concept of power-knowledge is explained in relation to Nietzsche's will to power. Truth, he argues, is not the most important question for us now, but this does not mean he sees claims to truth as merely rhetorical strategies in the contestation of power. Rather he traces the development of regimes of truth historically, connecting institutional and discursive structures.

10 A brief reflection upon the sets of practices around which **regimes of truth** are socially constructed forms a bridge into a consideration of the sociology

of science. The question of whether the production of scientific knowledges can be reduced to sociological determinants is engaged with in relation to the debates that have become known as '**science wars**'.

a   Scientists reject the explanation of their disagreements about theories, data interpretation, etc. in sociological or discourse analysis terms. They insist upon the importance of what their disputes between themselves are about, i.e. the content's relationship to the subject matter.

b   The problem of first-order knowledges is re-considered in relation to the scenario – physicists/first-order knowledges, sociologists/second-order knowledges. Again a foreshadowing of the final chapter's debates and arguments is given in that a **critical realist** view is implied in the acceptance of degrees of validity to both groups' claims in this debate.

DIALOGUE

Socrates: It's me again.

G.O.D.:   Who are you?

Socrates: What do you mean who am I? This is our seventh conversation. You can't have forgotten!

G.O.D.:   No, I haven't forgotten. But who are you? You told me you were a student and a woman but that's all.

Socrates: I thought personal conversations were out of bounds. Are you really interested in my personal life?

G.O.D.:   Personal information is not supposed to be exchanged through the philosophical reference service. It is supposed to be an academic resource rather than a counselling facility. However, the bureaucratically prescribed strict separation between the two tells us something about the philosophical assumptions underlying the service. It tells us something about the way that knowledge is conceived of by the powers that be, does it not?

Socrates: I guess it does. It has a certain similarity to the positivist conception of science.

G.O.D.:   Indeed it does. It also perhaps demonstrates some masculine gender bias.

Socrates: I can see how you could make an argument for that from a feminist perspective. So are you trying to break the rules?

G.O.D.:   That's debatable. I strongly believe that philosophy can be, and should be, relevant to people's lives, but sometimes it is presented as simply an abstract enterprise, with no connection to them. There are perhaps no more relevant questions to be asked than the ones that go to the core of the way people conceive of themselves. I mean by this, questions concerning identity. You are a student. You are a woman. You are many other things as well. You are different things at different times and different things to different people. How do you conceive of yourself?

Socrates: Do you want me to give you a list?

G.O.D.: Actually, no. But I want you to think about what might be on such a list. Your sexual preferences. Do you have a concept of your self in relation to them? Does that conception directly match behaviour or are there discrepancies? How much of your sense of self is related to past and present behaviour, to what you are doing and what you have done? To your accomplishments, hopes, dreams, failures?

And what about your race? Your nationality? Your religious and political beliefs? Do you belong to any organisations in relation to them? How important is such membership, or the lack of it, to your conception of yourself? Your family? Your community? Hobbies? Cultural tastes? Job? Well, okay, you are a student; the jobs you have held perhaps won't connect up to your sense of self in the same way as being a miner might to someone who has been 'down pit' for thirty years and just been made redundant. Your marital status? How much of your identity is your own and how much your husband's? Or if you are single now, how much does that feature in your sense of self in relation to the future? How much will (or does) motherhood affect your notion of yourself? How much does age figure in your self-identity? What about other people's perceptions? Some of the preceding list is perhaps used by others to construct a picture of who you are. Labels are put upon you that may or may not be more or less accurate. How much do some of these things change from situation to situation? I mean, for example, does your self-identification in terms of nationality change when you are abroad? Does it change in times of national crisis?

How much do any of these variables shift? How constant are they? Are you much more one thing at one time than at another? Is there some core 'you' that remains constant through time and situational change?

Socrates: Well, that's quite a list of questions. To tell you the truth, I haven't thought about it all that much. I suppose I have a sense of myself, something that is constant, something that is always still me, no matter what situation I'm in. I know that many of those things that you listed figure into that 'me' in some way, but I'm not exactly sure how. I'll give it some thought.

You know something though? This is more like what I thought philosophy was all about, asking and answering those sorts of questions. But I'm not sure how it connects up with our specific subject matter. I mean what do these questions have to do with the philosophy of social science?

G.O.D.: There are a great many connections. You remember that I presumed you were male because of the code-name you chose. Well, that is an aspect of identity that is chosen for us. There are male names and female names and a few that aren't gender-specific. Names certainly feature in relation to other people's ideas of us – even to expectations of what we might think, yes?

We touched on some of the issues related to this when discussing feminism. Well, let's carry on a little further with it. Gender seems to be a pretty fundamental category with respect to both how we conceive of ourselves and how others conceive of us. It is very much a social phenomenon insofar as gender is socially constructed. It is not something that is simply reducible to biological sex. And yet it is also a very personal thing. One of the most famous slogans of the 1960s women's liberation movement was that 'the personal is political'. The personal relations that women had with men and each other were understood to be socially constructed and therefore changeable. You can see that there are both ontological and political issues involved here. Yes?

Socrates: Yes.

G.O.D.: As a part of that political project women were attempting consciously to change their identities through a political/philosophical reflection upon the nature of what it means to be a woman. Their 'reconstructions of womanhood' were partially successful and partially not. That is, on a personal level, many women's lives, including importantly their conceptions of themselves, were profoundly changed. Society as a whole could be said to have also shifted profoundly with respect to some of its notions of gender. How much change actually occurred is debatable, but I think it is fair to say that much social change definitely occurred and also that many aspects of society stubbornly remained the same.

Sexism persists. Some of this is, of course, attributable to a power structure that opposed such fundamental social change. However, perhaps some blame could be laid at the doors of feminism itself. Some of it can be connected with issues of sociopolitical identity. Second-wave feminism articulated a notion of sisterhood as part of its reconstruction of female identity. But it was one that was soon perceived to be flawed.

Socrates: I'll certainly go along with that. But how so?

G.O.D.: Well, you actually put your finger on it yourself when you criticised feminist standpoint epistemology. You drew attention to a variety of other 'standpoints' that might be considered to be epistemologically privileged: race, class, sexuality and so on. Part of the feminist standpoint critique of the 'malestream' self-understanding of science was that it expressed as universal what was, in fact, only the partial vantage point of a particular social grouping. Under the guise of neutrality it actually represented a particular set of interests. Well, as your criticism implied, it appeared that feminists were doing the same thing. 'Woman' became an all-encompassing category that obscured some real and very important differences and interests between women.

Let me give you an obvious example. Women pressed for changes in legislation and company policies with respect to child-care provision so as to remove many of the obstacles to career development. They also attacked the ideology of the male breadwinner and the woman care and service provider roles. This went along with the critical attack upon the policies and ideology that prohibited female entry into traditionally male professions. This struggle was immensely successful. More and more areas of public life and career possibilities opened up to women.

But let us look at this in class terms. Middle-class women wanted to escape from the prison of the home to begin and continue careers, to enter 'public life'. They wanted someone to look after their children while they were doing this. Who was going to do it? Not their husbands! No, child-care would still be a female activity. It would just be done by other women . . . foreign women, black women, working-class women. Working-class women have always worked. They have run the home and worked outside it. The professional career barriers to women, with their related issues concerning child-care and so on, are not universal issues. Or rather they are issues that affect different groups differently.

All right, socialist feminism was there from the start in second-wave feminism. Socialist feminist analysis understood the relationship between capitalism and patriarchy quite differently from radical feminism. Marxist feminist analysis tended to see class structure and mode of production as predominant, while the radical feminists tended to see patriarchy as the dominant form of oppression. Political unity based upon different theoretical analyses has always been difficult. So there was a tension from the beginning between socialist feminists and radical feminists, and between both of these with liberal feminists. However, awareness of a much greater fragmentation began to surface with the black women's critique of feminism. It challenged the very notion of sisterhood upon which an ideology of feminist political unity depended.

Radical feminist theory locates the family as the primary site of patriarchal oppression. American black women objected strongly to this. It did not fit their experience. Home and family were sources of strength and bastions of support to American black women. Outside the home they faced a racist America. The home was if anything a refuge from oppression. Structural inequalities in America produced a situation whereby the black family, if not exactly matriarchal, at least had a structural interaction with patriarchy that was fundamentally different from the situation in which white middle-class American women found themselves. Black women identified more strongly with the struggle against racism. They felt more allied with their 'brothers'' struggle, than with that of their white 'sisters'.

I am drastically over-simplifying a complex history here as well as its accompanying theoretical issues and debates. But I think you can see a picture beginning to emerge. The over-reaching and essentialist notion of the identity of women as women began to seem increasingly inadequate. It distorted the plethora of different experiences, interests and subjective senses of identity possessed by those it was supposed to unite politically. If you remember the different issues we discussed earlier concerning cultural difference and judgment, you can see just how complicated the theoretical picture was becoming. Feminists were accused of everything from covert racism to ethnocentrism. They were accused of ideologically succumbing to the artificially constructed oppositions of patriarchy, i.e. of a kind of biological reductionism.

Gender is socially constructed and not reducible to biology. But if it is socially constructed, it is done so in the diverse contexts of an extremely complicated social reality. Women do not have a particular set of experiences of the family or anything else. This is variable according to class, race, ethnicity and even sexualities. A doctrine of pluralism emerged, and the charge of essentialism became the worst form of theoretical pejorative.

Socrates: I can see how this sort of thinking leads to problems concerning political activism and unity. 'Women of the world unite' becomes rather more difficult, if not impossible, once it is realised that they not only don't live in the same situations or have the same sorts of experiences but also have different interests in change. If they have radically different senses of self-identity, then you no longer have the basis upon which to unite politically. Yes, I see all that. In fact, it seems only obvious to me. I don't feel any great sense of unity with women who are performing clitorectomies upon one another. They live in a different world. I suppose I don't really care very much what they do there, as long as they don't want to do it to me. You see, I think this is only a problem for people like you.

G.O.D.: What, philosophers?

Socrates: No, feminists. So we're all different. It seems to me that that is how it should be. The categories you create are just straitjackets. You want to put us all into neat little boxes so you can change the world to suit your tastes. Actually, maybe it is philosophers who want to do that too. You've got some kind of passion for classification.

G.O.D.: Don't sociologists depend upon classification too? Do you really think theoretical classification is such a bad thing?

Socrates: Yes, I do. And maybe sociology doesn't have to be that way either.

G.O.D.: Hmm. It is interesting that you feel that way. I think you are going to have a great deal of sympathy for postmodernism. Perhaps you will like it for precisely the reasons I don't. It is seen by most of its proponents as being very radical politically. Yet ironically it seems to undermine the very possibility of radical change. Feminism is a case in point. Postmodernism's emphasis upon the differences, as opposed to the commonalties, in women's situations appears to be a very radical move. Yet it can just as easily be seen to uphold the status quo if it undermines the possibility of collective action based upon a notion of sisterhood.

Socrates: Aren't you committing a philosophical error here? You seem to be judging an epistemological position – postmodernism is an epistemological position, isn't it? – on the basis of its political implications. Shouldn't you be judging it on the basis of logical coherence and other philosophical criteria instead?

G.O.D.: Yes, you are quite right. However, that is not quite as straightforward as you might think. Yes, postmodernism is an epistemological position, or rather positions, as like all the points of view we have been discussing, there are many different takes upon it. But leaving these differences aside for the moment – that from a postmodernist perspective is a rather ironic thing to say – it is probably more accurate to describe postmodernism as an anti-epistemological position.

Socrates: What does that mean?

G.O.D.: Well, it can mean various things. But let us take it from the perspective you were taking a moment ago. You didn't like the way feminists and philosophers (and I added sociologists to the list) want to 'put people into boxes'. You would emphasise difference, plurality, the subjectivity and self-determination of individual identity. Yes? You liked the 'seeing is believing' idea inherent in the empiricist position, but you disliked its rigorous logical refinement in the form of positivism – another case of putting people into 'boxes'. You didn't like the imposition of value judgments upon another culture, except when you thought those cultural values were ridiculous. In short, it appears to me that you resent the necessity of being logically consistent. Postmodernism is somewhat similar to this: an anti-philosophy philosophy. That is why I think you'll like it. Not that that is the way postmodernists would describe themselves but . . .

Socrates: Now hold on. You're starting to accuse me of things again, of holding positions before I even know what they are. And you're becoming somewhat inconsistent yourself. You used to accuse me of being a positivist before. Actually, I'm not anything. Maybe I'll even become a feminist after I learn more about it. If I have logical inconsistencies in my 'position', it is probably because I don't really have a position yet. I'm just learning about these things. You're telling me these stories, and I know enough now to know that you're doing it from a somewhat biased perspective, and I'm somewhat sceptical of all of them. Some parts of these 'stories' seem to be true and some not. I'm just retaining some scepticism towards the overall picture each of them presents. I don't think I'm anti-philosophy. In fact, I'm just beginning to find it interesting. I can see now some of the effects it can have. But yes, I don't like being pigeonholed. What's wrong with that? Why do all these 'stories' have to fit together anyway? The world, as you say, is a complicated place. Who can say that they have the whole truth?

G.O.D.: You have just simultaneously articulated, and given empirical evidence for, the veracity of one postmodernist assertion anyway.

Socrates: I always knew I was good. Now tell me how I pulled off this double coup. What is this postmodernist assertion I made?

G.O.D.: We live in an age of scepticism towards **grand narratives**. Your own scepticism is evidence of that.

Socrates: What do you mean 'grand narrative'? I was using the word 'story' before in a very loose sense.

G.O.D.: Perhaps you were, but it provides a very good lead in to one postmodernist perspective at least. Language is very crucial to postmodernist views. You remember I told you that social science (and understandings of social science) had taken what came to be called 'the linguistic turn'? Well, postmodernism has taken this linguistic turn to extreme lengths. We are going to need to consider the relation of language to truth and reality and power from a number of different perspectives. One perspective, though, very crucially turns on an interpretation of all the various theoretical perspectives as quite literally being 'stories'.

There is the 'story of the Enlightenment'. There are various versions of it. But it links the emergence of science to the history of ideas and humanity's (Europe and America's at any rate) social, political and economic development. The growth of civilisation and a notion of progress form an integral part of this story. There are different versions of this story. Marxism, for example, would be one of these versions. It puts its own particular emphasis upon economic development but generally could be said to fit easily within this same overall narrative framework. The radical feminist versions of the historical development of patriarchy would be another such story. These 'stories' are theoretically all-encompassing. They perhaps don't explain all the detail of humanity's historical evolution, but the detail is expected to 'fit'. The 'story' can be modified, but its basic framework remains. This is the theoretical legacy of **modernism**. It produced, amongst other things, these grand narratives, metanarratives of the human condition.

Socrates: But isn't this simply another 'story'? I mean isn't this the 'story' postmodernists tell about the history of ideas, civilisation and our understanding of these things?

G.O.D.: Perhaps. I would definitely say so. But we will come back to that. First, let us look at its implication for science. Here I am giving you one book's particularly influential argument by the way – Jean Lyotard's *The Postmodern Condition: A Report on Knowledge*. He argues that science cannot validate itself. He appears here to accept some of positivism's perspective upon the separation of fact and value. But there is a very long-standing position in moral philosophy that asserts that you cannot derive ought from is.

Consider these two statements: 1) The door is open, and 2) Shut the door. They are of completely different orders. You cannot derive one from the other. The first is a statement of fact and may be true or false. The second is simply an imperative. It is neither true nor false, but rather it is a command that you obey or not.

Socrates: But the second must have some relation to the first. The command to shut the door, in order to be sensible at least, must be based upon at least the belief, if not the fact, that the door is open. The belief is thus related to the fact (or not) that the door is open. So they are connected.

G.O.D.: Yes, that is a very good point, and one that I will come back to, when I begin to give you some criticisms of postmodernist views. But you do see the sense in that they are quite different kinds of assertions? One is a statement about what is, the other about what ought to be done. Science, allegedly at least, tells us about what is. But it cannot speak to questions of value. Max Weber, amongst many others, also maintained this position, by the way. He believed that science was itself a value. So it cannot be said that Lyotard's position in this regard is in any way novel.

However, Lyotard goes on to ask, and answer, the questions concerning the source of this value. Science cannot legitimate itself (in its own terms) as a desirable social activity. That is not the sort of question with which it concerns itself. As Weber says, once a particular end is chosen, science can then help in determining the best means to arrive there, but it cannot pronounce upon the worth of the end itself. So, if the justification of the worth, value and desirability of science as a social activity cannot come from science itself, then the question arises as to just where the justification does come from. Lyotard argues that it comes from **narrative knowledge** that is expressive of social values.

We, society, tell ourselves stories. These serve to bind us together, to develop our senses of identity as members of a group and to transmit collective values. Narrative, then, is a form of knowledge. But it is a form of knowledge completely unlike scientific knowledge. Such knowledge would, in fact, be much more like the magic and witchcraft of the Azande. The problem is, Lyotard argues, that by the standards of science, such knowledge, that is narrative knowledge, is no knowledge at all! Science undermines its own legitimisation!

Socrates: He's arguing that the justification for science is not scientific and therefore pretty poor as a justification? We don't have good reasons for valuing science. But it goes on in spite of this. What's the problem?

G.O.D.:   Philosophical questioning, socio-economic and political developments, capitalism; Lyotard is a little unclear about exactly what the present-day mechanisms in operation are, that were not present previously, but at any rate we have now reached a situation whereby this insight has become all too apparent. That's the problem. It's not just that there is some kind of contradiction between scientific values and the value justification for science, but that collectively we have become aware of this. The old modernist stories are no longer believed! Capitalism and science together have contributed to the undermining of the ways in which they can be understood. Lyotard argues that we don't really have knowledge any more, at least knowledge in the sense of understanding. We have information – information unequally distributed throughout society. We have more or fewer pieces of the jigsaw puzzle, depending upon our access to information.

Socrates: So he's saying that no one has the whole picture? Some people have more of it than others. Capitalism, money, power, these determine who possesses access to information and who doesn't. That seems accurate enough as a description of how the world is. Again, I don't see the problem.

G.O.D.:   Yes, no one has the whole picture. No one knows everything.

There is no problem with that. As you say, that seems to be merely an accurate description of how things are. But that is not all there is to the argument. The picture not only looks different depending upon the perspective from which you are viewing it but may even be a completely different picture! It is not only that we don't have all the pieces of the jigsaw puzzle, but that not all of those that we do have fit together. The various theoretical perspectives, the informational 'facts' we possess, the stories we narrate are frequently radically incommensurable with one another. Irreducible differences remain. The important thing, so Lyotard argues, is to be tolerant of those differences, to keep dialogue open.

Socrates: I like that. What's wrong with it? In fact, it sounds to me a little bit like Habermas, only with more realistic expectations.

G.O.D.:   Actually, it is very unlike Habermas. He and Lyotard had many debates on precisely this issue. Habermas explains the sources of the different perspectives in terms of the distortive effects of power relations. He locates knowledge as arising from a finite number of fundamental human interests. Rational consensus exists as a theoretical possibility for him, however difficult it may be to achieve in reality. For Lyotard, the differences are irreducible.

Socrates: Okay, maybe I'm beginning to see the problem. What is the point of the dialogue if differences are never going to be overcome anyway?

G.O.D.: Well, Lyotard's answer would be that through continual dialogue we at least come to a greater (relative) understanding and thus greater tolerance of radically opposed points of view. But your question points to one of what I see as the many incoherent aspects of his philosophy. Interminable dialogue over irreconcilable difference seems to me merely to be a way of seconding diplomacy into the service of war, or worse, of seconding propaganda into the service of preserving power.

Habermas's point of view is much more optimistic (and coherent!). He sets our present power-distorted dialogues in both particular historical developments and fundamental aspects of the human condition. He grounds both dialogue and difference in an overall pattern that gives meaning to history through the identification of a purpose to knowledge: our common emancipatory interest in human freedom.

Socrates: It sounds to me both appealing and implausible. I just can't believe it. A good story, but I just can't buy it. Lyotard's depiction of irreducible and irreconcilable differences seems a lot more realistic.

G.O.D.: So you see your perspective on philosophy is rather like his. And it has the added virtue of being evidence for its veracity at the same time. You have bits and pieces of information that don't all fit together. Other people's bits of information may or may not fit with yours. This doesn't matter, because the time when such could all be put together to form a coherent understanding is now past – and was always illusory anyway. Such grand claims to knowledge belong to the age of modernity, and we are in a new period now. The human condition has become the postmodern condition. Knowledge is partial, fragmentary, contradictory. Our identities are diffuse, shifting and unstable.

Socrates: Wow. You're right, I do like postmodernism!

G.O.D.: I thought you would. But I haven't given it all to you as yet. I expect you will also really like Baudrillard's ideas. But I want to go back a bit first – to the linguistic turn. Both Winch and Lyotard were heavily influenced by Wittgenstein, but there is another source to our ideas about language that has been particularly influential in social science – the linguistic theory of Ferdinand de Saussure. It is upon his thinking that the school of thought known as **structuralism** was founded. And out of structuralism (more or less indirectly) came poststructuralism. Poststructuralism can be understood either as synonymous with postmodernism or not.

Socrates: I don't exactly know where I got this idea from, but I thought they were the same.

G.O.D.: It rather depends upon the attitude one takes to postmodernism – whether or not you are for or against it – and also the interpretations you accept and the judgments you make upon the quality of the insights of some of the seminal poststructuralist thinkers, two in particular: Michel Foucault and Jacques Derrida. Neither of them applied the label postmodernist to themselves. However, that is not at all decisive. Many postmodernists are disinclined to label their own work as such. The ideas associated with postmodernism are too loose and ill-defined for it even to be said to exist as a definite school of thought. It perhaps can be better understood as a rather nebulously floating intellectual orientation, loosely grouped together, insofar as they have a (often contradictory) connection to a number of specific arguments, propositions or key thinkers. It is something of a peculiar intellectual phenomenon. It undoubtedly exists but is difficult to pin down precisely – its rather negative attitude to pinning things down being precisely one of its characteristics.

Those sympathetic to postmodernism are not inclined to make a sharp distinction between poststructuralism and postmodernism. Those who are not impressed with the work of Foucault or Derrida are unlikely to be sympathetic to postmodernism either, and so are also likely to fail to make a distinction between poststructuralism and postmodernism. However, others would make a definite distinction.

Socrates: I have the feeling you're one of that last lot.

G.O.D.: Yes, I am. I am impressed with the work of both Foucault and Derrida but opposed to what I see as the fundamental effects of postmodernist theorising. I have my reservations about Foucault and Derrida as well but . . .

Socrates: Wait a moment. You haven't told me what's wrong with Lyotard yet. All you did was to contrast his thinking with Habermas's position. Was Habermas the only one to oppose Lyotard's account of postmodernity? Because if so, I'm afraid I really am a postmodernist. Habermas simply fails to convince me.

G.O.D.: You mean my rather potted account of his position fails to convince you. Perhaps if you actually read some of his own . . .

Socrates: Yeah, yeah. Of course. I will when I get the time.

G.O.D.: No, Habermas was not the only one to disagree with Lyotard. Many of the adherents of **Anglo-American analytic philosophy** simply never took either postmodernism in general, or Lyotard in particular, quite seriously. However, it did seem for a time that Habermas was the sole defender of Reason and the Enlightenment. As I said before, he describes modernity as an unfinished project. However, I'm going to give you plenty of criticisms of postmodernism. They'll be all the more potent, however, after I give you accounts of Derrida, Foucault and Baudrillard.

Socrates: Okay, let's start with Derrida then. He's a poststructuralist but not a postmodernist. Why isn't he one of the latter?

G.O.D.: This is a matter of interpretation but . . .

Socrates: Yes, yes, everything's a matter of interpretation. I wish you would just get straight to the point instead of always trying so hard to qualify what you're saying. I know all these things are subject to debate.

G.O.D.: I'm just trying to avoid misleading you. But okay. Neither Foucault nor Derrida are postmodernists by my definition because of where they stand on a particular fundamental issue. Or rather, because of their failure to take an explicit stand. The issue is truth. Both of them attack the issue obliquely through their work on different questions. These questions have appeared to some to provide definite answers of a most sceptical relativistic kind – the very reason why they are claimed by the postmodernist camp.

Socrates: So what you are saying is that postmodernists claim them as one of their own because of their position with respect to truth, and you would dispute that they actually hold such a position.

G.O.D.: Exactly. In order to make this clear I must give you some account of their thinking. But before I can do that I need to give you an account of another – Saussure. Structuralism before post-structuralism, yes?

Socrates: That seems logical.

G.O.D.: The 'linguistic turn' was profoundly affected by Saussure, perhaps more profoundly than by anyone else. He is widely regarded as the founder of modern linguistics and is also the originator of what has become known as semiotics or **semiology**. His understanding of language as a system of signs was expanded to a science of signs in general and applicable to many diverse fields – anthropology, psychoanalysis, film and media studies, and much else.

Socrates: Excuse me. What's a sign? Is it what I think it is?

G.O.D.: Notwithstanding the fact that I don't exactly know what you think it is, I would say yes and no. That is, yes, signs are all those things you probably see as signs in the world, either narrowly or more generally. So a stop sign is a sign. And so is a trembling hand frequently a sign of fear. However, there is a more technical understanding of the term as developed by Saussure. The explication of this is the key to understanding the revolutionary aspect of his theoretical accomplishment. A **sign** is the unity of **signifier** and **signified**.

The signifier is the sound, or visual mark, or mental impression of the sound or visual mark, which signifies to us a particular idea or image. When you read the letters grass, or hear the English word 'grass', what do you see in your mind?

Socrates: I see grass, long green stuff in front of the house, that maybe needs to be cut. That's the signified, eh? But wait a minute. You said written mark or sound. Those are signifiers. Fine. But you also said mental image of the written mark or sound. What do you mean?

G.O.D.: It is questionable how important this really is, but a lot of commentators on Saussure tend to forget it. You think in words and images. The written mark doesn't have to be actually physically written, it can just exist in your head, when you are composing a letter, perhaps you say the word to yourself before you write it. It is still a signifier whether physically manifest or not.

Socrates: I see.

G.O.D.: Much more importantly, you should not confuse the mental image of the signified with the **referent**.

Socrates: The referent?

G.O.D.: Yes, that real, physically existing, green plant growing in front of somebody's house. The signified is not that reality. Rather it is the mental image provoked by the signifier. A sign is the unity of signifier and signified.

Socrates: I see. So what is the relationship to the referent then?

G.O.D.: Well that in fact is controversial, very controversial. Some misinterpretations of Saussure tend to equate the signifier and the referent. This has quite important implications concerning truth. Saussure produced a theory of linguistic structure and meaning that has since been extended beyond its original remit to promote a particular version of epistemological relativism. Derrida, in fact, is often cited as a principal architect of this. However, we'll leave that for a moment.

The important thing for now is to understand Saussure's theory of language as a **system of differences**. Prior to Saussure, linguistics was principally a **diachronic** study. It concerned itself with linguistic change, the origins and derivations of words and so on.

Socrates: Diachronic means change over time?

G.O.D.: Yes, and **synchronic** means the direct opposite: without change over time. Saussure inaugurated the synchronic study of language, that is, the study of the structure of language. Now, of course, he was well aware that languages change; he simply bracketed that aspect of their existence off in order to analyse linguistic structure.

Socrates: What do you mean he 'bracketed it off'?

G.O.D.: Bracketing is a methodological device used by both philosophy and science. It is simply a useful way of dealing with unwieldy complexity. We perform an abstraction whereby an intentional over-simplification is made.

Socrates: I thought over-simplifying was bad.

G.O.D.: It depends on how it is done and for what purpose. Accidentally or unconsciously over-simplifying is likely to lead you to mistaken and over-simplified conclusions. However, if one does so consciously, and for a purpose, it can be a productive intellectual tool. When we bracket off a feature of some phenomenon we are wishing to understand, we are doing so only abstractly and temporarily in order to isolate the aspects of the phenomenon we are particularly interested in. This is what Saussure was doing when he conceptually divided language in two. He divided language into **langue** and **parole**. Langue was the structure of language. Parole, roughly translated, means speech. Actually reading or writing words, or actually speaking or listening, is parole. All the actual utilisation of language humans engage in would fall within the conceptual category of parole. Saussure chose not to concern himself with this. He argued that parole, all the actual language usage that ever was, or ever would be, is dependent upon langue. Langue is the structure of language, which at any given moment in time is required in order for meaning to be produced. Any actual speech presupposes the existence of a linguistic structure: syntax, grammar and so forth.

Socrates: So Saussure was a grammarian?

G.O.D.: No, not exactly. The grammarian studies the structure of particular languages. Saussure propounded a theory whereby such structures facilitate the production of meaning. Essentially, he produced a theory of the structure of such structures.

Socrates: Structure of structures? I don't know what you mean by that at all.

G.O.D.: Well, every language has its own syntactical rules, its own grammar, but Saussure's analysis is more fundamental. It explains how language, that is langue, is a system of differences, because the essential relationship between signifier and signified is arbitrary!

Socrates: What do you mean arbitrary?

G.O.D.: Well, let's consider Chinese pictogram writing. It has evolved over the years but originally the symbols resembled what they signified. That is, the pictogram character signifying house rather 'looked like' a house. It is a two-dimensional representation of a three-dimensional object to be sure, but still it 'pictures' the object.

Okay, another example: the sound of the word 'quack'. This is perhaps not a very accurate imitation of the sound ducks make, but nonetheless the similarity is more or less recognisable.

Socrates: What's arbitrary about that? Your examples don't seem arbitrary at all!

G.O.D.: Exactly. They're not. They are also unusual cases that do not express at all the basic relationship between signifiers and signifieds – that is, one of arbitrariness. Another way of putting it is that signifiers and signifieds bear no relationship to one another at all, other than that which is maintained by institution and convention.

Consider these two words and the letters that compose them: bag and fag. There is nothing intrinsic to the letters b, a and g that connects them up to our English language understanding of a particular kind of container. But put a b in front of the letters a and g, and we get this very particular meaning. Put an f in front of them instead and you get . . .

Socrates: You get the English colloquial expression for a cigarette. Bag and fag; how do you come up with these examples?

G.O.D.: Well, the one everybody seems to use is cat and mat. I got bored with it. Don't get distracted by absurdity. What is the significant thing concerning the letter f with respect to meaning?

Socrates: I don't know, nothing I guess.

G.O.D.: Nothing in itself! But it is significant insofar it is not b or c or o or g or any of the other letters of the alphabet. It stands in a relationship of difference to all the rest. The meaning derives from the fact that it is what it is and that it is not one of the others. The way in which letters or words or sounds may be combined with one another in order to generate meaning composes the structure of language. There are particular rules that govern the way the elements may combine and stand in relation to one another. These rules vary from one language to another but are present in all. Not all combinations are possible. But a potentially infinite number of combinations is possible nevertheless.

Socrates: Isn't that a contradiction?

G.O.D.: No. What does 'eht truck red fly ylf' mean? Nothing. There are rules in English (and in every language) that govern word order to be a possible sentence. Only certain combinations of letters form real words. There is a finite number of words in English at any given time. New words may come into existence and others fade away from current usage, but some combinations of sounds (or letters) are simply not English words. Nevertheless, the number of possible sentences, and combinations of sentences, that we may use to convey meaning is still potentially infinite.

Any particular utterance or written sentence, that is, any particular instantiation of parole, is dependent upon the structure of langue in order for meaning to be produced. We select from a range of vocabulary, cats or mats, fags or bags, or whatever, and put them together in a rule-governed way so as to convey our intended meaning.

All fluent speakers of a language 'know' these rules. They may not know them in the manner of a grammarian, i.e. the names for the parts of speech and the rules governing the relation between subject, predicate, adverbial clauses and so on. But they know them tacitly, practically. The potential for the creation of meaningful sentences depends upon this structural aspect of language. It depends on such tacit knowledge. Non-native speakers of a language will often make mistakes concerning word order, for example. Such mistakes can make the intended meaning of a sentence completely indecipherable.

Socrates: Yes, I see. The entire structure of a language is present at any given moment. It somehow exists prior to any particular example of language usage. The signifiers produce meaning, not through any resemblance to what they signify, but simply by not being something else in the system of differences that is the structure of the language. Is that it? I'm convinced, and I think I understand. I'm putting it that way, because though I find the argument convincing, it still has an aspect of oddity to it. It's the idea of 'difference' that strikes me as somehow peculiar. What about your first examples, the ones where the relation between signifier and signified seem not so arbitrary?

G.O.D.: Well, as I said they are a limited case. And perhaps there is some element of arbitrariness to them as well. When we imagine pictograms 'looking like' something it perhaps conceals a greater element of conventionality than one might first think. We are so used to interpreting two-dimensional images of three-dimensional objects in our culture, that we are inclined to naturalise this skill, to forget that it is a learned capability. Perhaps, if we examined more closely the Chinese symbol for house, we'd see that it doesn't look so very like one at all. That non-Chinese readers can recognise it as doing so speaks well for shared cross-cultural understanding. But it doesn't mean that such a symbol would be recognised universally.

A more amusing way of making this point would be to point out that apparently the sound French cows make is not 'moo' but something else. This perhaps says something as well about the present state of Franco-Anglo relations.

Socrates: What? You're kidding.

G.O.D.: I'm kidding. You may well think I'm kidding about the next thing as well. It has an absurd side to it; yet a perfectly serious point is there as well. Anyway, we'll see what you think of it in a moment. First, one last point about Saussure. He believed that this structural understanding of language, understanding it as a system of signifiers and signifieds, of differences, could be extended well beyond the sphere of what we ordinarily consider to be language. That is, it could be extended to any system of signs. Do you remember Winch's argument that understanding social phenomena is much more like understanding a language than explaining the working of a machine?

Socrates: Yes.

G.O.D.: Well, in some sense, virtually all social phenomena can be conceived of as a 'text', the particular product of a system of signs. Saussure intended his linguistic science as the particular case of a more general science of signs. Others made good his pioneering hope. Such a science now exists: semiology. A **semiotic** analysis of an amazing variety of social phenomena has been carried out.

Socrates: This is structuralism? Are structuralism and semiology (or semiotics) the same thing?

G.O.D.: Not exactly. Structuralism utilises the notion of structural relationships of difference as its prime theoretical orientation. It is thus more general. One can, in the field of anthropology for instance, discuss the structure of societies in terms of possible kinship relationships, as did Levi-Strauss. The science of signs, though, has been developed in different ways in film theory, psychoanalysis and other fields. Poststructuralism gives it a particular twist, a twist that may or may not be understood to be implicit within Saussure's work. Are you ready for this? It contains the element of absurdity I warned you about.

Socrates: Sure. Go for it.

G.O.D.: What do you do when you wish to know the meaning of a word you don't know?

Socrates: I look in a dictionary.

G.O.D.: And what would you do if within the dictionary entry there were one or more words that you also failed to understand, yet they were necessary to grasp the meaning of the definition?

Socrates: I'd look them up as well.

G.O.D.: And what if the same thing happened again. And again? And again?

Socrates: Okay. I'd be in an ongoing quest for meaning. But I think it would end sooner or later. Is that the point? That it would never end?

G.O.D.: Well, we're going in that direction. Consider this proposition; every signified is itself a signifier in another system of signification.

Socrates: What does that mean?

G.O.D.: Just a minute. I'm going to try to tell you by means of a self-demonstrative example. Did you understand the meaning of all the words in the proposition?

Socrates: Yes.

G.O.D.: And the way they were combined in the sentence?

Socrates: Yes.

G.O.D.: The whole sentence made sense to you?

Socrates: Yes.

G.O.D.: Yet you still asked me what it meant?

Socrates: Yes. I both understood what it meant on one level, and didn't, on another.

G.O.D.: Right. You were waiting, waiting for more words, in order to make complete the meaning of those that went before.

Socrates: I suppose so. Yeah. I was waiting for you to clarify what you said.

G.O.D.: Okay, another example. 'Jim Powell was a Jelly-bean'. Do you understand the meaning of that sentence? Do you know what a jelly bean is?

Socrates: Uh, yeah, I think so. A jelly bean is an American candy.

G.O.D.: That's right.

Socrates: Okay, so that sentence doesn't really make sense. Not on its own anyway. Jelly bean must mean something else.

G.O.D.: Yes, and you would know this if you were a part of a particular sub-cultural world at a particular time but very likely not otherwise. The sentence is in fact the opening to an F. Scott Fitzgerald story entitled *The Jelly-Bean*. He goes on to explain what one is in that particular context through his story. You have to wait to get the meaning. You have to wait before the signified connects up with the signifier. You not only have to wait for Fitzgerald to give you his description of its cultural meaning and definition; but really to understand that sentence, you have to read the whole story! And then afterwards think about it a bit.

Socrates: Excuse my impatience. But how long do I have to wait in order to get your meaning?

G.O.D.: Well, that is just the point. The deferral of meaning. Every signified is itself a signifier on another level, in another system. Meaning is given immediately but also deferred as these various levels are unfolded. The process is in theory infinite. Or at least, so Derrida would argue. He has developed a concept that performatively demonstrates this – its own meaning. The concept is called '**differance**'. Language is indeed a structured order of difference with respect to signifiers and signifieds. But incorporated into the very structure of language (langue, not parole) is a kind of temporality, the deferral of closure of meaning because of the signified's work as a signifier in another system of difference. Do you see?

Socrates: Not exactly. What's 'differance'? Did you make a spelling mistake?

G.O.D.: No. I didn't. But if we were speaking in French that would make no difference. In fact that is part of the point. This term, 'differance' (Derrida insists that it is both more and less than a concept), is pronounced identically to the French word for difference. In order to know what word is being used, one must wait for it to be contextualised, and this aspect of deferral to later contextualisation is in fact the meaning of the word. Its meaning is thus performative.

Socrates: Okay, I see its performative nature. I understand what it means.

But I'm still awaiting the full significance of where this is leading. We need to await contextualisation to understand fully the meaning of anything said or written. That seems obvious enough, but so what? I seem to be saying 'so what' to a lot of things. Is this me being stupid? Or is it that a lot of these distinctions that seem so important to you philosophers just aren't that important really?

G.O.D.: It's definitely not you being stupid. I do think, however, that subtlety, complexity, fine distinctions, things that are not immediately obvious, can nonetheless be very important. The fact that meaning deferral process is, in theory at least, infinite, means that full precise meaning is never achievable. I think that is very important if it is true. Derridean poststructuralists playfully assert (and/or seriously assert) that one can never really say what one means, or mean what one says. There is only the infinite play of signification, the juxtaposition of difference and deferral. I think that is a very significant claim.

Socrates: All right, meaning is always imprecise. I see that that is important, but not that important. Is that the major significance of this line of thinking? How are these ideas actually used? And just to keep us on the subject: how does all of this relate to the philosophy of science? In Lyotard's case the connection seemed clear enough, but this escapes me.

G.O.D.:   Derrida developed a technique for a particular form of analysis; well, again he and his followers would maintain that it is something much more than a technique, but at least it can be most easily explained as a technique – the technique of deconstruction. But first consider this. If we can conceive of many or most aspects of social reality as a 'text', a sign system that can be 'decoded' as it were, and if we are to believe that this is actually the best way to conceive of many aspects of social reality, then semiology should rightfully become the dominant mode of social scientific analysis. Yes?

Socrates: If . . . if it is the best way to understand social life.

G.O.D.:   Yes, well it certainly would be the case, if the argument could successfully be made that the whole of social reality is actually reducible to a form of textuality.

Socrates: Again that's a big if.

G.O.D.:   Yes, it certainly is. Now let's take this one step further. If we take seriously, and I think we must, this notion of signifieds themselves being signifiers, then rather than social reality being merely a text, it becomes a complex weave of inter-textuality – because that is what all texts are. The impossibility of the achievement of closure of meaning, its inherently slippery nature, thus places severe limits upon the possibilities of knowledge production, upon the authoritativeness of any claims to truth.

Socrates: Yes, I see that. It sounds like a very negative program.

G.O.D.:   Yes, many have thought so. Many have conceived of it as wholly destructive. And on a certain level they are entirely right to do so. Deconstruction has now so far entered the English language lexicon that many people now use it virtually synonymously with the word 'analysis'. This is a gross misuse of the term. Whether it is merely a technique or not, it is a very particular form of technique, with quite definite implications. One is going down the wrong road with deconstruction, as it were, if one thinks of it in terms of taking something apart to see how it fits together, so as the better to understand the meaning it has. It is more akin to taking something apart in such a fashion that it can never be put back together. Derrida has accordingly likened deconstruction to a computer virus.

It is thus quite right to see it as destructive. However, how one conceives of that destruction is dependent first upon how successfully one thinks of it as having been done, and second, whether one conceived of that which was deconstructed as being mainly a good or bad thing.

Socrates: I think you're getting ahead of yourself. It's getting a little too abstract. I think you'd better tell me what the technique is and then give me an example of what it is applied to. I think that's the only way I can make any sense, let alone make any judgments, about what you're talking about.

G.O.D.: All right, meaning derives from a system of differences – and deferrals. Derrida argues that what we have in most (all?) discourses is a series of binary oppositions, in that one term always occupies the dominant position. The meaning of the other term is suppressed or marginalised. You might wish to reflect back upon the discussions we had concerning feminism for examples of such oppositions. The deconstructive method is to take the marginalised term and reverse the order of dominance, thus demonstrating that the apparent meaning of the text in question is in fact dependent upon precisely the meaning of that which it suppresses. This radically transforms forever the meaning of the text. This is all the more potent and permanently destructive because centralising what is marginal is allegedly done in such a manner as to show that it always did occupy a position of centrality – this fact was merely hidden, so to speak. Thus, the deconstructive technique is only revealing what was there all along. The texts, as it were, deconstruct themselves.

Socrates: That sounds rather paradoxical to me.

G.O.D.: Yes, it is rather, and in a very subtle elusive manner, very difficult to argue against. Deconstruction shows in the texts that it analyses, a kind of circularity inherent within them – circularity that undermines the stated intentions and conclusions of the text in question. Frequently, deconstruction demonstrates textual **aporias** with respect to meaning. This would seem to be inevitable if the dominant terms emphasised in the text always are in fact dependent for their meaning upon the meaning of the terms they suppress.

I'll give you one of Derrida's examples that demonstrates the full import of this, and that perhaps also illustrates the rather grandiose nature of some of his claims as well. With respect to language, Derrida argues, speech has always been the dominant term; writing is held to be derivative of speech, i.e. writing is a mere representation of the more fundamental nature of language – the spoken word. The entire history of Western philosophy, Derrida argues, is premised upon this notion. It is, in his terms, '**phonocentric**' and '**logocentric**'. Derrida makes an argument for reversing this opposition. As Western philosophy, he argues, is so dependent upon logocentrism, it is thus irredeemably flawed.

Socrates: I can see an affinity here with Lyotard – the emphasis upon difference, a kind of scepticism concerning knowledge, a way in which he identifies Western philosophy as playing a particular kind of language game. Yes, I can see why some people wish to label him a postmodernist. In fact, I don't see why you don't.

G.O.D.:   I wouldn't deny that at least superficially the affinities are there. However, I didn't give you the detail, for example, of Derrida's speech/writing argument. We perhaps don't have time to go into it here, but I think it is far more powerful than Lyotard's argument about narrative knowledges and scientific legitimacy. However, I also don't think Derrida succeeds in problematising the whole of Western philosophy. Rather I believe he problematises the notion of meaning and linguistic structure as derived from Saussurian linguistics. The suppressed term, to use Derrida's own terminology, is reference. There is signifier, signified and referent. Saussure, if you remember, bracketed off the issue of reference. And if you also remember, bracketing is only supposed to be a temporary measure. The complexity of reality thereby removed from the abstraction is meant to be later reintroduced in the form of a more complete explanation. It seems that many people thought that this issue had already been satisfactorily dealt with. Or they confused and conflated the signified with the referent, or simply forgot about it altogether.

Socrates: Just so I don't make the same mistake – the signified is not the real world referent, it is our mental image or idea that is provoked by the signifier.

G.O.D.:   Right. The question of meaning is tackled both in structuralism and poststructuralism in a wholly social constructionist manner. Essentially, language games determine reality. Even more fundamentally, one could say that they are reality. There is thus little point in attempting to make comparative judgments between competing accounts. Derrida has apparently happily embraced the form of relativism that so troubled Winch full on. The key word there is apparently.

First, he never precisely articulates this conclusion; so whether the implicit conclusion troubles him or not is hard to say. He is in fact rather ambiguous. He says things like: 'We must inhabit logocentrism'. Second, his arguments, whether overly grandiose in their ambition or not, very definitely are successful in demonstrating some profound insights along the way. In fact, and this is the third point, they implicitly point out the need for a realist ontology to be incorporated within a theory of meaning and language. Derrida's poststructuralism takes us beyond the limits of adequacy of structuralist semiology and linguistics. The notion of the **floating signifier** has been taken beyond where it enlightens.

Socrates: Floating signifier?

G.O.D.:   Yes, signifiers that have a wide diversity of signifieds upon a variety of different levels, signifiers that are doing a plethora of different things at the same time. The simplest level upon which we can see that sort of phenomenon would be with the 'double entendre' – a word is used that has a simple practical meaning but also has perhaps a sexual connotation as well. Humour occasionally results, though perhaps not as often as the English seem to think. Floating signifiers multiply such effects; symbols lose a definite shared meaning and mean different things to different groups, different individuals; they mean many different things simultaneously, as well as changing their meaning over time. They have no definite signifieds; they 'float' indeterminately. This notion, while undoubtedly expressing some truth about the nature of signification, has been taken so far as to imply that there are no limits to the 'floating' process. But this is not true. Reality itself imposes limits upon possible meanings of signifiers.

Socrates: I don't quite see what you mean by that. Unicorn is a meaningful word. The fact that it is an imaginary being makes no difference. Where does reality come into it?

G.O.D.: Not in that way. Trust me, it does though. No, never mind. Don't trust me. Just be patient. I want to leave realism until last. I will attempt to tie everything together with it; then you can take it or leave it as you choose. There is still more to be said about postmodernism. First of all, there is Foucault to be considered. Actually before we can consider Foucault we need to consider another postmodernist thinker: Nietzsche. Actually if you look again at the epigraphs at the beginning of this chapter you will find a perfect juxtaposition of the modernist and postmodernist perspectives on truth, with the modernist view represented by Freud and the postmodernist view represented by Nietzsche.

Socrates: Isn't he a nineteenth-century figure? How can he be a postmodernist?

G.O.D.: He is a postmodernist *'avant la lettre'*. Actually, if we think of it from Baudrillard's point of view, the very notion of temporal historical succession collapses. But we had better leave that for a minute.

Socrates: That's fine with me. But what does *'avant la lettre'* mean?

G.O.D.: Literally it means 'before the letter'. Thus, Nietzsche was a postmodernist before his time, so to speak, or rather, before its time. Nietzsche had a rather neat and simple solution to the problem with truth. It is absolutely brilliant in its simplicity.

Socrates: What's that then? Is it simple enough that you can state it without first making all sorts of apologies for over-simplifying?

G.O.D.: I'll ignore your sarcasm. Yes, I think I can. He simply denies that we are really interested in truth at all. On one level, at least, and according to Nietzsche the most important level at that, truth is simply irrelevant. What is important to people is power. We all possess a 'will to power'. Some are strong and some are weak; in fact most are weak. Claims to truth are simply strategies in struggles for power. We must look at claims to truth carefully, suspiciously, so as to detect what really lies underneath them. What we find is not better or worse arguments or theories, in the sense of some being truer than others or more accurately describing reality. No, what we find is that better or worse arguments masquerading as truth are really only better or worse in the sense of rhetorical strategies, modes of presentation and powers of persuasion.

The brief synopsis that I have presented to you here would be a case in point. It is not at all how a Nietzschean would present his case. Nietzsche's own writing is a tour de force, a dazzling display of arrogance and wit – far more convincing. Philosophers have produced good writing and bad, clear straightforward expositions of very complex and subtle thought, and also jargon-laden convoluted prose as thick as porridge. But elegance, style and wit are rather rare in philosophical writing.

Socrates: I've noticed!

G.O.D.:   Yes, Nietzsche's philosophy is a work of art. One could say that he aestheticises philosophy, and doing so is very much a postmodernist virtue. But with respect to truth one can see here resonances with or a philosophical precursor for Wittgenstein's notion of language games – except that these games are expressions of the life struggle. Nietzsche was the first to develop what has been called a 'hermeneutic of suspicion'. Language is not held to be a neutral instrument. Power relations are embedded within it. One can see here resonances of Derrida's critique of Western philosophy's metaphysical heritage; he too demonstrates what could be termed a 'hermeneutic of suspicion'.

Socrates: Does Derrida write in this same sort of dazzling style?

G.O.D.:   Well, I'm not sure he even tries to. Perhaps some of his most devoted admirers might think so. But I think even amongst his supporters the consensus would be that if he tried, he most certainly failed. One would find more people making such a claim for Foucault, though I don't think many would claim he achieves Nietzsche's brilliance in this regard. His work, however, is in other respects perhaps the most contemporary manifestation of Nietzschean philosophy concerning truth.

Socrates: He denies the existence of truth then? Or the importance of asking questions about it?

G.O.D.:   Yes and no. He is rather ambiguous and arguably inconsistent.
Thus, realists, postmodernists and others can all make quite compelling claims for interpreting him one way or another based upon textual exegesis. On one level, from our point of view here, he simply sidesteps the whole issue by asserting that questions as to the validity of truth claims are not the most important things for contemporary society to address. Like Nietzsche, the important questions are those concerning power relations. However, such questions are transformed

in Foucault's work into more sociological and historical questions. Foucault hyphenates the concepts of knowledge and power. They form for him a single concept: **power-knowledge**. He examines the historical emergence and analyses the structure of discursive structures.

Socrates: The structure of discursive structures?

G.O.D.: Yes. Discourses do not simply float about in the world. They do not emerge as the individual products of individual producers. Knowledge is not the individual possession of an individual subject as knower. Rather there are what he terms '**regimes of truth**'. In his *Archaeology of Knowledge* he provides for us the rules of the formation of **discursive formations**.

Socrates: Regimes of truth? The rules of formation for discursive formations? I'm getting a glimmer here of what you're talking about, but you are going to have to be more specific.

G.O.D.: Yes, of course. Foucault's work is basically of two sorts. Familiarity with one sort is a distinct aid in coming to an understanding of the other. He develops his ideas abstractly and with a higher degree of generality in some works, while in others he provides a more specific concrete historical tracing of the emergence of these 'regimes of truth'. **Genealogy** is the term he uses for the tracing of the institutional development and disciplinary exercise of power concurrent with sets of ideas. For example, he traces the history of madness or rather the idea of madness. The notions of sanity and insanity, as behaviours and pathological forms of cognition, socially emerged as a set of material practices, institutionally defined disciplines complete with an entire range of theoretical concepts, tools and rules of judgmental criteria. Their practices, which are quite distinctly manifestations of power, are inseparable from the knowledges produced, including the criteria and standards of truth and knowledge. He does the same thing with respect to criminality and the penal system, human sexuality and so on. In all of these cases, he demonstrates how claims to truth are claims to power as well, and how the exercise of power carries with it a legitimation in terms of knowledge and truth claims.

Socrates: I see. Or rather, I think I do. So is he saying there is no such thing as madness or criminality, then?

G.O.D.: Not exactly. There are social behaviours, modes of cognition, that individuals display and that are categorised and labelled. We actually only know and understand such behaviours and modes of cognition through the manner in which they are categorised and labelled. There is a whole disciplinary array of conceptual apparatuses and practices through which this is done. This is, of course, an exercise of power through both knowledge and the practical techniques that accompany it.

Socrates: This is sounding very relativistic with respect to truth. People define rather than discover truth.

G.O.D.: Well, not actually people, or certainly not only 'people'. Foucault is often labelled a theoretical anti-humanist. This is because the very notion of individual subjectivity is transformed. The exercise of power, understood correctly, is inseparable from its actual practices. These have a history (or genealogy) that pre-exist us. Individuals do not think outside such frameworks of understanding. We are subjected to the disciplines, the regimes of truth. They penetrate us, form us as well as our understandings of ourselves. This is so even of our most intimate and personal thoughts and behaviours; for example, our sexuality.

Socrates: You keep inserting the term genealogy alongside the word history. What is the difference between the two?

G.O.D.: Well, genealogy is a much more modest term actually. Foucault wished to disassociate himself from the teleology connected with many of our understandings of history. He also wished to direct our attention away from the attempt to specify deeper, more all-encompassing accounts of broader structural processes as somehow underlying the specific conditions of development of the various areas of human life he investigated. Again, he always emphasised that questions concerning power could not be separated from the actual mechanisms whereby it was manifested. Likewise with knowledge, of course.

Socrates: Right. What's teleology again? And isn't the last bit contradictory with what you said earlier concerning structure, the rules of formation of discursive formations and so on?

G.O.D.: There has been a tendency to ascribe a purpose to human history, or if not exactly a purpose, to see it in terms of possessing an underlying direction, as a process in which we might determine the general 'laws' of its development. And you're quite right there is a contradictory aspect to his thought. This direction of our attention to the observably specific and localised manifestations of power, and his admonitions against attempts to describe phenomena in such terms as, for example, 'underlying historical tendencies', is one of the reasons why his work can be given an empiricist interpretation and labelling as well. As I said before, it rather depends upon which texts of his you read and how you choose to interpret his apparent inconsistencies.

Socrates: All right. The way I'm interpreting him, then, at least from your account of his work, is as a social constructionist. He would be a conventionalist with respect to the philosophy of science. Is this a 'respectable' interpretation of his work?

G.O.D.: Were you being self-consciously ironical in asking if your interpretation is respectable? Yes, it is, though of course it is something of an over-simplification.

Socrates: Of course! But what about nature, natural science? Where does he stand there? The social constructionist, or conventionalist notion of

| | knowledge and reality, somehow seems much more plausible when restricted to the social domain of reality. It possesses a dimension of absurdity when applied to nature. |

G.O.D.: Well, the boundary between these two domains is perhaps not so absolute as sometimes is supposed. In Foucault's work this is most obvious with respect to medical knowledges.

Socrates: Okay, I can see how that might work.

G.O.D.: Perhaps it is worth a brief digression from poststructuralism for a moment to consider briefly the sociology of science, particularly the so-called '**strong program of the sociology of science**'. It's perhaps not such a big digression, as poststructuralist-influenced semiological analysis has been very influential upon their work. Presently there exists an interdisciplinary dispute that has come to be called '**science wars**'.

Socrates: That sounds very Foucauldian or Nietzschean. Two disciplines duking it out in a struggle for power.

G.O.D.: It can be seen in that light, though to do so obscures some of the facts of co-operation and goodwill on both sides – though, of course, examples of hostility and bad temper are easy enough to find as well. The 'strong program' takes a very extreme interpretation of Kuhn's notion of paradigm and has proceeded to attempt to demonstrate it, not so much historically as in contemporary sociological research into the actual practices of the physical sciences. They observe laboratory work and communicative interchanges between scientists and so on. Their empirical investigation and discourse analysis of scientific communication in most cases support a sociological explanation of changes in scientific conclusions, interpretations of data and so on. That is, in its most extreme version, it propounds a sociologically reductionist account of the construction of scientific knowledges.

Socrates: You mean that changes in the scientific community's generally agreed theories about the way nature works can be explained entirely in terms of the social relations of the group of people involved?

G.O.D.: In the most extreme cases, yes, exactly so. You remember from earlier discussions that there is a problem with respect to observation statements?

Socrates: For positivism and empiricism, yes. Their account of science seems to depend very crucially upon their neutrality, upon there being uncontested assertions about what are 'facts' about the world. But the problem is that observations, and even more obviously statements about observations, are 'theory-laden'. But I thought that that was only positivism's problem. And you told me that even the positivists have realised it as a problem and taken steps to deal with it.

G.O.D.: Well, it is not only positivism's problem . . . and whether the steps they have taken to deal with it are adequate is another question. The 'strong program' in the sociology of science implicitly posits another way of dealing with it. But the problems with their way of dealing with it become all too apparent. You see, the point of their research program, at least ostensibly, is not simply to be destructive, but to be of some aid to the scientists whom they are studying. They show the gap between the scientists' reconstructions of what they are doing (usually cast in positivistic terms) and what they are actually doing – as viewed objectively by the sociologists.

Socrates: 'Viewed objectively' by the sociologists?

G.O.D.:   There, you see, you've got to the heart of the problem immediately. The accounts of what has taken place given by sociologists and, say, physicists for example, differ enormously. The procedures of repetition, and thus confirmation of experimental results (including of course confirmations of falsifications) according to many sociologists of science, don't actually seem to take place in the way they are alleged to. The 'objectively made' observations seem to be made differently by different laboratory teams for example.

Socrates: How so?

G.O.D.:   Well, modern science is a very complex business. Very little is now done by single scientists carrying out single experiments leading to sudden dramatic breakthroughs. Scientific work is carried out by vast teams of workers carrying out huge numbers of experiments, observations, selections and exclusions of data. A problem for empiricism, which I don't think we touched on before, is that of the use of instruments; that is, in essence, when we look at something invisible to the naked eye but visible to a microscope, do we count it, philosophically speaking, as a sensory observation or not? This constituted a philosophical problem for empiricists, if not for scientists themselves, who, of course, were quite willing to rule pragmatically in the observational results of increasingly sophisticated equipment. However, the very heights of complex development of such equipment have magnified the problem. Magnified it philosophically, that is, as scientists have taken the very same pragmatic attitude towards this. Computer modelling now plays an enormous role in physics.

All right, I don't want to go into too much detail here, but the complexity of modern scientific research has so far transformed scientific activity that it doesn't look very much at all like the recipe-following procedures of school kid chemistry experiments. Procedures are of course replicated, observations confirmed or not, by different research teams. But the element of selection in this procedure has magnified immensely.

So the disagreement between the two sides in the science wars essentially comes down to this: one side believes that the new techniques, the increased complexity of instrumentalisation, reliance upon modelling, interpretation of 'raw' data etc., is simply that:

increased complexity. They believe that the process of scientific agreement, disagreement, the building of consensus is an objective fact based on communicative enterprise. They are aware that subjective factors may sometimes come into play. But they also believe that there are guiding rules, norms of scientific procedure, in place to minimise this. The other side analyses carefully what actually occurs, in terms for example of discourse analysis, and demonstrates that what is allegedly happening (alleged by the scientists) is not! Rather something else is occurring – a competition of competing stories, whereby the rules of scientific procedure and so on are used as tropes in discursive strategies.

Socrates: Tropes? Never mind. Okay, if I understand you correctly, the two sides are simply using a different vocabulary to describe the same activities. Yes? The physicists are analogously in the position of the Azande in Winch's example. They are having their meaningful social actions re-described in sociological language. They don't like it. But so what? I don't see what the problem is. The Azande probably didn't much like the anthropologists' accounts either.

G.O.D.: There are a few more problems actually. I don't know whether the Azande liked or not the anthropological accounts that were given of them. But we could speculate as to whether they would or not and presume that if they could understand them they wouldn't – simply because these secondary accounts, implicitly or explicitly, very frequently challenge the veracity of their own.

Socrates: Yes, that's what I was getting at. But so what if they disagree?

G.O.D.: In the science wars case, there is no question about it. Many of the scientists find the language of discourse analysis well nigh unintelligible, but they certainly understand the conclusion, i.e. sociological reductionism. They understand it, and they wholeheartedly reject it. They also see a contradiction within the sociology of science enterprise. That is, they see the sociologists' claims concerning what is going on in scientific communication, for example, to be a claim to greater objectivity. Yet the majority of sociologists pursuing the strong program in the sociology of science are disputing the very possibility of objectivity as such. Scientists would see the sociologists' substantive claims as conflicting with their more general claims about the nature of communication and knowledge.

Socrates: This is basically the first-order and second-order knowledge claims problem, yes?

G.O.D.: Yes.

Socrates: If the second-order explanation is merely in different terms from that of the first order, then the question arises as to what is the point of merely re-describing in other terms what the participants already know. But if the second-order explanation is not merely a re-description, we are entitled to ask what greater purchase it has on reality, and where does it conflict with or diverge from the first-order explanation. We can also ask the second-order explanation to explain just why the participants (propounding the first-order explanation) believe what they do.

G.O.D.: Very good, please continue.

Socrates: And in this case, the second-order explanation, the sociology of science explanation, conflicts with the first-order explanation (the chemists', or nuclear physicists', or whatever) because ultimately it propounds their processes of reaching consensus exclusively in terms of rhetorical strategies, career moves, funding, the wider socio-economic processes in which scientific practice is situated, etc.– in short, in terms of anything and everything except the specific contents of scientific claims that the scientists see their disputes and agreements revolving around.

G.O.D.: Exactly. And this constitutes (or so it can be argued) a claim to a greater degree of objectivity than the first-order explanation grouping (the scientists) possesses.

Socrates: And this claim conflicts with the theoretical position upon objectivity that they begin with.

G.O.D.: Exactly so. The difference between the anthropologist studying the Azande and making claims as to the falsity of some Azande beliefs, and the sociologist studying a group of physicists, is that the physicists are better placed to respond to and challenge the sociologists drawing these conclusions.

They would make the claim that the sociologists are misunderstanding what they are in fact doing. The disputes over interpretation of data, the references to published studies as appeals to authority and precedent, the rhetorical strategies utilised in disagreements, are not to be understood primarily in terms of social competition and power relations. These may exist but the disputes are always about . . . something. It is this 'something' that they assert the sociologists are overlooking. They overlook it because ultimately they don't understand what the scientists are in fact doing.

Socrates: The Azande could say the same thing to the anthropologist.

G.O.D.: Yes, perhaps they could. But they are in a weaker position to do so. It would be as if they not only could believe and live by their system of magic and witchcraft but be able to simultaneously use it as the basis for mounting a Western philosophical critique against those who would judge them. We can see Winch and many others' efforts as, in fact, attempts to do this on their behalf.

Socrates: And the scientists, being of the West, can do it themselves. They can simply say to the sociologist of science that complex social processes may well be at work, but ultimately the scientific disagreements are disagreements over competing accounts of reality.

G.O.D.: Well, some of them would say that. That is, in fact, the realist position. Realists assert that the nature of scientific activity itself commits scientists to an at least implicit realist position. However, the scientists' philosophy is often naive on the one hand, but on the other hand too complicated. This can prevent them from clearly articulating what would seem to be the obvious rejoinder to the sociologist.

Socrates: Too philosophical but not philosophical enough, eh? You're painting a picture of scientists as simultaneously over- and under-educated witch doctors.

G.O.D.: I hope you are remembering that I'm giving you a heavily biased presentation here.

Socrates: That's possibly the one thing I never forget. I realise I'm talking to some feminist realist fanatic – probably a communist too!

G.O.D.: Yes, well, that's good. Because so far all I've done is characterise the debates, sketch out some of the major positions and provide you with the major questions. Later on I'm going to give you the answers!

Socrates: The answers?

G.O.D.: Some of *the* answers.

Socrates: One of my lecturers told me that in this subject there are no right answers or wrong answers.

G.O.D.: Well, he's wrong.

Socrates: Wow. I always thought you guys stuck together and backed each other up.

G.O.D.: Ask him if he thinks my answer to his assertion is wrong or not. I'm directly contradicting him, aren't I?

Socrates: Yes.

G.O.D.: So, he'd have to say I'm wrong.

Socrates: I'm sure he would. He likes telling people they've made an error in their reasoning.

G.O.D.: Well, then he is contradicting himself, isn't he?

Socrates: No, no. You're just making fun of me. What he says is that there are no right or wrong answers, but that there are better or worse answers.

G.O.D.: Well, he's certainly right as far as the last bit. But I think he has been over-exposed to the corrosive influence of postmodernism. It seems to have the effect of causing philosophers to be very bold in making the most absurd assertions yet be very timid about stating simple truths.

While I have given you a biased, and perhaps one could say rather ungenerous account of Lyotard's ideas and postmodernism generally, there is one thing about it that certainly *is* correct. While they are wrong about metanarratives in some ways, they are nonetheless correct about a couple of particular, and particularly influential, metanarratives. That is to say, they are correct about the very meta-narratives I have been giving you.

Socrates: What?! Now you're going to tell me you've been lying to me!

G.O.D.: No, no, or at least not exactly. I have given you two closely related 'stories'. One was an extremely abbreviated and selective history of

	science – Bacon and Newton – and all of that. The other was a history of the philosophy of science – rationalism and empiricism and the 'dethroning of God as an epistemological guarantee'.
Socrates:	These are what Lyotard would call the 'grand narratives' that allegedly we no longer believe.
G.O.D.:	Yes, that's right, and Lyotard would have us reject them just because they are universal claims. He is both right to insist upon this . . . and wrong.
Socrates:	Here we go again!
G.O.D.:	Both these narratives in their claims to truth have important things in common. First, they are quite widely believed by the public at large and also widely believed by experts in their fields, and thus are all the more powerful and compelling. Second, they do make a claim for some kind of universality. In the first case – the history of science – historians can be well aware of the 'situatedness of historical accounts'; they can know that historical evidence can only ever be partial, can only ever be less than comprehensive; they can know that their account of history is very crucially socio-culturally located; they can know all of that, and yet simultaneously be blind to it! That is precisely the case here.
Socrates:	Um, so what you're telling me now is that you have given me a blind historian's account of the history of science?
G.O.D.:	Exactly.
Socrates:	Why? Why would you do that?
G.O.D.:	Well, one reason is that the account I have given you is the 'standard account'. Even the postmodernists kind of accept it even as they attack it. The other reason is more personal: ignorance.
Socrates:	Wow! This is a day! You, admitting ignorance!
G.O.D.:	Yes, well it is true. There is a whole history of science that has largely been invisible to the Eurocentric eye . . . to *my* eye. In our next section I'm going to at least partially correct that ignorance. We are going to talk about some of this invisible history of science. Perhaps more importantly, as we are mainly focused upon the philosophy of science and social science, I'm going to supply some of the corrections to that account too. The 'story' as I have told it so far is misleading because of what has been left out.

DISCUSSION QUESTIONS

1   Who are you? Is there an essential you that remains constant and distinct from your various and changing social roles and relationships? How much of your identity derives from the various collective identities you have had and continue to have throughout your life? How do such questions relate to

the conception of knowledge, as something which is possessed by an individual knower?

2   In what sense can stories be said to be knowledge? Do we really live in an age of scepticism towards the 'grand narrative' of ever-increasing knowledge of science? Or do we perhaps possess a kind of 'double-think' about it, simultaneously sceptical and credulous?

3   Can we ever mean what we say or say what we think – precisely? Is meaning always changeable, precarious, ambiguous?

4   Are questions concerning truth and falsity inextricably linked to questions concerning meaning?

5   Are questions concerning truth really the most important at this point in history? Is it not more important to understand the power relations that are bound up with claims to truth? Aren't claims to truth themselves strategies in struggles for power? Is that all they are?

6   Why might a sociologist's account of a group of physicists' practices and debates differ significantly from those of physicists themselves? Is the sociologist perhaps simply failing to understand the content of the subject matter, which the physicists are debating? Or do the physicists misunderstand the nature of their own communicative practice and its underlying social features? Can the answers to these questions be generalised so as to give an answer to the problem of first-order and second-order knowledges discussed earlier in the book?

7   Reconsider question 6 substituting 'sociologists' for 'physicists'. Might a sociology of sociology paralyse the discipline or is it actually something that the discipline needs most in order to be truly self-reflective?

FURTHER READING SUGGESTIONS

Postmodernism (general)

Appignanesi, L. (ed.) (1989) *Postmodernism: ICA Documents*, Free Association Books, London.

Callinicos, A. (1989) *Against Postmodernism*, Polity Press, Cambridge – a strong Marxist critique, which among other things socio-historically locates postmodernism. It also summarises a very diverse field quite well.

Connor, S. (1989) *Postmodernist Culture*, Blackwell, Oxford.

Featherstone, M. (ed.) (1988) *Postmodernism*, Sage, London.

Jameson, F. (1984) 'Postmodernism, or the Cultural Logic of Late Capitalism', *New Left Review* 146 pp. 53–92.

Implications of postmodernism for sociology

Bauman, Z. (1997) *Postmodernity and Its Discontents*, Polity Press, Cambridge.

Calhoun, C. (1995) *Critical Social Theory: Culture, Politics and the Challenge of Difference*, Polity Press, Cambridge.

Dickens, D.R. (1994) *Postmodernism and Social Inquiry*, Guildford Press, New York.

Seidman, S. (1994) *The Postmodern Turn: New Perspectives on Social Theory*, Cambridge University Press, Cambridge.

Seidman, S. and Wagner, D.G. (eds) (1992) *Postmodernism & Social Theory: The Debate over General Theory*, Blackwell, Cambridge.

Simons, H.W. and Billig, M. (eds) (1994) *After Postmodernism: Reconstructing Ideology Critique*, Sage, Thousand Oaks, CA.

Woodiwiss, A. (1990) *Social Theory after Postmodernism*, Pluto, London.

Structuralism and poststructuralism

Althusser, L. (1969) *For Marx*, Allen Lane, London.

Althusser, L. and Balibar, E. (1970) *Reading Capital*, NLB, London – structuralist Marxism.

Barthes, R. (1967) *Writing Degree Zero*, Cape, London.

—— (1972) *Mythologies*, Cape, London – accessible and entertaining, shows some of the diverse subject matter which can be approached from a structuralist perspective.

Culler, J. (1982) *On Deconstruction: Theory and Criticism after Structuralism*, Routledge & Kegan Paul, Ithaca.

—— (1988) *Framing the Sign: Criticism and Its Institutions*, Blackwell, Oxford.

Ellis, J. (1989) *Against Deconstruction*, Princeton University Press, Princeton – accessible critique of Derrida, which deconstructionists would argue completely misunderstands him, but interesting nonetheless.

Hawkes, T. (1997) *Structuralism and Semiotics*, Routledge, London.

Jameson, F. (1972) *The Prison House of Language*, Princeton University Press, Princeton.

Levi-Strauss, C. (1968) *Structural Anthropology*, Allen Lane, London.

Nortis, C. (1983) *The Deconstructive Turn: Essays in the Rhetoric of Philosophy*, Methuen, New York.

—— (1985) *The Contest of Faculties: Philosophy and Theory after Deconstruction*, Methuen, London – gives a good overview of the debates which surrounded poststructuralist theory and demonstrates how these debates do not merely exist on some abstract theoretical plane but are framed within the perspectives of different institutional structures.

Sturrock, J. (1986) *Structuralism*, Grafton Books, London – a good overview of quite a diverse field and quite accessible.

Wollen, P. (1982) *Readings and Writings: Semiotic Counter-strategies*, Verso Editions, London.

Derrida

Derrida, J. (1976) *Of Grammatology*, John Hopkins University Press, Baltimore.

—— (1977) 'Limited, Inc. abc', *Glyph* 2 pp. 29–110.

—— (1978) *Writing and Difference*, Chicago University Press, Chicago.

—— (1981) *Positions*, Athlone Press, London.

Norris, C. (1987) *Derrida*, Harvard University Press, Glasgow – Derrida's own work is quite difficult. This book is perhaps the best available for presenting a clear picture of Derrida's project.

Foucault

Foucault, M. (1970) *The Order of Things and Archaeology of the Human Sciences*, Tavistock Publications, London.
——— (1971) *Discipline and Punish*, Penguin, Harmondsworth.
——— (1972) *The Archaeology of Knowledge*, Tavistock Publications, London.
——— (1980) *Power/Knowledge: Selected Interviews and Other Writings, 1972–1977*, Harvester Press, Brighton.
——— (1986) 'What Is an Author' in Paul Rabinow (ed.), *The Foucault Reader*, Penguin, Harmondsworth, pp. 101–120.
Gutting, G. (1984) *Michel Foucault's Archaeology of Scientific Reason*, Cambridge University Press, New York.
Lecourt, D. (1975) *Marxism and Epistemology: Bachelard, Canguilhem, and Foucault*, NLB, London.
Sheridan, A. (1982) *Michel Foucault: The Will to Truth*, Tavistock Publications, London.

Lyotard

Lyotard, J.F. (1984) *The Postmodern Condition: A Report on Knowledge*, Manchester University Press, Manchester.
Searle, J. (1964) 'How to Derive Ought From Is', *Philosophical Review* 73 pp. 43–58 – contradicts Lyotard's argument concerning the impossibility of doing so. No consensus has been reached on this topic.

Saussure

Saussure, F. (1974) *Course in General Linguistics*, Fontana, London.
Tallis, R. (1988) *Not Saussure*, Macmillan, Basingstoke – the book is an attack upon poststructuralism, and Derrida in particular, but manages as well to give a clear exposition of Saussure.

Sociology of knowledge

Mannheim, K. (ed.) (1936) *Ideology and Utopia*, Routledge & Kegan Paul, London – especially see 'Ideology and Utopia' by Mannheim himself.
Mannheim, K. (1952) *Essays on the Sociology of Knowledge*, Routledge & Kegan Paul, London.

Sociology of science

Barnes, B. (1985) *About Science*, Basil Blackwell, Oxford.
Bloor, D. (1981) 'The Strengths of the Strong Programme', *Philosophy of the Social Sciences* 11 pp. 199–213.
Frickel, S. and Moore, K. (eds) (2005) *The New Political Sociology of Science Institutions, Networks, and Power*, University of Wisconsin Press, Madison, Wisconsin.
Fuller, S. (1989) *Philosophy of Science and Its Discontents*, Westview Press, Boulder, CO.
Fuller, S., de Mey, M., Shinn, T. and Woolgar, S. (eds) (1989) *The Cognitive Turn: Sociological and Psychological Perspectives on Sciences*, Reidel, Dordrecht.

Knorr-Cetina, K.D. (1981) *The Manufacture of Knowledge: An Essay on the Constructivist and Contextual Nature of Knowledge*, Pergamon Press, Oxford.

Latour, B. (1987) *Science in Action*, Harvard University Press, Cambridge, MA.

Latour, B. and Woolgar, S. (1979) *Laboratory Life: The Social Construction of Scientific Facts*, Sage, Beverly Hills, CA.

Livingstone, D.N. (2003) *Putting Science in Its Place: Geographies of Scientific Knowledge*, University of Chicago Press, Chicago.

Woolgar, S. (1981) 'Interests and Explanations in the Social Study of Science', *Social Studies of Science* 11 pp. 365–394.

―――― (ed.) (1988) *Knowledge and Reflexivity: New Frontiers in the Sociology of Knowledge*, Sage, London.

―――― (1988) *Science: The Very Idea*, Tavistock, London.

CHAPTER 8

ISLAM AND SCIENCE: THE STARS ON A COMMON CELESTIAL GLOBE

I have to deplore the systematic manner in which the literature of Europe has continued to put out of sight our obligations to the Muhammadans. Surely they cannot be much longer hidden. Injustice founded on religious rancour and national conceit cannot be perpetuated forever. The Arab has left his intellectual impress on Europe. He has indelibly written it on the heavens as any one may see who reads the names of the stars on a common celestial globe.

John William Draper (1863)

We are at a point in our work when we can no longer ignore empires and the imperial context in our studies.

Edward Said

OUTLINE OF MAJOR POINTS TO BE COVERED

The chapters leading up to this have focused specifically on European-American contributions to the practice and philosophy of Science, mirroring the dominant narrative found in Western academia. This history is the result of intentional historical acts of erasure connected to European goals of political and cultural dominance. The legacy of this erasure leaves us with an incomplete and inaccurate knowledge of the genealogies of the ideas we engage with. This chapter draws attention to this reality and seeks to draw attention to its scope, including shedding light on predecessors of ideas that earlier chapters have explored Eurocentrically.

1   An outline is given of some of the ideas of Ibn Sina, living across the tenth through eleventh centuries. He contributed astoundingly to a range of fields, particularly medicine, and theorised laws distinctly similar to Newton's laws of motion, as well as a scientific method of inquiry.

2   A listing is given of a sampling of various Islamic thinkers and their contributions to science and the history of civilisation generally. Their absence, measured against the incredible scale of achievement is reflected upon.

3   An outline of many of the ideas of Ibn Khaldun is given. It focuses primarily upon his work, *The Muqaddimah*. Ibn Khaldun is given credit as the 'father of Sociology' though his new discipline would be divided into historiography

as well as sociology. Ibn Khaldun also sets out a scientific method for the social sciences. Other ideas in *The Muqaddimah* that are now well recognised include peak taxation principles, social cohesion (often translated as 'group feeling') and evolutionary theories mirroring Darwin's.

4   The chapter concludes with a reflection upon possible contradictions between religious faith and science. Reference is made specifically to the work of Al-Ghazili and Ibn Rushd in this regard, with the former making an argument against pursuing knowledge that is not of either an obvious practical benefit or of a religious nature. Ibn Rushd argues against this narrowness using numerous quotations from the Quran to show how it enjoins people to seek after knowledge. The very end of the chapter alludes to the way neo-pragmatists differently deal with the issue of faith and science and thus presages the next chapter.

DIALOGUE

G.O.D.:	Do you remember our discussion of Derrida?
Socrates:	Yes. But I'm not sure why we would bring him up at this point in our discussion.
G.O.D.:	I can understand why you might wonder. In some ways he is an odd choice for a starting point for where I am hoping to take us. In some ways he's quite an ironic choice.
Socrates:	Ironic?
G.O.D.:	Yes, because we are about to turn our minds eastward, middle eastward to be precise, and Derrida as you know, is very definitely a Western thinker, even if he is a critic of Western thought. But in some senses, we are going to make a typically deconstructive move. We are going to reverse the relationship of core and periphery and make what is peripheral central to our argument.
Socrates:	Okay, I'm with you. Arabic and Islamic thinkers have been marginalised in the Westernised history of thought.
G.O.D.:	Yes, precisely. Ramón Grosfoguel of the University of California goes so far as to call it an **'epistemicide'**.
Socrates:	As in genocide? Except instead of wiping out whole peoples, it is the wiping out of knowledges, whole bodies of knowledges.
G.O.D.:	Yes, exactly, the term indicates a kind of symbolic violence and very definitely a lack of innocence. What we are going to consider next, is on one level simply a correction of the historical record from a realist perspective. However, the original errors are not innocent, nor will their correction be. Both were, and are, political acts. Hence, bringing Derridean deconstruction into it; we are wishing to include in our considerations the dimension of power. There has been a *deliberate* exclusion of certain facts and certain thinkers. It is not a simple matter of knowledge and ignorance. Ignorance is involved,

my own included, but it is not innocent. Virtually all that we are going to consider next has been known quite a long time. That is, it has been known and not known at the same time.

Socrates: What do you mean by that, known and not known?

G.O.D.: I think the best way to explain what I mean here is simply to re-visit our earlier account of the history of science and the history of the philosophy of science. How well do you remember it?

Socrates: Pretty well, actually, or at least the bare bones of it. Most knowledge initially was pretty much a Church-supervised scholastic kind of thing. People interpreted religious texts because they were the word of God and God knew everything. And then God was dethroned by Man . . . and Woman, I would add! So I see how this story is, as you say, not innocent. The human abilities of reason and observation were then given pride of place, represented respectively by the schools of thought – rationalism and empiricism.

G.O.D.: Very good!

Socrates: Thank you. And then positivism evolved as a refinement of empiricism. We have the key thinkers of Descartes, a rationalist, and Locke, Berkeley and Hume as empiricists, and earlier still Francis Bacon, as both philosopher and scientist.

G.O.D.: Excellent. Okay, now here are some problems with the story. *Valerius Terminus: of the interpretation of Nature* is Francis Bacon's first real scientific work and was published in 1603. *Novum Organum* (New Method), which contains a great deal of Bacon's thinking concerning empirical inquiry, observation and experiment (not to mention the relationship of such-like to God) was published in 1620. But nearly six hundred years earlier Ibn Sina-Avincina was commenting upon deductive and inductive inference in relation to Aristotle's thinking.

Socrates: Really! Six hundred years earlier!

G.O.D.: Yes. I am going to tell you about Ibn Sina-Avincina. First, his full formal name is Abū ʿAlī al-Ḥusayn ibn ʿAbd Allāh ibn Al-Hasan ibn Ali ibn. The Islamic world has rather different naming conventions than the West and the full name is rather long . . .

Socrates: I'll say!

G.O.D.: So I will just refer to him as Ibn Sina. He wrote about Islamic theology and philosophy. He also contributed to medicine, astronomy, alchemy and the beginnings of a proper science of chemistry. His five volumes *Canon of Medicine* was the standard encyclopedic text throughout not only the Islamic world but Europe as well, all the way through to the eighteenth century. He also wrote about geography and geology, psychology, physics, logic and mathematics and . . . poetry. To this day poetry occupies a much more prominent place in Islamic culture than it does in the West. Some of our science/art oppositional thinking is quite alien to them. But it is his scientific ideas and his ideas about science that are of the greatest interest to us here.

Isaac Newton, as you know, is given pride of place in the Western history of science. Virtually single-handed, he developed most of the fundamental laws of physics. The Newtonian paradigm of physics, as named after him, lasted without fundamental alterations until Einstein came along with his general and special theories of relativity. We can speak now of there being an Einsteinian paradigm now whereby relativity and quantum mechanics can fit in.

Socrates: Paradigm? You mean like Kuhn's idea of paradigms . . . a kind of agreed-upon set of problems, methods and criteria of judgment . . . agreed-upon by the scientific community.

G.O.D.:   Yes, except that this would be *the* most fundamental paradigm of all. You could say it is the foundational scientific worldview, and it is to this day the one we refer back to, as the Einsteinian paradigm really only comes into play in the quantum realities of the very, very small and at the other end of the spectrum when we approach the speed of light. We still basically orient ourselves in the world through a Newtonian lens.

Socrates: Okay, I get that, but what has this to do with Ibn Sina?

G.O.D.:   Well, Newton lived from 1642 to 1727. Ibn Sina lived from 980 to 1037 and essentially developed what we know now as Newton's laws of motion. He asserted that an object set into motion does not require a continuation of that initial force in order to remain in motion, but gains a property that allows propulsion, what we would call inertia. Any changes in its trajectory must be the result of other forces applied to it. If such an object were set in motion in a vacuum, it would not cease but would continue without change.

Socrates: I see; so again he was way ahead of his time. Or maybe another way of putting it, we could say he was way ahead of the timeline of our Western story.

G.O.D.:   Yes, very good! He also reflected very consciously upon what he was doing. In the 'Al-Burhan' (On Demonstration) section of *The Book of Healing*, Ibn Sina discussed the philosophy of science and described an early scientific method of inquiry.

First he discusses Aristotle's *Posterior Analytics* and significantly diverged from it on several points. He criticises Aristotelian induction and sees the justification of inductive inquiry as problematic. This reasoning sounds familiar to you, yes?

Socrates: Yes, Hume, Popper, yes, it sounds very familiar.

G.O.D.:   Ibn Sina asks the question: how does one arrive at the basic axioms of a deductive science without inferring them from some more basic premises? He explains that the ideal situation is when one grasps that a 'relation holds between the terms, which would allow for absolute, universal certainty'. Ibn Sina then adds two further methods for arriving at the first principles: the ancient Aristotelian method of induction (**istiqra**) and the method of examination and experimentation (**tajriba**). Ibn Sina criticised Aristotelian induction, arguing that 'it does not lead to the absolute, universal, and certain premises that it purports to provide'. He promotes instead a rigorous methodological examination and experimentation as a means for scientific inquiry.

With regard to logic he endorsed the principle of non-contradiction, stating that anyone who disagreed should be beaten and burned until they acknowledge that to be beaten is not the same as to not be beaten, and to be burned is not the same as to not be burned.

Socrates: Beaten and burned?

G.O.D.: Yes, rather clever, don't you think? He makes the point rather dramatically with a very down to earth kind of example.

Socrates: Kind of like Samuel Johnson's famous refutation of Berkeley, kicking a stone and saying 'I refute it thus'.

G.O.D.: Well, yes I suppose, except that Johnson's stone kicking was not really a refutation of Berkeley. Touch is sensory perception just as much as sight or hearing. Whatever may be the merits, or lack thereof, of Berkeley's theory, Johnson did not successfully refute it. Ibn Sina's 'burned or not burned' quite successfully illustrates the principal of non-contradiction. Someone should have suggested that Derrida try it.

Socrates: Derrida . . . you're joking, right?

G.O.D.: Yes.

Socrates: Good. Okay, so to recap: Ibn Sina, he was engaging with what you described to me, quite a while back actually, as 'the problem of induction?' And he saw that, of course, induction could not ever lead to any absolute certainty?

G.O.D.: Yes, and his alternative of experimentation is quite similar to Bacon's in some ways and in others more akin to the Vienna School and Popper's critique of them. It was a kind of early falsificationism.

Socrates: So, what you are saying is that this guy was writing about this stuff hundreds of years before Bacon and Newton, let alone Popper.

G.O.D.: Yes, and his thinking had an interesting parallel to that of Descartes also. He developed a thought experiment, known as either the 'floating man' or 'flying man' experiment dependent upon the translation. Ibn Sina asks us to imagine a human being with absolutely no sensory experience. He then suggests that what this person with no experiences would know is that he himself exists – rather like the Cogito, yes? – and that person would be aware of themselves quite apart from needing experiences of other things. This he intended to conceptually demonstrate that Aristotle's axiom that there is nothing in the mind that was not first in the senses is incorrect. Rather there is at least one thing in the mind that is not dependent upon experience: self-awareness.

Socrates: That's pretty cool. So he did all this good thinking and was kind of just written out of the picture? How is it that you know of him then?

G.O.D.:   That's just it. He is known and not known. The knowledge is there; it is simply ignored, forgotten or intentionally omitted in the Western account. But he is not alone in this occurring to him. The early knowledge advancements of the entire Muslim, Persian and Arabic world largely go unrecognised. Yet a woman named Fatima Al-Fihri was the founder of the oldest still existing university in the world, in the Moroccan city of Fez in the ninth century. And did you know that algebra was invented in the Islamic world? Muḥammad ibn Mūsā al-Khwārizmī, who lived between 780 and 850 A.D., invented it. His name, which when Latinised is 'Algoitimi', is where we get the term 'algorithm' from.

Socrates: Really!

G.O.D.:   Yes. Why is that particularly interesting to you? I guess you know what an **algorithm** is.

Socrates: Well, not exactly. But I know that it is some kind of formula or something, which social media sites like Facebook use. They use them to determine automatically which posts will show up on your timeline and which not.

G.O.D.:   Okay, well, there are a few other uses for them as well. Anyway, al-Khwārizmī not only invented algebra, he used it in making astronomical calculations. And his *Book of the Description of the Earth*, with a table of the latitudes and longitudes of 2,402 cities and landmarks, formed the basis of an early world map.

Socrates: Quite the fellow!

G.O.D.:   Yes, and there were many, many more thinkers who made early important advances across a wide range of fields. Abū Bakr Muhammad ibn Zakariyyā al-Rāzī, from what would today be Iran, made discoveries and advances in both chemistry and medicine in the ninth century. He was the first to produce acids, e.g. sulfuric acid. He also was a pioneer in ophthalmology . . .

Socrates: In what?

G.O.D.:   Ophthalmology. It is the branch of medicine that deals with the eyes . . . their physiology and diseases. He also studied diseases like smallpox and chickenpox and was able to differentiate them, which if you think of the seriousness and fatality rates of a disease like smallpox is an extremely important achievement. The range of his medical interests is really quite impressive. He is also the author of the first book on pediatrics, for example.

Socrates: Yeah, I get it. It is impressive.

G.O.D.:   Such mastery of many fields is not really possible today because of the development of knowledge and its specialisations. But still these early thinkers quite amaze me with the variety of their interests. Abū Rayḥān Muḥammad ibn Aḥmad Al-Bīrūnī, born in 973, devised a method of calculating the radius of the earth and also employed spherical trigonometry in the matter of determining the direction of

Mecca from various distances. This, of course, is something rather key for Muslims who must face there for their daily prayers.

Socrates: I can see why that would be important to him. Were most of these advances motivated or driven by practical or religious concerns then?

G.O.D.: Well, that's a good question, and one I don't really know the answer to. You remember from our discussions of Weber that he felt that social science, at least, arose from a context of practical human concerns. And there have been many who have written about how capitalist interests drive the direction of contemporary scientific research. But still I think there is a place to put curiosity and maybe even a pure drive for scholarship.

Socrates: Really? That sounds pretty idealistic.

G.O.D.: Maybe. But let's consider Al Biruni some more. He was widely known in his day for an encyclopedic work describing the cultures and customs of India. Yet he was from a different part of the world entirely, from what today is called Uzbekistan. What practical interest did people in that part of the world have in India? Perhaps they did, but I don't know it. If you are curious, you could research it.

Socrates: Uhh . . . no. I'm not that curious. I'll go with your idealistic explanation. Is that all of them . . . of the early Islamic thinkers that made big contributions to knowledge?

G.O.D.: Oh, good heavens, no. There are a very large number of them. I'll just mention three more of them. There is Abū ʿAlī al-Ḥasan ibn al-Ḥasan ibn al-Haytham. He was a ninth- and tenth-century physicist who conducted experiments to determine how light travels. He correctly concluded that light enters the eye rather than emanating from it. He derived the equivalent of **'Snell's law of refraction'** (which Willebrord Snellius derived some six hundred years later in 1692). He used water in a glass orb to replicate raindrops and describe the dispersion of light in the formation of a rainbow. He created a model of light cast into a dark room, which would serve as the model for the modern film camera.

Socrates: Wow!

G.O.D.: Yes indeed. And you have probably heard of Omar Khayyám, full name Ghiyāth ad-Dīn Abu'l-Fath ʿUmar ibn Ibrāhīm al-Khayyām Nīshāpūrī?

Socrates: Uh, no. Why in the world would you think I would have?

G.O.D.: Because he is actually very well known in the contemporary Western world . . . but for his poetry rather than his science.

Socrates: Poetry. Yes, of course, I know lots about poetry.

G.O.D.: Don't be sarcastic. The *Rubáiyát*? 'A Jug of Wine, a Loaf of Bread and Thou?'

Socrates: Oh yeah, I've heard of that.

G.O.D.: And 'The moving finger writes and having writ moves on.'

Socrates: Yeah, I've heard of that too.

G.O.D.: It's actually better in context. 'The Moving Finger writes; and, having writ, moves on; nor all your piety nor wit, shall lure it back to cancel half a line, nor all your tears wash out a word of it.' Actually, we know lines like this mainly through the translations of Edward Fitzgerald who in 1859 published a number of his quatrains in English as *The Rubáiyát of Omar Khayyám*. They were an immediate hit, causing more of his quatrains to be published in later editions.

Socrates: Okay, so he was a great poet, but what about his scientific achievements?

G.O.D.: Well, the thing is that poetry is regarded quite differently in Islamic culture . . .

Socrates: Less of a kind of wimpy thing, you mean?

G.O.D.: I wouldn't put it like that, though I'm aware that there is a kind of notion of poetry being effete and feminine among the more ignorant members of Western . . .

Socrates: Hey!

G.O.D.: The important thing here is that art and science, poetry and science, religion and science are not regarded in quite the same oppositional way as perhaps they are in Western culture. So, it was not really unusual for Omar Khayyám to be both a poet and a scientist.

Socrates: Okay, so what did he do scientifically?

G.O.D.: Well, it is more mathematics really. He performed the first systematic study of how to solve cubic equations. Some historians say, it is perhaps disputable, but some historians say that he developed a general **binomial theorem**.

And with regard to astronomy, he was invited by the reigning Sultan to make the required observations and derive a most accurate calendar. His calendar, with eight leap years in every thirty-three, was actually more accurate than our current **Gregorian calendar**.

Socrates: The calendar we use now is the Gregorian calendar?

G.O.D.: The Gregorian calendar, also called the 'Western calendar' and the 'Christian calendar', is internationally the most widely used official calendar of governments and civil organisations. It is named for Pope Gregory XIII, who introduced it in 1582.

Socrates: So out of all this bunch, who is really the most important thinker? Omar Khayyám? Ibn Sina?

G.O.D.: I don't think that is a very productive way of looking at the history of thought. It isn't like we're at a beauty contest trying to pick a winner.

Socrates: Well, it is a bit like that. We're trying to figure out what is right, what is the best view to have.

G.O.D.: We are tracing the history of human thought, examining connections between different traditions, and critiquing and reflecting upon the ideas as we go along. The question of which is the most important thinker would really be a question deriving from one's perspective. So, given that ultimately we are interested in social science and perhaps sociology in particular, I guess what we would take as most interesting from the Islamic history of thought would be the thinking that most directly relates to social science. And in that regard, if we want to put it in your terms, we have a clear winner here, someone I was leaving until the end to mention: Abū Zayd 'Abd ar-Raḥmān ibn Muḥammad ibn Khaldūn al-Ḥaḍramī, or as he is less formally known: Ibn Khaldun. He can quite rightly be considered the 'father of modern Sociology'.

Socrates: What! I thought that was Auguste Comte.

G.O.D.: Well, yes, that is how the Western story goes. Comte developed a systematic and hierarchical classification of all sciences, including astronomy, earth science, chemistry and biology; and also, for the first time, introduced the term 'sociologie' in 1838. Ibn Khaldun, however, was a fourteenth century thinker – born in Tunis in 1332 and lived until his death in Cairo in 1406. In addition to having a better claim to the title of 'father of modern sociology' than Comte, he, arguably at least, was also a founding father of historiography, demography, and economics. He was a very profound and important thinker indeed!

Socrates: Ibn Khaldun, the father of sociology?

G.O.D.: Yes.

Socrates: Well, I just looked it up. Wikipedia says Comte was the founder of sociology.

G.O.D.: Wikipedia, yeah, well . . . Wikipedia is constantly improving. It used to be quite an unreliable source, but it has improved immensely, and it is constantly editing and re-editing its entries, but regardless of that it still ain't the Bible.

Socrates: The Bible?

G.O.D.: A little joke. It is not the absolute ultimate source to which we must accept.

Socrates: Okay, but other people call Dürkheim the father of modern sociology. Still others call Marx, Weber and Dürkheim the founding fathers.

G.O.D.: Ah yes, the 'Holy trinity'. We can't seem to get away from religious references here. Okay, two things: first, Marx not only never used the word 'sociology' but would have been most definitely against the disciplinary specialisation and separation of sociology and history and politics and economics, a perspective implicitly shared by Ibn Khaldun by the way, and second, this founding father mythology is a part of the *Western* story of history, a Eurocentric history we are trying to correct.

Socrates:	Okay, if you say so, Ibn Khaldun is the father of Sociology.
G.O.D.:	No, no, not because I say so! Let me tell you something of his thinking, and you then decide for yourself what claim he might have to such a title.
Socrates:	Okay then, what did he do that was such a big deal?
G.O.D.:	He wrote the **Muqaddimah**.
Socrates:	The *Muqaddimah*?
G.O.D.:	Yes, the *Muqaddimah* was actually intended as the introductory book of a series dealing with world history: the *Kitābu l-'ibari wa Dīwāni l-Mubtada' wal-Ḥabar fī ayāmi l-'arab wal-'ajam wal-barbar, waman 'Āsarahum min Dhawī sh-Shalṭāni l-Akbār*. Roughly translated this means *Book of Lessons, Record of Beginnings and Events in the history of the Arabs and Foreigners and Berbers and their Powerful Contemporaries*. But the *Muqaddimah*, translated as 'Introduction' came to stand on its own. It is essentially the first real work in the philosophy of history. It serves quite consciously as a foundation for a new discipline. Ibn Khaldun states that perhaps some future scholar will penetrate into such problems in greater depth than he was able to, but he justifies its various shortcomings by asserting that being comprehensive is not the task of the initiator of a new discipline. He states this common sense truth in such a way that it appears more as a modest acknowledgment of the impossibility of looking into all the new discipline's problems in sufficient detail, rather than as any kind of boast about being the father of a new science. Yet such he was. He anticipated the discipline growing incrementally as his successors added more problems. His task, he asserted, was rather to specify the subject of the discipline and its various branches.

This new discipline he invented covers what have essentially become two separate disciplines today: historiography and sociology. Ibn Khaldun opens *The Muqaddimah* with the problems of history and those who transmit it. He decries the frequency of partisanship; he laments the transmission of alleged facts through unreliable narrators; he criticises many of the narrators of events as having a lack of knowledge about the *purpose* of an event. Finally, and most important to him, he thought much of what had been hitherto written to suffer from a kind of provincialism, a lack of understanding about the civilisation being studied on a broader level.

While pointing out such common flaws in historians' approaches, he lays out the need for an intellectual and systematic approach to historical knowledge. This is what could be considered the introduction of a scientific method to the social sciences. He states that he is attempting to create a new independent science with its own specific subject matter: human civilisation and social organisation. As such, he acknowledges that it will have its own particular problems. The most important of these he argues are the conditions that attach themselves to the essence of civilisation.

The establishment of this discipline for Ibn Khaldun then seems rooted in questions of understanding not just present societies, but past ones, and in the ability of future societies to understand the present one, by building a body of knowledge about society.

Socrates: Ah, so there's the sociology part.

G.O.D.: Yes, but for him history and sociology are completely intertwined. One of the biggest criticisms he had of historical record was that it did not take into sufficient account the social environment of the times. He suggests that if accurate information about the context were known, it would be easier to distinguish spurious claims from valid ones, checking particular claims against general ones.

Socrates: This all seems very vague and general and more like philosophy than either history or sociology.

G.O.D.: Well, yes, it is both a philosophy of history and a philosophy of social science and sociology in particular. These are important areas to be explicit and conscious of; and he was perhaps the first to be so systematic about it. But he could also be very specific in applications of these philosophical generalities. He weaves in significant contributions to economics, demography and evolution. For example, he discusses taxation. He proposes that as taxation increases over time, the burden will grow to the point of inhibiting economic activity and result in a decrease in revenue. This resembles the modern economic concept known as the **Laffler Curve**.

Socrates: The Laffler Curve?

G.O.D.: The Laffler curve is named after the American economist Arthur Laffler, who was an advisor to the Reagan administration. It is a graphic representation of the relationship between an increasing tax rate and a government's total revenues. The relationship suggests that revenues decline beyond a peak tax rate. This is because after a certain point the tax burden works as a disincentive for people to work harder.

Socrates: Well, that makes sense.

G.O.D.: Yes, it does. He describes the economy more generally as being a series of interrelated value-adding processes. So, one takes a raw material and adds labour and skill to transform it into something else; this makes a product, which can be sold at a higher value than the original raw material. In this regard he is anticipating the labour theory of value held by the economists of Adam Smith's generation and even anticipating Marx's theory of surplus value, when he makes a distinction between 'profit' and 'sustenance', the latter being the value of labour, or in Marx's terms 'labour power'.

Socrates: What about classes? Did he have a theory of class?

G.O.D.: Well yes, but nothing like Marx's.

Socrates:	He didn't see class conflict then? He wasn't a 'conflict theorist'.
G.O.D.:	Well, actually he was a kind of conflict theorist. But he was writing from the perspective of his time . . . something that he was well aware of. He developed a dichotomy of sedentary life versus nomadic life, whereby the nomadic tribes come in and conquer the cities . . . and are later conquered, a history which repeats itself in cycles. When a society becomes a great civilisation (and, presumably, the dominant culture in its region), its high point is followed by a period of decay. This means that the next cohesive group that conquers the diminished civilisation is, by comparison, a group of barbarians. Once the barbarians solidify their control over the conquered society, however, they become attracted to its more refined aspects, such as literacy and arts, and either assimilate into or appropriate such cultural practices. Then, eventually, the former barbarians will be conquered by a new set of barbarians, who will repeat the process.
	He also developed a notion of 'group feeling' to explain social cohesion. He discussed the sense of tribalistic or nationalistic feeling of belonging required for unity. He emphasises in this regard people's affection and willingness to fight and die for each other. In his work we can see in an early formation virtually all the concepts worked with by later European and American sociologists, Weber, Parsons and so on. We have notions of social action and the necessity to 'understand' motivation; we have notions of social cohesion and social solidarity.
	And also, many, many years before Darwin, he developed a notion of evolution. He saw the elements of creation constantly changing, the various animal species being transformed and becoming more numerous in differences of kind on the one hand, and more highly evolved, on the other. He observed monkeys and saw intelligence within them and, though lacking in the capacity for reflection and real thought, he saw them as human precursors, the rung below the first stage of man. These ideas would seem to be a kind of proto-socio-biology.
Socrates:	Okay, all of that is very impressive. But he really was limited by his time wasn't he?
G.O.D.:	Well, yes, of course, all thinkers are conditioned by their historical place and time. But I have a feeling you're trying to get at something here.
Socrates:	I wasn't sure if I wanted to bring it up. But I read something on the web about him being a racist and his writing even being used by colonial powers to help justify slavery. I read that he asserted that the Negro nations, as he called them, are submissive to slavery. He apparently also asserted that they lack essential human qualities and are similar to dumb animals.
G.O.D.:	Well, I'm not sure of the accuracy of that. But yes, he wasn't immune to many of the prejudices of his time in attempting to extend his

ideas on evolution, which at the same time were very much in advance of his time. But let me ask you a question. You haven't gone and done extensive research on him, have you?

Socrates: No, I just spent a couple of minutes on the Internet.

G.O.D.: Well then, do you not think it odd that allegations of racism would be among the very first things you would learn about him? Do you think, for example, that if you were researching Thomas Jefferson's political views that among the first things you would learn would be that he was a slave owner?

Socrates: I don't know. Maybe. No, I guess probably not.

G.O.D.: I just checked the entry 'Jeffersonian Democracy' in Wikipedia, and they don't mention it.

Socrates: Okay, I get the point. This is part of that, what's the word again, for distorting history and writing out knowledges of cultures?

G.O.D.: Epistemicide. Yes, it is power applied to history and knowledge. It privileges certain narratives over others, and where the facts seem to contradict or not fit the story, then they are omitted or distorted, or perhaps certain other pieces of information are given prominence, so as to discredit people's achievements, for example. The narrative changes over time. Today's historical narrative is different from that of the early colonialists; their distortions and prejudices, their exotic picture of the Orient is different from that of the West's present day omissions and distortions, but that isn't to say that we are free of our own prejudices in our account.

Socrates: Okay, well after all that we just covered, you are going to think this is a terrible question, and I don't quite know how to put it into words. Um . . . Islam . . .

G.O.D.: Islam?

Socrates: Yes, the Muslim religion. Ibn Khaldun, Ibn Sina, all of these thinkers were believers in Allah, the whole thing, right?

G.O.D.: Yes, I believe so.

Socrates: Well, didn't they encounter contradictions? Contradictions between their faith with its various dogmas and the questioning spirit of philosophy? I mean some of their thinking seems so sophisticated, and yet they cling to these silly religious notions.

G.O.D.: Like believing in God?

Socrates: Yes.

G.O.D.: And you think that that is a ridiculous belief? Because you are an atheist?

Socrates: Well, yes. And isn't that really the educated view?

G.O.D.: And so after all we've just covered, you're reverting back to the Western superiority view over the 'ignorant superstitions of the inferior culture'.

Socrates: Well, no. I've just got a problem thinking this through. Things seem contradictory.

G.O.D.:	Okay, I didn't mean to make fun of you. You are certainly not alone with this perspective. But let me ask you a couple of questions.
Socrates:	Okay.
G.O.D.:	Back when we were considering Berkeley, *Bishop* Berkeley, didn't you think that his Christian faith inserted itself into his reasoning?
Socrates:	Well, yes, of course, and I thought it flawed for that very reason. 'Reality is all mind. God is universal mind'; no, I don't buy it.
G.O.D.:	Okay, and what about Descartes? He set about trying to doubt everything, and yet he still managed to reason his way back to God's existence.
Socrates:	Yes, exactly my point. His faith was corrupting his reason.
G.O.D.:	And yet, if you had been there at the time to point that out to him, he would have certainly disagreed . . . and not because of his Christian faith but because of his commitment to reason. Are you so sure you could have convinced him his reasoning was mistaken, that yours is better?
Socrates:	Well, no . . . but . . . I still think . . .
G.O.D.:	You still think you are right.
Socrates:	Yes.
G.O.D.:	All right. That is basically the default position of the academy.
Socrates:	Atheism?
G.O.D.:	I think secularism is a better word because it is more accurate. The academy is not simply atheist insofar as it unconsciously reflects its own traditions of thought. There is a significant Judeo-Christian element influencing the perspective of the West to the present day. Yes, while society at large – East, West, North, South, it doesn't matter, Christianity, Islam, Hinduism, Buddhism – religion permeates all cultures, all societies. Yet secularism is the default position of the academy. It doesn't matter how many important thinkers in the history of science, in the history of philosophy, have been serious Christians or Muslims or Hindus, the default position of Western philosophy is secularism. The default position is that regardless of the powerful conscious and unconscious religious influence upon Western academic culture, religion and science are seen as opposed.
Socrates:	So what you call 'the academy' – what do you mean by that exactly anyway? – agrees with me.
G.O.D.:	When I say the academy, I am referring to the world community of university scholars and thinkers. It is a world community, but it is one that has been dominated by the West. And yes, I guess you could say they basically are in agreement with you.
Socrates:	So, I'm right then!
G.O.D.:	Whoa, whoa there! I think that first of all the academy doesn't speak with a unified voice; and second, it would not put it as crudely as

you have done; and most importantly, it probably wouldn't really put it any way at all. It's something not explicit; it is just there, as something tacitly understood.

Socrates: Well, maybe it should be!

G.O.D.: Should be what?

Socrates: Made explicit.

G.O.D.: Yes. Assumed beliefs should always be questioned. Actually Islamic thinkers debated this issue as well. Their debate was framed somewhat differently, of course. Abu Hamid Al Ghazali took issue with the idea of knowledge for its own sake, as opposed to knowledge as a means to seeking God. He, of course, conceded the value of knowledge, of worldly things that had obvious use, the field of medicine, for example, but he saw as pernicious any theoretical space where application to solving material problems or seeking closeness to God were not the direct goals.

Socrates: Ah ha, just what I was saying about intolerance and contradictions!

G.O.D.: Yes, but his views did not go unchallenged. Ibn Rushd, his thinking is based in the same Islamic framework from which Ghazali's on legal grounds has drawn from the Quran. He produces numerous instances in it whereby the intellect is held up as a virtue and where there is an injunction to seek knowledge. Philosophy is seen as a sort of science; statements about the nature of the world are made upon solid observed premises and logically deduced from that point. On the other hand, he uses the word Hikma – translated as wisdom – to refer to philosophy as well; so these terms and arguments must be understood to take place within their own context whereby subtle distinctions are made, that perhaps the Western ear is not attendant to.

Socrates: Well, mine's certainly not.

G.O.D.: You don't understand what I've just been saying?

Socrates: No, I do; I was just making a little joke. You don't have a monopoly on it, you know.

G.O.D.: Don't I? Okay, there is another perspective on the relationship between religion and science, the perspective of the school of thought we are going to look at next. They think it is fruitless to ask questions whose answers have no practical consequences.

Socrates: And the issue of religious belief has no real consequence?

G.O.D.: Well, where science and religion apparently contradict one another, they believe there are no real practical consequences to that kind of debate. Of course, they frame it somewhat differently than you have.

Socrates: Of course! What is the name of this school of thought we are going to look at next then?

G.O.D.: Pragmatism and neo-pragmatism.

DISCUSSION QUESTIONS

1   In Western culture, science and poetry are typically thought of as radically different modes of thought, whereas in Islamic culture this opposition does not hold. Is such an opposition as found in Western culture actually useful or is it rather pernicious?

2   Do you think the concept of 'epistemicide' accurately reflects the way Western thought has taken Islamic thought and written it out of history? Do you think this may still be happening today?

3   Some of Ibn Khaldun's work has provoked accusations of racism. Many Western thinkers of the past have also provoked such accusations. Do you think it possible that even great thinkers can be blinded simply by the prejudices of their time?

4   A characteristic of not only today's sciences, but also humanities disciplines and social sciences, is very definite disciplinary boundaries. You find no such boundaries in the work of either Marx or Ibn Khaldun. Do you think this is detrimental to their work or a positive thing?

SUGGESTIONS FOR FURTHER READING

Islam and science

Rashed, Roshdi. (2002) *Science in Islam and Classical Modernity*, Al-Furqān Islamic Heritage Foundation, London.

Saliba, George. (2007) *Islamic Science and the Making of the European Renaissance,* MIT Press, Cambridge.

Sardar, Ziauddin. (1989) *Explorations in Islamic Science,* Mansell, London.

Islam and the philosophy of science

Kazi, M.A. (1997) 'Islamic Epistemology and Theory of Knowledge' in *Islamic thought and Modern Science*, Islamic Academy of Science, Amman, pp. 26–46.

Ibn Khaldun and sociology

Ibn Khaldun. (2005) *The Muqaddimah: An Introduction to History*, trans. Bruce Lawrence, Princeton University Press, Princeton. (Original work published in 1377) – this is a highly accessible translation of a book written in a straightforward manner.

Colonial distortions of the history of science and civilization

Grosfoguel, Ramon. (2010) 'Epistemic Islamophobia and Colonial Social Sciences', *Human Architecture: Journal of the Sociology of Self-Knowledge* 8(2) pp. 29–38.

Grosfoguel, Ramon. (2013) 'The Structure of Knowledge in Western Universities: Epistemic Racism/Sexism and the Four Genocides/Epistemicides of the Long 16th Century', *Human Architecture: Journal of the Sociology of Self-Knowledge* 11(1) pp. 73–90.

Grosfoguel, Ramon and Cervantes-Rodríguez, A.M. (2002) *The Modern/Colonial/Capitalist World-System in the Twentieth Century: Global Processes, Antisystemic Movements, and the Geopolitics of Knowledge.* Greenwood Press, Westport.

Said, Edward. (1991) *Orientalism*, Penguin Books, London.

CHAPTER 9

PRAGMATISM AND NEO-PRAGMATISM: FOUNDATIONS OF ANTI-FOUNDATIONALISM

Taylor and I both pride ourselves on having escaped that collapsed circus tent of epistemology – those acres of canvas under which many of our colleagues still thrash aimlessly about.

Richard Rorty

Truth is simply a compliment paid to sentences seen to be paying their way.

Richard Rorty

In the face of the idea that truth might afford the opposite of satisfaction and turn out to be completely shocking to humanity at any given historical moment, . . . the fathers of pragmatism made the satisfaction of the subject the criterion of truth. For such a doctrine there is no possibility of rejecting or even criticizing any species of belief that is enjoyed by its adherents.

Max Horkheimer

OUTLINE OF MAJOR POINTS TO BE COVERED

1   A description of the debate within critical realism about the intellectual consequences of Roy Bhaskar's 'spiritual turn' is used as a lead-in to the epistemology of pragmatism and neo-pragmatism.
   a   Bhaskar's 'proof' of reincarnation is given.
   b   Garry Potter's refutation of this proof is also given.
2   This debate within **critical realism** is contrasted with the pragmatism understanding of truth. Richard Rorty's argument concerning the lack of any important contradiction between religious faith and science is given. Scientists who are also religious believers are not in 'intellectual bad faith' because of apparent contradictions between the assertions of one with the other. Rather as Rorty puts it 'they are not candidates' for the same office.
3   The above argument goes along with a more general critique of a '**correspondence notion of truth**'. Such epistemologies are forms of '**representationalism**', a pernicious and widespread viewpoint in philosophy. Knowledge in the representationalist paradigm is dependent upon a misguided metaphor; it is held to 'mirror' nature.

197

4   A distinction is made between cruder and more sophisticated forms of pragmatism. A 'pragmatic attitude' or **'pragmatic stance'** is an approach disdainful of metaphysics and any pre-determined guiding theories. In politics this kind of position emphasises action. In social science it connects up with a **grounded theory** approach, whereby the theory is supposed to flow naturally from the facts. Many other theorists find this a crude and under-theorised approach.

5   A more sophisticated pragmatism and neo-pragmatism does not reject all epistemological questions. Rather it is more specifically focused upon the critique of representationalism and with finding better ways to proceed.

6   Potter's argument for a **pragmatic epistemological guarantee** is explained. It is shown how, that while it does have some (ironic) connections with pragmatism, nonetheless it is very different. It actually propounds an ontologically grounded epistemology and philosophy of science and correspondence notion of truth . . . exactly what pragmatism is most critical of.

DIALOGUE

Socrates:	So, neo-pragmatism then.
G.O.D.:	Yes, but I'm going to take a somewhat odd and indirect route into it.
Socrates:	Well, that is your usual way. I'm used to it.
G.O.D.:	Yes, I know, but this time it may seem even more convoluted than usual. I'm going to begin with critical realism.
Socrates:	But I thought that this kind of issue, epistemological realism versus non-realism, was just the kind of debate that pragmatists didn't get into.
G.O.D.:	Yes, that's quite right. And we are not going to now either. The critical realist epistemology or philosophy of science – that will come later – but we are just going to look at one aspect of it now as an illustrative example. It will lead, by contrast, into the pragmatist stance towards religious beliefs philosophically. We are going to look at Roy Bhaskar's arguments about God.
Socrates:	And Roy Bhaskar is, I presume, someone big in the critical realist school of thought. And we're going to consider the question of God because of what I said before in relation to Islam and Allah.
G.O.D.:	Yes, exactly. Bhaskar is generally acknowledged as the 'father of critical realism'. However, he is also a very controversial figure among those who would call themselves critical realists. His early thinking – two books in particular, *A Realist Theory of Science* and *The Possibility of Naturalism* – constitute the foundations of the critical realist philosophy of science and philosophy of social science respectively. We shall look very closely at these ideas later on. But Bhaskar's thought developed further later on until he reached a

crucial point, an intellectual position, which was quite simply a bridge too far for many of his colleagues and admirers. He articulated a realist argument for the existence of . . .

Socrates: God. He argued that God really existed.

G.O.D.: Precisely so, he gave a realist argument for God's existence.

Socrates: But surely people have been debating that for years, and surely some of them were putting forward intellectual arguments on the God side of the debate.

G.O.D.: Yes, that's true. There is quite a famous debate staged by the BBC in 1948 between the philosophers Bertrand Russell and F.C. Copleston in which they attempted to cover all the basic arguments, with Russell giving the atheist case and Copleston the believers (https://www.youtube.com/watch?v=hXPdpEJk78E). But the Bhaskar justification is somewhat different. It shows an evolution of thought from science and the philosophy of science to a kind of theology, which he asserted contained no contradictions with his earlier articulated arguments.

Socrates: But others disagreed.

G.O.D.: Yes, quite a number of people disagreed. He published a book called *From East to West: Odyssey of a Soul* that almost immediately split the critical realist school of thought. In it, he not only gave an intellectual argument for the existence of the soul and reincarnation, he described a series of his 'past lives'.

Socrates: And why did this disturb people so much? Because they don't accept reincarnation?

G.O.D.: Well, people disagreed for a number of different reasons. But yes, reincarnation, but not entirely; it was because in making arguments for reincarnation, the existence of the soul and so on, he was in effect fundamentally changing the basic definition of realism used by critical realists. Bhaskar argues that realism in philosophy asserts the existence of some disputed entity; **irrealism** denies it. Thus, one can allegedly be realist about causal laws and irrealist about God.

Socrates: Well, that sounds straightforward enough. Isn't that what realism is?

G.O.D.: No, it isn't, or at least the 'realism' in critical realism isn't that at all or wasn't until Bhaskar changed it. Realism asserts the nature of our relationship to reality. Ontologically, it asserts that existence is not dependent upon human perception, belief or knowledge. Reality exists independently of our perceptions of it . . . well, we'll go into all this later on in some depth. Bhaskar, in making his case for the existence of God, the soul and so on, had changed the nature of critical realism to an idealist philosophy from a materialist one.

Socrates: And he had caused offence by going against the 'default secularism' of the academic world, and that bothered people.

G.O.D.: Well, it certainly bothered the people that didn't 'buy the Kool-Aid', so to speak, the people who did not want to follow him on his journey to the East.

Socrates: Okay, what was his argument for the existence of a soul and reincarnation then?

G.O.D.: Well, are you really interested? It is slightly off the topic. I brought up this history of critical realism as a lead-in to neo-pragmatism.

Socrates: Well, it's a pretty convoluted lead-in; I've totally lost *that* plot line. But I do want to hear this argument for reincarnation.

G.O.D.: All right, Bhaskar explains it like this: the deduction of the necessity for reincarnation turns essentially on three features. First, that of universal causality; second, that of the emergence, i.e. causal and taxonomic irreducibility, of intentional states to the physical states through which they are manifest; and third, following on from the first and second, a) the causal explicability of intentional phenomena, presupposing the pre-existence and b) the causal efficacy of intentional states implying the post-existence of the being who is the subject of the intentional state. The continuant in question is commonly called the soul.

Socrates: I didn't quite follow all of that so let's see if I've got this right. People having intentions and acting on the world is an emergent reality. Rocks bouncing into other rocks can show a chain of cause but not intentionality. We can explain events, which are caused through intentionality, though. I 'intend' to move this rock, so I push it and it rolls down the hill. My intention, as well as my action and gravity, are all causes of the event.

G.O.D.: Yes, that's right so far.

Socrates: So being able, at least in principle, to explain intentional events, presupposes both the pre-existence and post-existence of an 'intender', the person or being that decides to push the rock and then pushes it . . . or as Bhaskar puts it 'the subject of the intentional state'.

G.O.D.: Yes, spot on so far.

Socrates: So, the mere existence of intentional events, of which there are indisputably many, implies a *continuity* of the subject. And he calls this continuant the soul.

G.O.D.: That's correct.

Socrates: Well, I don't see anything wrong with that. It seems like a sound argument to me.

G.O.D.: But it's not. Garry Potter points out the error in reasoning. Potter argues that it is true that intentions may be causally efficacious. But intentions are certainly not necessarily always efficacious. That intentionality may be causally efficacious is a real characteristic of it that may not be actualised in the form of an event in the future. There is thus no necessity for the subject of the intention to continue to exist. There need be no continuant. As the argument for reincarnation stands as a subset of this broader argument concerning intentionality and continuity, it too is refuted. There is thus no necessity for a 'continuant' (soul) to continue to exist after death, regardless of the fact that human beings are the subjects of intentionality. There may indeed be souls, but their existence (not to mention reincarnation) cannot be proved in this manner.

Socrates: I'll need to think about this some more. But what does any of it have to do with pragmatism?

G.O.D.: Do you remember what ontology is?

Socrates: Yes, it is the study of being or existence . . . or the conditions of being or existence . . . or what constitutes a state of being or existence. Is that right?

G.O.D.: Yes, and critical realism is an ontology-based philosophy of science and epistemology. For critical realists, ontological questions precede epistemological questions, and answers to the latter are dependent upon the answers to the former. Do you see?

Socrates: Uuh . . . no!

G.O.D.: Well, it is like this; when Bhaskar asserted the existence of the soul and God and so on, he shifted critical realism's ontology, and thus its epistemology and philosophy of science and social science and basically everything else, and he also argued that he did so *without contradiction*. That last point is key in relation to pragmatism. For the pragmatist, epistemological questions are not related to ontology . . . to what really exists or not. In fact, everything the critical realists on both sides of the God debate were tearing themselves apart over, to the pragmatist would be no more than perhaps an amusing intellectual diversion and of no importance to any important questions concerning science and knowledge.

Socrates: You mean pragmatists simply don't care whether God exists or not?

G.O.D.: Well, not exactly that, though it is probably less of an issue to them than some others. Rather they have a uniquely pragmatic way of engaging with the secular 'default positions' of believers and atheists in the academy and elsewhere. Richard Rorty, probably the most important representative of the school of thought now known as **neo-pragmatism**, presents us with an interesting perspective upon scientist religious believers and the apparent contradictions between their faith and their profession.

Socrates: You mean he asks how people can be both believers in the scientific approach to understanding nature and yet accept religious dogma?

G.O.D.: Well, kind of. But it is more he answers with an argument of his own as to how they can happily live with such apparent contradictions.

Socrates: That would be living in a sort of bad faith . . . at least intellectually, wouldn't it?

G.O.D.: Well, I'm inclined to think so. But Rorty has an argument that asserts that it isn't.

Socrates: I'd like to hear how he pulls *that* off.

G.O.D.: Well, his argument goes something like this. There is no truth, in the sense of corresponding to the real nature of **things-in-themselves**.

Socrates: Things-in-themselves?

G.O.D.: Yes, this would be a label for aspects of reality that simply are how they are, respective of our human interests in them. But pragmatists such as Rorty would insist that we never approach that kind of knowledge. Rather knowledge is simply a label for that which we produce about the world in relation to our different sorts of interests in the world. So, for example, most scientific knowledges would be about prediction and control of reality, whereas religious knowledges would be about our interests in consolation and happiness and so on. The two sorts of knowledges, he would assert, and he actually uses this metaphor, are like candidates running for different offices.

Socrates: Hmm.

G.O.D.: Yes, Rorty gives a hypothetical example of the scientist Professor Ryan.

Socrates: Professor Ryan isn't a real person then.

G.O.D.: No, but she serves as an illustrative example for many, many such cases. Rorty's Professor Ryan is an evolutionary biologist, who is a Catholic and on Sunday goes to Mass and takes communion. The stories of the formation and composition of the universe for her working life – Galileo, Newton, Darwin and so on – are rather different from that of her Sunday-go-to-church-life where truth is a matter of divine revelation. Ryan is aware but unruffled by the fact that her scientific colleagues have some level of disdain for her religious convictions. On the other hand, she shrugs off some of her priest's dogmatically derived views on homosexuality in the light of her own son's being gay. She doesn't worry much about the relation of one set of beliefs to the other. I have met many people who would fit Rorty's hypothetical Dr. Ryan. This, I suppose, would be an example of what you used the term 'bad faith' for a few minutes ago?

Socrates: Yes, absolutely. The one set of beliefs contradict the other. She has to be consistent.

G.O.D.: Why?

Socrates: Why what?

G.O.D.: Why does she have to be consistent?

Socrates: Because those are the rules of the intellectual game.

G.O.D.: Well, those are the rules of one intellectual game at least, and possibly others as well, but perhaps do not apply everywhere.

Socrates: But they must!

G.O.D.: Well, you know I want to agree with you, but I think we must fully appreciate Rorty's argument as well.

Socrates: Okay, you mean I'm missing something here.

G.O.D.: Yes, you are missing the detachment of ontology from epistemology here. Or perhaps even more fundamentally a change in what we have been seeing as ontological and epistemological questions. What we have been doing so far focuses upon ontology as existence, as the nature of what exists, as descriptors of things-in-themselves. We are inclined to see 'truth' as dependent upon the nature of things-in-themselves, upon the nature of reality. Pragmatists, William James, for example, instead sees ideas as true insofar as they help us to get into satisfactory relationships with other parts of our experience. You see how this works with respect to the religion versus science question and Rorty's hypothetical Dr. Ryan.

Socrates: Yes, I see that. Her 'religious truths' facilitate some aspects of living for her quite well and are therefore true; whereas her scientific beliefs facilitate quite different aspects of her life and thinking . . . and are thereby true for that reason. Ontology, the nature of things-in-themselves, doesn't even come into it.

G.O.D.: Yes, at least not ontology thought of in that way. Rather for Rorty, ontology is only about being, specifically *human being*, and not 'human beings' as existent objects in the world as they would be for realists. Rather it is about the conditions of humans *being* in the world; again, not human beings as phenomena but rather humans *being*. And it is a condition of our being that we always approach reality through our interests in relation to it. And it is another condition of our being that we always approach reality through language, and truth and falsity are properties of language. There is thus no 'thing-in-itself' about which we may have better and worse descriptions. But rather our knowledges are produced in language in relation to our purposes, sometimes quite variable in relation to different purposes. What counts as knowledge is what works best in the light of those purposes.

Socrates: I don't know why, but this is starting to remind me of Nietzsche and postmodernism.

G.O.D.: Well, the Nietzschean connection is there in the pragmatist philosophical roots. Nietzsche asserted that we – humanity – are not interested in truth, that we are only interested in power and that claims to truth are really only one strategy in the struggle for power. The pragmatists would go along with that insofar as they share a rejection of truth as defined in any kind of realist fashion. Rather Rorty asserts, following both James and Dewey in this, that what is actually going on when we call a belief true, is that there are no other competing beliefs that serve the same purpose equally well for us.

Socrates: So, I suppose that is practical enough, labeling something true if it serves people's purposes. But aren't they giving up on *really* understanding anything?

G.O.D.:   They wouldn't put it quite that way. But they are giving up on a notion of knowledge and truth as corresponding to the intrinsic nature of things. They would deny that things actually have an intrinsic nature, as opposed to the situation we live in whereby we produce more or less useful descriptions of things according to our various purposes.

Socrates: So, the utility of the beliefs in question is essentially the bedrock of pragmatism.

G.O.D.:   That is basically it. John Dewey described and labeled it as **instrumentalism**. Instrumentalism then, is the application of knowledge to interactions with the environment and surroundings. Knowledge is not gained by passive observation but through active engagement. The relevance of theorising comes in as a sort of rehearsal of ideas before the moment of engagement that is an inevitable part of learning. Logical principles are understood in terms of their utility in rehearsing these sorts of encounters. W.V.O. Quine argues that philosophy is not a distinctive discipline that looks in on science from the outside. Rather he conceives of philosophy as a science itself, rather than a practice that precedes science. Ontological questions then are like any physicist or chemist's questions, where defining the boundaries of the discipline too falls within the discipline. We'll find later on an ironic and curious affinity of this with critical realism's justification for its ontology.

But long before we come to that there is still a matter of making a distinction between the crude and more sophisticated variants of pragmatism. Cornell West criticises pragmatism with a critique focused upon its cruder formulations and applications. He famously called it 'the American evasion of Philosophy' and applied it to politics. Among the left, he argued, there is a hyper-pragmatism that is suspicious of abstract thought, that insists on a myopic focus, that extols activism as the highest good, and that deplores any debate among intellectuals as a waste of time while the world grieves. Confronted by any sort of intellectual critique, activist hyper-pragmatism responds by saying 'this doesn't matter; intellectuals criticizing other intellectuals is a trivial indulgence while we face serious problems like racism, economic inequality, and climate change'. Jeet Heer argued (*New Republic*, April 24, 2015) that if we accept the principles of hyper-pragmatism, then it's never a good time to think and argue, since the world is always full of evils that need to be protested.

Socrates: Okay, so that's the crude version of pragmatism applied to politics. You could call it a kind of 'leap before you look' philosophy.

G.O.D.:	Very good way of putting it! It shows in a single phrase what's wrong with it. But we can also find a crude pragmatism sometimes embedded in social scientific research. Steve Borgatti, one of the theorists of the grounded theory approach, defines grounded theory as a method of using empirical data without preconceived theories. He calls for a systematic rigour in building theory from the data. However, many researchers simply use "grounded theory" as an eclectic approach, basically a whatever-seems-to-work, under-theorized approach.
Socrates:	Why do I get the feeling here that proponents of pragmatism or grounded theory wouldn't be happy with the way you are describing it?
G.O.D.:	Yes, you are quite right; I'm sure they wouldn't be. But this is simply a condition of philosophising. It is something I have warned you about before. You need to read everything I tell you with a dose of scepticism; I am presenting arguments to you through the filter of my own biases, and I am not a pragmatist.
Socrates:	No, I didn't think so.
G.O.D.:	Actually though, the contemporary neo-pragmatist Patrick Baert makes a conceptual distinction between what he calls the pragmatic attitude or pragmatic stance, as opposed to pragmatism as a philosophy. The earlier pragmatist, William James, speaks of it as an attitude of orientation, of looking away from first things, principles, categories, supposed necessities; and of looking towards last things, fruits, consequences, facts. I would say that this pragmatic attitude corresponds with the cruder pragmatism and/or grounded theory that I was describing. The pragmatic stance implies that the choice of theories or techniques depends on the particular topic of investigation or situation at hand rather than on a well-articulated philosophical or theoretical position. Not only is the validity of ideas based upon their *consequences*; the value of distinguishing them, relies on there being *differences* in their consequences. Theories then become instruments, not goals. Pragmatism agrees with positivism in its disdain for metaphysical abstractions. I see this as an anti-intellectual tendency, particularly so with regard to ontology and epistemology but also with respect to methodology.
Socrates:	This is reminding me of something.
G.O.D.:	Paul Feyerabend, perhaps?
Socrates:	That's the guy. What was the name of his book called?
G.O.D.:	*Against Method*. The sub-title of the book is 'Outline of an Anarchist Theory of Knowledge'. The anarchism is a kind of epistemological anarchy, which removes the philosophical demand for consistency in doing science. Principally his argument is against a singular scientific method.
Socrates:	Oh yeah right, he is the 'anything goes' guy.

G.O.D.:   Well, actually in saying that he was really just poking fun at the monistic and rationalist philosophers of science. He was characterising the history of science as a history of quite diverse approaches. But I think he would actually be in agreement with what Baert was calling the pragmatic attitude and demonstrating its successful historical application by various scientists. This is actually consonant with critical realism as well . . . though articulated by them very differently . . . more along the lines of asserting that the scientific method must be appropriate to its object of knowledge.

But pragmatism *as a philosophy* is quite different. Baert takes as his base line William James' perspective: Pragmatism is sceptical of intellectual disputes, if taking one or another position has no practical consequences for anyone.

Socrates: That sounds to me pretty similar to your definition of crude pragmatism. I think I'm missing the distinction you are trying to make.

G.O.D.:   Think of it like this: the crude pragmatism is under-theorised because it is basically rejecting all attempts at having a consistent philosophy underlying one's research or critiques. Whereas, the more sophisticated pragmatism Baert wishes to promote does not do this blanket rejection of philosophy. Consistent with James' idea, he believes that intellectual disputes ought to be rejected if they have no practical consequences with regard to one position, as opposed to another. But he does not believe that this applies across the board with respect to meta-theoretical positions. Rather, his version of pragmatism anyway, is focused upon the practical irrelevance of a particular set of questions . . . mainly ontological questions. He argues that questions about inner essences or ontology are scholastic enterprises. Answering them in one way or another makes no real difference to how you would go about trying to achieve the practical answers to the questions the empirical sciences focus upon.

Socrates: So, it is just the ontological debates about truth that he sees as irrelevant.

G.O.D.:   Well, actually I think both Baert and Rorty before him would see the theories of knowledge focused upon ontology, critical realism for example, as even being pernicious. Critical realism would just be the latest in a history of epistemological positions that they call '**representationalism**'.

Socrates: That would be the idea that something represents something . . . oh never mind, I'm being silly.

G.O.D.:   Not really. You're closer than you might think. Representationalism for Rorty and Dewey, and Baert too for that matter, is considered a widespread view in the philosophy of social science; it is one that proceeds seriously with a misguided metaphor concerning research aims, even failing to see that the metaphor is a simply a metaphor and not some fundamental reality of the situation. Dewey called it the '**spectator theory of knowledge**'. Rorty spoke of it as theory of knowledge whereby it is a kind of 'mirroring', hence the title of his most famous book: *Philosophy and the Mirror of Nature*.

Socrates: So Rorty believes that our knowledges mirror the nature that they are supposed to be knowledges of.

G.O.D.: No, no, quite the opposite! This is, according to Rorty, a long-standing *misconception* in the history of epistemology and the philosophy of science.

Rather, representationalists, as Baert asserts, assume that social research aims to map or depict the social world as accurately and completely as possible. Social theory provides the necessary building blocks for this social cartography. Empirical research is regarded as fruitful if the theory used is shown to be applicable and to allow for the social mapping to take place effectively.

Socrates: So what's wrong with that?

G.O.D.: Well, let's take Rorty's 'mirroring' first. The mind is a mirror that 'reflects' reality is a long-standing notion in the history of philosophy since the seventeenth century. But what actually is mind? It is not the same as brain. Our brains are physical. Our brains are part of material reality, which would then make the mind immaterial. But while 'physical' and 'material' are synonyms, 'mental' and 'immaterial' certainly do not appear to be. Essentially, Rorty argues that such philosophy simply leaves us in a tangle of confusion.

Socrates: Well, I can relate to that . . . but carry on.

G.O.D.: Rorty argues that if we are unclear about what we mean by the term 'mental', then what we call 'philosophy of mind' is a series of rather odd and useless disputes. This is one side of the mirror, as it were. *Philosophy and the Mirror of Nature* gives a fairly persuasive critique of not only this imagery but the tradition of thought that used it un-reflectively . . . pardon the little joke.

Socrates: Excuse me?

G.O.D.: The metaphor of mirroring, of reality being reflected in the mind, I said on behalf of Rorty, was being used *un*-reflectively.

Socrates: Okay, got it. Ha ha.

G.O.D.: If you look in the mirror, you see that your mirror image looks like you, right?

Socrates: Yeah, so?

G.O.D.: Well, in what sense could you say that the knowledges, expressed in words or mathematical formulations, look like what they are meant to be knowledges of? The knowledge is either linguistic or mathematical, whereas the subject matter of the alleged knowledge is . . . well it could be many different things actually . . . it could be something material; it could be an action; it could be a condition; it could be a relationship or set of relationships . . . but definitely something other than the mathematics or language used to describe it.

Socrates: So the letters C A T don't look like the four-legged feline they are used to describe, and we are back to Saussure and his principal of arbitrariness?

G.O.D.:   Hmm. That is a tack on this I wasn't expecting. But, well, no, not really, it does connect up with a kind of non-representationalist philosophy of language that is also a non-representationalist episte-mology . . . but it would be Derrida rather than Saussure that it connects with, or certainly that Rorty connects with. But rather than go into that, I'll try and put this another way.

It is a rejection of any and all versions of a **correspondence theory of truth**. These epistemologies, formulated in a variety of ways, all see knowledges as in some sense 'corresponding' to reality. Truth is a matter of degree of relative correspondence. Pragmatists such as Rorty, usually express this idea in terms of a visual metaphor . . . like I just mentioned before; hence Dewey's expression: 'the spectator theory of knowledge'. And this is, according to the prag-matists, badly misguided! But correspondence need not be expressed, or believed to be accurately 'represented', by a visual metaphor.

Socrates: You're trying to be funny there: 'a correspondence being accurately represented'?

G.O.D.:   Good! I'm glad you're following me.

Socrates: Yes, but not only can I now see what is wrong with knowledges looking like what they are knowledges of, but I also can't see any other way of expressing degrees of correspondence in a theory of truth and knowledge. Basically, it is looking to me like the pragma-tists are right. But I know that is not what you believe.

G.O.D.:   Well, no, it isn't. But there is a measure of irony in the relationship between what I believe is correct and what pragmatists, Rorty in particular, believe about knowledge, truth, correspondence, and what is pragmatic. In his book *Contingency, Irony, and Solidarity* . . . yes, there is irony in that he uses irony as an important concept in his book as demonstrated by its title, but his notion of irony is not what we are interested in here. Rather we want to discuss his views on the relationship of language to reality, which he would say that, in a sense anyway, there isn't really one . . . or rather that any con-nection is accidental or contingent because of its very nature as a human creation. Descriptions of the world are not true or false by virtue of their relationships to the actual properties of the world being described but rather by human consensus. This I believe, by the way, is a terrible notion of truth! Truth is determined in this sense either by naked power or a kind of democracy. Is global climate change a real phenomenon? Well, the statement 'Climate change is a hoax' is true if enough people believe it.

Socrates: I'm still not sure what I think. But whatever it is I don't believe *that*. It's funny because just a moment ago I was thinking maybe the pragmatists were right. My ideas are shifting along with the way you put things. I've got to get a grip on this for myself.

G.O.D.: You will; don't worry. Give yourself time to intellectually digest things. Perhaps it is the way I put it, and perhaps it is that the way Patrick Baert puts it sounds more reasonable than Rorty. But anyway we have yet to get to the real irony of the relationship between Rorty's position and my own.

Socrates: Yours is a critical realist position, right? And it is based upon ontology, and pragmatists like Rorty don't think much of ontological based notions of truth . . . quite the opposite, in fact.

G.O.D.: Yes, you've got a better grasp of this than you give yourself credit for. And here is where the irony is: Garry Potter has defended the critical realist ontologically based notions of truth with what he calls '**the pragmatic epistemological guarantee**'.

Socrates: Okay, what's that then?

G.O.D.: All right, a little patience, the concept derives from an argument with quite a few steps. Do you remember the problem of induction? We considered it in relation to Popper and falsification.

Socrates: Yes, because conclusions about the world based upon inductive inference are logically unwarranted, and science relies upon inductive inference that implies that science, rather than being the wholly rational method of obtaining knowledge that it is reputed to be, is actually based upon irrational premises. Popper was unhappy with that conclusion and tried to show that science does not arrive at its conclusions from induction. This is where falsification comes in. We cannot absolutely prove something true no matter how many examples we have, but we can prove something false with only one instance. Science proceeds by making risky predictions and then trying to falsify them. Scientific laws are our best as yet un-falsified predictive assertions.

G.O.D.: Very good! I'm glad you remember all of that so well!

Socrates: I was drawing from my notes actually.

G.O.D.: Never mind. The important thing is that you *understand* the argument.

Socrates: I do; I get it.

G.O.D.: Okay, we'll come back to that in a minute. Potter's understanding of truth is a correspondence notion of truth; it is a notion of truth, like that which other critical realists have, that is grounded in ontology. The ontological description of reality that he uses is that reality is ordered and structured with different levels to it. He derives this ontological description from *scientific theoretical and empirical descriptions of reality*. So, that for example, the level of reality we mainly function on understands solid things – chairs, tables, ice, trees, whatever – as motionless material relatively opaque things without space within them. Yet we know that on the molecular and atomic level, there is constant motion and a great deal of space between the '**things**' – electrons, protons and so on – and though these descriptions would seem to contradict one another in a superficial linguistic sense, there is no real contradiction between them. This is because truth and knowledge correspond to a stratified reality with ontological depth.

So, these ontological descriptions of the critical realist actually derive, broadly speaking, from both scientific *and* more mundane everyday conclusions about reality.

Socrates: So, you're saying that critical realists derive their ontological notions from everyday and scientific practice and conclusions. But shouldn't the ontology precede the scientific practice and justify it as method? It sounds like critical realists, or Potter anyway, are doing it the wrong way around.

G.O.D.: What Potter is doing is this: instead of attempting to deny that scientific knowledge is based upon logically unwarranted inductive inference, as did Popper, Potter accepts that both science and our everyday knowledges are constantly utilising induction, but he then argues that our basing our knowledges upon induction and our notion of truth as corresponding with a reality that in broad strokes has the characteristics our science and everyday practices say it has, is actually logically warranted.

Socrates: He's arguing that inductive inference has the same rational, logical justification, as does deductive inference?

G.O.D.: No, he is not asserting that. Rather he is saying that ultimately all our alleged knowledges about the world have inductive inference caught up with them. He says that we are condemned to induction, as it were.

Socrates: To learn about the world we have to use induction?

G.O.D.: Yes. But we can then make a deduction about this circumstance.

Socrates: Yes?

G.O.D.: Yes. We can say that all our knowledges, whether of the everyday sort or the more rigorously derived scientific knowledges, are, because of doubts about induction, only *apparently* knowledge. We can, though, make a deduction about this situation, and we can do so without speaking to any *particular* knowledge claim. Either the world really is ordered, structured and stratified in terms of ontological depth or it isn't. He uses an arithmetic analogy to make his point here.

Socrates: Aw . . . just when I was thinking that this was going to be simple and straightforward.

G.O.D.: It is. Imagine an infinitely long sequence of numbers and then imagine taking a fairly large segment of that sequence and analysing it. Your analysis discovers patterns to the sequence, perhaps even rules for categorisation and predictions concerning the next number in the sequence. Okay, what is your situation now? Could this infinitely long sequence of numbers that we have analysed in part and found it to contain a repeating pattern, in fact *not have this pattern really*? It just has it *apparently*, because the particular part of the sequence being examined does.

Socrates: Yeah, okay, I guess that could be. You wouldn't know that the apparent pattern, was only apparently a pattern, until you saw more of the sequence, maybe even just one more number, and then you could see that it didn't repeat and your pattern didn't in fact exist.

G.O.D.:   And this is analogous to our situation in the universe; it is analogous to our relationship of knowledge to reality. We see only a small portion of the universe, but we have discovered patterns. So, the situation is either the patterns really exist or they don't. Either reality is structured or not. Either we have some knowledge about it or we have none. This we can deduce with respect to the *apparent*-patterns-situation that is our situation with respect to knowledge. We can *deduce* that we have a straightforward either/or situation to decide upon with regard to our alleged knowledges and the ontology that goes along with them. But this logical choice is not a *real choice*. This is because we can only make one of the choices if we are to even minimally function in the world. The pattern overall may or may not exist, but we have to assume that it does in order to be able to conclude anything and act upon our inferences. This is the pragmatic epistemological guarantee: we must accept that some of our knowledge, some of the rules and patterns we have inferred, really exist in order simply to function.

Socrates: All right, let me think about this for a moment. So his argument is that . . . and I'm putting it a lot more simply than you did . . . for purely practical reasons we *must* accept that our knowledge, some of it anyway, really is knowledge? And that means that we can deduce an ontological description of an ordered and structured reality.

G.O.D.:   Yep, you've got it.

Socrates: But isn't that too simple, a kind of trivial truth?

G.O.D.:   In one sense it is trivial; in another it is profound because a great deal can be built upon it. But then, as I keep telling you, I could be wrong. The pragmatists could be right; you could be right. Maybe even some of the postmodernists are right to assert there is no right and wrong.

Socrates: No, I know you well enough now to know that you think you're right and everyone else is wrong . . . most *particularly* the postmodernists. So, critical realism, the school of thought closest to your own views should be interesting. I'm looking forward to seeing what you really believe.

G.O.D.:   Well, that will be in our next session.

DISCUSSION QUESTIONS

1   Do you think science and religious belief systems are incompatible? When science and religious dogma are apparently in direct contradiction to one another, is it intellectually 'bad faith' to ignore this contradiction?

2   Do you think Richard Rorty's argument, that the frequent apparent contradictions between scientific 'truths' and religious 'truths' are only apparently so, is correct? That is, do you think that such 'truths' are not really in competition with one another, that they are satisfying different needs and therefore can both be 'true'?

3   More generally than the previous question, do you agree or disagree with Richard Rorty's argument that truth is not about 'mirroring' reality but rather a property of language in relation to different human concerns?

4   Do you think that a correspondence notion of truth contains a visual metaphor? That is, does our knowledge of reality somehow 'look like' what it is knowledge of? If not, then what else could 'truth corresponding with how reality really is' actually mean?

5   Do you think Potter's 'pragmatic epistemological guarantee' succeeds in doing the job it is intended to do? Does it really 'guarantee' that our alleged knowledges really are such?

FURTHER READING SUGGESTIONS

Journals

Contemporary Pragmatism (Brill)
European Journal of Pragmatism and American Philosophy (the journal of the European Pragmatism Association)

Pragmatism classics

Dewey, J. (2007) [1938] *Logic – The Theory of Inquiry,* New York: Saerchinger Press.
James, W. (1907) *Pragmatism, a New Name for Some Old Ways of Thinking; Popular Lectures on Philosophy*, Green & Co., Longmans.
Pierce, C. S. (author) Turresi, P.A. (ed.) (1997) *Pragmatism as a Principle and Method of Right Thinking,* State University of New York Press, Albany, New York – a collection of manuscripts for Pierce's lectures given at Harvard University in 1903.

Epistemological anarchism

Feyerabend, P. (1975) *Against Method Outline of an Anarchist Theory of Knowledge*, Verso, New York.

Grounded theory

Borgatti, Steve (2006) 'Introduction to Grounded Theory' on-line <http://www.analytictech.com/mb870/introtogt.htm>

Richard Rorty

Rorty, R. (1979) *Philosophy and the Mirror of Nature*, Princeton University Press, Princeton.
——— (1989) *Contingency, Irony, and Solidarity*, Cambridge University Press, Cambridge, UK.

Contemporary neo-pragmatism

Baert, P. (2005) *Philosophy of the Social Sciences: Towards Pragmatism*, Polity, Cambridge, UK.
Baert, P. (2011) 'Neo-pragmatism and Phenomenology: A Proposal', *European Journal of Pragmaticism and American Philosophy* III(2) pp. 29–40.

Critique of the pragmatic stance

Heer, J. (2015) 'Acting without Thinking: The Most Effective Protest Movements Have Been Enriched by Debating Ideas and Strategy', *New Republic* April.
Critical realist debates about Roy Bhaskar's "spiritual turn"
Hartwig, M (2009) '"Orthodox" Critical Realism and the Critical Realist Embrace', *Journal of Critical Realism* 8(3), Brill, pp. 233–257.
Potter, G. (2006) 'Reopening the Wound – Against God and Bhaskar', *Journal of Critical Realism* 5(1), Brill, pp. 92–109.

The pragmatic epistemological guarantee

Potter, G. (1999) *The Bet: Truth in Science, Literature and Everyday Knowledges*, Ashgate, Farnham, UK, pp. 7–14.

CHAPTER 10

HYPERREALITY AND CRITICAL REALISM, SIMULACRA AND SOCIAL SCIENCE

The simulacrum is never that which conceals the truth – it is the truth which conceals that there is none. The simulacrum is true.

> *Ecclesiastes* as quoted by Jean Baudrillard (but I think he just made it up)

All science would be superfluous if the outward appearances and the essences of things directly coincided.

Karl Marx

In fact the likelihood that sociology will disappoint or vex the powers that be rises to the extent that it successfully fulfils its strictly scientific function.

Pierre Bourdieu

OUTLINE OF MAJOR POINTS TO BE COVERED

1   Baudrillard's general notion that we have lost our collective hold upon reality and are now living under a tyranny of the image is elucidated using his provocative assertion that America is Disneyland. There are four successive stages of the image. First, it is seen as representing realities. Second, it is seen as distortedly representing reality. Third, it is falsely representing this representational process, signifying a linkage to reality (whether distorted or not) that no longer exists. Last, it is seen as wholly floating, connecting only to itself, i.e. to other images.

2   The political and social scientific significance of such a view is made through a contrast with the perspective of Bourdieu. In the latter theorist's work, an assertion, for example, 'that public opinion does not exist' stands first of all critically in a political sense. Second, it stands as a criticism of ideologically distorted *scientistic* social scientific practice. It is an assertion that both can be investigated and used as a guide for the improvement of future practice. Baudrillard's view, by contrast, is seen as nihilistic and paralysing. The comparison of these two points of view is used to illustrate what is at stake philosophically, scientifically and politically between postmodernism and critical realism.

3   A brief encapsulation of the book's central theme is provided. It is argued that if the understanding of the nature of natural science is re-conceptualised

along critical realist lines, then the objections of the humanist critique of positivist social science becomes irrelevant to the consideration of a possible unity of natural and social science. The critical realist notion of scientificity is such that hermeneutic understanding can be incorporated within it.

4   Realism is outlined as a **thing**-based ontology and ontologically based philosophy of science. It does not begin with epistemological questions. It asks instead what must reality be like for, first, scientific experimentation to be intelligible as a meaningful activity, and second, successful as such. This question is then broadened to ask what reality must be like for social life to be possible at all.

5   The above view is contrasted with the implicit ontology of empiricism and positivism. This ontology is shown to be impoverished. It leaves out a notion of real causal mechanisms as characteristics of 'things' and instead focuses upon constant conjunctures of events.

   a   Things are described as possessing causal powers which may or may not be exercised dependent upon their interaction with other things and the counter-acting forces of other causal powers. Non-events (absences) and potential are thus important features of realist ontology.

   b   The real is explained in terms of three domains: the empirical, the actual and the real. This last is the dimension of the unexercised causal powers which things possess and which is left out of empiricism's implicit ontology.

   c   Reality is understood to possess depth. Thus explanations are likewise addressed to different levels of reality.

6   Scientific laws are to be understood as **tendencies**. Prediction, while still desirable and important, is thus dethroned from its pride of place in the positivist conception of science. Falsification and confirmation are now understood as part, but only part, of science. Empirical observations are no longer decisive in the same way. This removes some of the objections to a unity of social and natural science.

7   There is no single scientific method. Methods must be appropriate to their objects. Again this removes some of the objections to a unity of science. Hermeneutic analyses can now be understood as scientific or not, according to different sets of criteria from before.

8   The realist philosophy of science is explained as being fallibilist. Reality is, however it is. But our ostensible knowledges of it are fallible and subject to improvement, revision and even upon occasion may be wholly false. Science is understood as a social practice. It is something that is engaged in by human beings collectively and thus subject to a whole range of social, economic, cultural and historical determinants, as well as individual error and culpability.

9   The critical element in critical realism is explained through a brief comparison of the differences and similarities between it and critical theory. Philosophy and science can frequently reveal the source of mistaken views about the nature of reality to lie within reality itself. Contradictions in scientific or

philosophical views are thus often expressive of real contradictions in reality. The exposure of such is thus linked to human emancipation, as it posits a need not only to change mistaken views, but to also change the reality, which gives rise to such views.

DIALOGUE

Socrates:	Why America?
G.O.D.:	Why America what?
Socrates:	I've been reading a little Baudrillard. He says first that L.A. is Disneyland, then he extends it to the whole of America. Why America? Why not England? Or Sweden or Japan?
G.O.D.:	I see. Do you understand his argument?
Socrates:	Well, I didn't read all of it and well . . . it seemed pretty strange to me.
G.O.D.:	Are you English?
Socrates:	No, I'm American. I guess that's why I'm asking. Is he casting some particular slur on my country?
G.O.D.:	I'll leave that for you to decide. Have you ever been to Victoria?
Socrates:	Victoria in London?
G.O.D.:	No, Victoria, British Columbia, Canada.
Socrates:	No, I've never even heard of it.
G.O.D.:	Well, its major industry is tourism. It sells itself to the potential American tourist as a little piece of England without having to cross the ocean. It has got an olde-English-style grand hotel, London double-decker buses with London place-names on the front of each of them (only they're not real city buses, they're tour buses), the old-fashioned red wooden telephone boxes they used to have in England – it's chock a block full of things like that. The downtown area can seem very much like a tourist theme park. It can seem a very Disneyland-type experience to the foreign visitors; particularly so if they happen to be English. A great many of its pubs are English-themed in this way. They look, in fact, more like English pubs than do real English pubs.
Socrates:	You mean they really seem more English, more authentic?
G.O.D.:	No, not at all! No one from England would ever think they were in a pub in England. But they'd recognise all the little touches. They would instantly see what I meant about them being more English than real English pubs.
Socrates:	Are you still answering my question as to why America?
G.O.D.:	Yes, I am. There is a chain of pub-style restaurants with an American theme to them in England; they may even be run by an American company.

Socrates:	And they don't seem authentically American either?
G.O.D.:	No, they don't.
Socrates:	But they seem more American than real American places?
G.O.D.:	No, they don't seem that either. That's the point. That's why America. Other places in the world have some of the features that America possesses to some degree. There seems to be a general process of the Americanisation of world culture occurring. But no place has the features of postmodernity to quite the same degree as America.
Socrates:	But didn't you say Victoria was in Canada?
G.O.D.:	North America. Anyway, it's a minor detail. The important thing is why he was saying that any place was Disneyland – other than Disneyland. Did you understand that?
Socrates:	Yeah, part of it anyway. Disneyland is a theme park. When you enter a theme park you are supposed to be entering a land of make-believe, of intentional illusions. You leave the humdrum of everyday reality behind you and participate in an experience of which illusion is very much a part. There is supposed to be a clear boundary with respect to this experience of illusion. Inside is the theme park. Outside is reality. But Baudrillard would say that that is itself an illusion. Disneyland functions as a comforting symbol for us in that manner. It symbolises the illusion that we have clear boundaries between reality and illusion. It falsely signifies for us the reality that is America. But it doesn't exist anymore, that reality. When we drive through America, we look out of the car window and say things like 'Wow, that looks just like the hillbilly country in the film *Deliverance*' or 'the Grand Canyon looks like the film set of *Thelma and Louise*'. Or you listen to a conversation and note with a sense of unreality that it sounds like something straight out of a commercial. Some people do have conversations comparing washing powders and recommend shampoos for dandruff problems. Reality looks like TV rather than TV looking like reality. Thus, America is Disneyland.
G.O.D.:	Good examples. Did you really hear people comparing laundry detergents?
Socrates:	That was my mom actually.
G.O.D.:	Okay, well, the Disneyland argument is just one example of a more general thesis concerning simulation. Did you read about Baudrillard's notion of the four successive phases of the image?
Socrates:	No, what are they?
G.O.D.:	The first is very straightforward. The image reflects reality. The animals and mountains in Disneyland, for example, are not real. They are to some degree supposed to be representations of real animals and mountains. The second order of simulation is that of ideology. The image masks and distorts reality. One can interpret Disneyland's 'Main Street' in this sense. It is a simulation of

small-town America, a representation of an idealised small-town American main street that symbolises many things about the American way of life. However, there is an element of distortion in the picture. It represents a past, perhaps the 1950s, that never was, and with that a notion of values and morality that is as hypocritical as it is untenable. Well, that is one way of looking at it anyway. The key aspect of simulation in this sense is of images as false representation.

The third order of simulation you articulated yourself concerning the illusion of boundaries, i.e. inside, the amusement park fantasy, outside, cold reality. It in effect simulates the other two phases of images and simulation. It simulates the first order signification process of signifiers representing signifieds connected to real world referents. It also simulates the second order of simulation, that is, of ideological simulation. It simulates a situation of boundaries between fantasy and reality, truth and falsity. It comforts us with notions of fantasy theme parks representing or falsely representing an undeniably real world outside their boundaries. The boundaries do not exist. Thus the third phase of the image is the making of an absence. But even here, there is implicitly some notion of reality in relation to the image. That is, the absence is a real absence. Something we, as human beings, are missing, as it were. Main street Disneyland connects up with a real nostalgia even though the past that its image represents is not a real past that we experienced. The fourth phase of the image is quite simply pure simulation. As Baudrillard puts it, 'It is its own pure simulacrum' (*America*, 1988, p. 170). We do not have simulations of real things; we have only simulations of simulations. Any grip on the reality principle is gone – if we ever had one. This is the domain of **hyperreality**. Does this notion appeal to you?

Socrates: I don't know. It seems to connect up with some of my subjective perceptions of life; it connects with perceptions I have sometimes. But something about it bothers me as well. I still feel there is a reality and some kind of sense of it as well. What does it mean to say that we don't? Now, before you start tearing this notion apart, will you give me some more examples or arguments for it? I want to think this over a little bit more. Also could you define 'simulacrum' and 'hyperreality' for me?

G.O.D.:   A **simulacrum** is an exact copy for which no original exists.

Socrates: Hmm. I quite like that. Can you give me an example of one?

G.O.D.:   Sure, Andy Warhol's prints. What is the original in a limited edition print run? That was part of Warhol's point concerning originality and authenticity in art actually. Another example of someone being postmodernist *avant la lettre*. And what about e-mail messages sent out to multiple recipients? Is one the original or are they all copies; and if they are all copies, copies of what?

Socrates: Hmm. I both like this notion and yet, as I said, something bothers me about it.

G.O.D.: Good. Because it is actually philosophically incoherent – from a realist point of view anyway. There would be other ways of explaining such examples that do not have such unsettling effects upon our common-sense notions of reality.

Socrates: I'm not surprised that you would say that. What about hyperreality?

G.O.D.: Okay, I'll illustrate this notion first of all with a story. I was with a group of friends in a pub when another friend suddenly arrived tearful and distraught. She imparted to us tragic news: Edith had died. Several other of my friends began to cry as well. However, Edith was not a real person. Edith was a character in a TV situation comedy. Baudrillard asserts that the world of signs, of simulations, is more real to us than reality.

Let's think about history for a moment. I told you before that Nietzsche was a postmodernist *avant la lettre*. Well, this '*avant la lettre*' concept is one that easily fits in with our usual notions of historical time. In Baudrillard's notion of postmodernity, of hyperreal history, the sequential notion of past and present collapses into an eternal present of simulations. We can roughly date the emergence of postmodernism – somewhere around the early 1970s. Aesthetically, postmodernism arrives on the scene after the decline of influence of modernism. Philosophically, postmodernity follows the demise of modernity – modernity roughly being understood as the period from the Enlightenment to twenty or thirty years ago. However, all of these periodisations and time-frames collapse in postmodernity. They are modernist ways of viewing history.

Socrates: I'm losing the thread here. What has the understanding of history got to do with your story about the death of Edith the situation comedy star?

G.O.D.: Not the star of the sitcom, the character! As far as I know, the actress who played her is still alive and well today. In fact, were it possible for the actress to have died, and the character to have survived, it is plausible to think a great many fewer tears would have been shed. If images of reality are more real than the real, then all one needs to do to travel backwards and forwards in time, is to change the channel. On one channel we're in the old West, on another in the Middle Ages, on another in *A Million Years BC*, a time when dinosaurs and human beings were contemporaries. You see what I mean? In George Orwell's famous book *1984* there is an ideological manipulation of history. The all-powerful 'big brother' government's 'Ministry of Truth' is engaged in a constant process of re-writing the events of history. One day they are at war with one country and at peace with another; the next day it is reversed – they have always been friends with the country they were at war with the day before and always at war with their previous friends. All historical documents are re-written to reflect that fact. Everyone believes it. In Orwell's negative utopia, this was plainly depicted as ideological deception. It was done for a malign purpose and enacted conspiratorially. In our postmodern hyperreal world, however, this is not at all the case. One tall story represents another. The historical depictions do not all agree. They do not falsely represent the truth of past events. There never was a truth of past events. We have only images. Images of images of images, more real than any hypothetical past, because the images are our present. They are our only experience. One could say that Baudrillard's notion of hyperreality is a more rigorous form of empiricism than the empiricists ever dreamt of.

Socrates: Ah, I see. I get it now. I understand why this view of things really bothers you. It's because you see this philosophy stuff as really being important.

G.O.D.:   Yes, of course. And you still don't? History as a more or less truthful account of the past disappears even as a goal to be striven for. You don't see a problem with that?

Socrates: Of course, I see a problem with that. But in some ways it does seem to be a relatively accurate description of my situation. My historical knowledge is relatively sketchy. Much of it comes from TV, and not from documentaries either. The same thing is true about my knowledge of what's happening around the world. I see pictures of foreign wars, famines, a host of tragedies, and they don't seem real to me. I don't know if I've ever cried over a sitcom character, but I've been deeply moved by a lot of films. I live my life. I can see the relevance of the philosophy of science, the importance of deciding some of these questions of truth and knowledge and reality. But still, that importance is only relative to other things in my life and thus relatively pretty minor. It seems to me that Baudrillard is only articulating what must be a pretty widespread condition.

G.O.D.:   Yes, I would agree with you there. He has also expressed the view that he sees himself as an intellectual terrorist but . . .

Socrates: Sorry to interrupt, but do you mean he advocates terrorism?

G.O.D.:   No, no, not at all! No, it is intellectual terrorism. He seems to be consciously trying to achieve what Derrida's worst enemies accuse deconstruction of doing. His exaggerations – I, at least, would call them exaggerations of features of contemporary life – are destructive in nature. They are destructive with respect to our coming to an understanding of social complexity.

I was going to say that his view of himself as performing this role is probably quite positive; very likely he sees himself as being something along the lines of a Socratic gadfly, destroying complacency. But I see his work as rather being symptomatic of deep social problems, of intellectual as well as political failures in coming to grips with them. As philosophy, I don't think Baudrillard's ideas stand up terribly well. Politically, though, they are disastrous.

Socrates: What are the political implications then?

G.O.D.: Well, you've actually articulated the battle cry of one of his strategies of resistance.

Socrates: Oh yeah, how's that?

G.O.D.: Well, virtually all the postmodernist philosophers, and here I am including poststructuralists as well, have situated themselves on the left politically. Most of them have come from a left-wing political background. And all of them in one form or another have articulated a concern about the relationship between knowledge and power that included a strategy of resistance. Baudrillard's 'strategy of resistance' is to be a couch potato. The 'masses', he believes, are adopting the only strategy possible in the face of the saturation bombardment of images – simply to go with the flow, to let them wash over you and through you, neither to believe nor disbelieve anything. Being apolitical, in this sense, is the ultimate act of political resistance. It seems that you were getting at something like that when explaining your attitude concerning the relative importance of philosophy.

Socrates: I don't know if I was actually singing the battle hymn of the couch potato exactly. I was talking about the relative importance of philosophical questions about truth in comparison with one's actual experience. We are being bombarded with images. There are problems with the idea of ideological distortion. I mean, you haven't explained critical realism to me yet, but you have said it doesn't entail a subscription to an absolutist notion of truth. So, we have different cultures that understand the world differently. One culture claims to have superior knowledge to the other. Yet how can they? The empiricist scientist, who believes that ultimately knowledge is based upon experience, wishes to deny the validity of the experience of others. As you said, it seems the postmodernist is more rigorously empiricist than the empiricist; it's simply that the experience is an experience of images of reality, rather than claimed to be an experience of reality itself. We have the poststructuralists talking about signification, about having not only to speak about reality through a system of signs but to think about it that way too. I don't see how you can escape that. So, language games, regimes of truth, language and knowledge are all related to the exercise of power. Well, when you make the claim to have a better understanding of reality than someone else, you will be doing so in language. When you make that claim to the superiority of your theory over another's, you are making a bid for power. I don't see how this can be resolved.

And what difference does it make? We began this whole exercise with the observation that scientists kept on doing science regardless of its apparent 'refutation' by Hume's arguments concerning induction. You've said many times that their actual practice is often out of synch with the way they conceive it. So, science will go on. Baudrillard wasn't claiming that it wouldn't, was he? So we go on, living our lives watching TV, having contradictory thoughts about truth and reality and a host of other things. So what?

I kind of feel we have come full circle from where we began. Now, I don't mean to say that I haven't found it interesting. I have. But you began by trying to convince me of the importance of the philosophy of science, and you succeeded for a time; but I think we have gone around so many of the related issues now, that you've undermined that project. That is, at first glance, the philosophy of science seems boring and abstract, then one can see the value in it, and as one goes further, the questions become kind of interesting. But the interest is connected to the relevance ultimately. And ultimately the relevance becomes undermined. There are twenty sides to every question, each side has its own argument and plausibility to some degree, but yet is less than wholly convincing – in part because of the plausibility of its competitors, in part because of the problems it seems to generate for itself, and all of it is extremely abstract!

And what does it do for social science? There are a host of social science approaches to a host of problems. It is done in a variety of different ways. There are a variety of points of view in the philosophy of social science too. Pick your social theory; pick your area of investigation; pick your philosophical framing of it too. Life goes on; science goes on. What difference does philosophy make? Except philosophy goes on too – for the professional philosophers. But you can't expect us all to be so enthusiastic about it.

G.O.D.:   Wow! That's the longest speech you've ever made. And you make a lot of good points too. But now I want to give you some answers. Or at least, I want to give you some last arguments in the hope of changing your mind.

Socrates: Oh yes, you said you were going to give me *the* answers. Well, I wait upon them sceptically.

G.O.D.:   I won't disappoint you. I mean, I won't disappoint you by refusing to give them, or to so over-qualify them that they seem more like questions than answers. Then we'll see what you think. But a question first concerning Baudrillard, though: what sort of social science could be based upon his notion of hyperreality? What might he recommend?

Socrates: I don't know; I've only read a little bit of him and heard what you've had to say.

G.O.D.:   Well, in his earlier writings he called for the development of a **political economy of the sign**. He combined a critique of Marxism with an analysis of contemporary capitalism to conclude the necessity of this. I'll spare you his critique of Marx's notion of production, but the proliferation of signs and symbols, the new technologies of communication we find in contemporary capitalism, makes the analysis of signification in relation to politics and economics seem obviously quite an important task. Yes?

Socrates: Yes.

G.O.D.: But I don't think he produced a political economy of the sign. He produced his works of intellectual terror instead. He gave us the notion of hyperreality. How does it connect with social science? Baudrillard gave us some explicit examples as a basis for comparison with more conventional views. Here are two controversial historical and sociological assertions: 1) Watergate must not be understood as a scandal, and 2) public opinion does not exist. Both Baudrillard and Pierre Bourdieu would propound these views. I really hesitate to call Bourdieu 'conventional'. It is so only in relation to Baudrillard's position. These two assertions are quite radical. However, they mean something very, very different in the mouth of one as opposed to the other. Do you remember the Watergate affair, by the way?

Socrates: I'm too young to remember it, but I read about it. There was a burglary in the Watergate Hotel, hence the name. Things were stolen from the Democrats. The burglary was ordered by the White House, and a cover-up was undertaken. The subsequent investigation led to many people resigning, including the President, and to a lot of people going to jail.

G.O.D.: That's right. Now, Baudrillard says that Bourdieu would apparently agree with him, that Watergate was not a scandal however much it was hyped up as such in the media. But Bourdieu would understand it in terms of ideology. It was not a scandal because to be a scandal something has to be unusual, outside the normal workings of the political sphere. The media are thus propagating an ideological mystification in their presentation of the Watergate affair as a scandal. By doing so, they conceal the real workings of power in a capitalist society. That is the real scandal!

However, Baudrillard would argue that Bourdieu is still clinging to an outmoded notion of ideological representation and truth. There is no distortion; there is no truth to be misrepresented; thus, there is no scandal; there is only power, power and images.

No matter whether one agrees or not, one can easily see what Bourdieu means. It is a clear thesis about the workings of government, the media and the workings of capitalism. It is a thesis that may be partially true, either in the sense of being banally obvious, or else being truly illuminating as to the nature of social reality. It is a thesis that may be adjudged in terms of relative truth or falsity and that may be completely false in its most important elements. It is a thesis that we can judge according to criteria of reasoning and evidence. In short, it is a scientific thesis, or at least potentially it could be formulated as such. This rather bold political claim thus can be easily translated into a practical social scientific research program.

But what does Baudrillard's assertion mean? There is nothing to be investigated. There is nothing to look for behind the scenes of the media representation. No, the media representation of Watergate is not truthful insofar as it represents Watergate as a scandal because it only presents us with images of scandal. But it is not false either because there is no truth underneath the representational layers. There is nothing to investigate! There is only the TV to be passively watched – the ultimate resistance to manipulation supposedly.

A second example: public opinion does not exist. Bourdieu asserts this. It superficially sounds very like a Baudrillardian assertion of postmodernity. But what does he mean by it? Does he mean that people have no opinions? No, he does not mean that. He means that public opinion, in the sense of being that which is measured in market or politically commissioned opinion polls, does not exist. He means the results of such allegedly scientific surveys do not measure what they purport to be measuring. He means that the pollsters have a different sort of agenda from that of the mass of people's opinions they are allegedly attempting to measure. He means that there is pseudo-science masquerading as science ideologically functioning in the service of existing power relations. He gives us reasons for making such assertions. Again, these can be evaluated in terms of relative truth and falsity. That is, he gives us a critique of scientific practice and scientific knowledge claims in terms of their scientific failures. Implicitly, this points to a way of going about things better. It is not a dead-end road.

Is it important to be able to make such judgments as Bourdieu makes? I think, at the very least, it is important not to rule them out of court by philosophical decree. Your arguments almost entail as much. They show the reason for postmodernism's popularity. They accord with a defeat when we are confronted with complexity. There are complex levels of signification and meaning. There are contradictions that immediately arise when we attempt to sort things out. Baudrillard does not accept Bourdieu's argument. Fine. He may be quite wrong with respect to the workings of contemporary capitalism and politics. Baudrillard may be right that signification is a more complex process in contemporary society than Bourdieu realises. Maybe. But the manner in which Bourdieu's analysis is formed enables one to challenge it: to confirm it, falsify it, reformulate it on a more sophisticated level. Baudrillard's thesis, however, cannot even be investigated. Accept it. Reject it. Do both. There are many contradictions. Let's leave them be. Let's celebrate them even.

Socrates: I take your point. However, it presumes that it is possible to sort them out. You keep saying you can do this. Well, let's see you try.

G.O.D.: All right. Well, first of all I don't start from a void, and I am not alone. The production of knowledge is a social process. It is also a historical process at a particular stage. We start with what has gone before. We can identify some broad themes out of which problems and contradictions emerged. We can begin with those that arise from a positivist and empiricist understanding of natural science. We can look at past critiques of positivism.

We see objections to it of two sorts. First, it is held that it is inapplicable or only partially applicable to social science. Causal explanation and understanding are felt to be two very different sorts of things. Second, not only is positivism riddled with all sorts of problems, but even more broadly speaking, empiricism is shown to be a shaky basis for knowledge. There are a host of problems ranging from induction, the utilisation of instruments for observation, to the imbrication of theory with observation. The history of natural science shows it to be inextricably bound up with its social relationships.

Well, let's just begin by saying that empiricism is inadequate as a philosophical basis for knowledge in general and thus that all its positivist derivatives, including falsificationism, are accordingly inadequate conceptualisations of the nature of natural scientific explanations, laws and so forth. This partially solves our first big problem at a stroke. The question as to whether the positivist notions of law and explanation are applicable to social science is now irrelevant.

Now, of course, we still have to provide arguments for this claim, and an alternative way of conceiving of natural scientific explanation and so on. But the question of the applicability of scientific explanation to social phenomena must now await the elaboration of this new conception of natural science. So too with respect to all the other problems. Perhaps, for example, now that we have included the contributions of Islam to the history of scientific progress it can now be explained in such a way that it can no longer be seen as an idealised story that has many discrepancies with its apparent historical reality.

Socrates: Perhaps, perhaps! Okay, you've said before that realism provides a different account, not only of social science, but of science more generally. All right, what is it? I see how that changes the framework for all the other debates. But exactly how it changes them is going to depend upon the detail of the account of natural science it gives.

G.O.D.: Fair enough. Realism begins from ontology rather than epistemology. Its first questions are not about the nature of knowledge, either scientific or any other sort. Rather it takes as a given that we have some scientific knowledges. I'm not referring here to any particular theory or knowledge claim but to scientific knowledges in general.

Second, we also start from the realisation that science is a human activity. You'll see later how important that rather obvious observation is. We ask ontological questions about the nature of reality. What must it be like, what must be so, in order to make scientific activity intelligible? Rom Harré and Roy Bhaskar ask these questions about scientific experimentation. What presumptions need to be made about the nature of reality to give such activities a sense and purpose? What must reality be like in order for such activity to be relatively successful? These questions, one can see, are actually implicit in science's actual practice. They are assumptions that underwrite scientific activity.

Socrates: I realise you haven't got very far in developing your argument yet, but I see a problem already. You're asking what must reality be like in order for scientific experiment to produce knowledge successfully. Isn't there some circularity in this procedure? Aren't you putting the cart before the horse? How do we know it's successful? Also, isn't that the pragmatists argument?

G.O.D.:   Okay, first of all, no, it is very definitely *not* the same as the pragmatist's argument. They justify something as true on the basis of whether it works. This is not what we are doing here. We are asserting that our knowledge *is* knowledge of the world. You are replying to an ontological question with an epistemological one. Success. Hmm. What is it? It is a good question. But it illustrates the very different approach realism takes. You, and I mean here generations of philosophers as well, begin asking the question of scientific knowledges: how do we know they are in fact knowledges? This is a very important question. It is in fact an epistemological and scientific question rolled into one – if we are discussing any particular claim to knowledge. But there are more sensible approaches to the question of scientific knowledge in general. Scientists act as though their activity will potentially produce real knowledge about the world. We act as though scientific knowledge is in fact knowledge every time we use a piece of technology. Every time we step on to a plane to fly us across the ocean (or board a ship for that matter) we are assuming that the applied scientific knowledges of its design are in fact knowledges. We believe that the plane really will fly, don't we?

Socrates: Yes, of course. So you're saying that practically we don't doubt whether or not natural science has produced knowledge or not. And you're also saying that scientists engage in experimental procedures assuming that they will potentially achieve something by this. You're then asking what would make such assumptions warranted.

G.O.D.:   Exactly! For it to be possible for scientific experiments to produce knowledges successfully, reality *must* possess certain features. The very activity of performing a scientific experiment thus also assumes that it must possess these features.

Socrates: So this is like Potter's argument for his pragmatic epistemological guarantee then. Do all critical realists accept this view?

G.O.D.: No, they definitely don't. But nonetheless they do argue that reality must possess certain features to make scientific practices intelligible or successful. The question of intelligibility is a somewhat different criterion than success, but they come to the same thing in the end; they support the same ontological claims. Reality *must have* certain features.

Socrates: What features are they then?

G.O.D.: Well, before elucidating them I want to present them negatively first. The positivist empiricist view of scientific knowledge also has an underlying ontology. Or rather it has two. It has one that corresponds with its formal epistemology, and it has a second that corresponds with the activity of science. The two don't hang together consistently. The epistemology concerns itself with a description of the formal properties of scientific laws for example. As we shall see, this description implies some things about the nature of what exists, what counts as real. However, the model of activity for the empiricist implies the existence of some aspects of the real that seem to be ruled out by the formal epistemology.

Experiments produce empirically observable, constant conjunctures of events. They either succeed or fail to produce their expected outcomes in accordance with hypotheses or theories. Either way they tell us something. But what? We observe constant conjunctures of events and generalise from them universal laws. We can move either way on this. We either observe sufficient repetitions (whatever number that might be) to confirm our generalisation from our sample and thus solve the problem of induction in some rough and ready pragmatic fashion. Or we consider our explanations and laws as unfalsified hypotheses. However, either way we are left with an ontological problem.

We have an event-based ontology with two categories of reality – the empirical and the actual. Observations are held to be the basis for knowledge. However, the observations are supposed to give us knowledge of events beyond merely those that were experimentally observed. An experiment, for example, shows us that A causes B. Well, a law or explanation must extend beyond the experiment to include other examples, in fact all the other instances of A and B. A always causes B. That is, the law is either confirmed or falsified. The ontology underwriting the law thus has its two categories: 1) the observed A causing B, and 2) A causing B throughout the whole of reality. This is what gives the experiment a point, from the empiricist position, a greater reality of A's and B's beyond the limited sample experimentally observed. Otherwise the experimental activity would tell us nothing beyond itself.

But this is of course an absurdity. It not only demonstrates an impoverished ontology, but also neither explanations nor laws are actually to be found in this form. If they actually were, then an enormous portion of the complexity of the reality to be found outside the experiment would intentionally be excluded from it. In fact, this is frequently the whole point of experiments, to restrict artificially, that is by human activity, the number of variables that will interact. In the experiment only A and B are considered, but the causal relationship between them is supposed to be explanatorily applied to the wider reality where a host of other variables are to be found. The causal relationship between A and B is still supposed to hold even if no event occurs.

Socrates: I'm afraid you've lost me. You are saying that experiments induce the occurrence of events, and that empiricist epistemology then asserts that explanations consist of generalisations beyond the experiment from these observations. This, then, is to project an ontology, that is, a description of what in theory exists in reality, as two sorts of events: those that occur and then (as a subset of these) those that are observed to have occurred. Laws and explanations are generalisations from the latter to the former. Yes? I mean that's what you said. I'm a little confused.

G.O.D.:   You're quite right. What are you confused about?

Socrates: I don't know exactly. What is wrong with that?

G.O.D.:   Well, it would seem that on such a basis the old saying 'what goes up must come down' would be a good scientific law or at least a pre-scientific formulation of the law of gravity.

Socrates: Yeah? What's wrong with that? Okay, positivism is criticised for equating explanation and prediction. 'What goes up must come down' is certainly predictive, easily falsified and so on. I can see that it doesn't really explain why things behave that way. But still it tells us something.

G.O.D.:   I'm certainly not denying that the generalisation tells us something. But even the empiricist would have to concede that that is not quite the way scientific laws are formulated. Also as a universalisation the proposition is quite false. We've shot some things into space which are never coming down!

Socrates: Yeah, okay, so it's not a law. Or rather, it's a law that has been falsified.

G.O.D.:   It's a form of explanation from which one could never build upon sufficiently to have made a paper airplane fly, let alone shoot a rocket into space.

Socrates: Why do you say that?

G.O.D.:   Because there is a huge dimension of reality that is being left out. All the things that are intentionally excluded in a scientific experiment are to be found, of course, in the open system outside the controlled experimental situation. These other variables are always potentially at hand to causally influence the occurrence or non-occurrence of events outside the experimental situation. The experiment is a part of a process (that includes theorisation) to attempt to arrive at causal explanations. Scientific laws are generalisations of our understanding of causality based upon these explanations. The explanations apply to the non-laboratory situations, to the interactions of experimentally excluded variables.

Socrates: I don't see the distinction you're making here. This sounds more or less like the understanding of explanations and laws that you gave me about positivism.

G.O.D.: The difference between the realist and positivist understandings of laws and explanations is profound. Let me see if I can put it in terms of gravity and paper airplanes. Why do the planes fly? There are a variety of reasons that can be identified at a variety of levels. Why some planes fly further and faster and in different directions to others is dependent upon a complex interaction of **causal mechanisms**. We may use experiments in an attempt to understand particular causal mechanisms in isolation from other variables. But this, in effect, is to create a closed and restricted system. Reality itself is an **open system**. The paper airplane may meet with forces, say for example a heavy driving rain, that will severely limit its capacity for flight. The rain was not present in the child's construction of the experimental situation.

Socrates: The child? I thought we were talking about science here.

G.O.D.: We are using a very simple example, and I think it is useful not to create artificial divisions at the outset between scientific and everyday knowledge production. It is easy enough to reflect upon the methodological refinements that divide any scientific discipline's recommended practices from the more rough and ready 'experiments' of daily life. In cases where the same principles hold, I think simple examples may prevent us from mystification in our notions of science. The reason why 'what goes up must come down' does not qualify as a scientific law is not its simplicity, its existence as an old common-sense adage, or because as you suggested it has been falsified. It is because it is utterly detached from any explanation of causal mechanism. This is the problem with astrology by the way. Its empirical observations are not connected up with the other empirical observations (human behaviour) required to support its notions of causal mechanism, i.e. that the stars affect us.

But back to gravity. The bodily attraction of gravity's force is a causal mechanism that interacts with other causal mechanisms at any given time. This interaction produces a variety of events and sometimes non-events. Gravity may be the cause of our falling down, but we are not falling down all the time. Yet gravity is present even when no event is empirically observed. Not only is it present when no events are observed, but it is present even when events fail to occur. Potential events fail to occur because they are prevented from doing so by other causal mechanisms.

Socrates: You keep saying **causal mechanism**. This is a key realist term, I presume. I get the feeling that you think that simply because you keep repeating it I'll understand what you are on about here. But I don't! Remember all this may be very familiar to you, but it isn't to me.

G.O.D.: Okay, fair enough. I'll take another tack. In broad terms, realist ontology consists of three domains: the empirical, the actual and the real. The first two are familiar enough to you. Throughout this book we have been constantly referring to them. The empirical is simply a subset of the actual. Many events occur that have not been observed, yes? You don't have a problem with that.

Socrates: No. The empirical is part of the actual. The domain of the actual (actuality?) consists of all the events in the universe that really occur. That's it, right?

G.O.D.: Yes. So what's missing?

Socrates: Just a minute. Both the empirical and actual are real, yes?

G.O.D.: Yes.

Socrates: Okay, then I don't understand. Forget about the empirical. Does a tree make a sound in the forest even if there is no one there to hear it? Yes, it does. Okay, fine, no problem there. But if the actual is real, then it follows that what isn't actual isn't real. Yes?

G.O.D.: No. This is precisely the difference between a realist and an empiricist ontology. Here is another approach to make this clearer. Realism is a 'thing-centred' ontology; empiricism is, implicitly at least, an 'event-centred' ontology. This is where its problems originate. Let us instead conceive of reality as consisting of 'things' that have characteristics. These 'things' exist in sets of relations with other 'things'. 'Things', of course, may be very different from what we might commonly take to be things, i.e. the physical things that we perceive, rocks, logs, houses, etc. are not the only sorts of things. They may in many cases be very unlike such things as these. I spoke of things existing in sets of relations with other things. Well, the things may, in fact, simply be the sets of relations. Social structure would be an example of that sort of thing. Dürkheim was very much on the right track when he spoke of social forces and so on as things. Things possess causal powers. Causal power is one of the character- istics that 'things' may possess. However, this causal power may only be exercised in certain sets of circumstances. That is, things possess causal power whether exercised or not. What determines whether the causal power may be exercised is the set of relationships and interac- tions it enters into with other things. Are you following this?

Socrates: Maybe. Give me some illustrative examples.

G.O.D.:   Okay. You have two chemicals. If the two chemicals are kept separate from one another they are quite stable. They could sit side by side for years with no event occurring as long as something acts as a buffer zone between them. But, if they come into contact with one another, a violent explosion immediately occurs. If such occurs, and we see it, the event is in both the empirical and actual domains. But what of the years when nothing happens because the two do not come into contact with one another? No event occurs. But the potential for such an event, the explosion, was always present. This potential is real! The characteristics, the powers of each of the things, were always possessed even if unexercised.

There are other reasons why an explosion may not occur. Let us suppose that some third chemical or combination of chemicals, if applied to both of the first two, will prevent explosions even if the two combine with one another. All right, again no explosive event occurs in such situations; yet the explosive potential of the two chemicals is nonetheless still real.

Science is not about merely observing explosions and generalising about their occurrence in the isolated cases induced by experimental closure. Reality is an open system. Our universalisations, our scientific laws, are supposed to be about reality, about the nature of reality, and not merely refer to restricted cases. Potentiality is an important dimension of the real. Science is primarily engaged in identifying the underlying structure of reality, the nature of **things-in-themselves**, their causal powers and the sets of relationships, actual and potential, which affect the exercise (or not) of these causal powers.

Socrates: Two things. Just say a little more about 'things' and about the term you used, 'things-in-themselves'. And give me one more example. I'm almost there, I think. If I've got this right I'll have some objections. But I'm not sure yet.

G.O.D.:   All right. First, there are two prime tenets of realism. One is accepted by all realists, while the other is more controversial, even amongst realists themselves. The first tenet is that 'things' exist independently of us; they are as they are, regardless of what we believe about them, whether we see them or don't see them, whether we even exist or not. Human beings gave the heavenly bodies names, but they existed before us. Their existence, the manner of it I mean as well, not merely the fact of existence at all, is how it is, regardless of whatever we allege to be knowledge of the stars, planets and so on. This is **ontological realism**. The 'thing-in-itself' is merely a philosophical label signifying the elements of this independently existing reality. It is possibly not the best label for it either. The term 'thing-in-itself' has an earlier and different but related philosophical usage, which can be confusing. However, I don't think that will bother you too much, as you're not seriously over-burdened with Kantian philosophy.

Socrates: No, I'm certainly not that.

G.O.D.:   The second tenet of realist philosophy is that we can achieve knowledge of reality, that we have knowledge of reality. Some realists, myself amongst them, express this in terms of a **correspondence notion of truth**. That is, knowledge is relatively true or false according to the degree in which beliefs or propositions 'correspond' to an independently existing reality. Other realists, perhaps the majority of today's critical realists, do not want to express this in terms of a correspondence notion of truth. This is because of some of the problems raised by Wittgenstein, the poststructuralist philosophy of knowledge and so on that we have briefly engaged with already. However, the variety of ways in which realists engage with these problems have at least one thing in common. Our knowledge, for it to be considered really knowledge, is knowledge of the real.

Socrates: What else could it be?

G.O.D.:   You are forgetting the idealist philosophical point of view. You are forgetting the position of the extreme sceptic. You are forgetting all the variations of empiricism and cultural relativism that we have considered already. There are other philosophical viewpoints – rationalism, nominalism, phenomenonalism and a host of others – that we haven't touched. Realism itself has been propounded in a variety of forms throughout history. But it certainly has not been and still isn't the most popular viewpoint amongst professional philosophers.

Socrates: Oh yeah? But it just seems so uncontroversial and banal. Knowledge is knowledge of reality. Wowie!

G.O.D.:   Well, it is not so obvious as all that. Yes, it corresponds well with common sense. Many philosophers have seen it as suspect for that very reason. And perhaps more importantly, a great deal follows from it. It has many implications.

Socrates: Yeah, like what?

G.O.D.:   Actually, I have given you some of them already. The first is a form of epistemological relativism – a form of relativism that has nothing whatsoever to do with the other judgmentally paralysing defeatist forms of relativism we have considered in other epistemologies. Second, we have radically transformed the notion of scientific law. Instead of seeing laws as expressions of empirical invariance, we now have to conceive of them as **tendencies**. From these implications, other implications follow.

Socrates: I don't remember you saying either of those things before. I think I know what you mean by laws as tendencies and why you'd say so. But I don't know what you mean by 'epistemological relativism'.

This doesn't seem to go along with what you said about a correspondence theory of truth. If your statement corresponds with reality then it is true. This doesn't sound relativist to me, it sounds absolutist!

G.O.D.: I'll make the relativism clearer in a moment. Realism keeps some of the positivist understandings of law, explanation, confirmation, falsification and so on. It just restricts them, transforms them and changes the emphasis. For example, realism keeps some of the sense of the 'covering law', deductive-nomological notion of scientific law. It is seen as a good thing if we can deduce connections between the various scientific laws. The hierarchical notion of laws being deducible from ever more basic laws connects up with the realist ontological notion of a stratified reality. Reality possesses levels, depth. It is complex. But realism would shy away from the demand that every scientific law must fit into a deductive hierarchy. Laws should not contradict one another obviously, but realism is much more **epistemologically cautious**, more aware of the limitations of what we have achieved and what we can achieve, concerning knowledge. It is asking too much to demand that every putative scientific law immediately fit into a deductive hierarchy.

The understanding of laws as tendencies implies a greater complexity to reality and thus an added necessity for epistemological caution. Taking 'un-actualised potential' very seriously into account, taking the extraordinary possibilities of future occurrence implicit in the notion of reality as an open system, makes one more cautious in claiming full explanations of causality. Realism recognises the place of experimental falsification. But this place is far more circumscribed when your notion of law refers to tendencies. If laws are expressions of invariance then theoretically they are easily falsified. This is not so of tendencies. The apparent counter-examples, the anomalies left by the current state of scientific knowledges, are often quite rightfully to be left as anomalies. This, of course, is the point whereby Popper's theory diverges from the actual history of scientific practice. The realist understanding of law and explanation fits that practice and that history. Tendencies may be subject to counter-tendencies. This dethrones prediction's pride of place. There will be many cases where the expected does not occur. We will not necessarily know if such should count as a falsification of the hypothesised explanation or not. There always is the possibility that there are factors at work that we have not taken account of, of which we may even be wholly unaware.

Socrates: Hmm. You're getting me confused. Where before I said you sounded pretty absolutist, now I'm hearing you as a relativist.

G.O.D.: I am – of a sort.

Socrates: No, I'm hearing you as the same sort as all the others we've discussed so far. I would even go so far as to say that your assertion of there being an independently existing reality implies a fairly radical relativism with respect to knowledge. There's reality, right? It is however it is. But how can we ever know that our claims with respect to it are true? I'm taking on board your notion of laws as tendencies here. 'Whatever goes up has a tendency to come down' says person A. Whatever goes up tends to stay up' says person B. How do we decide between the two? As you said, there may be a host of factors in reality that affect the tendencies. Observing whether things come back to earth or hang in the air won't resolve anything, will it?

G.O.D.:   Okay, you've made a good point. But you've made an error as well. I said earlier that there were reasons why scientific laws are not framed in the form of generalisations with respect to events; that is exactly what you have done with your example. All right, realism asserts that all scientific knowledge claims are fallible. This is part of its relativism. But this does not mean that there is no rational basis for judging between competing knowledge claims. In some cases there will not be. In some cases we do not have sufficient information to judge. But more frequently, we can make comparative judgment. In the case of your two contradicting propositions, we need not take either one of them. There is some partial truth in both of them, as expressed in the laws of gravity and inertia respectively.

How do we form judgments? There are some general rules. We utilise reason and we take into account empirical evidence. So, prediction carries some weight. But it is not synonymous with explanation. Falsification carries some weight. But it is not entirely decisive. Our epistemological caution, our awareness of reality's complexity, suggests the possibility that the apparent decisive falsification of a theory may not really be such. Perhaps the theory can simply be re-worked somehow, to express a greater knowledge, which would include an understanding of the apparent anomaly and yet retain its earlier expression of partial truth about reality.

There are two important features of knowledge to be kept in mind. First, that scientific knowledges are more accurately conceived of in terms of shades of grey (and the scientific utilisation of mathematics does not contradict this) than in terms of black and white. Second, truth and falsity are not symmetrical. We may find some theories to be absolutely, completely false. Absolutely true ones are a different story. This corresponds to what we discussed earlier, with respect to induction, amongst other things. It also corresponds well with scientific history. Scientific theories are continually being superseded by better theories. The newer theory is truer than the previous one, but it still isn't true in an absolute sense – at least, we cannot know this. And it doesn't necessarily mean the previous theory was totally false; it may have been, but more likely it was partially true as well. The new theory can be shown to avoid the elements of falsity in the old theory and thus be a truer more complete explanation. This gives us a notion of scientific progress with respect to knowledge. However, it also demands some humility. If we look back at the past, we see that yesterday's knowledge is not today's. It thus seems almost certain that today's will not be tomorrow's either.

Socrates: I think I get it now, but I still have some problems. And by the way, you forgot to give me some more examples. Okay, any knowledge claim is fallible. The history of science reflects that, and it also suggests that we keep this in mind with respect to current knowledge claims. But I don't think you have given a satisfactory answer as to how to judge between theories. Maybe the past theory was actually better, truer, than the theory held today. Why couldn't that be the case? Maybe the Azande's magic more closely corresponds to how the world really is than our Western view. Or at least, maybe it more closely corresponds to how the world really is for them! What is there in realist epistemology to preclude such a view?

All right, you've referred to empirical observation and reason, but you haven't been very specific. What is the scientific method? I'm asking that because I'm presuming you are still wanting to give some special pride of place to scientific explanation as opposed to any other kind. Yes? It seems to me that you are believing that this realist position gives you some kind of happy medium between absolutism and relativism. But it strikes me that it is completely the reverse. You are completely relativist about knowledge on the one hand, and yet extremely elitist on the other. The West is the best! Science rules!

G.O.D.: No, I don't think that's true.

Socrates: Well, you wouldn't would you?

G.O.D.: I have reasons for my belief. Right, let's get a couple of things straight and then I will give you some examples. No, there is not a single scientific method. Nor is there a single set of criteria for assessing scientific theories. But there are some general features of science that distinguish it from non-science. These general features have evolved in the particular disciplines to become quite specific methodological guidelines. Not only are specific scientific explanations and theories mutable, but so too are the specific methodological criteria. We spoke of the linguistic turn in social science that occurred earlier this century. This came about for two interrelated reasons. First, there was a greater understanding of the manner in which language, and more broadly speaking sign systems, are structured and operate. Second, there was a better understanding not only of the importance of language in social reality, but also of the manner in which social reality is like a language. These two realisations came about, more or less, together. They brought with them changes in terms of the sort of criteria by which to judge social scientific theories.

What is the difference between scientific and everyday knowledges? Or rather, what is the difference between the way scientific knowledge is produced and the process by which common-sense understandings of the world are produced? Broadly speaking, we can say that scientific procedures are more rigorous. But what do we mean by that? Well, in one sense it is precisely its utilisation of the refined methods that have developed in each discipline's history. Okay, that is circular in a sense. So more generally, what would be meant by that? In a general sense, science is really no different from the process of everyday knowledge production – at its best! Both are social processes. Both utilise induction, deduction, **retroduction** and empirical observation. Both are active attempts to develop knowledge. That is, both are processes of construction as well as discovery. The knowledges of both are fallible. **Fallibilism** is a crucial component of critical realism. Our knowledges can always be in the light of better practices, new facts or a number of reasons be shown to be either partially or completely false. Truth and falsity though, frequently are more questions of true and truer . . . or even less false, than black and white one or the other.

We can point out the differences with respect to all the above factors as well. It is a question of degree. Let us take fallibility first. As we have seen, the history of science shows it to be a less than perfect exercise in terms of its own self-conception of what it is doing. Theories and theorists really do triumph over their rivals because of reasons that have nothing to do with either evidence or logic. This can be entirely due to sociological factors. Science is affected by economics. Science is affected by ideology. Some allegedly scientific theories are nothing more than ideological mystification. All that is so. However, science, collectively, is also a very self-aware social activity. It has a very powerful ethos that directly runs counter to power-influenced judgment and behaviour.

Imagine something like Habermas's ideal speech situation. Equal access to relevant knowledge. Equal opportunity to express it. Rational discussion and appeal to relevant evidence are given pride of place over rhetorical power. Scientific consensus is determined after a long democratic process of discussion (amongst the specialists, I mean), with the discussion being somewhat like Popper's notion of conjectures and refutations. All knowledges are capable of being disproved and then by democratic understanding and consensus abandoned. No sacred cows are held to exist.

	Is science really like this? No, of course not! But it does have something like this as a regulatory ideal that has some causal power.
Socrates:	Excuse me. But now it is sounding like Popper's view – a kind of conventionalist falsificationism.
G.O.D.:	There are many good things in Popper's understanding of science that I don't want to abandon. I told you that when we were looking at his work. But there are important differences too. Let me just continue with the differences between science and everyday knowledge practices a little longer. You brought up the Azande. Well, one of Winch's points about their practices of agriculture and so on, was that they were actually quite practical in Western terms. From a realist point of view, they would have to be. Otherwise they would starve. Or if there were substantial differences in practical terms between their view and ours, one of us would have to have the better view. This is because the knowledges of nature are really knowledges of nature. There is not an Azande nature and a Western nature. Nature is how it is. Our respective conceptions of this are relatively true or false. But science has the realist notion of fallibility built into its practice. It knows (in practice anyway) some of its presently cherished beliefs may have to be discarded in the light of further evidence or better theorising. In daily life we also make pragmatic readjustments to our theories in the light of problems that arise. But the imperative to do so is not so systematically worked out, consistently maintained or rigorously enforced. The evolution of disciplinary methodologies is in part the development of procedures to do just these things – systematically to maintain and enforce the guidelines for change of belief. It does not always live up to its own standards. But the standards are there. Thus, in theory at any rate, scientific explanation is far more amenable to change because of rational argument and evidence than is 'common sense'. It is also, again in theory only, far more resistant to sociological determinations of consensus.
Socrates:	Okay, I've got a host of questions. Some are questions of clarification, points where I'm not sure I understand you, and some are critical. Let's start with the Azande. Now, when you are considering Azande beliefs about the natural world, you are **bracketing** off the way such beliefs function socially. Yes? So, for example, Azande beliefs about what causes rainfall are considered entirely without reference to the wider complex set of social beliefs in which 'rainfall causality' is situated. Yes? But the Azande beliefs about the natural world are not analytically separated from social beliefs in the way Western philosophy and science make this separation. Isn't that right? I mean you said their beliefs about magical forces are seamlessly inserted into the fabric of life. The boundary between the natural and social worlds is certainly not

something absolute, if it exists at all. Okay, well I don't really know anything about what the Azande really believe, but my point should stand regardless. There could be a tribe somewhere with such beliefs. And so in making comparisons between respective beliefs about 'rainfall causation' you are not comparing like with like.

G.O.D.:   Very good points! Actually, I don't know much about the Azande belief system either. However, you are somewhat mistaken concerning the separation of nature and culture within a realist framework. And not only realists. If you remember in our discussions about feminism and postmodernism, some of the traditional Western philosophical analytical oppositions are rejected – nature and culture being foremost amongst them. Realists, feminists and poststructuralists, and maybe even the Azande, would all be together on that point. It perhaps could be said to be one of the points of agreement of all post-positivist philosophies of social science. But postmodernists and realists differ as to how this is to be understood. The realist position, that there is an independently existing reality that we can have knowledge of, makes all the difference with respect to this problem.

A poststructuralist would assert that we are trapped in language, discourse, culture. This is both true and misleading. It is certainly true in a banal sense. As T.S. Eliot said, 'I gotta use words when I talk to you'. Our beliefs, about the causes of rainfall or anything else in particular, are located in particular discourses, which in turn are located more broadly within other discourses situated within particular socio-economic historical processes. All of this frames and determines the way we can talk about anything. But this does not mean that the reality of what we are talking about can be reduced to this complex socio-historical process, or to language, or to anything else. Its reality simply is how it is. Some ways of talking about it, interacting with it, describing it and so on, simply have more purchase on it than others. The Azande way of doing this may indeed have some greater purchase on the interaction of rainfall with their daily life than does Western meteorology. But in other ways it is extremely limited. The Chinese were able to make rockets and fireworks without the benefit of Newtonian physics. The knowledge required to do so, however, would share some features of the Newtonian formulation of physical laws. Insofar as these laws are relatively accurate descriptions of underlying physical reality, they would be in agreement with the quite differently framed Chinese 'firework-making' knowledges. They would have to be; otherwise the fireworks would not go bang.

Socrates: So, the Azande descriptions of nature are partially true but not as true as Western meteorology?

G.O.D.:   Yes. And as I said, some aspects of their descriptions may even be truer in a sense. First off, because knowledge is not simply descriptive. It involves active cognition. That is, it prescribes certain ways of acting in the world, that is, interacting with the natural and social world. It might be a very difficult exercise to compare directly Azande and Western views upon a host of subjects. But there would be an overlap where comparison in a limited fashion would be possible. And though expressed in quite different language, there would be points of agreement, as well as difference, within that overlap.

Socrates: But you would still maintain a sense of scientific superiority, though, wouldn't you? You would still have something of the arrogance of the 'civilised' Westerner dealing with the primitive savage, wouldn't you?

G.O.D.:   I certainly wouldn't put it like that.

Socrates: No, you wouldn't because you are too worried about being 'politically correct'.

G.O.D.:   No, that's not it. You are right to say that I have a belief in the superiority of science's account of nature over rival belief systems. But it is a notion of superiority whereby the 'arrogance' as you call it has been severely curtailed – humbled even. In the first place, while one could write a history of science set to triumphal music, and even justify the tone, one could equally paint a dark picture of ignorance and shame. We had 'scientists' filling skulls with ball bearings and counting them to make comparative judgments about black and white intelligence. Was this bad natural science or bad social science? Was it really 'bad'? Yes, I would have to say. It followed some of the strictures of scientific inquiry. But it was undoubtedly ideologically loaded.

We have a huge industry of medical research. New drugs are rigorously tested to determine their curative powers and the risks of negative side effects. But it is an industry. Thus, herbal remedies handed down through generations of folk wisdom are not scientifically tested. Why not? Because patenting regulations and the possibilities of profit determine the allocation of research funding. This is one of the aspects of the critical realist understanding of science. It is seen as a human activity, a social activity. Thus, there are definite points of agreement that realism has with the social constructionist and conventionalist accounts of science. Critical realism posits a need for a sociology of science. It merely does not reduce scientific knowledge claims to sociological determinants. However, because it does take those determinants on board, very seriously on board, its point of comparison with other cultures' knowledges is not directly one of unbridled superiority. Its point of comparison with lay actors' own accounts of their activities is not one of unbridled superiority either.

Socrates: How so? I mean we considered first-order and second-order knowledges and came up against a problem, didn't we? If the account given by social science is not in some way superior to the lay actors' account of their actions, then what is the point of the social scientific account? It seems to me that you want to have it both ways and that there is a contradiction there somewhere.

G.O.D.: The realist account of social science takes seriously the call for hermeneutic understanding. The hermeneutician does not wish to call his or her activity scientific, however refined and rigorous their interpretative techniques have been developed. This is because they have taken on board the positivist account of science. Between hermeneutic understanding and positivist causal explanation there is an enormous conceptual gap in the way of looking at things. Understanding is to do with social rules, human reasons; explanation is entirely to do with causality. This opposition is transformed and transcended in the realist perspective.

In the realist conception of laws as tendencies, the difference between the eternally enduring (we think) nature of gravitational force and the temporally limited nature of any set of social rules becomes less significant. Reasons are definitely to be understood as causes within the realist understanding of social science. Overall, the conceptual gap between understanding and causal explanation is greatly diminished. However, the notion of epistemological caution also comes into play here. In the standard hermeneutic rejection of scientificity, the very complexity of the social world is used as a crucial argument for the impossibility of science. In the realist account this becomes merely an awareness of the limitations of the scientific observer, theorist and scientific community generally.

In Winch's objections to the possibility of social scientific explanation of other cultures, the cultural participants' cultural knowledges are emphasised. So they should be. Human beings not only act but reflect upon their actions. To obtain a knowledge, an understanding, of a group of social actors' own understandings of their activity is difficult. The knowledge the social scientist obtains is fallible; perhaps it is relatively true but perhaps it is wholly false. At any rate, it is unlikely to be as deep and comprehensive as that of the lay actor – in one sense. That is, the second-order knowledge of the social scientist consists in part of an alleged knowledge of what the first-order knowledge is, i.e. the knowledges of the social actors. However, because both first-order and second-order accounts of social action, social structure, social reality are fallible, it is not only the social scientist who has the possibility, indeed the likelihood, of making some errors, but the lay actor as well. That is, the participants of a sub-culture in a sociological study, or another cultural grouping in an anthropological study, only partially know what they are doing.

Their knowledge of their own social reality is incomplete and, in some senses, sometimes, inaccurate.

Socrates: How can you say that? You're back to your old arrogance again!

G.O.D.: No, I'm not. Unless you wish to assert that social reality is nothing more than the sum of social actions undertaken and the sum of the individual social actors' own understandings of what they are doing. But social reality is a lot more than that.

Socrates: Is it? I think a good case could be made for saying just the opposite. Isn't that Weber's argument?

G.O.D.: Yes, it is. But he is inconsistent in his own practice in this regard. The realist view is that reality, both natural and social, possesses depth. It is stratified. For example, we have a table. It is solid and motionless. In some frames of reference this would be an accurate description, at least in part. However, if we want to talk about molecules or atoms or electrons, motion is invoked. Does the motion, in one frame of reference, contradict the immobility of the table, in another. No, it doesn't. Reality possesses depth, and our knowledges of it are on different levels with different frames of reference.

More than one thing can be happening simultaneously. Or rather the same thing can be happening but must be described quite differently relative to different frames of reference. An extraordinary rise in retail sales figures occurs one December. Were the shoppers consciously engaging in a collective activity designed to boost the retail sales index? No, they were just going Christmas shopping. They each had their own reasons for spending what they spent. However, social and economic forces were at work that they may or may not have had any awareness of. Just because they were unaware of these, do we really wish to say they do not exist?

Socrates: Aren't you simply saying that there are intended and unintended consequences of actions?

G.O.D.: That is part of it but not all. We have yet to speak of social structure. Sociology has long had a debate (some would say a sterile debate) between structure and agency. Realism can provide a meta-theoretical basis for going beyond the oppositions of theories of structure and theories of social action. I said earlier that realism asks the ontological questions about what reality must be like for certain things to be possible. In providing a philosophy of natural science these questions were first of all asked about scientific experiments. The question was asked about what assumptions about the nature of reality were required to make such an activity intelligible. Certain conclusions are made about the nature of reality: that it possesses complexity, order, depth and so on. These also allow for and depend upon the tremendous successes of natural science. Social science does not heavily rely upon experiment, and its knowledge producing successes are not so dramatic. Certainly they do not have the same obvious technological applications as natural science. So we need a different basis for grounding the possibility of social science.

Socrates: But not all natural science relies upon experiment. And some of its currently held theories don't have any apparent technological applications either.

G.O.D.:   That's true. What sciences and theories did you have in mind here?

Socrates: Well, biology developed as a science primarily through classification, didn't it? Observation rather than experiment would be astronomy's primary method, wouldn't it? Theories about black holes aren't likely to have many technological applications. I don't know, there are lots of examples.

G.O.D.:   Very good. The close examination of scientific experiment out of which Roy Bhaskar developed his version of realism merely reflects its origins as a critique of positivism, which, as we have seen, tends to concentrate upon a particular model of scientific activity. Science is actually far more diverse. But at any rate, Bhaskar changes his ground when he turns his attention to the possibility of social science. Your objection too becomes transformed when we consider realism's foundational arguments about social science. That is, the examples you gave concerning other sorts of scientific activity only serve to make the argument for the possibility of naturalism stronger. More of the alleged fundamental differences between natural and social science are eliminated. The realist philosophy of science is not based upon any particular scientific technique such as experiment. Rather it is based upon the conditions of possibility of social life.

Socrates: Sorry, you said 'the possibility of naturalism' and then later said 'the possibility of social life'. I'm getting confused with all these 'possibilities'.

G.O.D.:   It is as well you keep them clearly separated. One is, as it were, the conclusion of a philosophical argument, i.e. naturalism. The other is the philosophical premise of the argument – the possibility of social life.

Socrates: Naturalism means . . . what?

G.O.D.:   In this context it simply means that we can have a unified conception of science including both natural and social science.

Socrates: Okay, what makes social life possible? Isn't that a sociological question rather than a philosophical one?

G.O.D.:   It can be both. However, they are different sorts of questions. I've said to you before that many theorists confuse ontological questions with substantive questions to the detriment of their specific theories. Conflating the two involves a shifting of levels of argument. Meta-theoretical questions are given theoretical answers and vice versa. Beginning with Dürkheim and Weber, sociology as a discipline has been particularly prone to do this. I should mention as well that philosophers have thrown their own pinch of semantic confusion into the pot, by sometimes speaking of scientific ontologies. Well, I'm certainly not in the position to legislate language usage, but I think this has been a very unhelpful utilisation of the word 'ontology'.

Socrates: I know we've been through this before, but what is the difference between a substantive proposition and an ontological one?

G.O.D.: Tell you what, I'll simply begin my argument for a realist ontology of social reality, and then through example show the difference between it and any substantive proposition about society. Okay? What is the first thing that society must consist of?

Socrates: People, I suppose.

G.O.D.: We have already seen that there are ontological positions that would assert that that is all there is – well, they would also add on people's actions and people's conceptions of their actions. But other things as well must exist in order for social life to be possible.

Socrates: They must exist? Why?

G.O.D.: Because our actions are framed with reference to things outside ourselves.

Socrates: Yes, other people and nature.

G.O.D.: And what about meanings?

Socrates: People create the meanings.

G.O.D.: Okay, so far we can go in either Dürkheim's direction or Weber's. For the latter, the meanings transcend our individuality and for the former we have a concept of sui generis structure. We have been through this before, yes?

Socrates: Yes.

G.O.D.: Well, let us utilise our notion of ontological depth. The actions humans engage in are on the surface level of reality. They are within the empirical domain. Yes? They are observable.

Socrates: They are observable, but the meaning of them is not.

G.O.D.: Well, there is a surface level of meaning as well. If we want to know why someone performed a particular action we could simply ask them. Yes?

Socrates: Sure. Except that they might not know all the reasons why they performed it. They might also lie.

G.O.D.: Let's leave lying aside. People might not know all the reasons why they did something. Well, that takes us in two possible directions. It could take us in the direction of psychoanalysis. The conscious reasons people have for performing their actions may not be all there is to it. There may be unconscious reasons as well. So, if we go in this direction we are leaving the level of empirically observable realities and going deeper to a level we cannot observe. We are essentially deducing the existence of this deeper level from our observation of the empirical. If our conscious reasons for performing any given action are not sufficient to explain why we did it, then something like the Freudian unconscious must exist. This is a transcendental realist argument to an ontological conclusion. All right, I used the phrase 'something like' to qualify the term 'Freudian unconscious'. Freudian theory is dependent upon a transcendental realist argument to demonstrate the existence of the unconscious. However, the particularity of Freudian theory's explanation of how that unconscious is structured, and how it operates and so on, is substantive rather than ontological. It is dependent upon a whole body of argument and evidence. We will hold its conclusions with an appropriate degree of epistemological caution and be willing to alter our conclusions in the light of further evidence and argument. So do you appreciate the difference between substantive theory and ontology in this case?

Socrates: In this case, I do.

G.O.D.: That's fine. There will be another example that will clarify the difference further. All right, we moved from the surface of meaning and action in one direction, now let us go in the other. Dürkheim makes exactly the same sort of realist argument for the existence of social structure. He speaks of its pre-existence and externality. His two prime examples are language and the economy. His strongest argument for their sui generis reality is that of constraint. However, reflecting upon this further, we can see that constraint is not their only feature. They enable as well. In fact, if we reflect deeply enough upon the human condition, we can see that social structure is a fundamental condition of possibility for there to be any meaningful action at all. Language as we have seen is structured. The whole process whereby meaning is produced is conditioned by the structure of signification processes. We have also seen that we cannot reduce linguistic structure to examples of its utilisation. The structure of language is the condition of possibility for any particular case of language use. We can extend this to meaningful social action. Social structure is the condition of possibility for any meaningful social action. Languages change, meanings change; that is, the structures enabling and constraining action, and the linguistic structures enabling and delimiting the production of meaning, change. How? They change over time as a collective result of individual meaningful social actions and particular utilisations of language. Thus, structure is both the condition of possibility of social action and its outcome.

Socrates: That seems to boil down in the end to the individual.

G.O.D.: That's true on one level. No individuals, no social structure. But it is quite false to say that the social structure at any given time is simply the outcome of all the individual actions of that time. There are, for example, the effects upon the present left over from the past.

Also there is a process of emergence involved, whereby different levels of existence take on new characteristics not possessed by the elements that compose it. Water has a particular chemical structure. We can analytically break it down into hydrogen and oxygen. However, in combination these elements possess characteristics quite different from either hydrogen or oxygen. We can also say: no atoms, no water. But this informs us very little about the characteristics of either.

Socrates: All right, I don't know if what I'm going to say next is right or not; I just don't want to agree too quickly. But let's say I give you language and meaning (for the moment). Well, doesn't that still leave open an idealist interpretation? Language is structured. So that we can say there is a structure to meaningful social action – a discursive structure. Isn't this what the poststructuralists are arguing? And doesn't that leave the structure of social reality as essentially discursive?

G.O.D.:   It would, if language were the only sort of human activity to which we could apply the same sort of argument. We know that human beings, as well as interacting with each other, must interact with nature. The fact that we also know that this interaction is a social interaction, involving and dependent upon meaning construction, is in itself a powerful argument for breaking down the absolute dichotomy between nature and culture. Well, at any given time, humanity is engaged in changing the natural world – by and large this is economic activity – but that world pre-exists that moment and has already been not only physically changed but changed with respect to the meanings it possesses for us.

Socrates: Isn't that a Marxist argument? Was Marx a realist?

G.O.D.:   I think he is best interpreted that way. But we have a long history of Marxist philosophy, social science and scholarly interpretations of Marx's own work. Many different sorts of spins can be put upon it. I believe, though, that realist meta-theory can be most productively utilised in conjunction with it.

Socrates: 'Utilised in conjunction with it'? I thought the meta-theory is supposed to ground the substantive theory. It is supposed to be analytically prior to it.

G.O.D.:   Quite so. It is analytically prior to it, but it is not necessarily temporally prior to it. I can read Marx as being implicitly a critical realist. However, just like Dürkheim and Weber, he is not entirely consistent. And I don't think his philosophical meta-theory can be wholly decided by scholarship. Many interpretations have been given of Marx's work; each has their textual justifications. Realism grounds the best of him, I think. It does so in such a way as to make his insights more useful in our present-day context. For example, a teleological understanding of history can be derived from Marx's work that assigns to history a definite direction and inevitability of outcome. Realist meta-theory with its stress upon reality as an open system contradicts this view. It gives us a guideline for how to appreciate Marx. We need not take him lock, stock and barrel. We take what is useful and defensible and scrap the rest. Marx's own scientific aspirations would have endorsed such an application of his work I believe.

We can use Marx as another example to demonstrate the difference between ontological and substantive claims. Marxism has a fundamental postulate that is actually a realist meta-theoretical assertion, an ontological claim essentially: human beings must interact with nature and each other socially. Thus, we find expressed in Marxist language, the realist ontology of social reality as being both structured and inextricable from nature. Marxism is committed to the realist notion of social structure as being both the outcome and condition of possibility of human action. The interwoven aspect of nature and social life is an ontological description of the Marxist insistence upon the importance of the economic sphere.

However, while thus far one could say realism and Marxism are one, Marxism makes further claims. It claims a causal primacy of the economic sphere in its explanation of human history. This is a substantive claim that must be judged with respect to its relative truth or falsity by the available evidence and the theoretical logics that are applied to that evidence. This is a subject matter beyond the scope of philosophy to pronounce upon.

Socrates: Okay, so there is a kind of intellectual division of labour between the scientist and the philosopher.

G.O.D.: Exactly. The philosopher has a particular service to perform in relation to science. This is the critical realist position anyway. It sees itself as an 'under-labourer' to science. One can contrast this to the 'master scientist' conception that casts philosophy in a much grander role. However, though reasonably modest in its claims for what philosophy can achieve, the role is still seen as potentially valuable. Realism, so critical realists believe anyway, is implicit in the practice of science anyway – good scientific practice that is. Being conscious of the implicit realism in scientific practice can only improve that practice. There is pragmatism in it. But it sets limits to that pragmatism. That is, it allows of a methodological pluralism but it stops short of 'anything goes' or of judging the relative truth of a theory solely in terms of how well it does in terms of prediction, or in terms of technological or any other sort of applications. It retrospectively allows us to detect meta-theoretical contradictions in theoretical projects and thus enables us not only to recast the projects in terms that rest on more secure philosophical foundations, but also to guide the project away from errors and to proceed with practices more likely to be substantively successful.

As we have seen, there is a kind of relativism within it and an inherent epistemological caution. But its awareness of the relativity of truth and falsity stops short of an all-embracing scepticism or judgmental paralysis. It can definitely pronounce upon some theories as false, simply because of their philosophical assumptions. While with others, it leaves such judgment to the particular scientific disciplines. It gives respect to everyday knowledges, the cognitive achievements and understandings of social actors, but is not bound to leave them with the last word.

Socrates: Yes, I can see its virtues. I can see that it has an answer to most of the problems we have encountered. Overall it both accords with common sense and leaves room for scientific specialisation. It is a softer conception of science basically. Okay, one last question – I think it's the last anyway. You keep saying realist, but sometimes you say critical realist. All right, I understand that realism has a long philosophical heritage, and you are referring to a much more recent development. Critical realism is the label for this development. But what does 'critical' refer to, in the label? Is there a connection with critical theory? With Habermas?

G.O.D.:   This is a difficult question to answer on one level and relatively easy on another. The second level is far more crucial. On the first level, it is purely a socio-political strategic question. It is a kind of flag. And the strategic question is: do you want to fly it? If you choose to use it, it locates you in relation to other theorists, most importantly in relation to Bhaskar. However, many people, myself amongst them, have important differences with Bhaskar. I alluded to one earlier – a correspondence theory of truth. Other people who also call themselves critical realists would have other differences. For example, Rom Harré profoundly disagrees with Bhaskar concerning the **causal powers** of social structures. So, using the label for one's own position or not, may depend upon which audience one is addressing. Or it may depend upon just how crucial one finds such philosophical differences relative to other positions. This is true of most schools of thought – it is an ongoing question just how broad a church the school of thought is. But this question, while not without importance in playing the particular language game of the politics of academic debate, is really not too crucial here. It really can't be answered, except insofar as you are a fully-fledged player in the game. As such, you then contest the membership of the teams and debate the rules as well.

The other level of this, which I presume your questions are really addressed to, is far more important. It also can be far more easily and definitely answered. The realist emphasis upon ontology gives rise to a whole new perspective upon truth and falsity. Ideological discourses that are laden with error can also be situated within social reality in such a manner that erroneous conceptions of social reality can be seen to have their source within social reality itself.

Let us take Baudrillard's ideas up again for a moment. They have a certain attraction. They are plausible up to a point. But underneath them is a social reality whose relationship between capitalism and signification is such that the notion of unreality (implicit in the notion of hyperreality) that arises from the intense bombardment of images within which we live our daily lives makes his notions of simulation seem plausible. However, there is a reality – the reality Baudrillard might have been able to theorise if he had actually produced his political economy of the sign – which supports the erroneous nature of the hyperreality conception. The particular nature of contemporary social reality's complexity is such as to give rise to a theory that simultaneously celebrates significatory complexity and is defeated by it.

Realist ontology, which accepts the reality of erroneous conceptions of reality as part, but only part, of that reality, places an implicit demand to perform a double judgment in choosing between competing theories. In choosing one theory over another we should also be able to see the source in reality for the plausibility of the surpassed theory. Very frequently this can be seen to arise from the social conditions that produced the relatively false theory. You can see here the resonance with critical theory, yes?

Socrates: Yes, but it is not simply a question of procedures used to produce either theory. There seems to be some notion of reality being inherently misleading. This isn't the same as in Habermas's viewpoint though, is it?

G.O.D.: Well, the degree of similarity or compatibility between critical realism and Habermas would itself be one of the points of contention within critical realism. However, I think you are basically right. Both points of view would argue that the power relations involved in the production of knowledge are the source of much error. Both points of view insist that a recognition of the aspects of social reality that generate falsity in terms of understanding give rise to an emancipatory interest. If certain social conditions are seen as the source of misleading views about the nature of social reality, then it follows that one should wish to change those conditions. This is, by the way, another area of dispute amongst critical realists. They can lean either way on this point – towards a more Marxist perspective or a more Habermasian one. The Marxist view would be more inclined to emphasise other interests, the desire to overcome human suffering for example, than merely questions of truth. It comes down in some respects to the question of how far philosophy can go. It is rather analogous to drawing the line between ontological questions and substantive social scientific ones, except that in this context the question is the dividing line between questions of political philosophy and 'real politic' motivations.

Socrates: I'm not quite sure I can appreciate the distinction exactly.

G.O.D.: Well, it doesn't matter that much. It will become important if you go further with this. But you do see where the 'critical' in critical realism comes from though?

Socrates: Yes, I understand that. Locating the sources of the distortions in the knowledge production process within reality itself generates the imperative to transform that reality. That's it, isn't it?

G.O.D.: Yes. But now I have a last question for you.

Socrates: What's that then?

G.O.D.: Are you convinced?

Socrates: Of what?

G.O.D.: Of critical realism being able to provide the best philosophical underpinning for science, for social science in particular.

Socrates: Well, yes and no. I followed the reasoning in the case you made for it. And right at the moment I can't find any flaws in it. But I don't think that necessarily means there aren't any. I mean, why isn't everyone a critical realist then? I mean by that, all the philosophers of social science anyway. Never mind, you'd have an answer for that, I know. But the thing is, I can feel that my grasp on these questions is superficial really. I feel like I need to go back and think over some of these discussions. I also want to read some of the thinkers we've spoken about. Basically, I think I need to read and think some more before I am convinced of anything.

G.O.D.: Very good. You are living up to your namesake then.

Socrates: What do you mean?

G.O.D.: Socrates was told by the Goddess of Delphi that he was the wisest man in Athens because he knew that he knew nothing.

Socrates: Well, I guess I'm on the right track then.

DISCUSSION QUESTIONS

1   Is reality irrelevant if our most usual and our most profound experiences are experiences of media images? If this is even partially true, it is somewhat disturbing. Is there anything which could be done about it?

2   We might wish to assert that there is an independently existing reality, which is however it is, quite apart of how we describe it. But it is necessary to use language even to make that assertion. Does this make the independent nature of reality irrelevant to our knowledge of it? If not, why not?

3   What might be meant by hermeneutic realism? Are thoughts, meanings, beliefs, etc. real? Do collective beliefs, discourses, discursive structures, etc. really exist?

4   What is the difference between a realist framed relativism concerning knowledge, and the sort of relativism that accords equal claim to validity of all belief systems?

5   Critical realists would assert that strictly speaking there are no applications of the empiricist or positivist philosophies of science because they are fundamentally incoherent, and attempted applications are thus bound to be contradictory. They would further argue that all good scientific practice is realist. What is meant by such assertions?

6   Does the critical element in either critical realism or critical theory lead to any particular strategy for human emancipation? If so, what is it? If not, what good are they?

7   Is the philosophy of social science important?

FURTHER READING SUGGESTIONS

Baudrillard

International Journal of Baudrillard Studies (electronic publication: <http://www2.ubishops.ca/baudrillardstudies/>)
Baudrillard, J. (1983) *Simulations*, Semiotexte, New York.
———— (1988) *America*, Verso, London.
———— (1992) *Selected Writings*, Blackwell, Oxford.
Kellner, D. (1994) *Baudrillard: A Critical Reader*, Blackwell, Oxford.

Bourdieu

Bourdieu does not usually specifically engage with epistemological questions on the level of abstraction with which this book has been concerned. However, his work certainly seems to imply an implicit realism. I have him listed here primarily as an example of sociology at its best. His works cover a diverse selection of fields and are too numerous to list here. The first one listed below is a reflection upon methodology and the second more general reflections upon sociology as a discipline.

Bourdieu, P. (1990) *The Logic of Practice*, Polity Press, Cambridge.
———— (1993) *Sociology in Question*, Sage, London.

Critical realism in general

Journal of Critical Realism (Taylor & Francis)
Archer, M., Bhaskar, R., Collier, A., Lawson, T. and Norrie, A. (1998) *Critical Realism: Essential Readings*, Routledge, London – covers the development of critical realism through its various stages through thematically organised essays by many of its most prominent proponents. It is pitched at a higher level of technical detail, however, than would be desirable for a first introduction to critical realism.
Benton, T. (1981) 'Realism and Social Science', *Radical Philosophy* 27 pp. 13–21.
Chalmers, A. (1988) 'Is Bhaskar's Realism Realistic?', *Radical Philosophy* 49 pp. 18–23.
Frauley, J. and Pierce, F. (eds) *Critical Realism and the Social Sciences: Heterodox Elaborations,* University of Toronto Press, Toronto, Canada.

Manicas, P. (2006) *A Realist Philosophy of the Social Sciences: Explanation and Understanding*, Cambridge University Press, Cambridge, UK.

Norris, C. (1996) *Reclaiming Truth: Contribution to a Critique of Cultural Relativism*, Lawrence & Wishart, London.

Outhwaite, W. (1987) *New Philosophies of Social Science*, Macmillan, London – engages with the relationship between critical realism and hermeneutics, especially with critical theory and Habermas.

Potter, G. (1999) *The Bet: Truth in Science, Literature and Everyday Knowledges*, Ashgate, Hampshire, Avebury Series in Philosophy.

Sayer, A. (1984) *Method in Social Science: A Realist Approach*, Hutchinson, London.

Critical realism and postmodernism

Lopez, J. and Potter, G. (2001) *After Postmodernism: An Introduction to Critical Realism*, Bloomsbury, London, UK.

Critical realism and God dispute

Hartwig, M. (2009) 'Orthodox' critical realism and the critical realist embrace', *Journal of Critical Realism* 8(2) pp. 233–257.

Potter, G. (2006) 'Re-opening the Wound: Against God and Bhaskar', *Journal of Critical Realism*, Taylor & Francis 5(1) pp. 92–109.

Bhaskar

Most people find Bhaskar's work very difficult, particularly the later writings. Andrew Collier's book listed below is an excellent, clearly written exposition. However, the first three chapters of Bhaskar's *The Possibility of Naturalism*, if read carefully, will take you a long way, e.g. Chapter 1 is more or less a summary of the argument put forward in *A Realist Theory of Science*.

Bhaskar, R. (1986) *Scientific Realism and Human Emancipation*, Verso, London.
———— (1989) *The Possibilities of Naturalism: A Philosophic Critique of the Contemporary Human Sciences*, Harvester Wheatsheaf, London.
———— (1989) *Reclaiming Reality*, Verso, London.
———— (1998) *The Possibility of Naturalism*, Routledge, London.
———— (1999) *A Realist Theory of Science*, Routledge, London.
Collier, A. (1994) *Critical Realism: An Introduction to Roy Bhaskar's Philosophy*, Verso, London.

Harré

Harré, R. (1970) *Causal Powers*, Blackwell, Oxford.
———— (1972) *The Philosophies of Science*, Oxford University Press, London.
———— (1986) *Varieties of Realism: A Rationale for the Natural Sciences*, Blackwell, New York.

Socialism

Brown, A. and Roberts, J.M. (2001) *Critical Realism and Marxism*, Routledge, London, UK.

Collier, A. (1988) *Scientific Realism and Socialist thought*, Harvester Press, Hemel Hempstead.

Signification and reference

Nellhaus, J. (1998) 'Signs, Social Ontology and Critical Realism', *Journal for the Theory of Social Behaviour* 28(1) pp. 1–24.

Potter, G. (1998) 'Truth in Fiction, Science and Criticism', *Journal of Literary Semantics* 27(3) pp. 173–189.

Putnam, H. (1960) *Word and Object*, MIT Press, Boston, MA.

TERMINOLOGY GLOSSARY

The definitions of the terms that follow are not dictionary definitions. The definition of philosophical and social scientific terminology is a complex business as their meanings in many cases are far more fluid and context-dependent than those of most ordinary words. However, this glossary attempts whenever possible to locate the terms in the theories, debates, etc. in which they are frequently used as well as to indicate where they are most significantly (rather than first) used in this book. It is intended that cross-referencing between the entries should be used by the reader as a way of deepening and more richly contextualising the meaning of the term in question.

Abstraction: Concept formation process (or result of that process) whereby limited and specific features of reality are first selected then generalised in a specific representational form. For example, a circle is an abstraction as it is first of all only one feature of any circular thing, and second as a concept it is general in nature as it signifies no particular circular thing but is applicable to all circular things. A somewhat different example would be masculinity. Masculinity is an abstract concept because it signifies a limited set of characteristics (though exactly what these are may be contested) and is used as a way of generalising about gender. Weber's notion of ideal types specifies the nature of a particular sort of process to produce a particular sort of abstraction. See ideal type.

Algorithm: A procedure or formula for solving a problem.

Analogues to the role of experiment: Experimentation is the key feature of some sciences. However, for a variety of reasons it is simply not possible in others. Social scientists have searched for and found various techniques that (arguably) are analogous to experimentation. For example, sociology and other disciplines use quantitative techniques of statistical comparison.

Anglo-American analytic philosophy: There is a division between continental European philosophy and the Anglo-American tradition that still persists to this day, though some of the barriers of mutual incomprehension and lack of interest seem to be breaking down. The continental tradition is more literary, speculative and historical in nature, often dealing with very big and very fundamental aspects of the human condition and history. The Anglo-American tradition by contrast is more precisely focused and rigid with respect to the analytical rigour demanded. John Searle is a prominent American representative of this style of philosophising and can be used to demonstrate the contrast in contemporary terms. Some of Searle's work has been focused upon a very close analysis of 'speech acts', the question of what is involved in making a promise for example. Jacques Derrida is also very concerned with language. However, by way of contrast to Searle's quite precise and narrow focus of analysis, Derrida has been involved in attempting to 'deconstruct' the entire history of Western philosophy. See deconstruction. Some other prominent names associated with analytic philosophy are Austin, Carnap, Frege, Moore, Popper, Quine, Russell, Ryle and Wittgenstein. Please note that some of the names listed are neither American nor English. The division, though having some correspondence with geography, is much more significantly to do with philosophical approach and style, and the sort of problems that are engaged with.

Anomaly: This is an experimental result or observation that cannot be explained in terms of generally accepted scientific theory. Strictly speaking such results 'should be' seen as thus refuting the particular theory guiding the experiment in question or as casting doubt upon the wider theoretical framework that guided the experiment undertaken. However, in practice such results are frequently ignored. Anomalous results perhaps most frequently only indicate some trivial mistake made somewhere and thus are not always particularly serious. However, if such results occur repeatedly, or if they begin to accumulate, they usually then begin to attract serious attention and often precipitate profound changes in scientific perspective. The fact that this has not always occurred with perhaps the speed that is warranted is one of the principal arguments of those who maintain that scientific judgment is merely a matter of social convention. See conventionalist philosophy of science and paradigm.

Aporia: This is the point in an analysis whereupon you cannot go further because you have been brought face to face with the fact that you have found that you assumed your conclusion in your initial premises or that you have reached a point of fundamental contradiction. It is one of the goals of deconstruction to demonstrate textual aporias.

A posteriori: This is knowledge that is derived from observation and experience. It can be contrasted with its exact opposite *a priori. A priori* knowledge is knowledge analytically prior to experience.

A priori: *A priori* knowledge is knowledge analytically prior to experience. It is not dependent upon empirical or observational proof. It can be contrasted with its exact opposite, the term *a posteriori.*

Binomial theorem: A formula for finding any power of a binomial without multiplying at length. A binomial is a reduced expression of two terms. An example would be: $x + x + 3$ can be re-written as $2x + 3$.

Bracketing: This is a theoretical tool for reducing complexity to a manageable level. Aspects or dimensions of the subject matter being investigated are conceptually put to one side, so to speak. This allows for a theorisation of an artificially simplified model of reality. However, once a certain degree of understanding has been achieved using this procedure, the next step is to re-insert the previously bracketed off complexity into the theorisation.

Bridging operation: Within the hypothetico-deductive model of scientific explanation there is a necessary theoretical step, or bridging operation, to be made linking observational and theoretical concepts. Another level of theorisation is undertaken, providing the bridge principles or correspondence rules for the linkage between observational and theoretical variables. In this book we have talked about scientific theory and practice in a kind of abstract simplicity. Actual scientific theories can be very complex and the bridging operation likewise so. The philosophical importance of this notion is that it indicates that it is not necessarily straightforward or easy either to demarcate the theoretical from the purely observational, or having apparently done so, to connect them up with one another.

Causal mechanism: A key term for the critical realist philosophy of science. It is a property of things, or combinations of things that causes events to occur. The reality of the mechanism, however, is not dependent upon events actually occurring. For example, gravitational force is the causal mechanism responsible for the occurrence of a great many events. However, it is also at work even when no event occurs because of counter-acting causal mechanisms. The significance of this observation cannot be made apparent in a short definition. See final chapter on critical realism.

Causal powers: One of the properties of things is that they possess causal powers. These may be exercised or not. Reason and will, for example, are causal powers that humans possess, which are not always exercised. However, even the exercise of a causal power does not guarantee an event will take place. For example, a person may exercise his causal powers of will and physical strength to try to lift an object yet fail. The exercise of these causal powers is counteracted by the causal powers of gravitational force exercised by the earth and the object. The reality of causal power is thus not dependent upon events actually occurring.

Closed system: The sense of this term derives from its opposition to the term open system. Scientific experiments attempt to produce a controlled interaction of a restricted number of variables so that the identical experiment may be repeated. The same experiment, if carried out correctly, should produce the same results each time it is performed. Reality, however, is an open system. There is no limit to the possible interactions of variables, and thus while events may apparently frequently repeat themselves (e.g. the sun rises and sets each day), there is no guarantee that they will continue to do so (e.g. it is possible some event of cosmic proportions could cause the earth to detach itself from the sun's orbit). The future occurrence of novel events is a continual possibility. The distinction between reality seen as an open system and experiment seen as an artificial (humanly initiated) production of a closed system is crucial to the realist understanding of scientific experimentation and the nature of knowledge production generally.

Cogito (the): Cogito ergo sum – I think, therefore I am. The fundamental truth Descartes discovered that he could not doubt.

Consensual theory of truth: This is to define truth by virtue of agreement upon it. It can be argued, for example, that Habermas's understanding of truth is of this kind. He does not argue, of course, that any socially agreed belief is true. But he bases his notion of truth in terms of the procedures used to arrive at it, of which equal access to knowledge, democratic admission to discussion and un-coerced agreement are the principal features. See ideal speech situation.

Constant conjunctures of events: This phrase is frequently used in discussions of causality. The same sequence of events is seen to occur repeatedly – a 'constant conjuncture' of such. On the basis of this observed repetition causality is inferred. For example, every time events A, B and C occur together, another event D occurs. The earlier three events are then believed to cause D. Positivist understandings of scientific laws and causality rely heavily on such inferences in one way or another. Laws can be understood as inferential generalisation from the repeated observations of such constant conjunctures. However, such conjunctures as can be observed are most frequently produced through controlled conditions, i.e. experimental closure. Realist critique suggests that the identification of causal mechanisms involves much more than this. It cannot be exclusively 'event-centered' because of the complexity of possible counteracting influences that are to be found in open systems. Causal mechanisms have a dimension of potentiality to them that is not easily understood in event-centered ontologies and notions of causality. The strength of such critique is what gives the theoretical significance to the phrase. See open systems and causal mechanism.

Conventionalist philosophy of science: The more extreme versions of this understanding of science assert that what counts as scientific knowledge and what are considered acceptable methods and criteria of judgment are reducible to the social conventions of the scientific community. More moderate viewpoints are reluctant to admit that science can be reduced to a matter of social convention but yet cannot find other criteria acceptable to them to justify the special status of science's knowledges and procedures. They would assert that scientificity is ultimately a matter of social convention but that even so, there are good reasons for accepting its standards of judgment, even if these cannot be ultimately philosophically justified.

Correspondence theory (notion) of truth: This is a realist epistemological view not accepted by many critical realists, most notably Roy Bhaskar. It asserts first of all ontological realism – reality is however it is, independently of our beliefs, perceptions etc. Second, it asserts that we can and do have knowledge of that reality. Statements, beliefs, etc. about reality are true if they correspond to it. This notion of truth can be understood very naively or in a quite sophisticated manner. A naive view, for example, would be to understand the correspondence between statements about reality and reality as unproblematic. Establishing just what might be meant by such a correspondence is notoriously difficult. Nonetheless, there are good arguments available that attempt to do just that. Their success is subject to debate.

Cosmology: 1) Philosophical and/or scientific views (the distinction has become somewhat blurred with more speculative physics) upon the nature of the physical universe. 2) A related but somewhat looser usage of the term to refer less precisely to a general overview of the nature of reality. For example, one might wish to refer comparatively to European versus Eastern cosmologies.

Critical Realism: A (relatively) new realist philosophy of science, which like positivism propounds a unity of natural and social science, but unlike positivism it does so with a different notion of scientific explanation and laws that can include the dimensions of understanding propounded by the humanist tradition. See humanist tradition, understanding, explanation and most importantly the final chapter of this book.

Critical reason: See emancipatory interest.

Critical Theory: This school of thought originally had an institutional home in the Frankfurt Institute for Social Research (founded 1923), but its prominent members were forced into exile in America by the rise of fascism in Germany. Theodore Adorno, Max Horkheimer, Herbert Marcuse and Eric Fromm were among these. The breadth of work they engaged in was quite broad. It encompassed a negative critique of the rationalism inherent in modernity, an empirical study and diagnosis of the rise of fascism and a critique of mass culture. They attempted a theoretical marriage of the insights of Marxism and psychoanalysis, and the success or lack of it in this endeavour is still controversial today. Jürgen Habermas is the next generation's prominent representative of this school of thought, though he is not only innovative but also considerably more optimistic than his predecessors. In recent years there has been something of a revival of interest in the first generation of theorists, principally in Adorno's work. People use the term 'Frankfurt School' as an alternative way of referring to this school of thought.

Cultural relativism: This perspective asserts that differences between cultures in terms of beliefs and practices are not a matter upon which we can make comparative judgments. Generally, this is meant to be understood in moral and ethical terms, i.e. we cannot condemn the practices of other cultures in terms of our own moral standards. However, an even stronger cultural relativist case is sometimes made, which would assert that we cannot make any cognitive evaluations of the beliefs of other cultures either. That is, we cannot say that a belief in witches, for example, is false. Instead, the cultural relativist would argue, we must attempt to understand such a belief from within the terms of reference of the culture in which such a belief is to be found. The most extreme version of cultural relativism would assert that such a task is impossible. We could never understand the overall belief system sufficiently as to make the belief in witches fully intelligible; hence passing any judgment as to its truth or falsity would be not only morally reprehensible but also foolish. Overall this point of view has been a healthy corrective to the conceits of imperialistic anthropology, which judged all cultures relative to their own and evaluated them entirely in their own terms. However, cultural relativism violates most people's moral intuitions, generates a great many philosophical problems and would create a number of ethical dilemmas if people attempted to act upon it consistently. See ethnocentrism.

Deconstruction: This is a technique of reading and analysing texts that originated with the work of Jacques Derrida. Derrida and many of his supporters imply that it is much more than a mere 'technique', and the profound effect Derrida's work has had upon a variety of intellectual disciplines would seem to support this. However, as a technique it is relatively straightforward to explain if not to actually practise with skill. It is argued that most (all?) texts are most significantly organised around some key terms and concepts. These in turn stand upon definitions in terms of their opposites. These opposing terms are implicitly present in the text, though they are repressed or marginalised by the dominant term. A deconstructive reading simply reverses the oppositions; the marginal is made central and that which is repressed by the text is uncovered and re-presented as the dominant term in the hierarchy of definition. The process of doing this exposes the inherent contradictions within the text. The argument for understanding deconstruction as being something more than a mere (and slightly odd) technique of analysis rests upon the notion that this deconstructive reading is already there with the text implicitly; that is, it contains its own deconstruction. If the preceding sentences you have just read, for example, seem in some sense ambiguous and possibly contradictory, this is not due to any failure of comprehension on your part but rather intrinsic to the very nature of signification. Or so deconstructionists would maintain. See logocentrism. It also should be noted that the verb 'to deconstruct' has crept into everyday language and is frequently used as a synonym for 'analyse'. This usage is technically incorrect, though it is also used in this fashion by academics that should know better.

Deduction: Logical inferential process dependent upon moving from a universal to the particular. It is generally held to be the only truly logical form of inference. See logic, syllogism and induction.

Deductive-nomological or covering law theory of explanation: 'Nomological' as a term on its own refers to the notion of scientific laws. Scientific explanations attempt ultimately to produce knowledge in the form of scientific laws. The relation between scientific laws must be deductive in nature. Thus, we have a hierarchy of scientific laws of ever broader and more basic natures, from which more specific laws may be deduced. Hence the more colloquial term 'covering law'. Laws understood in this sense are propositions expressing relationships of empirical invariance. This understanding of scientific explanation is associated with positivism and has been challenged from a variety of perspectives.

Diachronic: A diachronic analysis is one that is conducted over time and significantly focused upon change.

Differance: This is Jacques Derrida's term used to illustrate performatively the notion of deferral and difference in relation to meaning. In French, the performative nature of the meaning of this term derives from the fact that the French word for 'difference' is pronounced identically to the word 'differance'. Thus, one needs to await contextualisation before one can decide which of the two words and respective meanings is intended by the speaker.

Discursive formations: This is a related collection of discourses that emerge at a particular time and last for unspecified periods. They are structurally related to one another and bear ideological family resemblances, though neither the underlying structural relations at work during their formation nor the resemblances immediately obvious. Discourse and discursive as used here mean more than merely expressions in language but refer as well to sets of practices. Furthermore, the structural relations referred to above involve linkages with institutions. The term is associated with the work of Michel Foucault.

Eduction: A special form of inductive inference, whereby the inference moves from instances of the particular to a conclusion that the next instance will be the same. For example: the only six apples I have ever seen were red, therefore the next one I see will also be red. Not a valid form of inference according to the rules of formal logic, which must be deductive in nature. See deduction and induction.

Emancipatory interest: In Habermas's theory of the relation between knowledge and human interest he posits three forms of rational knowledge production correspondent to three forms of collective cognitive interest. Our knowledge production process is distorted through the inequalities of power relations existing in society; thus ideology is not merely cognitive error but has its roots in actual contradictions in social reality. Critical reason develops out of the fundamental nature of the communication process itself and the contradiction with its socially distorted nature. It reflects the emancipatory interest we have in changing that reality. See empirico-analytic sciences, hermeneutic sciences, ideal speech situation and critical theory.

Empirical: That which can potentially be observed or detected directly through the senses or their instrumental enhancement. There is some lingering mild controversy concerning instrumental enhancement but generally speaking such phenomena are accepted as being empirical. Empirical evidence is observational (direct or instrumentally enhanced) evidence. Unobserved or unobservable aspects of reality believed to exist are not considered empirical. For example, neither the Freudian id nor atomic sub-particles are empirical. We have utilised empirical observation in theorising their existence, but strictly speaking they are not of the empirical domain of reality. (Not to be confused with the term empiricism, which is the label of a school of thought.)

Empiricism: A theory of knowledge that locates the source of all knowledge in experience. It is a very broad category of the philosophy of science and has been enormously influential. See positivism.

Empirico-analytic sciences: In Habermas's theory of the relation between knowledge and human interest he posits three forms of rational knowledge production correspondent to three forms of collective cognitive interest. The empirico-analytic sciences correspond to our practical interest in understanding the natural world. These sciences utilise the sort of object manipulation calculation understood by the earlier Frankfurt School theorists as instrumental reason. Habermas's characterisation of this form of rationality is less negative. It is harmful only when it is extended beyond its rightful domain of application (which of course it is). See hermeneutic sciences, emancipatory interest and critical theory.

Enlightenment (the): This refers to the eighteenth-century explosion of new thinking in philosophy, politics, economics, literature, art, etc., fundamentally affecting how life was generally understood on a variety of levels. The Enlightenment is generally understood as inaugurating the modern era.

Epistemicide: This is a form of symbolic violence done whereby there is a *deliberate* exclusion of certain facts and thinkers coming from a particular culture, so as to eradicate from history the knowledge they produced.

Epistemological caution: The realist philosophy of science asserts that all knowledge claims are fallible. Epistemological caution is a frequently used term to indicate awareness of this fact. Realism is a kind of epistemological relativism but a very different sort from that which takes this relativism to such an extreme that rational judgment cannot be made between conflicting knowledge claims. Epistemological caution thus stands in opposition to a notion of epistemological scepticism taken to absurdity. Epistemological caution suggests that we treat knowledge claims in the awareness that they may not be wholly correct and that they are likely to be superseded later on by better, more complete explanations. The possibility that the knowledge claim in question may be wholly mistaken is also taken on board in theory but held in check by a scientific and philosophical common sense. Perhaps the laws of gravity, inertia, etc. as they are presently understood may not be absolutely accurate and they may even be wholly wrong. However, this latter possibility is not very seriously entertained as we hold some knowledges with considerable confidence that they are not wholly wrong. We distinguish between new and as yet not securely established theories, and others that are more securely founded. The judgmentally paralysing form of extreme relativism by contrast takes its scepticism to the point of asserting that any and every knowledge claim may be wholly false, and thus one is equally sceptical of everything. There is, of course, some philosophical basis for such scepticism but it is a wholly unhelpful way of looking at human knowledge production and suggests instead that the manner in which epistemological questions are being framed is being very badly done.

Epistemology: Theories of what knowledge is, what it is possible to have knowledge of, how it is possible to have knowledge at all, etc. Epistemology asks and attempts to answer questions such as: how can we really know that what we think we know actually is knowledge? What is the source of knowledge? What does it mean to say we know something? What criteria should be used to judge something as being knowledge? It is a long and established principal sub-division in philosophy, which is given particular prominence in most philosophies of science where the knowledge referred to in such questions as the above is scientific knowledge.

Ethnocentrism: This is the tendency to judge other cultures' beliefs and practices entirely from within the terms of one's own culture. The early ethnocentric anthropology that went hand in hand with colonial conquest tended to judge other cultures in terms of a hierarchy, with the cultural values of the colonial power at the top of the pyramid. It is generally regarded as unacceptable today. See cultural relativism.

Explanation (scientific/causal): Explanations of cause and effect. The terms explanation and understanding are frequently used to point up the contrast between the causal explanations of natural science and the interpretive understanding of some sorts of social science. There are limitations to causal explanation in social science, whereby understanding includes dimensions of meaning and subjectivity (arguably) not accessible in cause and effect terms.

Expressive totality: This term refers to an understanding of social reality such that not only is every aspect of social reality interconnected but that one can find within any particular aspect an expression of the form of the totality. Thus, for example, one can find in capitalism's capital/wage labour relationship the essence of human oppression.

Fallibilism: This is an epistemological position asserting that theories and beliefs can never be absolutely and conclusively justified in terms of their truth. Rather theories, very importantly including scientific theories, must be always seen as open to potential improvement in relation to a notion of truth that is not an absolute binary with falsity but rather a matter of degrees, true and truer beliefs and theories. It is an important term in critical realist discourse. It was used much earlier in a looser sense as a general indication of fallibility with respect to knowledge.

Falsificationism: There are two ways of understanding the falsificationist theory of scientific explanation. Scientific knowledges consist of propositions from which specific empirically observable consequences may be deduced. These predicted observable consequences are the test of the theory. However, no number of observations of the correctly predicted consequences can ever be sufficient to confirm absolutely the truth of the theory. But one contradictory result is enough to (logically) falsify it. Thus, our scientific knowledges and laws are our best-to-date unfalsified hypotheses. The two sorts of falsificationism depend on how the above is interpreted. Naive falsificationists believe this chain of reasoning is sufficient to solve the problem of induction, as they believe the scientific explanations thus arrived at stand purely upon deductive reasoning. They are wrong about this; hence the qualification 'naive'. The second sort of falsificationism recognises this and instead sees the falsificationist procedure as both an accurate description of good scientific practice and desirable. This second form of falsificationism is thus a form of conventionalism.

Feminist standpoint theory: An epistemological theory that privileges the experience and socio-politically repressed position of women in society with respect to producing more objective knowledge of society. Note that the very meaning of objective is transformed in this epistemology. Objectivity in this context does not mean value-free. Rather the new meaning of objectivity would transcend previous understandings of the conceptual opposition between objectivity and subjectivity.

Feminist successor science: This term refers to the possibility of constructing a better, more objective science (because it would not be imbued with sexist assumptions and practices). There are various formulations of this possibility. Some would see this in terms of a reform of present practice, while others would attempt to ground such a science upon the superior vantage point with respect to knowledge that women's experience and position in society affords. See feminist standpoint theory.

Floating signifier: This is a signifier that has multiple signifieds on a number of different levels simultaneously. The relationship between signifier and signified is not fixed but may be read quite differently by different people and groups as well as possibly having multiple meanings for any one of them. A certain amount of ambiguity is thus built into such signifiers. The limits of this ambiguity in the case of floating signifiers, as well as the limits (or the lack thereof) to the fluidity of meaning in general, are subject to debate. Many poststructuralists take relatively extreme positions on this point, stressing the 'infinite play of signification'.

Genealogy: This is Foucault's term for the historical tracing of the formation of discursive formations or the emergence of regimes of truth. Knowledges and claims to truth socially evolve in conjunction with sets of practices and institutions. The term may be juxtaposed to the term 'history' because Foucault wanted to caution us against attempting to theorise the past in terms of a totality of interconnections and some overall logic governing these interconnections. Genealogy as a practice is thus more limited and focused than Foucault believed is implied by the term 'history'.

Grand narrative: See metanarrative.

Gregorian calendar: Also called the 'Western calendar' and the 'Christian calendar', is internationally the most widely used official calendar of governments and civil organisations. It is named for Pope Gregory XIII, who introduced it in 1582.

Hermeneutics: Originally the term referred to the interpretative study of sacred texts, but this meaning has now been expanded to include any text. As human social life can (arguably) be understood as a text, hermeneutics can also be understood as the interpretative study of the meaning of human actions. See interpretative understanding, humanist tradition, structuralism and poststructuralism.

Hermeneutic sciences: In Habermas's theory of the relation between knowledge and human interest, he posits three forms of rational knowledge production correspondent to three forms of collective cognitive interest. The hermeneutic sciences correspond to our practical communicative interest. That is, we need to understand how we communicate with and understand one another, as social life depends upon this. See empirico-analytic sciences, emancipatory interest and critical theory.

Human interests: 1) The term interests is frequently used in the sense of human beings possessing objective interests as opposed to purely subjective desires, i.e. a person could be misinformed about what their real interests are. Interest in this sense is used in the chapter on feminist epistemology. 2) Human interests as a term, is also used more specifically in reference to Habermas's theorisation of the relation between knowledge and human interests. He breaks down our collective interests into three categories in relation to different sorts of knowledge production. See the entries on empirico-analytic sciences, hermeneutic sciences, emancipatory interest and critical theory for specific detail.

Humanist tradition: This is the tradition within social science that stresses the uniquely human features of the subject matter. It thus sees the practices and types of causal explanation of natural science as being either wholly inappropriate or at least not adequate to what is required by social science subject matter. See explanation, understanding and interpretative understanding.

Hyperreality: This is the term used by Jean Baudrillard to indicate our present state of 'civilisation' whereby we are dominated by images and have totally lost hold of the reality principle (if we ever had it). Images now represent reality, neither accurately nor inaccurately. They no longer represent it at all. They are instead now totally self-referential. That is, images refer to images, which refer to images, and this is our dominant experience of reality. We experience it through reference to images, which refer to other images. This is a concept and theory that is, on the one hand, highly suggestive. It certainly expresses some partial truths of the present state of affairs. On the other hand (from a critical realist, as well as many other philosophical points of view), it is philosophically incoherent.

Hypothesis: A supposition used in an argument. In science, hypotheses are used in the building of scientific theories, i.e. as explanations, which possibly are relatively accurate. In empiricist philosophies of science, such suppositions are held to be potentially subject to either confirmation or falsification through reference to empirical observations. Hypotheses are understood to be a key feature of science by realists as well, though their relative confirmation or falsification does not rest so un-problematically upon empirical observations.

Hypothetico-deductive model of scientific explanation: Scientific explanations are to be treated as hypotheses from which consequences can be deduced, which could easily be falsified through empirical observation. After rigorous experimental attempts to produce such empirical falsifications and failing, the explanation is then accepted. However, all scientific explanations are only accepted in a provisional sense, i.e. even scientific laws are only such by virtue of being our best hitherto un-falsified generalisations.

Ideal speech situation: Habermas theorises the fundamental basis of communication as consisting of a free and open-ended exchange with the goal of being understood. He does not believe that that is how communication usually is because he sees it as subject to systematic distortion. Rather he sees the sincere mutual exchange as implicit in the very nature of communication itself. His ideal speech situation, the unlimited rational exchange of views where everyone has equal access to relevant knowledge and is allowed to participate, is not intended as a naive Utopia. Rather, it is intended as an ideal standard by which we can criticise actual communication and its usage in domination.

Ideal type: This is a theoretical tool designed to aid in sociological research, first elaborated by Max Weber. The ideal type is an abstraction based upon a selection of 'typical' characteristics of the phenomenon being investigated and carries no moral connotations whatsoever, e.g. it would be as feasible to construct an ideal type serial killer as anything else. The 'typical' aspects of the phenomenon selected are perhaps similar to, but not identical with, some kind of averaging. They are not identical to an average, however, as the research project is usually only interested in certain aspects of a phenomenon. Thus, there could be a great many different ideal types of serial killer, for example, none of which would be the 'average' serial killer. Ideal types are intended for use as an empirical research tool. A process of re-adjustment thus occurs as one moves from abstraction to empirical observations and back to abstractions. The ideal type both directs the empirical observations and is reformulated in the light of the findings.

Idealism: A philosophical position in which reality is conceived as being a phenomenon of mind. This can be understood in very different ways as the work of the following three famous idealist philosophers illustrates: Hegel, Plato and Berkeley. Berkeley is also famous as an empiricist – he was an empiricist epistemologically but an idealist ontologically.

Immanent criteria: Immanent criteria for judgment would be criteria that are within the terms of the discourse to which that which is being judged belongs. This would be directly contrasted with transcendent criteria, which would come from outside the terms of the discourse. To criticise an argument using immanent criteria is to criticise it without reference outside its logic and premises. For example, to criticise on logical or empirical grounds, an argument for the existence of miracle that is based entirely upon divine revelation and faith, would be said to be using transcendent, rather than immanent, criteria of judgment.

Incommensurability: Incommensurable discourses or arguments are those with clearly contradictory or opposing viewpoints, but where the contradictions or oppositions cannot be expressed in terms that the opposing sides can understand in their own framework of meaning. The idea of this can be grasped in everyday terms when we assert that two people are 'talking past one another'. This frequently happens in scientific discourses and is one of the bases of Kuhn's notion of paradigms. Scientists operating from within different paradigms do not understand each other's fundamental assumptions to the degree that real communication between them can be held to be impossible. This, however, is an extreme interpretation. Lyotard uses it in a slightly different sense when he maintains that in some cases positions are so radically different that the differences can never be resolved. Therefore their respective points of view are incommensurable.

Induction: A form of reasoning whereby we generalise from particulars. For example, three hundred observations of A are B, therefore all A are B. People often speak of inductive logic, but strictly speaking inductive inferences are not logically warranted. As our experience is always of a limited number of observations, induction thus constitutes a philosophical problem if we wish to ground scientific knowledge in experience. See deduction.

Instrumentalism: This is a methodological approach to science and acquiring knowledge more generally that is associated with philosophical pragmatism. According to this approach, theories are tools or instruments that identify reliable means-end relations found in experience; methods are chosen through their past utility.

Instrumental rationality or instrumental reason: This is a form of reasoning exclusively focused upon calculating the best means for achieving a particular end. It is also indicative of an attitude taken towards this with negative connotations. Instrumental rationality applied to nature transforms it into objects to be exploited for human benefit. It is a term used in the work of Max Weber, in the context of the historical rationalisation of human social life, and in the work of the Frankfurt School. See critical theory and the discussion in Chapter 5.

Interpretative understanding: This is the goal of humanist social science. It is an understanding that goes beyond cause and effect explanation to include subjectivity, emotion, reasons, meaning, etc. See explanation, understanding, humanist tradition, hermeneutics and Verstehen.

Irrealism: This is a term signifying the exact opposite of realism. Realism asserts the (real) existence or some disputed entity; irrealism denies it. Roy Bhaskar has used this way of understanding realism in his arguments concerning the existence of God, the soul, etc. Though Bhaskar was the 'father of critical realism', critical realists do not all accept such an understanding of realism, and accordingly are unlikely to use the term 'irrealism'.

Istiqra: This is the Arabic word for the Aristotelian method of induction.

Laffler Curve: It is a graphic representation of the relationship between an increasing tax rate and a government's total revenues. The relationship suggests that revenues decline beyond a peak tax rate.

Langue: Saussure divided language into two conceptual domains: langue and parole. He focused his concern upon langue, the synchronic structure of language. Parole on the other hand is the domain of actual instances of language use. The distinction between the two domains is absolutely crucial, as his structural account of the basis for meaning in signification depends upon it.

Liberal feminism: Feminist politics advocating reforms of specific inequalities, whether legal, cultural or economic. In terms of analytic perspective, it is not really a theory as such. Rather the term would apply to a diverse collection of analyses of specific injustices. It is critical of a very great deal of the existing status quo but does not offer a fundamental critique of society in general.

Linguistic turn (the): A dramatic re-assessment of the nature and importance of language within social science was undergone this century. The work of Wittgenstein and Saussure are seminal in this regard. Each of them greatly influenced a change in our understanding of the nature of language and meaning, and each directly and indirectly effected a massive shift in the way social theorists approached their subject matter. See structuralism and poststructuralism.

Logic: 1) The study of the rules and forms of reasoning with an emphasis upon determining what is correct reasoning. It is a part of the subject matter of the philosophy of science in considering how to relate observations to hypotheses and conclusions, the different elements of theory to one another and so on. See deduction, induction, eduction and retroduction. 2) The form of inference being utilised, e.g. 'the logic of your argument is circular' or 'your logic appears to be inductive'.

Logical atomism: Scientific (and ordinary language) statements may be reduced to the simpler more elementary propositions that constitute them. The elementary components (or logical 'atoms') are so simple as to derive their meaning directly from their referents, i.e. perhaps simply by enunciating the word and pointing at that to which it refers. This theory of meaning is no longer in vogue but was once associated with positivist philosophies of science. The arguments for this philosophy of language were developed by Russell, Moore and Wittgenstein. Note: Wittgenstein later profoundly changed his views upon the nature of language and meaning from those associated with this school of thought. It is his later ideas that influenced Peter Winch and the line of thinking considered in Chapter 5.

Logical positivism or logical empiricism: The positivism espoused by the Vienna Circle of philosophers who eschewed metaphysics and tried to develop a philosophy of language and logic which was consistent with a strict empiricist philosophy of science. They considered such problems as the meanings and relationships of observation statements and theoretical statements, inductive inferences, probabilistic inferences, and the ways in which the social sciences might achieve scientificity. A few of the prominent names associated with this school of thought are Carnap, Reichenbach and Neurath.

Logocentrism: (synonym – phonocentrism) Jacques Derrida produced a rather original thesis concerning Western philosophy's consistent logical privileging of speech over writing in its understanding of meaning. He alleges that Western philosophy thus conceals an implicit understanding of meaning whereby meaning is just somehow immediately present and transparent in the act of utterance. Meaning thus is anchored outside the text. This he believes to be illusory and idealist. This is an error he believes runs through the entire Western history of philosophy. Logocentrism is the term for this misguided philosophical orientation.

Malestream science: Critical and derogatory term applied by feminists to mainstream science alleging male bias and dominance past and present, which systematically excludes women and marginalises their perspectives and concerns.

Materialism: 1) A philosophical position in which reality is conceived of having a 'material' composition. Matter or material in this context can be interpreted as either something very like our common-sense notions of what something being physical implies or in a more sophisticated manner as a philosophical category signifying reality's independent existence to our ideas, perception or beliefs about it. In this latter case, materialism can be understood virtually synonymously with realism. 2) Dialectical materialism and historical materialism – the Marxist understanding of nature and history respectively. Note: readers should be sensitive to the context the term is employed in, as among the different possible shades of meaning, there is a lack of consistent usage in the term's history. Recently, the differences and affinities of critical realism with Marxism and post-Marxism have further clouded an already cloudy view of precisely how and how not to use this term.

Metanarrative: Metanarratives or grand narratives are the stories by which a culture makes sense of its present in relation to its history. Western European (North American, etc.) culture has a story of ancient times, the dark ages and the modern era for example. The modern era (usually dating from the Enlightenment) commences a progressive history of increasing civilisation associated with rationality, science, technological advance and the accumulation of knowledge, leading to the present and pointing towards further such progress in the future. There are many possible versions and variations on this general theme. Marxism is a frequently cited example of such a metanarrative. Humanity acquires ever-increasing knowledge, including significantly understanding the laws governing the historical process itself, and through self-conscious activity we emancipate ourselves through socialist revolution. Lyotard argues that we have now reached a new stage in history, the postmodern era, whereby we no longer can believe such grand narratives, whether Marxist or otherwise.

Metaphysics: One of the earliest branches of philosophy, it can be understood in two ways as regard its object of inquiry. The first object of inquiry is all that lies beyond or behind any possible empirical inquiry, i.e. inquiry into an abstract or spiritual domain not accessible even indirectly by any form of observation. The second object of inquiry can be understood as inquiry into the nature of what exists, what can be known etc.; in other words, some of the most fundamental questions of epistemology and ontology. Positivists and others have rejected metaphysical speculation as pointless and to some extent meant by this both senses of the term. They are thus rather ironically contradicting their own intentions, i.e. to rule out metaphysical inquiry as meaningless is itself a metaphysical position.

Methodology: This can be used in two senses. In the first sense it can be (loosely) understood as synonymous with the word method except insofar as it is usually used in a broader more general sense. The second sense is more accurate – the study of method. This involves both a reflection upon the nature and form etc. of what particular methods are and a consideration of the applicability (or inapplicability) and virtues (or drawbacks) of the utilisation of particular sorts of methods for particular problems. For example, some sorts of sociological subject matter would not be amenable at all to quantitative methods and a particular qualitative method would arguably be the best. Methodology as a subject area considers such questions.

Modern era (the) (or modernity): Historical period running from the Enlightenment to the present. Modernity and pre-modernity can be seen as a historical demarcation reflecting very broad ways of conceiving of life – socially, politically, culturally, etc. History can be further periodised in these terms, e.g. we are presently in 'late modernity'. Alternatively, the present can be understood in terms of an even more radical periodisation, i.e. postmodernity rather than late modernity. This implies that beginning somewhere around the late 1960s or early 1970s, society underwent such fundamental changes that we can no longer be said to be in the modern era.

Modernism: 1) Modernism is a fairly broad school (perhaps too broad and controversially defined to be called a school at all) of aesthetic theory and artistic practice. One can date it from the turn of the century (or slightly earlier or later) and it persisted until after the Second World War (how far after is also debatable). It is defined somewhat differently in the various artistic disciplines, i.e. painting, literature, photography, architecture, etc. 2) A fundamental worldview and set of assumptions colouring the whole way people think. Broad notions associating civilisation, progress, knowledge, science, rationality, etc. allegedly form this worldview, which was inaugurated with the Enlightenment. Whether it persists to this day is subject to debate, i.e. are we still in modernity or are we in postmodernity? It is also debatable as to the worth of this basic worldview, with postmodernists generally finding modernism's outlook and assumptions to be pernicious.

Muqaddimah: Arguably this is the first real work in the philosophy of history. Written by Ibn Khaldun, it is the introductory chapter of a series of books intended as a comprehensive world history titled (in translation): 'Book of Lessons, Record of Beginnings and Events in the history of the Arabs and Foreigners and Berbers and their Powerful Contemporaries'.

Naive falsificationism: See falsificationism.

Narrative knowledge: This is the knowledge produced through stories. Its form is radically different from the form which scientific knowledges take. Narrative knowledge is a term used by Jean Francois Lyotard in this manner (though he gives his own unique and rather peculiar formulation of it) for his argument that science has undercut its own strategy of legitimation.

Neo-pragmatism: This is the term for the philosophies associated with more recent proponents of pragmatism beginning with Richard Rorty. There has been a subsequent greater emphasis upon language in the work of these later pragmatists. See pragmatism.

Non-trivial universalisations: This expression is used in discussions concerning the nature of scientific explanation and law to rule out examples of valid generalisations (in the formal logic sense), which are patently absurd as candidates for consideration as scientific laws. For example, the statement 'all the walls of my house are made of wood' may be perfectly true, yet it would certainly not qualify as a scientific law. It is a trivial universalisation in the sense that it does not speak beyond itself, i.e. it does not really tell us anything beyond its own specifically limited boundaries. Yet on the other hand, it is a universalisation in another sense. This issue constitutes a problem for some forms of positivism insofar as the criterion demanding the 'speaking beyond itself' feature is rather more difficult to specify than it might first appear.

Normal science: This is a key concept in Thomas Kuhn's theorisation of the discontinuous history of science. It signifies the 'puzzle-solving' activity, which most science consists of. It works within a single paradigm, a single set of assumptions concerning criteria of judgment, methods and general framework of problems and fields of investigation. It can be contrasted with the periodic revolutionary upheavals that occur when new paradigms are formed which challenge quite fundamental assumptions of the older paradigms.

Novum Organum: This book can be translated as 'New Method' and was published in 1620. It contains many of Francis Bacon's thoughts concerning empirical inquiry, observation and experiment.

Ontological realism: Quite diverse epistemological positions may be paired up with ontological realism. It asserts the existence of a reality wholly independent of our perceptions, beliefs, statements, etc. Reality is however it is. It is arguable whether or not we can have knowledge of this reality, and ontological realism does not speak to this question. Scientific realists will, of course, be ontological realists as well. However, in direct contradiction to their view, it is sometimes argued that ontological realism logically implies epistemological scepticism.

Ontology: The inquiry into the nature of being or existence. It is in the sense of inquiring into the nature of what sort of entities could be said to exist that the word is used most often in the philosophy of science. For example, is social structure something that exists in its own right (see sui generis) or is it merely a convenient fiction with no existence or characteristics other than those of the actions of individuals? Or for a different example, we can ask: do circles or squares exist in the sense of being ideal abstract entities or do only material things exist, which may be circular or square? See substantive assertion for an important distinction between it and ontological assertions.

Open system: The sense of this term derives from its opposition to the term 'closed system'. See closed system.

Operationalise: To operationalise a concept is to translate it into practical workable terms. Frequently this is held to mean turning it into something that can be measured. For example, to operationalise the concept of heat is to turn it into measurable units of a thermometer reading.

Oxygen/phlogiston problem: The gas which today we call oxygen was once known as dephlogisticated air, corresponding to a wider chemical theory pre-dating and at odds with today's. The gas was isolated (discovered) before the theory that explained it as a chemical element – oxygen. It is philosophically interesting because it was one of Kuhn's original examples to illustrate science's discontinuous nature and is used in this book as an example of how a paradigm shift can be explained from a realist perspective, i.e. a perspective that demonstrates an underlying continuity within science's discontinuous history.

Paradigm: A set of assumptions consisting of agreed-upon knowledges, criteria of judgment, problem fields and ways to approach them. This is a key concept in Thomas Kuhn's depiction of science's discontinuous history, which has since come into wide usage. Normal science proceeds accumulating knowledge within a single paradigm for a time but then periodically enters a period of scientific revolution wherein a new paradigm is formed which competes for a time with the old one until it replaces it. Kuhn never completely made it clear how broadly or narrowly to define the term and was rather inconsistent in his own use of it. This lack of definitional clarity persists to the present day. Readers must therefore pay close attention to the context of its usage as it is frequently not precisely defined but nonetheless used as though it had a single unambiguous meaning.

Parole: Saussure divided language into two conceptual domains: langue and parole. Parole, literally translated, means speech. It refers to actual speech or writing. Langue, on the other hand, is the synchronic structure of language upon which parole depends in all instances to make meaning possible.

Phonocentrism: (synonym – logocentrism) See logocentrism.

Political economy of the sign: Baudrillard argued the necessity for this in his earlier writings. What he meant by it was that the process of signification is so thoroughly imbricated in politics and the economy as to make them virtually inseparable. Thus, economic analysis needs to be undertaken from a semiological point of view. The reasons for this seem obvious if one attempts to try and understand what real human needs and desires are, that is, in the light of such apparently being created by image and advertising.

Positivism: An empiricist philosophy of science, which sees a unity of the natural and social sciences. See the Chapter 2 summary for a list of its most important features.

Postmodernism: There have been so many profound socio-economic political and cultural changes within recent years that it is necessary to characterise the present in terms of a qualitative break from the past. We now allegedly live in a postmodern world. The term 'postmodernity' is, of course, dependent upon a characterisation of what came previously as the modern era, roughly dated from the time of the Enlightenment and lasting until the late 1960s or early 1970s. Many refuse the significance and degree of change as involving such a deep and qualitative break from the past. Instead they may use the term 'Tate modernity' as a description of the present (and also as an indicator that they are not post-modernists). Others refuse this categorisation of historical periodisation entirely and see it as too broad and thus too vacuous to be helpful. The theorisation of the various factors that characterise the present as unprecedented and unique is the philosophical common ground for the very diverse philosophers, sociologists, historians and others to whom the label postmodernist is applied. This easy categorisation process is complicated, however, by the fact that some of the most prominent thinkers associated with the term refuse it as a label to describe their own position. There is considerable disagreement, for example, as to whether Michel Foucault or Jacques Derrida are postmodernists or not. Two of the most prominent names associated with postmodernism are Francois Lyotard and Jean Baudrillard, the former being the author of *The Postmodern Condition*. See meta-narrative and hyperreality.

There is also an aesthetic dimension to the term whereby postmodernism is contrasted with twentieth-century modernist aesthetic theory and practice. There is considerable ambiguity here as well, as things are understood differently in connection with the different media being considered. Even more confusing is the fact that many of postmodernism's allegedly most definitive characteristics are sometimes also characteristic of modernism, e.g. pastiche. However, a number of contrasts may be observed. For example, notions of depthlessness and surface are celebrated by postmodernism, while modernism's concern with 'authenticity' is antithetical to a postmodernist perspective. The two dimensions of postmodernism, the philosophical and the aesthetic, are profoundly interconnected. In many respects postmodernist philosophy can be seen as an aestheticisation of philosophy, as questions of style occlude questions of truth.

Post-positivist era: Positivism was once the dominant philosophical understanding of both natural and social science. It is under increasing challenge as a theory of natural science and is no longer dominant as the understanding of social science. Hence, we are in a post-positivist era.

Poststructuralism: Perhaps the most significant feature of the diverse thinking that might be characterised as poststructuralist is its emphasis upon language. Science, art, the everyday practices by means of which we attempt to understand the world, are all language-borne activities. However, language is not simply a neutral tool, which we may use and turn however we please. Rather it is determinant of our most basic understandings of reality. Poststructuralists have all been profoundly influenced by the work of Saussure (hence the 'structuralism' in 'poststructuralism'), though they have taken it in different directions to structuralist theorists. Because of the diversity of poststructuralist perspectives, it is difficult to characterise it in general terms; however, Jacques Derrida and Michel Foucault have perhaps been the most influential names associated with this term. Other poststructuralist thinkers have usually been profoundly influenced by aspects of their work. See deconstruction, genealogy and regimes of truth.

Power-knowledge: Michel Foucault hyphenates power and knowledge to form a single term to indicate the inextricable linkage between them. The production of knowledge always involves the exercise of power and vice versa. Knowledge always involves sets of practices, and these always involve the exercise of power. See regimes of truth and discursive formations.

Pragmatic Epistemological Guarantee: This is the label given by Garry Potter to his conclusion that we are apparently left with a choice coming from the recognition that ultimately all knowledge derives from induction and therefore may *all* be illusory, that is to say, not really knowledge at all. However, Potter argues that while *logically* this is the case, in fact there is no actual choice to be made, because we *must* choose to believe that some of the world's apparent order and rules of order, that some of our knowledge *really is* knowledge. We 'must' make that choice because it is a necessary assumption in order to function in the world, hence the word 'pragmatic' in the term.

Pragmatism: This term refers to a philosophy advocating that we should make our decisions concerning procedures, explanations and knowledge on the basis of their practical successes. It should be noted that in the past many theories have been quite successful in terms of their applications and in producing further knowledge yet retrospectively can be seen to have been rather spectacularly false about quite important things. There is a historical time dimension involved with respect to the production of knowledge. That is, a theory that is in practical terms quite successful for a time may also be blocking further developments, which depend upon drastically revising our view of alleged knowledges. Thus, practical successes can be seen to be sometimes quite historically relative. Pragmatism thus fails to make some philosophical distinctions with respect to knowledge and truth, which ironically are quite useful. There have been a variety of formulations of pragmatism that deal with such problems and criticisms in different ways. William James was an important early advocate of this view, and Richard Rorty is a prominent contemporary exponent. Paul Feyerabend's 'anything goes (almost) argument' in his famous book *Against Method* is a kind of methodological pragmatism.

Radical feminism: The political solutions as well as the social analyses it offers are quite varied. However, a patriarchy theory of some sort is intrinsic to it. Women's oppression is not a contingent feature of present social reality. Rather, socially constructed gender divisions and power inequality are seen as fundamental in present society, as well as historically. Some radical feminists, but certainly not all, connect biology with their socio-economic historical analysis as well.

Rationalism: A theory of knowledge that asserts that our capacity for rational thought is the principal source of all knowledge. It can be contrasted with empiricism, which posits experience as the basis for knowledge. Empiricists would assert that we cannot acquire knowledge of the world merely through thought but must instead make close observations. This stark contrast when applied to their respective trends within the philosophy of science must be moderated. Science is dependent upon both experience and the capacity for rational thought. Within the respective traditions we find merely different degrees of emphasis upon one or the other.

Realism: Ontological realism asserts the independent existence of reality apart from any of our statements and/or beliefs about it or perceptions of it. Epistemological realism asserts that we can and do possess relative knowledge about the nature of reality. Scientific realism asserts that scientific practices are successful in producing such knowledges and that scientific practices can only be rendered intelligible in terms of making the attempt to do so. Thus, all good scientific practice is implicitly realist whether the practitioners themselves subscribe to this understanding of their activity or not. See critical realism.

Reductio ad absurdum: This is a strategy used to discredit a position whereby it is shown that obviously ridiculous conclusions apparently logically follow from it.

Referent: The referent is the term signifying something in reality to which signs, signifiers and signifieds are meaningfully connected. The signifier is a symbol (sound or inscribed mark) that produces one or more signifieds (meaningful mental images). The referent is that to which the unity of signifier and signified (the sign) is referring to in the real world. Note: The meaning of the term is very much bound up with the particular theory of meaning and reference to which one subscribes. The preceding description is very much a realist form of definition.

Reformation (the): Martin Luther issued a theological challenge to the accepted doctrines of the European Catholic Church in the seventeenth century with implications that ultimately went far beyond theological interpretation. Protestantism was born of this challenge, and a lengthy period of social and political unrest in many European countries occurred in relation to this.

Regimes of truth: Foucault theorises the relationship between knowledge and power as inseparable. Every discipline not only builds up a reservoir of knowledge but also associated practices. These practices involve an exercise of power. Every systematic exercise of power associated with an institution also has a discursive formation of associated knowledges. Thus claims to truth to the degree that they are accepted are always associated with regimes of truth.

Relativism (epistemological): 1) A philosophical position that sees as a reasonable implication of the impossibility of absolute certainty with respect to knowledge that therefore all knowledge claims are equally valid and that comparative judgment as to truth or falsity is impossible. There are many sophisticated arguments supporting this absurd conclusion (though it may not be stated so boldly and nakedly as above). 2) Epistemological positions can be relativist in the sense of recognising the inherent fallibility of knowledge claims and also in the additional sense of degrees or approximations of truth, i.e. knowledge is partial and thus knowledge claims may be true but others truer still. Rational comparative judgment between knowledge claims is certainly possible from within this position of philosophical relativism.

Representationalism (1): This is an epistemological point of view that sees our knowledge(s) as 'representing' reality. The question of just what 'representing' in this context means is variable between exponents and critics of this point of view alike. Often it is unspecified. However, most frequently, critics of representationalism use a visual metaphor for 'representing' and argue that such is usually unconsciously adopted by representationalists, to the degree that it is not realised that the metaphor actually is only a metaphor and not simply a description of reality. See spectator theory of knowledge.

Representationalism (2): This is a slightly different usage of the term representationalism. It is similar to representationalism (1), insofar as it tends to make much of the unconscious use of visual metaphor as a criticism. But it is used in the context of theories of signification, whereby representationalism is seen as locked into an older (and mistaken) paradigm of language based upon the relation between words and things, instead of more properly that between signifier and signified.

Retroduction: (synonym for abduction) This is arguably a third form of inference, being neither wholly deductive nor inductive. Many critical realists utilise this term to connect up the inferential processes used in scientific reasoning with the epistemological caution intrinsic to realism. The classic formulation of retroductive inference is roughly syllogistic in form: 1) a collection of data D is undertaken; 2) the hypothesis H is proposed, which if true would explain D; 3) no other hypothesis available to us now can explain D as well as H; 4) therefore, we conclude that H is probably true and hold it to be knowledge. Note that the conclusion of this reasoning takes into account the possibility that a better explanation may be produced later on. Two other points should also be noted. First, that this form of inference is also used frequently in everyday life. Second, it is arguable that this is really a distinctive form of inference at all. Rather it is merely a combination of deduction and induction combined with an awareness of the fallibility of the conclusion.

Science wars: The research results of, and the way they are presented by, the strong program in the sociology of science, has provoked controversy. Their description of what is occurring in scientific discussions, disagreements and experimental practice is hotly disputed by the scientists themselves, who refuse the sociologists' descriptions of their activity.

Scientific method (the): Non-existent. This is an erroneous and outmoded way of attempting to understand science's diversity of actual practice. There is commonly believed to be a single (broadly defined) method in science. However, these features must be so broadly defined in order to be applied to all the diverse and various practices of exceedingly specialised scientific disciplines as that to speak of them, as being a method at all, is virtually nonsensical. That is, we can accurately speak of science involving close and careful observation, classification, and a rigorous and systematic reasoning whereby theory and practice are closely and sensibly united. On the other hand, the features of science can be more specifically described relative to the various specialisms as a single method. This results in either most presently recognised scientific disciplines failing to qualify as such; or worse still, basing their scientificity on restrictive and rather poor approximations of criteria not really applicable to the practices of the specific discipline in question. Such descriptions of the scientific method can still be commonly found as inaccurate descriptions of disciplinary specialised practices in introductory texts to a host of disciplines.

Scientific ontologies: Scientific ontologies need to be distinguished from ontology in general (note the singular and plural usage here). Ontology is the general philosophical description of what is believed to exist whereas a scientific ontology is rather more specifically focused. Thus, a specialism with biochemistry may have its own ontology and quantum physics and sociology quite different ones. Scientific ontological description is on another level from that of ontology in general as it is not a completely *a priori* account (or argument) concerning what exists or must exist. Rather it uses the state-of-the-art scientific conclusions of any given moment to produce an ontological description useful to a particular specialism in clarifying some of its future working assumptions and assessing the implications of past results. The borderlines between substantive assertions and scientific ontologies are quite frequently less than clearly distinct. For example, the nature of light is both a substantive and ontological question. General ontology, the description of reality in terms of things possessing causal powers and so on, is arrived at *a priori* and is not going to be affected by any particular scientific theory or experimental result. However, the scientific ontological questions concerning whether to consider light in terms of particles or waves, or some hybrid of the two, is going to be profoundly affected by new scientific theories and experimental results. Nonetheless, there is still a distinction to be made between a scientific ontological assertion and a substantive one. A sociological example can be used to clarify this point. Within realist discourse there is a dispute concerning the causal power of social structure. This dispute would fall within the category of general ontology. The relationship between economic structure and culture may be articulated theoretically at a level of generality by a particular school of thought as an ontological description of that relationship. This logically derives (or should!) from some of the basic assumptions and conclusions of that particular school of thought. However, at this level, the empirical evidence required to make more specific claims remains to be scientifically processed. That is, there are limits to how far one can go with ontology and a significant amount of empirical evidence must be produced to support substantive assertions about the subject matter at hand.

Scientific revolution (the): The seventeenth century saw an explosion of scientific achievements. Science pre-exists this period, of course, but it is in this century that it really manifests the extent of its explanatory power.

Scientific revolutions: This is Thomas Kuhn's term to indicate the sudden fundamental shifts of perspective that science has undergone in its history. It is a term bound up with a viewpoint that stands in direct contrast to the view that science is a gradual accumulative process of gathering knowledge and that its history could be expressed in a linear fashion.

Scientism: Most frequently used as a term of abuse. But it is used as such in quite different senses. First, it can be used pejoratively, to imply an exaggerated respect for science by those who have no such respect. It can also be used (again pejoratively) to describe a fetishisation of the superficial trappings of science at the expense of a real understanding of it. Similarly it can be used as a term of abuse to attack the belief that the methods and explanations of science are the only ones worthwhile, i.e. the view that only scientific knowledge is real knowledge.

Semiology: Semiotics or semiology is the science of signs. The subject matter of this discipline focuses upon the production of meaning through the interrelationship of signifiers and signifieds.

Semiotics: See semiology.

Sign: The union of signifier and signified as used in Saussurian linguistics and semiology.

Signified: The meaningful mental image or idea produced by a signifier (a sound or inscribed mark). The signifier and signified together form a sign. The relationship of the sign to reality (the referent) is theorised very differently by various different schools of thought in linguistics and the philosophy of language.

Signifier: The written mark or sound(s) that provokes a meaningful mental image – the signified. The signifier may also be the mental image of the written mark(s) or sound(s), as for example when one thinks in words. The signifier provokes a mental image and thus is directly connected to the signified (not to the real world referent!).

Simulacrum: An exact copy for which no original exists. First coined by Plato but more frequently associated with Baudrillard's notions of simulation and hyperreality. Arguably the term is philosophically incoherent. However, an example that could arguably fit such a definition would be Andy Warhol's series of prints. Is there one Marilyn Monroe print that is the original and of which the others are copies? No. Hence they are all simulacra.

Snell's law of refraction: This is a formula used to describe the relationship between the angles of incidence and refraction, when referring to light or other waves passing through a boundary between two different isotropic media, such as water, glass or air.

Social rules: Social rules strongly influence human behaviour not only insofar as constraining us, but also as formulating the meaning system whereby we make choices. They are thus enabling as well as constraining. In terms of the debates covered in this book, the distinction between social rules and laws of nature is very significant. Traditional positivist versus humanist debate tends to cast the latter in terms of invariability and the former in terms of human choice. This opposition is transcended in the realist account of laws as tendencies. See entries for constant conjunctures of events and tendencies.

Social totality: This is a concept that indicates an interconnectedness to every aspect of social reality and is the sum of those elements and their interrelations.

Spectator theory of knowledge: This is a term used by pragmatists (first by Dewey, then later taken up by Rorty) to critique 'representationalism'. See representationalism (1). Knowledge does not 'look like' what it is alleged to be knowledge of; rather it is of a different order entirely.

Straw man argument: This refers to a critical attack upon an alleged position held by an intellectual opponent, which the opponent does not in fact hold, i.e. the argument is addressed to a 'straw man' rather than the real position held.

Strong program in the sociology of science: This has become a school of thought within the sociology of science. It studies science not in its own terms but rather looks at the practice of science using the conceptual tools of sociology and semiology. It tends to be extremely relativistic, reducing scientific dispute to sociological determinations. This is not always overtly stated but is implied through the refusal to consider the content and subject matter at the heart of natural scientists' disagreements.

Structuralism: This is a very broad school of thought with many different applications in different disciplines. Its central insights stem from the work of Ferdinand de Saussure, who originated the structural analysis of language out of which grew the discipline of semiology, the study of signs. Structure, very loosely, can be understood in terms of a system of differences whose elements derive their meaning from the system of relations between them. While Saussure's work profoundly affected the study of language (he is known as the 'father of modern linguistics') and directly led to the development of semiology, it had a more diffuse but still substantial effect upon sociology, anthropology, film theory, literary criticism and other disciplines. The analysis of kinship systems undertaken by Claude Levi-Straus, for example, utilises similar notions of relation and opposition, as does Saussure's analysis of language. See semiology. Structuralist theory, in whatever discipline, also very importantly emphasizes a notion of depth. Structure is seldom found to be immediately perceptible but rather is an underlying reality beneath the surface of observable phenomena.

Substantive assertion: This would be any assertion about the nature of reality that is not abstract in the sense in which ontological assertions are. The bricks are square is a substantive assertion. The ontological questions concerning whether squares are material or ideal are of a different nature and are posed upon a different level of abstraction (see ontology). The difference between ontological assertions and substantive assertions may seem only obvious in this example, but in other cases it is far less so and quite easy to make category mistakes.

***Sui generis* reality:** Society exists in a *sui generis* fashion. Some entities such as society are believed not to exist in their own right but are believed to be no more than the sum of the elements that compose them. To say that one of these sort of entities has a *sui generis* reality is to directly contradict this view. The whole is not only more than the sum of its parts but is something quite different as well, with its own special characteristics and properties. Society thus is a perfect example of such an entity according to people such as Dürkheim. However, society's *sui generis* existence can be challenged as it can also be argued (as did Weber) that it is really nothing more than people and their actions and a convenient (though fictional) way of referring to this.

Syllogism: This is the classic, as well as the simplest and most straightforward form of deduction: All x are y, this is an x, therefore it is y. For some interesting thoughts on this form of reasoning from a rather contentious feminist perspective, see Chapter 6.

Synchronic: A synchronic analysis is a structural analysis of a phenomenon that brackets off change over time. Saussure's analysis of language divides it into two: langue and parole. The focus upon langue is not concerned with historical change or actual instances of language use but rather the structural aspect of language that governs the possibility of such usage.

System of differences: This term signifies the fundamental notion of how meaning is produced in Saussurian linguistics and semiology. Between signifier and signified there is no inherent natural connection. Rather their relationship is arbitrary. The individual elements in this structural theory of meaning derive their identity through a system of differences. That is, the letter P is such not merely because it is P but because it is P and not Q or Z or A, etc.

Tajriba: This is the scientific method of examination and experimentation proposed by Ibn Sina.

Tautological (tautology): A tautological statement is one that is true necessarily because of the logical form of its expression. For example, you are either finished or you are not. This is tautological, as it is equivalent to the logical law of the excluded middle. Something can either be P or not P; it cannot be both simultaneously.

Teleology: Teleological processes are those which are structured in relation to a given end. An example would be the growth of a plant from a seed. The mature plant is in a sense present in the seed. It is arguable that human history is such a process. Some versions of Marxism, for example, assert that history is a process governed by identifiable laws and moving towards socialism – 'the end of history'. Such views are no longer popular even within Marxist discourse. Lukács's version of Marxism, however, is (as discussed in Chapter 6) an example of teleology. See expressive totality.

Tendencies (in reference to scientific laws): It is through the use of this term that the different notions of scientific laws in the realist and empiricist philosophies of science can be placed in clearest contrast to one another. For the realist, laws are to be understood as tendencies. They do not express a natural necessity for the occurrence of any particular sort of event. This is because the scientific laws are explanatory expressions of the relations of causality and real causal power may be exercised without any event actually occurring. This is because the tendency that the law expresses may frequently be counteracted by other causal mechanisms. Scientific law in the empiricist conception is also intended to express relations of causality but fails to take into account this counteractive possibility. That is, the empiricist description of scientific laws is in terms of generalised invariance from the observation of constant conjunctures of events. It is thus inaccurate as a description in a very fundamental way. The law of gravity if expressed in this way would have everything falling out of the sky. Fortunately actual scientific practice in the formulation of laws is far superior to the idealised model proposed by empiricist description.

Things-in-themselves: This term is best understood as a philosophical category indicating an independent reality because our knowledge of that reality is both fallible and changeable. In realist philosophical discourse the term may be used interchangeably with the less cumbersome word 'thing'. It is sometimes used in contexts instead of this shorter term to remind the reader that the 'things' of realist discourse may be quite different from our everyday conception of things as objects. They are whatever actually is real and may thus be everyday objects but also quite unlike them. They may be forces, charges, structures, sets of relationships or even in some cases be quite beyond our powers to imagine and conceive of. They simply are whatever they really are. We have various alleged knowledges and beliefs about stars, for example, but the star 'thing-in-itself' simply is however it really is. Note: there is also a Kantian usage of this term, which frames all that has been just said above quite differently. So one must attend closely to the discursive context of its usage. It is never used in the Kantian sense in this book however.

Things: See things-in-themselves.

Understanding: This term is used in the philosophy of social science by way of contrast with the term explanation. Explanation refers to causality while understanding is of the human dimension of reasons, meanings, emotion, subjectivity, etc., which (arguably) cannot be captured in terms of cause and effect explanation. See humanist tradition, explanation, interpretative understanding.

Verstehen: This German term (strongly associated with Max Weber but pre-dates him in the work of Dilthey) indicates the method of interpretative understanding whereby we can understand the specifically human mode of life, i.e. motivations, reasons, meaning, etc. It is used sometimes (though not by Weber!) to indicate understanding by means of emotional empathy. See the glossary entries for interpretative understanding and hermeneutics for an indication of how it is used in philosophy of science debate.

Vienna Circle: A group of prominent philosophers initially associated with the University of Vienna who were very influential in developing and expounding the ideas of logical positivism. Members included M. Schlick, R. Carnap, H. Feigl, P. Frank, K. Gödel, H. Hahn, V. Kraft, O. Neurath and F. Waismann. Karl Popper was both critical of the thinking of this school of thought and profoundly influenced by it.

INDEX